ANNUAL DIGEST OF PUBLIC INTERNATIONAL LAW CASES 1931-1932

(INTERNATIONAL LAW REPORTS, Volume 6)

GROTIUS PUBLICATIONS LTD.
PO BOX 115, CAMBRIDGE CB3 9BP, UK

International Standard Book Number 0 949009 20 2

Reprinted in 1987 by photolitho in Great Britain
by Gomer Press, Llandysul, Dyfed

DEPARTMENT OF INTERNATIONAL STUDIES OF THE
LONDON SCHOOL OF ECONOMICS AND POLITICAL SCIENCE
(UNIVERSITY OF LONDON)

ANNUAL DIGEST OF PUBLIC INTERNATIONAL LAW CASES

Being a Selection from the Decisions of International and National Courts and Tribunals given during the

YEARS 1931 and 1932

(INTERNATIONAL LAW REPORTS, Volume 6)

EDITED
BY
H. LAUTERPACHT, M.A., LL.D.
WHEWELL PROFESSOR OF INTERNATIONAL LAW IN THE UNIVERSITY OF CAMBRIDGE; OF GRAY'S INN, BARRISTER-AT-LAW

BUTTERWORTH & CO. (PUBLISHERS), LTD
BELL YARD, TEMPLE BAR, LONDON
1945

This reprinted edition published by
GROTIUS PUBLICATIONS LTD.
CAMBRIDGE
1987

CAMBRIDGE
UNIVERSITY PRESS

University Printing House, Cambridge CB2 8BS, United Kingdom

Cambridge University Press is part of the University of Cambridge.

It furthers the University's mission by disseminating knowledge in the pursuit of education, learning and research at the highest international levels of excellence.

www.cambridge.org
Information on this title: www.cambridge.org/9780521463515

First published 1945
First Grotius Edition 1987
6th printing 2016

Printed in Singapore by Markono Print Media Pte Ltd

A catalogue record for this publication is available from the British Library

ISBN 978-0-521-46351-5 Hardback

ADVISORY COMMITTEE

CONTRIBUTORS

DECISIONS OF INTERNATIONAL COURTS AND TRIBUNALS:

Permanent Court of International Justice United States and Mexico: Claims Commission Great Britain and Mexico: Claims Commission Upper Silesian Arbitral Tribunal and other awards of international tribunals and arbitrators	The Editor
Germany and Mexico: Claims Commission	Dr. A. H. Feller
League of Nations Administrative Tribunal	Mr. C. W. Jenks

DECISIONS OF NATIONAL COURTS:

United States of America	Professor Edwin D. Dickinson
Latin-American Countries: Argentina Brazil Chile Cuba Guatemala Mexico Panama Peru Venezuela	Mr. William W. Bishop, Jr.
Austria	Professor A. Verdross
Belgium	Professor F. de Visscher
British Dominions and Colonies	Professor H. A. Smith
Czechoslovakia	Dr. J. Sĭmák
Danzig	Dr. L. Gross
Egypt	Mr. J. M. Jones

France	Professor C. Rousseau
Germany	Dr. von Tabouillot
Great Britain	Mr. B. E. King
Greece	Professor C. G. Ténékidès
Holland	Professor J. H. W. Verzijl
Hungary	Professor F. Faluhelyi Dr. F. A. Váli
Italy	Professor G. Balladore Pallieri
Lithuania	Dr. J. Robinson
Norway	Dr. C. Kruse Jensen
Poland	Professor L. Ehrlich
Rumania	Professor N. Dascoviçi
Sweden	Dr. E. Sandström
Switzerland	Professor Dr. D. Schindler
Syria	Professor N. Bentwich
Transit and Communications	Dr. J. Hostie
Yugoslavia	Dr. S. B. Gavrilović

PREFACE

THE present volume follows the arrangement and, in general, the method adopted in the preceding volumes. I say "in general," for there is one change which, although as yet not conspicuous, may become more prominent in the future. The verbatim extracts from the cases reported in the present issue of the *Digest* are both fuller and more frequent than in the previous volumes. Whenever feasible, paraphrasing of decisions has given place to literal quotations from the judgment.

Like its predecessors, the present volume includes digests of decisions which are concerned with the interpretation of municipal statutes on matters bearing upon international law. This applies in particular to questions of jurisdiction, nationality, and extradition. A municipal statute and the way in which it is interpreted in a specific case do not, of course, constitute in themselves a direct source or an authoritative illustration of international law. In view of the fact that a considerable number of cases of this description have been reported in the *Digest*, it is advisable to draw the attention of the reader to this point. At the same time, however, such cases are clearly of interest as showing how international law is understood and applied by various countries and how far there exists a uniform international practice on any given point. As such they are of importance for ascertaining whether and to what extent any particular question is, in the language of Article 38 of the Statute of the Permanent Court, governed by one of the "general principles of law recognized by civilized nations." And there may be room for the view that, to use again the language of Article 38 of the Statute, they are evidence of that "general practice accepted as law" which constitutes international custom.

With the exception of the decisions given by the German-Mexican Claims Commission (which have been digested by Dr. A. H. Feller, of the United States Department of Justice), the Editor is responsible for the digests of cases decided by the Permanent Court of International Justice and by all other international tribunals and arbitrators. Digests of decisions given by the municipal courts of various countries have been prepared by the contributors named on pp. vii and viii, and I am glad to have this opportunity of conveying to them the warm thanks and the appreciation of the Advisory Committee and of the Editor for their collaboration.

I am deeply indebted to Sir Cecil Hurst, Sir John Fischer Williams, Mr. Beckett, Professor Brierly and Dr. McNair who, in their capacity as members of the Advisory Committee, read large portions of the manuscript and made valuable comments and suggestions.

The Trustees of the Carnegie Endowment for International Peace and the Governors and the Director of the London School of Economics and Political Science have continued undiminished their support of the *Digest*. Without their help the publication of the *Digest* would not have been possible. The Advisory Committee and the Editor desire to put on record their deep sense of appreciation of the value of that support.

I wish to express my sincere thanks to Mrs. G. Lyons, B.Sc.(Econ.), who has done valuable work in a secretarial capacity and in reading the proofs. She is also responsible for the preparation of the Tables of Cases and of the Index.

H. LAUTERPACHT.

LONDON SCHOOL OF ECONOMICS AND POLITICAL SCIENCE,
ALDWYCH,
LONDON, W.C.2.
MAY, 1938.

TABLE OF CONTENTS

(*See also* CLASSIFICATION)

TABLE OF CASES DIGESTED

(ALPHABETICAL)

(The figures in heavier type indicate the actual digests. The ordinary type indicates the page on which the digest appears as a cross-reference.)

[References are to pages.]

[References are to pages.]

[References are to pages.]

[References are to pages.]

[References are to pages.]

TABLE OF CASES DIGESTED

Arranged according to courts and tribunals (international cases) and countries (municipal cases).]

I. DECISIONS OF INTERNATIONAL COURTS AND TRIBUNALS

The figures in heavier type indicate the actual digests. The ordinary type indicates the page on which the digest appears as a cross-reference.)

Permanent Court of International Justice

Judgments

Advisory Opinions

Orders

Germano-Roumanian Mixed Arbitral Tribunal

Germany and Mexico : Claims Commission

[References are to pages.]

[References are to pages.]

II. DECISIONS OF NATIONAL COURTS[1]

[References are to pages.]

[1] As in some countries it is not the practice to state the names of the parties in reporting cases, we have ventured to invent titles for these cases in the interest of convenience of citation.—[ED.]

[References are to pages.]

[References are to pages.]

[References are to pages.]

TABLE OF CASES CITED

(or otherwise mentioned in this volume)

LIST OF ABBREVIATIONS

OF TITLES OF COLLECTIONS OF DECISIONS, LAW REPORTS, TREATISES, PERIODICALS, ETC., QUOTED IN THE TEXT

A.C.	= British House of Lords and Judicial Committee of the Privy Council.
A.J.	= American Journal of International Law.
Boh.	= Collection of the Decisions of the Czechoslovak Supreme Administrative Court (Sbírka nalezû nejvyššího spravniho soudu). Edited by Bohuslav. This Collection contains two series: decisions in administrative matters, abbreviated "adm.", and decisions in financial matters, abbreviated "fin."
Bulletin	= Bulletin de Législation et de Jurisprudence Égyptiennes.
B.Y.	= British Year Book of International Law.
Ch.	= Chancery Division of the English High Court of Justice.
Clunet	= Journal du droit international.
Dalloz	= Recueil périodique et critique de Jurisprudence, de Législation, et de Doctrine (founded by Dalloz).
D.L.R.	= Dominion Law Reports.
F. (or Fed.)	= Federal Reporter (United States).
Hague Recueil	= Recueil des cours de l'Académie de Droit International de la Haye.
H.L.R.	= Harvard Law Review.
K.B.	= King's Bench Division of the English High Court of Justice.
L.N.T.S.	= League of Nations Treaty Series.
Martens, N.R.G.	= Martens, Recueil de Traités (Nouveau Recueil Général).
M.L.R.	= Michigan Law Review.
Moore, Digest	= Moore, A Digest of International Law.
O.S.P.	= Orzecznictwo Sądów Polskich (an unofficial collection of decisions of Polish Courts).

P.	=	Probate, Divorce and Admiralty Division of the English High Court of Justice.
P.C.I.J.	=	Publications of the Permanent Court of International Justice. Series A—Judgments. B—Advisory Opinions A/B—Judgments, Advisory Opinions and Orders given since 1931. C—Acts and Documents relating to Judgments and Advisory Opinions given by the Court. D—Collection of Texts governing the Jurisdiction of the Court. E—Annual Reports. F—General Index.
Q.B.D.	=	Queen's Bench Division of the English High Court of Justice.
R.G.	=	Revue générale de droit international public.
R.G.B.	=	Reichsgesetzblatt.
Rivista	=	Rivista di diritto internazionale.
Sirey	=	Recueil général des lois et des arrêts (founded by Sirey).
T.L.R.	=	Times Law Reports.
U.S.	=	United States Reporter (Supreme Court).
Vaz.	=	Collection of the Decisions of the Czechoslovak Supreme Court of Justice (Sbírka rozhodnutí nejvyššího soudu). Edited by Vážný. The Collection contains two series: decisions in civil and commercial matters, abbreviated "civ.," and decisions in criminal matters, abbreviated "cr."
Y.L.J.	=	Yale Law Journal.
Zb.O.S.N.	=	Zbiór Orzeczeń Sądu Najwyższego (Collection of the Decisions of the Polish Supreme Court).
Zb.W.N.T.A.	=	Zbiór Wyroków Najwyższego Trybunału Administracyjnego (Collection of the Decisions of the Polish Supreme Administrative Court).
Z. für a. ö. R. und V.	=	Zeitschrift für ausländisches öffentliches Recht und Völkerrecht.

CLASSIFICATION

PART I

INTERNATIONAL LAW IN GENERAL

I. NATURE AND BINDING FORCE.

II. EXTENT.

III. SOURCES. *See also* PART X, ARBITRATION: The Law Applied by Arbitral Tribunals.

IV. SUBJECTS OF INTERNATIONAL LAW. *See* PART VI, THE INDIVIDUAL IN INTERNATIONAL LAW: In General; *and* PART VIII, TREATIES: Operation and Enforcement of Treaties.

V. RELATION TO MUNICIPAL LAW. *See also* PART VIII, TREATIES: Operation and Enforcement of Treaties.

VI. INTERNATIONAL COMITY.

VII. MISCELLANEOUS.

PART II

STATES AS INTERNATIONAL PERSONS

A. IN GENERAL

I. BEGINNING OF STATE EXISTENCE. (For RECOGNITION, *see below*, D.)

II. SOVEREIGNTY AND INDEPENDENCE—

i. In Foreign Relations. *See also below*, Recognition of Acts of Foreign States and Governments; PART IV, JURISDICTION; *and* PART VIII, TREATIES: Interpretation of Treaties—Restrictive Interpretation.

ii. In Matters of Domestic Jurisdiction.

iii. Acts of Sovereignty and Transactions of a Private Character. *See also* PART IV, JURISDICTION: Exemptions from.

III. EQUALITY OF STATES.

IV. RECOGNITION OF ACTS OF FOREIGN STATES AND GOVERNMENTS. *See also* PART IV, JURISDICTION: Territorial; *and below*, Recognition of States, Governments and Belligerency.

V. Continuity of States. *See also* State Succession.

VI. Extinction of States.

B. COMPOSITE AND DEPENDENT STATES AND TERRITORIES.

I. Unions of States—

i. Federal States and Confederations.
ii. Other Unions (including Customs Unions).

II. British Commonwealth of Nations.

III. Protected and Vassal States and Protectorates.

IV. Mandates—

i. Sovereignty over Mandated Territories. Status of the Mandated Territories.
ii. Rights and Duties of the Mandatories.
iii. Rights and Duties of the League.
iv. Equality of Opportunity.
v. Nationality in Mandated Territories.
vi. Other Matters.

V. Territories under Joint or International Government.

C. NEUTRALISATION AND DEMILITARISATION

I. Of States.

II. Of Parts of State Territory.

III. Of Parts of the High Seas. *See also* Part III, Canals.

D. RECOGNITION. *See also above,* Recognition of Acts of Foreign States and Governments ; *and* Part IV, Jurisdiction : Territorial.

i. Of States.
ii. Of Governments.
iii. Of Insurgency.
iv. Of Belligerency.
v. Conditional Recognition.

E. STATE SUCCESSION

I. Succession to Rights.

II. Succession with regard to Contractual and other Obligations, and Concessions.

B. PARTS OF STATE TERRITORY

I. BOUNDARIES—

i. Land Boundaries.
ii. Water Boundaries.

II. RIVERS—

i. National Rivers.
ii. Multi-national Rivers.
iii. International Rivers.
(*a*) The Principle of Freedom of Navigation on International Rivers.
(*b*) Functions and Competence of International Commissions on International Rivers.
iv. The Utilisation of the Flow of Non-National and International Rivers.

III. TERRITORIAL WATERS—

i. Nature of the Maritime Belt.
ii. Breadth of the Maritime Belt.
iii. Jurisdiction in the Maritime Belt.
iv. Coasting Trade and Fisheries. *See* PART IV, JURISDICTION : Territorial.

IV. NATIONAL WATERS.

V. STRAITS.

VI. BAYS.

VII. CANALS, INTERNATIONAL—

i. In Time of Peace.
ii. In Time of War.

VIII. LAKES AND LAND-LOCKED SEAS.

IX. ISLANDS.

X. STATE SERVITUDES.

C. MISCELLANEOUS

PART IV
JURISDICTION

A. IN GENERAL. TERRITORIAL AND PERSONAL

I. TERRITORIAL—

i. Over Territory in General and Persons and Property Situated therein. Expropriation of Alien Property.
See also PART II, RECOGNITION OF ACTS OF FOREIGN STATES AND GOVERNMENTS, *and* RECOGNITION OF FOREIGN STATES AND GOVERNMENTS.

ii. Criminal Jurisdiction over Foreigners.
iii. Over Ports and National Waters. *See also* PART III, TERRITORIAL WATERS.
iv. At the Maritime Frontier. Hovering Laws. *See also below,* C, HIGH SEAS.
v. Coasting Trade.
vi. Fisheries.
vii. Exemptions from and Restrictions upon Territorial Jurisdiction.
(*a*) Foreign States. *See also* PART II, SOVEREIGNTY AND INDEPENDENCE: Acts of Sovereignty and Transactions of a Private Character.
(*b*) Heads of Foreign States.
(*c*) Public Ships and other Property of Foreign States.
(*d*) Foreign Armed Forces.
(*e*) Diplomatic Immunities. *See* PART VII.

II. PERSONAL—
i. Over Subjects in Respect of Crimes Committed Abroad.
ii. Over Nationals Abroad or on the High Seas and their Property Abroad.

B. EXTRATERRITORIAL JURISDICTION

I. CONSULAR JURISDICTION. RÉGIME OF CAPITULATIONS. MIXED COURTS. JURISDICTION AND ORGANISATION.

C. HIGH SEAS

I. CONCEPTION OF THE HIGH SEAS AND OF THE FREEDOM OF THE SEA.

II. JURISDICTION ON THE HIGH SEAS.
i. For ensuring the Safety of Traffic. Collisions. Salvage.
ii. For Enforcement of International Conventions.
iii. Visit, Search and Arrest by Men-of-War in Time of Peace.
iv. The Law Governing the Flag. Ship's Papers.
v. Right of Pursuit.
vi. Enforcement of Hovering, Revenue and other Municipal Laws.
vii. Piracy.

See also PART III, TERRITORIAL WATERS, BAYS *and* STRAITS.

III. SUBMARINE CABLES—
i. In Time of Peace.
ii. In Time of War.

D. MISCELLANEOUS

PART V

STATE RESPONSIBILITY

A. WHERE DOES RESPONSIBILITY REST IN FEDERAL AND OTHER COMPOSITE STATES?

B. NATURE AND KINDS OF STATE RESPONSIBILITY

I. In General. Absolute Responsibility and Responsibility based on Fault.

II. For Breaches of Treaty Obligations.

III. For Revocation of, or Interference with, Concessions or Concessionary Contracts.

IV. For Debts.

V. For Other Breaches of Contractual Obligations.

VI. For Wrongs Unconnected with Contractual Obligations—

i. Acts and Omissions of State Organs and Officials.
(*a*) Denial of Justice. Exhaustion of Legal Remedies.
(*b*) Executive Action or Inaction.
(*c*) Connected with Legislation.
(*d*) Connected with Use of Adjacent Land or Water. *See also* Part III, Rivers.
(*e*) Plea of Non-Discrimination against Foreigners.
See also Part IV, Territorial Jurisdiction: Expropriation.

ii. Acts of Insurgents, Rioters and Private Individuals in General.

VII. For Acts and Omissions of Revolutionary or *de facto* Governments.

C. CLAIMS

I. In General.

II. Nationality of Claims.

III. Assignment of Claims.

IV. State Control over Private Claims.

D. PRESCRIPTION (EXTINCTIVE PRESCRIPTION)

I. Before International Tribunals.

II. Effect of Municipal Statutes of Limitation.

III. Effect of War.

E. DAMAGES (MEASURE OF DAMAGES)

I. Award of Damages in General. Grounds for Awarding Damages.

II. Indirect Damage and Damages for Loss of Profits.

III. Punitive and Exemplary Damages.

F. INTEREST

I. In General.

II. Rate of Interest. Compound Interest.

III. The *Dies a Quo*. The *Dies ad Quem*.

G. MISCELLANEOUS

PART VI

THE INDIVIDUAL IN INTERNATIONAL LAW

A. IN GENERAL

I. Position of Individuals in International Law. *See also* Part I, International Law in General: Relation to Municipal Law; *and* Part VIII, Treaties; Operation and Enforcement of Treaties.

II. Before International Tribunals.

B. NATIONALITY

I. In General. Proof of Nationality.

II. Acquisition of Nationality. Nationality as Affected by Changes of Sovereignty.

III. As Determining the Right of Protection of Citizens Abroad.

IV. Protected Persons and *de facto* Subjects.

V. Naturalisation.

VI. Expatriation. Loss of Nationality.

VII. Denationalisation.

VIII. Double Nationality.

IX. Option.

X. Statelessness.

XI. Nationality of Corporations. *See also* Part XI, War and Neutrality: A, VI. Enemy Character.

C. ALIENS

I. Admission of Aliens.

II. Position of Aliens—

- i. Subjection to Territorial Sovereignty of the Receiving State.
- ii. Protection by the National State.
- iii. Treatment by and Responsibilities of the Receiving State. *See also* Part V, State Responsibility.
- iv. Plea of Non-Discrimination. *See also* Part V, State Responsibility.
- v. Respect for Property. Expropriation. *See also* Part IV, Jurisdiction: I. Territorial.

III. Expulsion of Aliens—

- i. Rights of Expulsion.
- ii. Procedure of Expulsion.
- iii. Reception of Expelled Nationals.

D. EXTRADITION

I. In General.

II. Extradition of Nationals.

III. Conditions of Extradition. Extraditable Crimes.

IV. Procedure of Extradition.

V. Political Criminals.

E. MINORITIES (PROTECTION OF MINORITIES)

I. Minorities Treaties and their Interpretation.

II. Enforcement of Minorities Treaties through the League of Nations and Procedure with regard to Protection of Minorities.

III. Conception of Minority.

IV. Protection of National, Racial and Linguistic Minorities.

V. Treatment of Minorities Apart from Treaty.

F. MISCELLANEOUS

PART VII

DIPLOMATIC AND CONSULAR INTERCOURSE AND PRIVILEGES

A. PERMANENT DIPLOMATIC ENVOYS

I. Appointment and Reception of Diplomatic Envoys.

II. Position and Functions of Diplomatic Envoys.

III. Privileges and Immunities of—

i. Diplomatic Envoys and their Staff.
ii. Subordinate Members of the Diplomatic Staff.
iii. The Family and Retinue of Diplomatic Envoys.
iv. The Official Residence of a Diplomatic Envoy.

IV. Termination of Appointment of Diplomatic Envoy.

B. SPECIAL ENVOYS: DELEGATES AT INTERNATIONAL CONFERENCES: TRADE DELEGATIONS

C. RIGHT OF OTHER PERSONS TO PRIVILEGES AND IMMUNITIES

I. Officials of the League of Nations.

II. Representatives Sent by and Accredited to the League.

III. Delegates of States Attending the Assembly or International Conferences Convened by the League of Nations or the International Labour Organisation.

IV. Officials of the International Labour Office.

V. Judges and Officials of the Permanent Court of International Justice and other International Tribunals

VI. Members of International Commissions, and Officials of International Unions and Similar Bodies.

D. CONSULS

I. Appointment and Exequatur.

II. Position and Functions of Consuls.

III. Privileges and Immunities of Consuls.

E. MISCELLANEOUS

PART VIII

TREATIES

I. Conception and Function of Treaties.

II. Forms of International Agreements and Methods by which they are Concluded.

III. Multilateral Treaties.

IV. Conditions of Validity of Treaties. Registration of Treaties.

V. Parties to Treaties. Right to Conclude Treaties. Composite and Dependent States and Territories.

VI. Constitutional Limitations.

VII. Reservations.

VIII. Ratification of Treaties. Entry into Force.

IX. Operation and Enforcement of Treaties. Necessity of Municipal Legislation. *See also* Part I, International Law in General: V. Relation to Municipal Law; *and* Part VI, The Individual in International Law: A. In General.

X. Effect of Treaties on Third Parties.

XI. Termination of Treaties—

i. By Operation of Law.

(*a*) In General.

(*b*) Extinction and Dismemberment of Contracting Party.

(*c*) Outbreak of War. *See also* PART XI, WAR AND NEUTRALITY.
(*d*) The *clausula rebus sic stantibus.* Reconsideration of Treaties under Article 19 of the Covenant.
(*e*) Merger in Subsequent Treaty.
ii. By Act of Party.
(*a*) In General.
(*b*) Mutual Consent.
(*c*) Unilateral Denunciation. Result of Non-Performance by the Other Party.
iii. Effect of Termination.

XII. INTERPRETATION OF TREATIES—
i. Agencies of Interpretation. Construction in Accordance with the Intention of the Parties.
ii. Restrictive Interpretation.
(*a*) Restrictions of Sovereignty.
(*b*) Interpretation against the Party Responsible for the Drafting.
iii. Bilingual Treaties.
iv. Consideration of Preparatory Work.
v. Various other Rules of Interpretation.
vi. Miscellaneous.

XIII. SPECIAL KINDS OF TREATIES—
i. Commercial Treaties. Most-Favoured-Nation Clause.
ii. Peace Treaties. *See also* PART XI, WAR AND NEUTRALITY.

XIV. MISCELLANEOUS.

PART IX

INTERNATIONAL ORGANISATION AND ADMINISTRATION

A. LEAGUE OF NATIONS

I. CHARACTER OF THE LEAGUE.
II. THE ASSEMBLY.
III. THE COUNCIL.
IV. INTERPRETATION OF THE COVENANT OF THE LEAGUE.
V. THE SECRETARIAT OF THE LEAGUE.
VI. THE LEAGUE AND NON-MEMBER STATES.

B. INTERNATIONAL LABOUR ORGANISATION

I. ORGANISATION AND CONSTITUTION.
II. CONCLUSION AND INTERPRETATION OF LABOUR CONVENTIONS.
III. ENFORCEMENT OF LABOUR CONVENTIONS.

C. OTHER ORGANS OF INTERNATIONAL ADMINISTRATION. *See also* PART II B (Territories under Joint or International Government), *and* PART III B (Functions and Competence of International Commissions on International Rivers).

D. MISCELLANEOUS

PART X

DISPUTES

A. ARBITRATION

I. IN GENERAL—

i. Conception and Function of Arbitration.
ii. The Law Applied by Arbitral Tribunals. Arbitration and Judicial Settlement.
iii. The Arbitration Treaty. Appointment and Withdrawal of Arbitrators.

II. PROCEDURE—

i. Procedure before the Tribunal (Oral and Written Arguments).
ii. Competence. Competence to Determine Jurisdiction.
iii. Intervention.
iv. Counter-Claim and Set-Off.
v. Exceptions and Demurrers.
vi. Costs.
vii. Injunctions and Interlocutory Orders.
viii. Experts.

III. RULES OF EVIDENCE. BURDEN OF PROOF. (As to Consideration of Preparatory Work in the Interpretation of Treaties *see* PART VIII, TREATIES: XII, Interpretation of Treaties.)

IV. ADMISSION OF LIABILITY. WAIVER. ESTOPPEL.

V. THE AWARD—

i. Scope and Binding Force of the Award.
ii. *Res Judicata.*
iii. Appeal and Revision.

B. PERMANENT COURT OF INTERNATIONAL JUSTICE

I. ORGANISATION OF THE COURT.

II. RELATION OF THE COURT TO THE LEAGUE.

III. CONTENTIOUS JURISDICTION—
- i. Competence.
- ii. Procedure.
- iii. Law Applicable.
- iv. Judgment.

IV. THE ADVISORY OPINION—
- i. Competence.
- ii. Procedure.
- iii. Law Applicable.
- iv. Opinion.

C. CONCILIATION

I. BY THE COUNCIL OF THE LEAGUE.

II. UNDER SPECIAL TREATIES.

III. NEGOTIATION.

D. UNILATERAL MEANS OF REDRESS SHORT OF WAR

I. RETORSION.

II. REPRISALS.

III. PACIFIC BLOCKADE. BLOCKADE UNDER THE COVENANT OF THE LEAGUE.

IV. INTERVENTION.

E. NEGOTIATION

F. MISCELLANEOUS

PART XI

WAR AND NEUTRALITY[1]

A. WAR IN GENERAL

I. DEFINITION AND TECHNICAL MEANING OF WAR. INSURGENCY.

II. COMMENCEMENT OF WAR.

III. REGION OF WAR.

IV. BELLIGERENT FORCES.

V. EFFECTS OF OUTBREAK OF WAR—
- i. In General.
- ii. On Treaties.
  - (*a*) During the War.
  - (*b*) After the War.

[1] As it is not intended to digest decisions of Prize Courts save in so far as they raise questions of general international law, War and Neutrality are only dealt with in this Classification in very general terms.

iii. On Private Contracts.
iv. On Enemy Subjects with regard to—
(*a*) Their Personal Status in the Territory of the Belligerent. *Persona standi in judicio.*
(*b*) Their Property and other Rights.
v. On Enemy Merchant Ships in Port.
vi. On Neutral Persons and Property. Embargo. The Right of Angary.
vii. Trading with the Enemy.

VI. Enemy Character—

i. Of Individuals.
ii. Of Corporations.
iii. Of Vessels.
iv. Of Goods.

VII. The Binding Force of the Laws of War.

VIII. Enforcement of the Laws of War—

i. Reprisals.
ii. Punishment of War Crimes. Defence of Superior Orders.
iii. Compensation and Reparation.

IX. Prisoners of War.

X. Non-Hostile Relations between Belligerents, Especially Armistices.

XI. Termination of War.

XII. Effects of Treaties of Peace—

i. In General.
ii. Amnesty.
iii. Revival of Treaties.
iv. Miscellaneous.

XIII. Performance of Peace Treaties.

B. WARFARE ON LAND

I. Measures and Instruments of Force.

II. Appropriation, Utilisation and Destruction of Enemy Property.

III. Occupation of Enemy Territory—

i. Nature and Effects of the Occupation.
ii. Legislative, Judicial and Administrative Functions of the Occupant.
iii. Respect of Private Property. The Public Property of the Enemy State. Requisitions and Contributions.
iv. Inhabitants. Services. Deportations. Hostages.

C. WARFARE AT SEA

I. Measures and Instruments of Force.

II. Visit, Search, Capture, and Destruction—

(*a*) Of Enemy Merchantmen.
(*b*) Of Neutral Merchantmen.

III. Restrictions on the Right of Capture (Hospital Ships, etc., Postal Correspondence, Property under Neutral Flag).

IV. Prize Law—

i. Nature and Extent of Jurisdiction in Prize Courts.
ii. Procedure.
iii. Indemnities and Damages.

D. AIR WARFARE

E. NEUTRALITY IN GENERAL

I. Nature of Duties of Neutrality.

II. Neutral and Military and Naval Operations and Preparations.

III. Neutral Asylum.

IV. Supplies, Loans and Services to Belligerents.

V. As Affected by the Covenant of the League.

F. CONTRABAND

I. Conception of Contraband. Absolute and Relative Contraband.

II. Carriage of Contraband and Doctrine of Continuous Voyage.

III. Penalty for Carriage of Contraband.

G. BLOCKADE

I. Establishment of Blockade, Conditions of Validity.

II. Breach and Penalty

III. Blockade and the Doctrine of Continuous Voyage. For Neutralisation *see* Part II, *above*.

PART I

INTERNATIONAL LAW IN GENERAL

II.—Extent

International Law—In General—How Far Applicable to Disputes between Members of Federal States.

See Case No. 57 (*Connecticut* v. *Massachusetts*).

III.—Sources

[See also Part X, ARBITRATION : *The Law Applied by Arbitral Tribunals.*]

International Law—Sources—Treaties—Interpretation in the Light of Customary International Law.

See Case No. 205 (*The Kronprins Gustaf Adolf; The Pacific. United States and Sweden*).

International Law—Sources—Miscellaneous—Bases of Discussion of Codification Conference—Answers of Governments.

See Case No. 110 (*In re Eschauzier*).

V.—Relation to Municipal Law

[See also Part VIII, TREATIES : IX. *Operation and Enforcement of Treaties. Necessity of Municipal Legislation* ; and Part VI, THE INDIVIDUAL IN INTERNATIONAL LAW : (A) *In General.*]

International Law—Relation to Municipal Law—The Law of the United States—Abrogation of Treaties by Subsequent Statutes—Necessity of Clear Intention to that Effect—Negotiations Leading to the Treaty—Jurisdiction of Municipal Courts with regard to Seizures Effected in Violation of Treaties. **Case No. 1**

THE MAZEL TOV.

(Cook *v.* United States).

United States District Court, D. Rhode Island; United States Circuit Court of Appeals, First Circuit ; United States Supreme Court.

May 16, 1931, *March* 18, 1932, *January* 23, 1933.

(Letts, District Judge ; Bingham, Wilson, Circuit Judges, and Brewster, District Judge ; Hughes, C. J. ; Van Devanter, McReynolds, Brandeis, Sutherland, Butler, Stone, Roberts, Cardozo, JJ.)

Case No. 1 ***Contd.***

The Facts.—This was an action *in rem* brought by the United States against the British vessel *Mazel Tov* to enforce the collection of certain penalties assessed against the master for alleged violations of the Tariff Act of 1930. On November 1, 1930, the *Mazel Tov* was boarded by officers of the United States Coast Guard off the coast of Massachusetts, eleven and one-half miles from the nearest land. The sole cargo of the vessel consisted of whisky. Section 581 of the Tariff Act of 1930 (c. 497, 46 U.S. Stat. L. 590, 747) provided that the officers of the Coast Guard were authorised to stop and board any vessel at any place within four leagues (twelve miles) of the coast of the United States "to examine the manifest and to inspect, search and examine" the vessel; and if it should appear that any violation of any law had been committed by reason of which the vessel or merchandise was liable to forfeiture, it should be the duty of such officers to seize the same. The vessel was taken in tow to the port of Providence and a penalty, among others, was assessed by customs officials for having on board merchandise not described in the manifest (Section 584 of the Tariff Act of 1930, 19 U.S.C.A. §1584).

The speed of the *Mazel Tov* did not exceed ten knots per hour. The master of the *Mazel Tov* contended that the seizure was made beyond the three-mile limit and not within an hour's run of the vessel to the nearest shore, as prescribed in the Treaty between the United States and Great Britain of May 22, 1924 (43 U.S. Stat. L. 1761), and that in so far as the provisions of Section 581 of the Tariff Act of 1922 (19 U.S.C.A. §481), re-enacted in 1930 (19 U.S.C.A. §1581), fixed the distance of four leagues from the shore within which a vessel bound for the United States might be boarded and seized, they had been abrogated by the Treaty relating to intoxicating liquors. The preamble of the Treaty recited that the purpose of the Convention was "to aid in the prevention of the smuggling of intoxicating liquors into the United States." Article 1 asserted the intention of the parties "to uphold the principle that three marine miles . . . constitute the proper limits of territorial waters." Paragraph (1) of Article 2 provided for the boarding and examining of vessels of British registry. Paragraph (3) of Article 2 provided: "The rights conferred by this article shall not be exercised at a greater distance from the coast of the United States its territories or possessions than can be traversed in one hour by the vessel suspected of endeavoring to commit the offense." The action was brought in the District Court.

Held (by the District Court, *per* Letts, District Judge): that the action must be dismissed. The Treaty dealt completely with the subject of the limits within which search and seizure of British vessels could be made in the enforcement and application of the laws of the United States for the prevention of the importation or smuggling of liquor, and it excluded all extra-territorial seizures (that is, beyond the three mile limit) not made in conformity with the terms of the Treaty. A treaty may qualify or limit an Act of Congress. Wherever there was an inconsistency between an Act of Congress and a treaty, the provisions most recent in time must prevail: *Ribas y Hijo* v. *United States*, 194 U.S. 315; *Rainey* v. *United States*, 232 U.S. 310. The only difficulty here was that the Treaty was negotiated in 1924, and the present action was brought under the Tariff Act of 1930. The enforcement provisions of the latter, however, were substantially verbatim re-enactments of like sections in the Tariff Act of 1922 (42 U.S. Stat. L. 858). It could not be assumed, therefore, that Congress had any intention of altering the status and effect of these Treaties when it re-enacted in 1930 the enforcement provisions prevailing at the time when the British and other treaties were entered into. On appeal to the Circuit Court of Appeals,

Held (*per* Bingham, Circuit Judge): that the judgment must be reversed. It was apparent from the situation of the parties to the Treaty between the United States and Great Britain of May 22, 1924, and from the provisions of the Treaty, that the United States was contracting for the privilege of boarding and examining British vessels outside the three-mile limit for the purpose of ascertaining whether such vessels had imported, were importing, or were attempting to import alcoholic beverages into the United States in violation of its laws prohibiting the importation of alcoholic beverages. There was nothing in Article 2 of the Treaty or its subdivisions to indicate that the United States was to acquire any right or privilege as to the enforcement of its customs-revenue laws as exemplified in Sections 581 and 584 of the Tariff Act of 1922 (19 U.S.C.A. §481, 486) which were the same as the like numbered sections in the Tariff Act of 1930 (19 U.S.C.A. §§1581, 1584). Neither the Tariff Act of 1922 nor that of 1930 prohibited the importation of alcoholic beverages. It could not be said, therefore, that the contracting parties were undertaking in Article 2 of the Treaty to stipulate with reference to the United States customs-revenue laws. The case was taken to the United States Supreme Court on *certiorari*.

Case No. 1 ***Contd.***

Held (Opinion read by Brandeis, J.): that the decree of the Circuit Court of Appeals must be reversed and that of the District Court affirmed. It was suggested on behalf of the Government that the power to search and seize within the twelve-mile zone conferred upon officers of the Coast Guard by §581 of the Tariff Act of 1922 was unaffected by the Treaty, save that the British Government agreed not to protest where the seizure was within an hour's sailing distance of the coast. In construing the Treaty its history should be consulted. Compare *United States* v. *Texas*, 162 U.S. 1; *Oklahoma* v. *Texas*, 260 U.S. 606; *Nielsen* v. *Johnson*, 279 U.S. 47, 52. Both its language and its history indicated that the high contracting parties did not intend so to limit its operation. The preamble stated that they entered into the Treaty "being desirous of avoiding any difficulties which might arise between them in connection with the laws in force in the United States on the subject of alcoholic beverages." The history of the negotiations revealed that serious difficulties had arisen between the two Governments in that connection and that, for the purpose of resolving them, the parties determined to deal completely with the subject of search and seizure, beyond territorial limits, of British vessels suspected of smuggling liquors.[1] Being later in date than the Act of 1922, the Treaty superseded the Act in so far as the two were inconsistent: *Whitney* v. *Robertson*, 124 U.S. 190, 194. In a strict sense, the Treaty was self-executing in that no legislation was necessary to authorise executive action pursuant to its provisions. The purpose of the provisions for seizure in Section 581, and their practical operation as an aid in the enforcement of the laws prohibiting alcoholic liquors, left no doubt that the territorial limitations there established were modified by the Treaty. The Treaty was not abrograted by the re-enacting of Section 581 in the Tariff Act of 1930 in the identical terms of the Act of 1922. A treaty would not be deemed to have been abrogated or modified by a later statute unless such purpose had been clearly expressed: *Chew Heong* v. *United States*, 112 U.S. 536.

The Court was unable to accept the contention of the United States that, as the facts showed a violation of the law for which the penalty of forfeiture was prescribed, the United States could, by asking for forfeiture, ratify an otherwise illegal seizure. "It is true that where the United States, having possession of property, files a libel to enforce a forfeiture

[1] The Court gave a detailed account of the circumstances which led to the conclusion of the Treaty of 1924.

resulting from a violation of its laws, the fact that the possession was acquired by a wrongful act is immaterial. *Dodge* v. *United States*, 272 U.S. 530, 532. Compare *Ker* v. *Illinois*, 119 U.S. 436, 444. The doctrine rests primarily upon the common-law rules that any person may, at his peril, seize property which has become forfeited to, or forfeitable by, the Government; and that proceedings by the Government to enforce a forfeiture ratify a seizure made by one without authority, since ratification is equivalent to antecedent delegation of authority to seize. *Gelston* v. *Hoyt*, 3 Wheat. 246, 310; *Taylor* v. *United States*, 3 How. 197, 205-206. The doctrine is not applicable here. The objection to the seizure is not that it was wrongful merely because made by one upon whom the Government had not conferred authority to seize at the place where the seizure was made. The objection is that the Government itself lacked power to seize, since by the Treaty it had imposed a territorial limitation upon its own authority. The Treaty fixes the conditions under which a 'vessel may be seized and taken into a port of the United States, its territories or possessions for adjudication in accordance with' the applicable laws. Thereby, Great Britain agreed that adjudication may follow a rightful seizure. Our Government, lacking power to seize, lacked power, because of the treaty, to subject the vessel to our laws. To hold that adjudication may follow a wrongful seizure would go far to nullify the purpose and effect of the Treaty. Compare *United States* v. *Rauscher*, 119 U.S. 407." *The Richmond*, 9 Cranch, 102, and *The Merino*, 9 Wheat. 391, must be distinguished. These were cases not of violation of a treaty, but "merely violations of the law of nations because made within the territory of another sovereign."

[Report: 51 F. (2d) 292; 56 F. (2d) 921; 288 U.S. 102; *A.J.*, XXVII (1933), p. 559.[1]]

International Law—Relation to Municipal Law—Effect of Treaties which have not been made Part of Municipal Law —Rights of Individuals under Treaties—Construction of the Ashburton Treaty of 1842 between Great Britain and the United States—Interpretation of the Term "Free and Open"—Non-Discrimination against Aliens (Note). **Case No. 2**

Re Arrow River & Tributaries Slide & Boom Co. Ltd.

Canada, Supreme Court. March 15, 1932.

The Facts.—The appellants, a company incorporated in

[1] See also *A.J.*, XXVII (1933), p. 305; *Boston University Law Review*, vol. XIII, p. 375.

Case No. 2 ***Contd.***

Ontario, had constructed certain works for facilitating the passage of timber in the Pigeon River, which is a boundary river of Canada and the United States. By Article 2 of the Ashburton Treaty of 1842, which fixed the boundary line, it was provided "that all the water communications, and all the usual portages along the line from Lake Superior to the Lake of the Woods, and also Grand Portage, from the shore of Lake Superior to the Pigeon River, as now actually used, shall be *free and open* to the use of the citizens and subjects of both countries." The Treaty had never been made part of an Imperial or Canadian statute.

The Company constructed in the Canadian half of the Pigeon River certain works designed to facilitate the floating of timber, and applied to a judge in Ontario, in accordance with Section 52 of the Lakes and Rivers Improvement Act of that Province, to approve a scheme of tolls for the use of these works. The respondents, who were engaged in the timber industry on both sides of the frontier, denied that any tolls could be levied and maintained that Section 52, being contrary to the Treaty, was invalid.

Held, reversing the decision of the Supreme Court of Ontario and restoring the decision of the Judge in Chambers: that Section 52 of the Act, although running contrary to the provisions of the Treaty, was valid. The Court said (*per* Lamont, J.): "In my opinion the treaty alone cannot be considered as having that effect. The treaty in itself is not equivalent to an Imperial Act and, without the sanction of Parliament, the Crown cannot alter the existing law by entering into a contract with a foreign power. For a breach of a treaty a nation is responsible only to the other contracting nation and its own sense of right and justice. Where, as here, a treaty provides that certain rights or privileges are to be enjoyed by the subjects of both contracting parties, these rights and privileges are, under our law, enforceable by the Courts only where the treaty has been implemented or sanctioned by legislation rendering it binding upon the subject. Upon this point I agree with the view expressed by both Courts below, 'that in British countries treaties to which Great Britain is a party are not as such binding upon the individual subject, but are only contracts binding in honour upon the contracting states.' In this respect our law would seem to differ from that prevailing in the United States where by an express provision of the constitution, treaties duly made are 'the supreme law of the land' equally with Acts of Congress duly passed. They are thus cognisable in both the Federal and State Courts. In the case before us it is not suggested that any legislation, Imperial or Canadian, was ever passed implementing or sanctioning the provision of the treaty that the water communications above referred to should be free and open to the subjects of both countries. That provision, therefore, has only the force of a contract between Great Britain and the United States which is ineffectual to impose any limitation upon the legislative power exclusively bestowed by the Imperial Parliament upon the Legislature of a Province. In the absence of affirming legislation this provision of the treaty cannot be enforced by any of our Courts whose authority is derived from municipal law. *Walker* v. *Baird*, [1892] A.C. 491; *Re Carter Medicine Co.'s Trade-Mark*, [1892] 3 Ch. 472; *U.S.* v. *Schooner 'Peggy'* (1801), 1 Cranch, p. 103; *The Chinese Exclusion Case* (1888), 130 U.S.R. 581; Oppenheim's *International Law*, 4th ed., pp. 733-734."

Before deciding that point Lamont, J., dealt with the contention of the appellants to the effect that the words "free and open" did not mean free from tolls or charges for improvements to navigation, but meant "available," "accessible," or "without discrimination." The learned Judge rejected that contention, and said: "In my opinion the meaning of these words in the clause is that the citizens of both countries are to be at liberty, as a matter of right, to travel these waters on both sides of the fixed boundary line without let or hindrance from anyone, or having to pay anything for so doing. This seems to me to be the natural and ordinary meaning of the words and the meaning which, at the time of the treaty, the subjects of both countries would place upon them."

[Report: [1932] 2 *Dominion Law Reports*, 250.]

NOTE.—Anglin, C. J., considered that Article 2 of the Ashburton Treaty did not exclude the imposition of tolls, provided that they were applied impartially. He was of the view that the provision in question "was merely meant to ensure to the citizens of both countries equality of rights in regard to the water communications, portages, etc., and that it never was intended thereby to provide that in no event should either party to the treaty be at liberty, as regards citizens of its own nationality, to impose tolls for the use of improvements lawfully to be made thereon. In other words, where either party to the treaty saw fit to impose tolls upon its own citizens, in regard to such improvements, it should be at liberty to impose like tolls (but none greater) on citizens of the other country for the use of the improvements so made. Otherwise, it would

Case No. 2 *Contd.*

follow that neither country could impose any tolls whatsoever upon its own citizens, because that would interfere with the water communications, portages, etc., being "free and open" to the use of the subjects and citizens of both countries." Rinfret and Smith, JJ., were of the opinion that the Treaty did not apply to non-navigable portions of boundary rivers.

Case No. 3

International Law—Relation to Municipal Law—Treaties—Applicability of Treaties Prior to Incorporation into Municipal Law—Retroactive Effect of Municipal Laws—Brussels Convention on Salvage of December 23, 1910.

OLIVO *v.* MORDINI, GIOVANNI AND OTHERS.

Italy, Court of Cassation. July 28, 1932.

THE FACTS.—On June 14, 1925, an Italian law came into force giving municipal effect to the Brussels Convention on Salvage of December 23, 1910, to which Italy had adhered. The present case, which was a claim for salvage, arose out of salvage operations which took place prior to June 1925. The Court of Appeal of Genoa upheld the claim. On appeal to the Court of Cassation,

Held: that the Brussels Convention was not applicable.

1. With regard to the internal applicability of international conventions, the Court said: "An international treaty is an instrument which aims at establishing the reciprocal rights and duties of the adhering States in matters regulated by the treaty; it does not aim at modifying the internal legal system of those States with regard to the matters regulated by it. . . . For this purpose a municipal law for the execution of the treaty is necessary. The object of such a law is to comply with a promise made by the State when giving its assent to the treaty. . . ."

2. On the question as to whether the municipal act of incorporation of the Convention by the Italian State had retroactive effect and applied to facts occurring prior to the municipal law for the execution of the Treaty, the Court said: "Italy conformed to the Convention by the Law of June 14, 1925, which, since it is posterior to the matter which is the subject of the present dispute, is certainly not applicable to it. . . . The decision of the Court below attempted to justify the retroactive applicability of this Law of June 1925 by regarding it as interpreting the pre-existing state of the law in the matter of assistance and salvage of ships. However, the state of the law which was supposed to form the object of this legislative

interpretation could not have been created by the regulations of the international convention, which, for reasons already given, could not have had any force" in Italy.

[Report : *Diritto marittimo*, 1932, p. 469.[1]]

International Law—Relation to Municipal Law—Treaties—Operation of—Municipal Laws Inconsistent with Treaty Obligations. **Case No. 4**

SOCIÉTÉ RÉGIE *v.* GREEK GOVERNMENT.

Greece, Areopagus. 1932.

THE FACTS.—In September 1897, after the termination of the war between Turkey and Greece, there was established an international control of certain Greek revenues, including those of the salt tax, for the benefit of the Ottoman Public Debt. In pursuance of the Treaty in question the Greek Government, by an agreement with a company, Société Régie des revenus affectés à la Dette Publique Hellénique, made on July 14, 1925, and ratified on July 18 by a decree-law, the Greek State handed over to the plaintiffs (the Société Régie) the collection of these revenues. Subsequently, the Greek Government issued another decree-law the effect of which, according to the Société Régie, was to change the terms of the agreement of 1925. In the present action the Société Régie maintained that the new decree-law violated the agreement of 1925, which was of an international character by reason of its connection with the Treaty of 1897, and that the State could not disregard obligations which it had assumed in pursuance of an engagement of an international character.

Held : that the Société Régie had no remedy.

1. According to Article 807 (2) of the Code of Civil Procedure, an appeal to the Areopagus on account of a wrongful application or interpretation of an agreement between the State and juridical or physical persons, lay only in the case of "provisions establishing rules of objective law," as distinguished from provisions bearing directly upon the rights of the ordinary parties. The agreement of July 14, 1925, did not establish "rules of objective law."

2. A legislative act was not invalid because it was contrary either to general legal principles or to a former undertaking

[1] The decision of the Court of Genoa of March 14, 1930, reversed by the Court of Cassation, is reported in the same periodical, 1930, p. 492, with a note by Vassallo.

Case No. 4 *Contd.* of the State. It did not matter that the undertaking in question was entered into with regard to another State. There was no municipal remedy against the violation of such undertakings; the remedy must be an international one.

[Report: *Thémis*, vol. 44, p. 97.]

NOTE.—The learned reporter of this decision inclined to the view that the Court was guided in the first part of the judgment by the distinction between law-making treaties and other treaties. The analogy appears to the editor to be somewhat remote, but the circumstances of the case seem to warrant its inclusion in the *Digest*.

Case No. 5

International Law—Relation to Municipal Law—Treaties—How Far Abrogated by Subsequent Inconsistent Statutes.

In re BROOKS.

Panama, Supreme Court. May 21, 1931.

THE FACTS.—This was a petition for *habeas corpus*, against surrender to Honduras on a request for extradition. The petition was based on the fact that the Honduran Government had failed to remove the petitioner within thirty days after he was placed at its disposal. Article 7 of Law 44 of 1930 provided that an accused person shall be set free if he is not removed within thirty days.[1] On the other hand, Article 367 of the Bustamante Code,[2] put into force by Law 15 of 1928, allowed three months.

Held: that the petition must be refused. It did not matter that the Law of 1930 was later in time and therefore apparently derogated from the effect of the Law of 1928. The Court said: "The said Law 15 of 1928 adopted in all its parts the Convention approving the Code of Private International Law signed at Havana on February 13, 1928. That Convention was signed by the representatives of all the American countries and constitutes an international treaty whose fulfilment is obligatory for all the countries which signed and ratified it, according to the conditions indicated therein. These countries included Panama and Honduras. . . . Article 1 of this Con-

[1] That Article provided as follows: "If, after extradition has been granted and 30 days have passed from the time when the accused has been placed at the disposal of the requesting State, the latter does not remove him, the accused shall be set free."

[2] For the Bustamante Code, or Code of Private International Law, see *League of Nations Treaty Series*, vol. LXXXVI, p. 111; and Hudson, *International Legislation*, vol. IV, p. 2283.

vention reads: 'The contracting Republics accept and put into force the Code of Private International Law annexed to the present Convention.' . . . . Since the Code of Private International Law is the result of an agreement entered into between all the American States, no one of them has the power to add to it or to alter it in any way, and thus ignore the other signatory States. Accordingly, it is not possible for Law 44 of 1930 to modify or alter the provisions of the said Code, approved by Law 15 of 1928. . . . The provisions of Law 44 of 1930 are only applicable to extradition requests presented by countries not signatories of the Convention signed at Havana on February 13, 1928. The provisions of the Code of Private International Law, approved by Law 15 of 1928, are therefore of obligatory application in the present case."

[Report : 29 *Registro Judicial*, 487.]

International Law and Municipal Law—Relation between Extradition Treaty and Extradition Law.

See *In re Ciarletta*, decided by the German Supreme Court for Criminal Matters on January 18, 1932, where the decision was based largely on the consideration that as "the German Extradition Law contained no express provision concerning the relation between the Act and the existing treaties with respect to matters of legal assistance . . . it was a rule of international law, which had been recognised by Article 4 of the German Constitution, that international conventions cannot be altered or abrogated unilaterally by the legislature of one of the contracting States."

[Report : *Entscheidungen des Reichsgerichts in Strafsachen*, vol. 66, p. 87 ; *Juristische Wochenschrift*, 1932, p. 2344.]

International Law—Relation to Municipal Law—Treaties—Necessity for Municipal Legislation.

The view contained in some previous decisions (see *Annual Digest*, 1925-1926, Case No. 5, and *ibid.*, 1927-1928, p. 18), to the effect that the stipulations of international treaties have no binding force upon individuals if not incorporated in municipal law, was re-affirmed by the Supreme Administrative Court of Czechoslovakia in its decision of October 17, 1931, No. 13.900 (Boh. 9427 adm.).

International Law and Municipal Law—Municipal Validity of Acts Contrary to a Treaty.

See Case No. 7 (*Interpretation of the Statute of the Memel Territory*, (3)).

International Law and Municipal Law—Legal Nature of a Municipal Enactment Forming Part of an International Convention—Legal Nature of the Statute of the Memel Territory.

See Case No. 7 (*Interpretation of the Statute of the Memel Territory*, (2)).

International Law—Relation to Municipal Law—State Legislation and Constitutional Provisions as a Source of International Responsibility.

See Case No. 104 (*Treatment of Polish Nationals and Other Persons of Polish Origin or Speech in the Danzig Territory*).

International Law—Relation to Municipal Law—Enforcement of Legislation Contrary to International Law.

See Case No. 82 (*Croft v. Dunphy*).

International Law—Relation to Municipal Law—Construction of Municipal Statutes with a view to Avoiding Conflicts with International Law.

See Case No. 229 (*Royal Holland Lloyd v. United States* (c)).

International Law—Relation to Municipal Law—Treaties—Ratification—Treaties Passed by Parliament but not Ratified.

See Case No. 196 (*German-Polish Revaluation Convention Case*).

International Law—Relation to Municipal Law—Individuals—Position in International Law—How far Benefiting Directly under a Treaty regardless of Municipal Legislation—The Crown as Trustee for the Subject.

See Case No. 118 (*Civilian War Claimants Association, Ltd. v. The King*).

International Law—Relation to Municipal Law—Treaties as the Supreme Law of the Land.

See Case No. 38 (*Flensburger Dampfercompagnie v. United States*. Note).

International Law—Relation to Municipal Law—Restrictive Interpretation of Treaties—Treaties and Subsequent Statutes.

See Case No. 212 (*Clark v. Pigeon River Improvement Slide & Boom Co.*).

International Law—Relation to Municipal Law—Article 4 of the German Constitution.

See Case No. 179 (*Afghan Minister (Consular Activities) Case*).

International Law—Relation to Municipal Law—Operation of Treaties—The Doctrine of Transformation.

See Case No. 199 (*Public Prosecutor v. J.V.*).

International Law—Relation to Municipal Law—Indirect Repeal of Municipal Law by Subsequent Treaty.

See Case No. 198 (*Rennert v. Ministry of the Interior*).

VI.—International Comity

International Comity—Deportation of Aliens—Acquiescence of Country of Origin.

See Case No. 154 (*Re Janoczka*).

PART II

STATES AS INTERNATIONAL PERSONS

A—IN GENERAL

State—Notion of—In a Municipal Statute—As Distinguished from International Law—Expression "Foreign Country." **Case No. 6**

BURNET *v.* CHICAGO PORTRAIT COMPANY.

United States, Supreme Court. February 23, 1932.

(Hughes, C. J.; Van Devanter, McReynolds, Brandeis, Sutherland, Butler, Stone, Roberts, JJ.)

THE FACTS.—This was an income tax case. The Chicago Portrait Co., an Illinois corporation, owned 51 per cent. of the capital stock of the International Art Co. of Sydney, Australia, a foreign corporation. The Chicago Portrait Co. received dividends from the International Art Co., and sought credit for a proportionate part of the income tax paid by that Corporation to the Commonwealth of Australia, to the State of New South Wales, and to the Dominion of New Zealand. Section 238 (e) of the Revenue Act of 1921 (42 U.S. Stat. L. 227, 258, 259) permitted credit in the case of such tax paid "to any foreign country." Credit was allowed on account of the tax paid to the Commonwealth of Australia and to the Dominion of New Zealand, but was refused as to that paid to the State of New South Wales. The Board of Tax Appeals held that the respondent was entitled to the credit with respect to the last mentioned payment also ; the Circuit Court of Appeals affirmed that decision : 16 B.T.A. 1129 ; 50 F. (2d) 683. On *certiorari* to the United States Supreme Court,

Held : that the judgment must be affirmed. In delivering the Opinion of the Court, Mr. Chief Justice Hughes said : "The sole question is whether New South Wales is a 'foreign country' within the meaning of the applicable statute. The word 'country' in the expression 'foreign country,' is ambiguous. It may be taken to mean foreign territory or a foreign government. In the sense of territory, it may embrace all the territory subject to a foreign sovereign power. When referring more particularly to a foreign government, it may describe a foreign State in the international sense, that is, one that has the status of an international person with the rights and responsibilities under international law of a member cf the family of nations ; or it may mean a foreign government which has authority over

Case No. 6 ***Contd.*** a particular area or subject-matter, although not an international person but only a component part, or a political subdivision, of the larger international unit. The term 'foreign country' is not a technical or artificial one, and the sense in which it is used in a statute must be determined by reference to the purpose of the particular legislation." (285 U.S. 1, 4.).

The Court concluded that the word "country" in the statute in question was manifestly used in the sense of "government"; and that the purpose of the statute was to mitigate the evils of double taxation, which would be the same whether the tax was levied by a foreign power which could be considered an international person, or by a subordinate political entity. Consequently, the Court determined that the expression "foreign country" was intended to include a subordinate political entity having authority to levy taxes and that it was therefore unnecessary to determine the status of New South Wales in its relation to the Commonwealth of Australia. [Report: 285 U.S. 1.]

NOTE.—See *Proctor & Gamble Manufacturing Co.* v. *United States*, decided by the United States Court of Customs and Patent Appeals on March 30, 1932 (19 Court of Customs and Patent Appeals 415). In that case the Court, after quoting the passage cited in the case digested above, held that a cargo of whale oil from a Norwegian company which produced the oil upon the high seas on a Norwegian vessel was liable to duty under Section 1 of the Tariff Act of 1930, which provided that duties "shall be levied, collected, and paid upon all articles when imported from any foreign country into the United States."

I.—Beginning of State Existence

[For *Recognition*, see below, D.]

Establishment of New States—Coming into Existence of the Czechoslovak State—Effect of the Treaties of Peace—Recognition.

The view embodied in some previous decisions of Czechoslovak courts (see *Annual Digest*, 1919-1922, Cases Nos. 5 and 6, *ibid.*, 1925-1926, Case No. 8, and *ibid.*, 1927-1928, Case No. 94) to the effect that the establishment of the Czechoslovak State was independent of the Treaties of Peace, which merely granted international recognition to Czechoslovakia, was reaffirmed (with regard to the territory of Sub-Carpathian Russia) by the Czechoslovak Supreme Court of Justice in its decision of February 4, 1932, No. Zm IV 604/31 (Váž. 4366 tr.).

II.—Sovereignty and Independence

i.—In Foreign Relations.

[See also below, *Recognition of Acts of Foreign States and Governments*; Part IV, JURISDICTION; and Part VIII, TREATIES: XII. *Interpretation of Treaties.*]

Sovereignty—In Territory Subject to an Autonomous Régime by Virtue of a Treaty—Whether Sovereignty Divided—Legal Nature of a Municipal Enactment Forming Part of an International Convention—Question of Interpretation—Convention concerning Memel of May 8, 1924—Statute of the Memel Territory—Municipal Validity of Acts Contrary to a Treaty—Form of Applications Instituting Proceedings before the Court.

Case No. 7
PERMANENT COURT OF INTERNATIONAL JUSTICE.

INTERPRETATION OF THE STATUTE OF THE MEMEL TERRITORY.

Judgment of August 11, 1932.[1]

THE FACTS.—In Article 1 of the Convention of Paris of May 8, 1924, Great Britain, France, Italy and Japan transferred to Lithuania the sovereignty over the Memel Territory subject to the conditions contained in the Convention. Under Article 2 of this Convention the Memel Territory was to constitute, under the sovereignty of Lithuania, a unit enjoying legislative, judicial, administrative and financial autonomy, within the limits prescribed by the Statute which was annexed to the Convention and which, as an annex, was to be considered under Article 16 of the Convention as constituting for all purposes part of the Convention.

Article 7 of the Statute of the Memel Territory, which formed part of the Convention, provided as follows:

> "The affairs which, under the present Statute, are not within the jurisdiction of the local authorities of the Memel Territory shall be within the exclusive jurisdiction of the competent organizations of the Lithuanian Republic."

The first two paragraphs of Article 17 of the Statute provided as follows:

> "The Directorate shall exercise the executive power in the Memel Territory. It shall consist of not more than five

[1] The Court was composed as follows: Guerrero (Vice-President, acting as President); Baron Rolin-Jaequemyns, Count Rostworowski, Fromageot, de Bustamante, Altamira, Anzilotti, Urrutia, Adatci, Sir Cecil Hurst, Schücking, Negulesco, van Eysinga, Wang (Judges); Römer'is (Judge *ad hoc*).

Case No. 7 ***Contd.***

members, including the President, and shall be composed of citizens of the Territory.

"The President shall be appointed by the Governor and shall hold office so long as he possesses the confidence of the Chamber of Representatives. The President shall appoint the other members of the Directorate. The Directorate must enjoy the confidence of the Chamber of Representatives and shall resign if the Chamber refuses it its confidence. If, for any reason, the Governor appoints a President of the Directorate when the Chamber of Representatives is not in session, it shall be convened so as to meet within four weeks after the appointment to hear a statement from the Directorate and vote on the question of confidence."

In December 1931, the Lithuanian Government dismissed the President of the Memel Directorate on the ground that he had engaged in unauthorised negotiations with the German Government; they appointed as President of the Directorate a Lithuanian subject, and dissolved the Memel Diet. The four Powers, referred to above, were of the opinion that these acts were not in accordance with the Statute of the Memel Territory. They therefore brought the matter before the Council of the League and subsequently, in accordance with Article 17 of the Convention, instituted proceedings before the Court. In their application they asked the Court to decide, *inter alia*,

"(1) whether the Governor of the Memel Territory has the right to dismiss the President of the Directorate;

(2) in the case of an affirmative decision, whether this right only exists under certain conditions or in certain circumstances, and what those conditions or circumstances are;

(6) whether the dissolution of the Diet, carried out by the Governor of the Memel Territory on March 22nd, 1932, when the Directorate presided over by M. Simaitis had not received the confidence of the Diet, is in order."

Held (by ten votes to five, Judges de Bustamante, Altamira, Schücking, van Eysinga and Anzilotti dissenting): "(1) that the Governor of the Memel Territory is entitled, for the protection of the interests of the State, to dismiss the President of the Directorate in case of serious acts which violate the Convention of Paris of May 8th, 1924, including its annexes, and are calculated to prejudice the sovereignty of Lithuania, and if no other action can be taken; (2) that the dismissal of the President of the Directorate does not by itself involve the termination of the appointments of the other members of the Directorate; . . . . (6) that the dissolution of the Chamber of Representatives of the Memel Territory which was carried out on March 22nd, 1932, by the Governor of the said Territory when the Directorate presided over by M. Simaitis had not received the confidence of the Chamber, was not in order." (At p. 337.)

(1) *Sovereignty in Territory Subject to an Autonomous Régime by Virtue of a Treaty. Whether Sovereignty Divided.*—The Court interpreted as follows the effect of Articles 1, 2 and 7 of the Memel Convention:

"When, under the Convention of Paris, these four Powers transferred to Lithuania all the rights and title acquired by them from Germany, under Article 99 of the Treaty of Versailles, over the Memel Territory, and Lithuania undertook to secure to that Territory autonomy within the limits fixed by the Statute of Memel, it certainly was not the intention of the Parties to the Convention that the sovereignty should be divided between two bodies which were to exist side by side in the same territory. Their intention was simply to ensure to the transferred territory a wide measure of legislative, judicial, administrative and financial decentralization, which should not disturb the unity of the Lithuanian State and should operate within the framework of Lithuanian sovereignty.

"Whilst Lithuania was to enjoy full sovereignty over the ceded territory, subject to the limitations imposed on its exercise, the autonomy of Memel was only to operate within the limits so fixed and expressly specified.

"It follows that the sovereign powers of the one and the autonomous powers of the other are of quite a different order in that the exercise of the latter powers necessitates the existence of a legal rule which cannot be inferred from the silence of the instrument from which the autonomy is derived, or from an interpretation designed to extend the autonomy by encroaching upon the operation of the sovereign power." (At p. 313.)[1]

[1] But see the Joint Dissenting Opinion of de Bustamante, Altamira, Schücking and van Eysinga, where it was said: "If we disregard non-treaty international law and treaties binding Lithuania with the exception of the Paris Convention, this sovereignty is simply the residue left to the exclusive jurisdiction of Lithuania by the Convention of Paris. And as the Statute annexed to the Convention reserves—in terms which, as stated above, are as precise as possible—to the Memel Chamber of Representatives, and not to the Governor, the right to dismiss the President of the Directorate, Lithuania's sovereignty over the autonomous unit of Memel does not include the right to dismiss the President of the Directorate." (At pp. 346, 347.)

Case No. 7 ***Contd.***

"Given the terms of this Article, it is impossible to adduce the silence of the Statute in regard to any matter in order to restrict the sovereignty of Lithuania in favour of the autonomy of Memel, or to deny to the former the exercise of certain rights simply because they are not *expressly* provided for in the Statute of Memel. Moreover, the purpose of the Statute was not to confer rights on Lithuania, but to fix the limits of the autonomy which the Parties to the Convention of Paris of 1924 intended to establish in favour of the Memel Territory.

"The Court holds that Memel's autonomy only exists within the limits fixed by the Statute and that, in the absence of provisions to the contrary in the Convention or its annexes, the rights ensuing from the sovereignty of Lithuania must apply." (At p. 314.)

The Court could not adopt an interpretation of Article 17 of the Statute to the effect that the President of the Directorate was irremovable so long as he had the support of the Chamber. To do so would mean that the President would be able "to violate the Statute and to flout the authorities of the Lithuanian Government so long as he carried the Chamber with him. Such an interpretation would destroy the general scheme of the Convention of Paris of 1924 and the Statute annexed to it, under which Memel was to enjoy autonomy within defined limits, but was placed under the sovereignty of Lithuania. Both the autonomy as defined and the sovereignty were intended to be effective. . . It was not the intention of the Statute that the Lithuanian Government should be left with no protection against a violation of the Statute on the part of the Memel executive authorities and, further, that in cases where the Courts cannot interfere, the possibility of treating such acts as *non avenus* may be no sufficient protection." (At pp. 317, 318.)

(2) *The Legal Nature of a Municipal Enactment Forming Part of an International Convention. Question of Interpretation.*—The Court rejected the contention of Lithuania that as the Statute of the Memel Territory had been enacted as a Lithuanian law, it should be regarded and interpreted as such. It held that, for the purpose of the proceedings before the Court, the Statute of Memel must be regarded as a conventional arrangement binding upon Lithuania, and that it must be interpreted as such.

(3) *Municipal Validity of Acts Contrary to a Treaty.*—After having arrived at the conclusion that the dissolution of the Chamber was not in accordance with the Treaty, the Court

said: "It does not thereby intend to say that the action of the Governor in dissolving the Chamber, even though it was contrary to the treaty, was of no effect in the sphere of municipal law. This is tantamount to saying that the dissolution is not to be regarded as void in the sense that the old Chamber is still in existence, and that the new Chamber since elected has no legal existence." (At p. 336.) (However, it appears that the Court proceeded to qualify the preceding statement by pointing out that the four Powers, in submitting this question to the Court, did not intend to question the validity of the newly-elected Chamber, and that they merely intended to obtain an interpretation of the Statute which would serve as a guide for the future.)

(4) *Form of Applications Instituting Proceedings before the Court.*—Before dealing with the merits of the question the Court drew attention to the inconvenience resulting from the fact that some of the questions submitted to it were formulated as abstract questions without reference to the facts of the dispute which had arisen. The Court said: "If it was the dismissal of M. Böttcher which was the origin of the dispute and which led up to the other acts complained of, viz. the appointment of a new Directorate and the dissolution of the Chamber, the convenient and appropriate method in which to bring the difference of opinion before the Court would have been by means of submissions directed to the legality of these particular acts, leaving the Court to enunciate in its decision the principles on which that decision was based." (At pp. 311, 312.)[1]

[Report: *P.C.I.J.*, Series A/B, No. 49.]

[1] Judge Anzilotti was apparently inclined to take a more serious view of the irregularity referred to above. He was of the view that the Court ought to have declared the application inadmissible on the ground that it "does not embody the essential features of a claim for legal redress and tends to force the Court to deviate from the fundamental rules governing the activities of a judicial body." He said: "In its judicial capacity, the Court cannot answer questions; it must pass upon claims. The application mentioned in Article 40 of the Statute and Article 35 of the Rules is a claim for legal redress; and in such a claim the specification of the subject of the dispute can only be a statement of that which the Applicant wishes to obtain from the Court and of the reasons of law or of fact on the basis of which he feels entitled to obtain it (*petitum et causa petendi*). A properly constituted action at law is only possible if a claim is presented in this form, for an action is hardly conceivable unless there is a person who makes against some other person a claim upon which it is for the judge to pass according to law." (At p. 350.)

Case No. 8
PERMANENT COURT OF INTERNATIONAL JUSTICE.

Independence—Customs Union—Inalienability of Independence—Interpretation of Treaties—Equivalence of Consideration as an Element of Interpretation—Article 10 of the Covenant of the League—Rules of Interpretation.

CUSTOMS RÉGIME BETWEEN GERMANY AND AUSTRIA.

(Protocol of March 19, 1931.)

Advisory Opinion of September 5, 1931.[1]

THE FACTS.—Article 88 of the Treaty of St.-Germain of September 10, 1919, provides as follows:

> "The independence of Austria is inalienable otherwise than with the consent of the Council of the League of Nations. Consequently Austria undertakes in the absence of the consent of the said Council to abstain from any act which might directly or indirectly or by any means whatever compromise her independence, particularly, and until her admission to membership of the League of Nations, by participation in the affairs of another Power."

In a Protocol signed at Geneva on October 4, 1922, in connection with a guaranteed loan to Austria, Great Britain, France, Italy and Czechoslovakia declared "That they will respect the political independence, the territorial integrity and the sovereignty of Austria; that they will not seek to obtain any special or exclusive economic or financial advantage calculated directly or indirectly to compromise that independence; that they will abstain from any act which might be contrary to the spirit of the conventions which will be drawn up in common with a view to effecting the economic and financial reconstruction of Austria, or which might prejudicially affect the guarantees demanded by the Powers for the protection of the interests of the creditors and of the guarantor States; . . ." The same Protocol provided that the Austrian Government "Undertakes, in accordance with the terms of Article 88 of the Treaty of St.-Germain, not to alienate its independence; it will abstain from any negotiations or from any economic or financial engagement calculated directly or indirectly to compromise this independence. This undertaking shall not prevent Austria from maintaining, subject to the provisions of the Treaty

[1] The Court was composed as follows: Adatci (President); Guerrero (Vice-President); Kellogg, Baron Rolin-Jaequemyns, Count Rostworowski, Fromageot, de Bustamante, Altamira, Anzilotti, Urrutia, Sir Cecil Hurst, Schücking, Negulesco, van Eysinga, Wang (Judges).

of St.-Germain, her freedom in the matter of customs tariffs and commercial or financial agreements, and, in general, in all matters relating to her economic régime or her commercial relations, provided always that she shall not violate her economic independence by granting to any State a special régime or exclusive advantages calculated to threaten this independence."

In a Protocol signed at Vienna on March 19, 1931, Austria and Germany agreed to enter into negotiations for a treaty "to assimilate the tariff and economic policies of their respective countries" in accordance with the principles laid down in the Protocol. In the Protocol the Parties affirmed the independence of the two States and their desire to observe fully their international engagements. They undertook to agree upon a common tariff law and customs tariff to be put into force simultaneously and concordantly in Germany and Austria, the customs receipts to be apportioned according to an agreed quota. As between the two countries export and import duties and export or transit prohibitions were, in principle, to be removed. While the two Parties retained in principle the right to conclude commercial treaties on their own behalf, it was provided that such treaties should not be contrary to the purpose of the proposed customs union. The treaty was to be concluded for an unspecified duration, but could be denounced after three years.

On May 19, 1931, the Council of the League of Nations adopted a Resolution submitting to the Court for an Advisory Opinion the following question:

> "Would a régime established between Germany and Austria on the basis and within the limits of the principles laid down by the Protocol of March 19th, 1931, the text of which is annexed to the present request, be compatible with Article 88 of the Treaty of Saint-Germain and with Protocol No. 1 signed at Geneva on October 4th, 1922?"

Held (by Judges Guerrero, Rostworowski, Fromageot, de Bustamante, Altamira, Anzilotti, Urrutia, and Negulesco, the following Judges dissenting: Adatci, Kellogg, Rolin-Jaequemyns, Sir Cecil Hurst, Schücking, van Eysinga, and Wang): that the régime established on the basis of the Austro-German Protocol of March 19, 1931, would not be compatible with the Geneva Protocol of October 4, 1922.

(1) *Customs Union and Inalienability of Independence.*—While that régime did not in itself constitute an act alienating Austria's independence and while, in view of the reciprocal

Case No. 8 ***Contd.***

character of its provisions and the possibility of denunciation, Austria legally retained the possibility of exercising her independence, "it is difficult to deny that the projected régime of customs union constitutes a 'special régime' and that it affords Germany, in relation to Austria, 'advantages' which are withheld from third Powers." (At p. 52.) As such it was contrary to the terms of the Geneva Protocol. "If the régime projected by the Austro-German Protocol of Vienna in 1931 be considered as a whole from the economic standpoint adopted by the Geneva Protocol of 1922, it is difficult to maintain that this régime is not calculated to threaten the economic independence of Austria and that it is, consequently, in accord with the undertakings specifically given by Austria in that Protocol with regard to her economic independence." (At p. 52.)

(2) *Interpretation of Treaties. Equivalence of Consideration as an Element of Interpretation. Article* 10 *of the Covenant.*—As to the contention advanced by Austria and Germany that, as the first part of the Geneva Protocol constituted an affirmation on the part of Great Britain, France, Italy and Czechoslovakia of the obligations of Article 10 of the Covenant with regard to the guarantee of territorial integrity and political independence, and, as such, was merely a re-affirmation of the obligations of the Treaty of Saint-Germain not to participate in any act incompatible with the inalienability of the independence of Austria, Austria's undertakings ought to be regarded solely as the exact counterpart of the undertakings of the other Powers, *i.e.*, as a mere repetition of Article 88 of the Peace Treaty, the Court held that that contention could not be accepted. "The Covenant of the League of Nations, however, while it certainly contains an undertaking to respect the territorial integrity and political independence of each Member and even to preserve as against external aggression this territorial integrity and political independence, . . . contains neither any undertaking on the part of States not to alienate their own independence, of which they alone are in principle entitled to dispose, nor any undertaking not to seek economic advantages calculated to compromise the independence of another State which is free to dispose of it as it pleases." (At pp. 48, 49.)

[Report : *P.C.I.J.*, Series A/B, No. 41.]

NOTE.—I. Judges Guerrero, Rostworowski, Fromageot, Altamira, Urrutia and Negulesco held that the proposed Union would also be incompatible with Article 88 of the Treaty of St.-Germain.

II. Judge Anzilotti, in a Separate Opinion, held that the

proposed Union was primarily incompatible with Article 88 of the Treaty and that it was therefore incompatible with the Geneva Protocol which, in his view, merely applied the Treaty to a particular matter. He said, with regard to the terms "independence" and "inalienable" as used in the first paragraph of Article 88 : "With regard to the former, I think the foregoing observations show that the independence of Austria within the meaning of Article 88 is nothing else but the existence of Austria, within the frontiers laid down by the Treaty of Saint-Germain, as a separate State and not subject to the authority of any other State or group of States. Independence as thus understood is really no more than the normal condition of States according to international law ; it may also be described as *sovereignty* (*suprema potestas*), or *external sovereignty*, by which is meant that the State has over it no other authority than that of international law.

"The conception of independence, regarded as the normal characteristic of States as subjects of international law, cannot be better defined than by comparing it with the exceptional and, to some extent, abnormal class of States known as 'dependent States.' These are States subject to the authority of one or more other States. The idea of dependence therefore necessarily implies a relation between a superior State (suzerain, protector, etc.) and an inferior or subject State (vassal, *protégé*, etc.) ; the relation between the State which can legally impose its will and the State which is legally compelled to submit to that will. Where there is no such relation of superiority and subordination, it is impossible to speak of dependence within the meaning of international law.

"It follows that the legal conception of independence has nothing to do with a State's subordination to international law or with the numerous and constantly increasing states of *de facto* dependence which characterize the relation of one country to other countries.

"It also follows that the restrictions upon a State's liberty, whether arising out of ordinary international law or contractual engagements, do not as such in the least affect its independence. As long as these restrictions do not place the State under the legal authority of another State, the former remains an independent State however extensive and burdensome those obligations may be.

"This is obviously the standpoint of the Treaty of Saint-Germain when it proclaims the independence of Austria despite the many serious restrictions it imposes upon her freedom in the economic, military and other spheres. These restrictions do not put Austria under the authority of the other contracting States, which means that Austria is an independent State within the meaning of international law. This is the independence which Article 88 declares to be 'inalienable'." (At pp. 57, 58.)

He then examined the arguments of the German and Austrian Governments to the effect that the second sentence of Article 88

Case No. 8 ***Contd.***

merely drew the consequences from the first sentence and that therefore the acts from which Austria must abstain can only be acts of alienation or acts amounting to alienation. He said: "It is a fundamental rule of interpretation that words must be given the ordinary meaning which they bear in their context unless such an interpretation leads to unreasonable or absurd results.

"If we give to the words in the second sentence of Article 88—disregarding for the moment the last clause—the meaning they normally bear in their context, it is hard to admit that the acts in question are only acts of alienation or acts amounting to an alienation of independence. The ordinary meaning of the word 'compromise' is certainly not 'to alienate'; an 'act which might compromise . . . independence' is, in the ordinary meaning of the words, an act calculated to place independence in danger. If we take the ordinary meaning of the words in their context, an act may very well compromise a State's independence directly or indirectly or by one means or another, but I do not see how all this can be made to apply to alienation.

"Quite clearly the normal meaning of the words in the context of the second sentence of Article 88 is not the meaning given to them in the arguments of the German and Austrian Governments. If we interpret the words according to the meaning they would normally bear in their context, the conclusion is rather that Austria is obliged to abstain from certain acts which are not or are not necessarily acts alienating her independence, but which are calculated to expose that independence to danger." (At pp. 60, 61.)

III. The seven dissenting Judges (see above, p. 27) held that the proposed Customs Union was not incompatible either with Article 88 of the Treaty of St.-Germain or with the Geneva Protocol. They said, with regard to the terms "independence" and "inalienability" as used in the Treaty: "Independence is a term well understood by all writers on international law, though the definitions which they employ are diversified. A State would not be independent in the legal sense if it was placed in a condition of dependence on another Power, if it ceased itself to exercise within its own territory the *summa potestas* or sovereignty, *i.e.* if it lost the right to exercise its own judgment in coming to the decisions which the government of its territory entails.

"Restrictions on its liberty of action which a State may agree to do not affect its independence, provided that the State does not thereby deprive itself of its organic powers. Still less do the restrictions imposed by international law deprive it of its independence.

"The difference between the alienation of a nation's independence and a restriction which a State may agree to on the exercise of its sovereign power, *i.e.* of its independence, is clear. This latter is, for instance, the position of States which become Members of the League of Nations. It is certain that membership imposes upon them important restrictions on the exercise of their independence, without it being possible to allege that it entails an alienation of that independence.

"Practically every treaty entered into between independent States restricts to some extent the exercise of the power incidental to sovereignty. Complete and absolute sovereignty unrestricted by any obligations imposed by treaties is impossible and practically unknown.

"The 'alienation' of the independence of a State implies that the right to exercise these sovereign powers would pass to another State or group of States.

"The word 'compromise' in the second sentence of Article 88 implies 'involve danger to,' 'endanger' or 'imperil.' For an act to 'compromise' the independence of Austria it must be one which would imperil the continued existence of Austria as a State capable of exercising within its territory all the powers of an independent State within the meaning of independence given above." (At pp. 77, 78.)

They held, contrary to the Opinion of the majority, that "it was not enough that the proposed arrangement should be the grant of a special régime or exclusive advantages. The grant must be calculated to threaten Austria's independence." (At p. 81.)

Independence—Respect of—Hostile Expeditions against a Foreign State—Nullity of a Contract connected with the Organisation of a Revolution in a Foreign State. **Case No. 9**

In re FLÖRSHEIM.

France, Civil Tribunal of the Seine. July 2, 1932.

THE FACTS.—This was an action on a contract made on June 4, 1929, at Paris for the supply of arms and munitions for a "*coup d'Etat*" in Venezuela. The arms and munitions were carried to Venezuela, under the orders of General Delgado, by the German steamship *Falke*, which left Gdynia (Poland) on July 19. On August 12 the *Falke* took on board in the Bay of Cumana a contingent of 200 insurgents, and proceeded up the River Mançanarès. The "*coup d'Etat*" failed as a result of the intervention of the forces of the Venezuelan Government. The cargo was thrown overboard, the rebels were disembarked at Granada (in the Windward Isles), and the ship was interned a few days later by the British authorities at Port of Spain (Trinidad). Later the captain and the owners of the *Falke* were prosecuted in the German courts in accordance with Article 234 of the German Penal Code. As a result of a judgment delivered on June 4, 1930, the Maritime Office of Berlin de-

Case No. 9 *Contd.*

prived the captain and his second-in-command of their navigation certificates, stating that in aiding and abetting an armed revolt against the regular Government of Venezuela they had committed a grave breach of duty. In an action on the contract,

Held: that the contract was null and void. "Any act, agreement or contract the execution of which may disturb the established order in the territory of a State, is contrary to international public order and, therefore, illegal." This applied to the present contract, which sought to prepare and carry into effect a "*coup d'Etat*" designed to overthrow the government of a foreign State.

[Report: *Sirey*, 1934, Part 2, p. 73, with a note by Niboyet.]

NOTE.—See also a similar decision of the Commercial Tribunal of Luxembourg of March 8, 1930 (*Clunet*, 58 (1931), p. 429; *Annual Digest*, 1929-1930, Case No. 4), given in connection with the attempt of Dr. Dorten to establish a separatist régime in the Rhineland. On the *Falke* affair, see Ch. Rousseau in *R.G.*, 38 (1931), pp. 341-344.

Case No. 10

Act of State—French Practice—Assistance given by the Allied Powers from 1918 to 1921 to the Government of Admiral Koltchak—Agreement of March 14, 1919, on the Creation of an Interallied Railway Committee—Requisitioning of Coal by the Koltchak Government—Lack of Competence of the French Courts.

In re SOBIESZCZANSKI.

France, Conseil d'Etat. February 11, 1931.

THE FACTS.—The Allied Powers, by an Agreement of March 14, 1919, set up an Interallied Railway Committee to meet their needs with regard to railway transport in pursuance of their own and Admiral Koltchak's strategic plans. Representatives of the Siberian Government, France, Great Britain, Italy, Japan, and the United States sat on the Committee, which was given control over the operation of the railways. Payments for the transport of troops for the Allied Powers were due to the Siberian Government.

The plaintiff, formerly the owner of mines near Irkoutsk, claimed from the Allied Powers, and especially France, payment for coal which had been requisitioned for the Tomsk-Transbaïkalia railway. He invoked, *inter alia*, a decision of June 15, 1921, whereby the Interallied Railway Committee recognised his right to an indemnity on account of the total of the sums due for the transport of French troops.

Held: that the Conseil d'Etat had no competence in an action which raised questions concerning "military operations and the international relations of the French State."

[Report: *Recueil des arrêts du Conseil d'Etat*, 1931, p. 137.]

NOTE.—Compare the following decisions of the Conseil d'Etat: February 27, 1929, *In re Pancrazi* (same *Recueil*, 1929, p. 240); June 15, 1929, *In re Tokatlian* (*ibid.*, p. 754); October 31, 1930, *In re Klein* (*ibid.*, 1930, p. 874). See Duez, *Les actes de gouvernement* (1935), especially pp. 52-78.

Act of State—International Bodies—Reparation Commission—Legal Status of the French Agents of the Commission—Lack of Competence of the French Courts. **Case No. 11**

In re DAME ADRIEN AND OTHERS.

France, Conseil d'Etat. July 17, 1931.

THE FACTS.—The Conseil d'Etat was petitioned by certain French employees of the Reparation Commission to annul decisions given by the French Minister of Foreign Affairs, who had rejected their request for their official classification in the service in accordance with Article 18 of the Law of April 26, 1924.

Held: that the Conseil d'Etat had no competence to hear the petition. The petitioners belonged to an international organisation and their position was determinable only by international public law.

[Report: *Sirey*, 1932, Part 3, p. 81, with a note by Mlle. S. Basdevant.]

NOTE.—The decision is in accordance with other French decisions on the subject. For the legal status of the French officers sent to Upper Silesia in 1919-1921 as agents of the Plebiscite Commission, see the decision of the Conseil d'Etat of October 14, 1928, *In re Lamborot* (*Recueil des arrêts du Conseil d'Etat*, 1928, p. 1304, and *Revue du droit public*, 1929, pp. 116-127, with the conclusions of Rivet, Commissioner of the Government); for the position of officials of international organisations established at the time of the occupation of the Rhineland see decisions of the Conseil d'Etat of June 15, 1928, *In re Antin* (same *Recueil*, 1928, p. 764, and *Sirey*, 1929, Part 3, p. 45); April 24, 1929, *In re Marthoud* (same *Recueil*, 1929, p. 408); June 25, 1930, *In re Godard* (same *Recueil*, 1930, p. 648). It should be noted that the decision in the present case adopts as a test of the international status of an official the previous existence of an international agreement. (For a similar practice see the decision of the Conseil d'Etat of March 14, 1928, *In re Courmes* (same *Recueil*, 1928, p. 357). The case con-

Case No. 11 Contd. cerned the legal status of the Director of the Port of the Principality of Monaco. In its decision the Conseil d'Etat observed that the Director performed his duties "by reason of an agreement between the two Governments concluded in the general interests of the protection of public health.")

Case No. 12 **Act of State—Jurisdiction of Consular Officials—Treaty of Tien-Tsin of June 27, 1858, between China and France—Judicial Powers Granted to French Consuls in China by Article 35 of the Treaty—French Administrative Courts—Competence to Hear Cases concerning the Legality of Decisions Taken by French Consuls in the Exercise of these Powers.**

In re BANQUE DE L'UNION FRANCO-CHINOISE.

France, Conseil d'Etat. July 8, 1932.

THE FACTS.—Article 35 of the Treaty of Friendship, Commerce and Navigation between France and China, signed at Tien-Tsin on June 27, 1858, granted to French consuls in China the right of jurisdiction in actions relating to private rights. The Banque de l'Union Franco-Chinoise denied the legality of a consular order issued in accordance with this provision, and petitioned the Conseil d'Etat to annul it.

Held : that the Conseil d'Etat had no competence to hear the petition. The Conseil d'Etat had no powers with regard to the consular order, made under Article 35 of the Treaty of June 27, 1858, since it dealt with matters concerning the jurisdiction of the consular authorities.

[Report : *Dalloz,* 1933, Part 3, p. 7 ; *Sirey,* 1934, Part 3, p. 14.]

NOTE.—See with regard to the matter the conclusions of Rousselier, Commissioner of the Government, in *Dalloz* and *Sirey, loc. cit.* In cases concerning the act of a French diplomatic or consular agent, the Conseil d'Etat seeks to discover in what capacity the agent acted—as a diplomatic agent, or as a judicial authority (as in the present case), as arbitrator, as registrar of births, marriages and deaths, as bailiff, as notary public, etc. This often involves the question of the competence of the ordinary courts (Tribunal des Conflits : April 6, 1889, *In re Ville de Chateaubriant,* (*Recueil des arrêts du Conseil d'Etat,* 1889, p. 483) ; March 25, 1911, *In re Rouzier* (*Sirey,* 1911, Part 3, p. 105, with a note by Hauriou ; *Dalloz,* 1912, Part 3, p. 1, with a note by Mérignhac ; *Revue du droit public,* 1911, pp. 663-684, with a note by Jèze) ; Conseil d'Etat, March 26, 1924, *In re Taizon* (*Recueil des arrêts du Conseil d'Etat,* 1924, p. 330)) ; and, on other occasions, the competence of the Conseil d'Etat (Conseil d'Etat, November 14, 1923, *In re Lautier* (same *Recueil*, 1923, p. 723)), or its lack of competence (Conseil d'Etat, June 23, 1928, *In re Davin* (same *Recueil*, 1928, p. 786 ; *Dalloz*, 1929, Part 3, p. 21, with a note by Capitant ; *Sirey*, 1929, Part 3, p. 36)).

Act of State—Conclusiveness of Statements of the Executive—Statements of German Ministry of Defence as to the Limits of Foreign Bays—How far Binding upon German Courts.

See Case No. 61 (*The Senator Schröder*).

Act of State—Decisions of International Authorities—Occupation of the Territories on the Rhine by the Allied Armies (1919-1930)—Validity of the Measures of the Interallied High Commission for the Occupied Territories. **Case No. 13**

BORRÉLY *v.* DEPARTMENTAL ADMINISTRATION OF THE BOUCHES DU RHÔNE RAILWAY.

France, Court of Cassation, Civil Chamber. January 4, 1932.

THE FACTS.—In two decisions of the Court of Appeal of Aix, dated July 16, 1927, the exceptions made by the Interallied High Commission to the Convention of Berne of October 14, 1890, concerning traffic to the Rhineland, were declared illegal and invalid.

Held : that the decisions should be rescinded. "The courts have no authority to question the obligatory character of measures taken by an interallied organisation concerning traffic to territories occupied in virtue of Article 248 of the Treaty of Versailles."

[Report : *Gazette des Tribunaux*, March 27, 1932.]

NOTE.—The judgments of both the ordinary courts and the administrative tribunals have always recognised the Interallied High Commission as an international organisation whose decisions bound the French authorities (Conseil d'Etat : June 15, 1928, *In re Antin* (*Sirey*, 1929, Part 3, p. 45) ; April 24, 1929, *In re Marthoud* (*Recueil des arrêts du Conseil d'Etat*, 1929, p. 409) ; June 25, 1930, *In re Godard* (*ibid.* 1930, p. 648)).

Sovereignty—Treaties Involving Restrictions upon—Interpretation of—Abuse of Rights.

See Case No. 202 (*Case of the Free Zones of Upper Savoy and the District of Gex*, Note II.).

Sovereignty—Limitation of—Interpretation of Treaties.

See Case No. 205 (*The Kronprins Gustaf Adolf; The Pacific. United States and Sweden*).

Sovereignty—Limitation of—Effect on State Responsibility —Responsibility of Egypt for Acts of Mixed Courts.

See Case No. 98 (*Salem Case: United States and Egypt*).

iii.—Acts of Sovereignty and Transactions of a Private Character.

[See also Part IV, JURISDICTION: I. *Exemptions from.*]

Case No. 14

States—Acts of Sovereignty and Acts of a Private Character —Criteria for Deciding whether the Property of a Foreign State is Subject to the Common Rules of Private Law or Entitled to Special, Privileged Treatment—Public Loans.

FRENCH MINISTRY OF FINANCE *v.* BANCA ITALIANA DI SCONTO IN LIQUIDATION.

Italy, Court of Cassation. February 4, 1932.

THE FACTS.—In 1924, the French Ministry of Finance deposited with the Banca Italiana di Sconto the sum of 19,113,414 lire, obtained by a public loan issued in Italy and intended for the settlement of outstanding war debts. The money was to have been paid into the Banca Commerciale by the Banca Italiana di Sconto, but payment could not be made owing to a moratorium, *i.e.*, a legally authorised suspension of payments, by the latter. On August 8, 1924, the French Ministry of Finance took out a summons asking for a declaration that the sum should be considered, not as money paid into an ordinary current account, but as money derived from a public loan and allocated to a purpose of a public nature, the return of which would not be prevented by a provision of Italian municipal law authorising suspension of payments.

Held: that the summons should be dismissed. The Court held that the sum deposited by the French Ministry should be dealt with in the same way as other deposits on current account. The Court said: "The State, although it is *par excellence* an entity of public law whose normal activity falls within the functions of government, can nevertheless, in order to achieve its purpose, perform acts which fall within the sphere of private law. The function of sovereignty is not involved in such undertakings of a private law [*patrimoniale*] character. . . . Our legal system does not confine such undertakings to trading activities. . . . In France there has never been any doubt that the State can conclude, for its own purposes, transactions which are essentially of a private law nature. . . . It must therefore appear that the French Government, in the agreement for the negotiation of the loan, could properly enter into a contract of special deposit with the Banca Italiana di Sconto, and that, the transaction having been arranged and executed in Italy, it was governed by Italian law."

[Report : *Rivista italiana di diritto internazionale privato e processuale*, 1932, p. 386; *Giurisprudenza italiana*, 1932, p. 441.]

States—Acts of Sovereignty as Distinguished from Acts Done in a Private Capacity.

See Case No. 85 (*Brasseur and Associates* v. *The Republic of Greece*).

IV.—Recognition of Acts of Foreign States and Governments

[See also Part IV, JURISDICTION : I. *Territorial* ; and below, *Recognition of States, Governments and Belligerency*.]

Sovereignty and Independence—Recognition of Acts of Foreign States and Governments—Recognition of Decisions concerning Nationality—Provisions of the Treaties of Versailles and St. Germain concerning Nationality—Recognition by Austria of the Treaty of Versailles. **Case No. 15**

ETTINGER *v.* MINISTRY OF THE INTERIOR.

Poland, Supreme Administrative Court. January 22, 1932.

THE FACTS.—Under Article 4 of the Treaty between the Principal Allied and Associated Powers and Poland of June 28, 1919, Poland declared to be Polish nationals, *ipso facto* and without the requirement of any formality, persons of German, Austrian, Hungarian or Russian nationality who were born in Polish territory of parents habitually resident there. The plaintiff contended that he was a Polish national by virtue of this article. He had acquired in 1904 the right of domicile in Vienna. On May 4, 1927, he had obtained from the competent municipal authorities in Vienna a certificate to the effect that as from July 16, 1920 (the date of the coming into force in Austria of the Treaty of St. Germain) he had lost his Austrian

Case No. 15 *Contd.*

nationality and that as from that date he must be considered a Polish national by virtue of the Treaty. The Polish Ministry of the Interior, on the other hand, refused to recognise that the plaintiff was a Polish national. It considered that he retained Austrian nationality by virtue of Article 70 of the Peace Treaty of St. Germain which provided that every person possessing rights of citizenship (*pertinenza*) in territory which formed part of the territories of the former Austro-Hungarian Monarchy shall acquire *ipso facto*, to the exclusion of Austrian nationality, the nationality of the State exercising sovereignty over the territory in question. It held that the certificate of the Vienna authorities of May 4, 1927, was contrary to the Treaty of St. Germain since the Austrian authorities were not entitled to base their decisions on the Treaty of Versailles, which Treaty had been neither signed nor promulgated by Austria. Finally, the Ministry held that "the initiative in matters of nationality in concrete cases does not lie with Austria. Consequently the case must be taken up by one of the contracting parties to the Treaty, since Article 230 of the Treaty of St. Germain provides that 'Austria undertakes to recognise any new nationality which has been or may be acquired by her nationals under the laws of the Allied and Associated Powers and in accordance with the decisions of the competent authorities of those Powers pursuant to naturalisation laws or under treaty stipulations, and to regard such persons as having, in consequence of the acquisition of such new nationality, in all respects severed their allegiance to their country of origin.' "

In the present action the plaintiff pleaded Articles 64, 87 (2), and 91 of the Treaty of St. Germain. Those articles provided as follows:

> *Article* 64: "Austria admits and declares to be Austrian nationals *ipso facto* and without the requirement of any formality all persons possessing at the date of the coming into force of the present Treaty rights of citizenship (*pertinenza*) within Austrian territory who are not nationals of any other State."
>
> *Article* 87 (2): "Austria undertakes to recognise the full force of all treaties or agreements which may be entered into by the Allied and Associated Powers with States now existing or coming into existence in future in the whole or part of the former Empire of Russia as it existed on August 1, 1914, and to recognise the frontiers of any such States as determined therein."

By Article 91 Austria renounced all rights and title over territories situated outside her new frontiers and undertook to accept the settlement made in regard to those territories, particularly in so far as concerned the nationality of the inhabitants.

Held (on appeal): that the claim of the plaintiff was well founded. The certificate of the administration of the City of Vienna of May 4, 1927, evidently had in view the rule contained in Article 64. This followed indirectly from a comparison of the text of that article with the reference, contained in the certificate, to July 16, 1920, which was the date of the coming into force in Austria of the Peace Treaty, as well as with the reference, also contained in the certificate, to the Polish nationality of the plaintiff. Apparently the Ministry was of the view that the Austrian authorities, in considering whether in any concrete case Austrian nationality had been acquired by virtue of Article 64, could not on their own initiative take into consideration the question whether the person concerned was a national of another State and particularly of a State which was one of the Allied and Associated Powers. That supposition was erroneous. "For it follows from the essence of the sovereignty of a State that the question whether a certain person is the national of a State must be decided by that State. Thus the decision whether the plaintiff is, by virtue of Article 64, an Austrian national, lies with the Austrian authorities. An authority which is competent to make a decision is *ipso facto* competent, unless specific legal provisions stipulate the contrary, to take into consideration all facts which are material for the decision. Consequently, the administration of the City of Vienna was entitled to take into account, for the purposes of its certificate, the question whether the plaintiff is a 'Polish national'." No limitations in this respect could be found either in Article 64 or in Article 230. The first of these two articles denied the possibility of acquiring Austrian citizenship not to persons whom their own State required to be excluded from acquisition of Austrian nationality, but to persons who were citizens of other States irrespective of whether the State in question did or did not require Austria not to recognise such citizens of the other State as citizens of Austria. In Article 230 Austria undertook to recognise the nationality of an Allied or Associated Power which had been or might be acquired by an Austrian national in accordance with the laws of such Power and by virtue of decisions of the competent authorities of such Power. Austria did not,

Case No. 15 Contd. however, in that article, undertake to recognise the acquisition by her nationals of the nationality of any of the Allied or Associated Powers except such acquisition as might result from a decision of the authorities of an Allied or Associated Power. In consequence, where acquisition of Polish nationality took place *ipso jure*, as was the case where nationality was acquired by birth in virtue of Article 4 of the Treaty of Versailles, Article 230 was not a sufficient basis for refusing to Austria the right to assume, for the purpose of deciding the question of Austrian nationality, that the person concerned had acquired Polish nationality.

"With regard to the . . . view . . . that Austrian authorities are not entitled to take note of the Treaty of Versailles . . . since Austria neither signed nor promulgated it, it must be noted that the duty which Austria has under Articles 87 (2) and 91 of the Peace Treaty [of St. Germain] of recognising the Treaty of Versailles, is not made dependent upon Austria's signing or promulgating it . . ."

[Report: *Zb.W.N.T.A.*, X (1932), No. 483 A, p. 27.]

NOTE.—See also *Löwenheck* v. *Eber*, decided on October 8, 1931, by the Third Division of the Supreme Court: *Zb.O.S.N.*, III (i), Part 2, No. 178, p. 70.

V.—Continuity of States

[See also below, *State Succession*.]

Case No. 16 **Continuity of States—Juridical Identity of Czarist Russia and the Union of Soviet Socialist Republics—Continuance of Treaty Obligations in Case of Non-Recognition of New Government—Convention concerning Civil Procedure of July 17, 1905—*Cautio judicatum solvi*—Effect of Suspension of Diplomatic Intercourse—Absence of Denunciation.**

LOWINSKY *v.* RECEIVER IN BANKRUPTCY OF THE EGYPTISCH-TÜRKSCHE HANDWERKSIGARETTENFABRIEK "JAKA", LTD.

Holland, District Court of Amsterdam. June 7, 1932.

THE FACTS.—See Case No. 17. In this case the plaintiff, a Russian subject, claimed, in virtue of the Hague Convention on Civil Procedure of July 17, 1905, to be exempt from the rule requiring security for costs (*cautio judicatum solvi*) from aliens.

Held: that the security was not due. "In conformity with an established principle of public international law, changes in the form of government of a State have no influence on its rights and obligations under the Law of Nations so long as its existence as a State and, therefore, as an international person, remains unimpaired. This is the case with the U.S.S.R., which has to be looked upon as a sovereign federal State embracing by far the greater part of the territory and the population of the former Russian Empire. On this ground the Court holds that the Convention on Civil Procedure is still in force between the Netherlands and the U.S.S.R., so that exemption from the obligation to give security for costs must be granted to the plaintiff (defendant in the interlocutory proceedings). No decisive importance ought to be attributed to the absence of diplomatic relations between the Netherlands and the Soviet Government seeing that, though the suspension of diplomatic intercourse may cause insuperable difficulties in regard to the execution of a judgment in costs against a Russian plaintiff, the treaty obligations between the contracting States remain in full force as long as they are not cancelled by means of a regular denunciation in conformity with Article 29 of the Convention."[1]

[Report: *Weekblad van het Recht*, No. 12572; *Nederlandsche Jurisprudentie*, 1933, p. 1111.]

Continuity of States—Juridical Identity of Czarist Russia and the Union of Soviet Socialist Republics—Continuance of Treaty Obligations in Case of Non-Recognition of New Government—Convention on Civil Procedure of July 17, 1905—*Cautio judicatum solvi*—Effect of Suspension of Diplomatic Intercourse. **Case No. 17**

N. AND M. SHIPOFF *v.* ELTE.

Holland, Cantonal Court of The Hague. July 6, 1931.

THE FACTS.—Two Russian dancers engaged by a revue theatre at The Hague were given notice, and claimed damages for wrongful dismissal. In the course of interlocutory proceedings the defendant asked for security for costs (*cautio*

[1] The same divergence of opinion concerning the exemption of Russian plaintiffs from the *cautio judicatum solvi*, which appears from the two cases Nos. 16 and 17, and which has not yet been settled by a final judgment of the Supreme Court, revealed itself in an earlier case, which came before the District Court of Amsterdam. The Court's decision of October 16, 1925, in *Wirbelauer* v. *De Handelsvennootschap onder de Firma Lippmann Rosenthal en Co.* (*Weekblad van het Recht*, No. 11441; *Nederlandsche Jurisprudentie*, 1926, p. 775: cf. *Annual Digest*, 1927-1928, Case No. 36) was the same as in the judgment of 1932 cited above, but the grounds were somewhat different. The Court considered that, irrespective of the question whether the Convention of 1905 could be regarded as binding upon the two Governments concerned, their nationals had in any case acquired independent rights under the Convention

Case No. 17 *Contd.*

judicatum solvi). The plaintiffs claimed to be exempt from this rule in virtue of the multilateral Convention on Civil Procedure of July 17, 1905, to which both the Netherlands and Russia were parties. At the time of the action Holland had not recognised the government of the U.S.S.R. It was maintained by the defendant that, in view of this, the Convention of 1905 was not applicable.

Held: that the claim for security for costs must be allowed. "The engagements entered into by them [Holland and Russia] during the then existing monarchical form of government in Russia must be held to have remained in force after that form of government had been modified even though the new Government has not been recognised by the Netherlands. Consequently, the said Convention has maintained its binding force between the State of the Netherlands and the U.S.S.R. . . . The contracting parties, by concluding the said Convention, aimed at bringing about uniformity in the solution of questions relating to the law of international proceedings. On the other hand, it is apparent from the terms of the Convention that in many cases they considered that solution possible only between States which mutually entertain diplomatic relations. [Reference was made here to Articles 1, 9, 10, 19 and 21, prescribing or assuming the collaboration of consular officers and, if necessary, of the diplomatic agents of the requiring State.] It follows, then, that the contracting States at the time intended that the treaty provisions should be binding upon them only when, and as long as, diplomatic intercourse should exist between them, and that, therefore, the Treaty should not be operative so long as that intercourse is suspended."

[Report: *Weekblad van het Recht*, No. 12366; *Nederlandsche Jurisprudentie*, 1931, p. 958.]

NOTE.—For the contrary view see Case No. 16 and the comments on that case.

and were therefore entitled to its benefits. In a note to that case Professor Verzijl criticised the view that Russian subjects could derive independent rights from a Convention said to have ceased to be in force as between the two Governments or States. However, he supported the conclusion on the ground that the Convention had never been officially denounced by either of the parties in question, and continued therefore to be in force. In the case reported above the District Court seems to have adopted this view.

Cf. also the decision of the Federal Tribunal of Zürich of February 2, 1923, in *Re Lepeschkin* (*Annual Digest*, 1923-1924, Case No. 189; also printed in the annex to an article by Professor Kosters in *Bulletin de l'Institut Intermédiaire International*, IX, pp. 1 *et seq.*, 31 *et seq.*).

Continuity of States—State Succession—Treaties—Dismemberment of the Former Austrian Empire—Position of the Austrian Republic—Effect of Treaties on Third Parties—Treaty of St. Germain. **Case No. 18**

BILLIG *v.* HANDELSVENNOOTSCHAP ONDER DE FIRMA S. EINHORN'S SÖHNE.

Holland, District Court of Amsterdam. January 23, 1931.

THE FACTS.—Billig, a Roumanian national domiciled in Vienna (Austria), plaintiff in an action against a Dutch copartnership, invoked the Hague Convention on Civil Procedure of July 17, 1905, to obtain exemption from the rule requiring security for costs (*cautio judicatum solvi*) from aliens. Holland and Roumania were both parties to the Convention. The parties in the present case disagreed on the question whether the Austrian Republic, which came into existence after the collapse of the Austrian Monarchy, was a party to the Convention.

Held: that the exemption must be allowed. The Austrian Republic must be held to be a party to the Convention on the sole ground that it appeared to have declared that it considered itself bound by the Convention, in consequence of the signature thereof by the former Austrian Monarchy. That Treaty had never been denounced. The Court refused to take into account either the Treaty of St. Germain of September 10, 1919, to which Holland was not a party and which contained provisions concerning certain pre-war multilateral treaties, or the possible existence of treaties between Austria and Roumania concerning the *cautio judicatum solvi*, since in the case under consideration the Dutch Courts were not concerned with treaties which were not binding upon Holland.

[Report: *Weekblad van het Recht*, No. 12335; *Nederlandsche Jurisprudentie*, 1931, p. 710.]

NOTE.—Compare, however, *Czechoslovakian Co-operative Society* v. *Otten* (*Annual Digest*, 1923-1924, Case No. 42) concerning a similar question with regard to Czechoslovakia, which was held not to be bound by the Convention of 1905.

States—Continuity of—Russian Empire and Soviet Russia.

See Case No. 69 (*Lazard Brothers & Co. v. Midland Bank, Ltd.*).

B.—COMPOSITE AND DEPENDENT STATES AND TERRITORIES

I.—Unions of States

i.—Federal States and Confederations.

Federal States—Disputes Between Members of—Law Applicable.

See Case No. 57 (*Connecticut v. Massachusetts*).

Federal States—How Far Succeeding to Rights of State-Members—Prussia and Germany

See Case No. 38 (*Flensburger Dampfercompagnie v. United States*).

Federal States—State-Member of a Federation—Lack of International Status—Loan Contracted in France—Competence of the French Courts.

See Case No. 84 (*State of Céara v. d'Archer de Montgascon*) and *Annual Digest*, 1927-1928, Case No. 21 (*State of Céara v. Dorr and Others*).

ii.—Other Unions (including Customs Unions).

Customs Unions—Compatibility with Independence of States—Proposed Austro-German Customs Union.

See Case No. 8 (*Customs Régime between Germany and Austria*).

II.—British Commonwealth of Nations

Case No. 19 **British Dominions — Treaty - Making Power — Canada — Power to Implement Treaties in Matters not Expressly Reserved to the Federation.**

(a) *In re* THE REGULATION AND CONTROL OF AERONAUTICS IN CANADA.

British Empire, Judicial Committee of the Privy Council. October 22, 1931.

(Lord Sankey, L.C., Viscount Dunedin, Lords Atkin, Russell of Killowen, and Macmillan.)

(b) *In re* THE REGULATION AND CONTROL OF RADIO COMMUNICATION IN CANADA.

British Empire, Judicial Committee of the Privy Council. February 9, 1932.

(Viscount Dunedin, Lords Blanesburgh, Merrivale, Russell of Killowen, and Sir George Lowndes.)

[Both cases on appeal from the Supreme Court of Canada.]

THE FACTS.—The British North America Act, 1867, Sect. 132, provided that: "The Parliament and Government of Canada shall have all powers necessary or proper for performing the obligations of Canada, or of any Province thereof, as part of the British Empire, towards foreign countries arising under treaties between the Empire and such foreign countries." The points at issue in these cases were, *inter alia*, whether this section conferred power on the Dominion Parliament and Government (as distinct from the Provincial Parliaments and Governments) to implement the obligations incurred by Canada as a whole as a party to (a) the International Air Convention, 1919, (b) the International Radiotelegraph Convention, 1927.

(a) The International Air Convention was drawn up in Paris at the Peace Conference, and dated October 13, 1919. It was subsequently signed by representatives of the Allied and Associated Powers, including Canada, and was ratified by His Majesty on behalf of the British Empire on June 1, 1922.

Held: that the International Air Convention was a treaty "in force between the British Empire and seventeen other States" within the meaning of Sect. 132 of the British North America Act, 1867. The Parliament and Government of Canada had therefore exclusive legislative and executive authority under this section for performing the obligations of Canada, or of any Canadian Province, under the Convention.

(b) The International Radiotelegraph Convention, 1927, was concluded between the Governments of about 80 countries, including Great Britain, the Dominion of Canada and other Dominions, British India, and various Colonies. The representatives of Canada were appointed by the Governor-General in Council, and with the other signatories were described in the preamble as "the plenipotentiaries of the countries named." The Convention and Regulations were ratified and confirmed on behalf of His Majesty's Government in Canada by an instrument dated July 12, 1927, and signed by the Secretary of State

Case No. 19 ***Contd.*** for External Affairs, Canada, which stated that the Convention had been "signed by the representatives of His Majesty's Government in Canada and of the other Governments specified therein." They were ratified and confirmed on behalf of His Majesty's Government in Great Britain by an instrument in the same form signed by the Secretary of State for Dominion Affairs.

Held: that the Convention was not a treaty within Sect. 132 of the Act. ". . . It is said with truth that, while as regards aviation there was a treaty, the convention here is not a treaty between the Empire as such and foreign countries, for Great Britain does not sign as representing the Colonies and Dominions. She only confirms the assent which had been signified by the Colonies and Dominions who were separately represented at the meetings which drafted the convention." [Nevertheless, the Parliament and Government of Canada had power to implement the Convention under the general words of Sect. 91 of the British North America Act, which assigns to the Government of the Dominion the power to make laws "for the peace order and good government of Canada in relation to all matters not coming within the classes of subjects by this Act assigned exclusively to the legislatures of the Provinces".]

[Report: (a) *L.R.* [1932] A.C. 54; (b) *L.R.* [1932] A.C. 304.]

NOTE.—In *Attorney-General for British Columbia* v. *Attorney-General for Canada and Others* ([1937] A.C. 326) the Privy Council held that the power conferred on the Dominion Parliament and Government under Section 132 (or Section 91) did not extend to the implementing of obligations incurred by the ratification of International Labour Conventions. *Per* Lord Atkin, delivering the judgment of the Board: "The obligations are not obligations of Canada as part of the British Empire, but of Canada by virtue of her new status as an international person, and do not arise under a treaty between the British Empire and foreign countries. This was clearly established by the decision in the Radio case, and their Lordships do not think that the proposition admits of any doubt."

III.—Protected and Vassal States and Protectorates

Free City of Danzig—Constitution of—Protection by the League of Nations. **Case No. 20**

PERMANENT COURT OF INTERNATIONAL JUSTICE.

For a statement by the Permanent Court of International Justice to the effect that "the League, as guarantor of the Constitution, is therefore concerned not merely with the text of the Constitution, but also with the proper application of it"; and that "the League of Nations, as guarantor of the Constitution of the Free City, has the right—which, in practice, it exercises through the Council—as well as the duty, to intervene in the event of an erroneous application by Danzig of its Constitution"[1], see Advisory Opinion of February 4, 1932.[2] (*Treatment of Polish Nationals and Other Persons of Polish Origin or Speech in the Danzig Territory*): *P.C.I.J.*, Series A/B, No. 44, p. 21. See also Case No. 104.

Protectorates—Morocco—Moroccan Budget—Distribution of Financial Power Between the State Exercising Protection and the Protected State. **Case No. 21**

In re GRANGE AND LE GLAY.

France, Conseil d'Etat. December 16, 1932.

THE FACTS.—The Director of Public Debts at the French Ministry of Finance ordered the Treasurer-General of Morocco to provide for the payment of a debt in the Moroccan budget.

Held: that the order should be annulled, on the ground that an official of the French Ministry of Finance could not issue an order of that nature to the Treasurer-General of Morocco, "who acts on behalf of the Moroccan Government."

[Report: *Dalloz hebdomadaire*, 1933, p. 151.]

NOTE.—The establishment of a protectorate involves a division of legislative, executive and judicial powers between the State exercising protection and the protected State. The decision of the

[1] The Court relied here largely on the Resolution adopted by the Council of the League on November 17, 1920, to the effect that the guarantee of the League implied:

"(1) that this Constitution will have to obtain the approval of the League of Nations;

"(2) that the Constitution can only be changed with the permission of the League of Nations; and

"(3) that the constitutional life of the Free City of Danzig must always be in accordance with the terms of this Constitution."

[2] For the composition of the Court see p. 209.

Case No. 21 Contd. Conseil d'Etat applies this distinction to the financial and budgetary régime. On the financial régime in French Protectorates see Rolland and Lampué, *Précis de législation coloniale* (1936), pp. 489-492.

Free City of Danzig—Status of—Constitutional Provisions and Acts of Legislation—State Responsibility.

See Case No. 104 (*Treatment of Polish Nationals and Other Persons of Polish Origin or Speech in the Danzig Territory*).

Protectorates—Right of Foreign Courts to Enquire into the Relationship Between the Protecting State and the Protectorate — Treaties — Enforcement of — Agencies of Interpretation.

See Case No. 195 (*Sarasin and Pictet v. Fournier*).

IV.—Mandates

i.—Sovereignty over Mandated Territories. Status of the Mandated Territories.

Case No. 22 **Territories under "B" Mandates—The Cameroons—The Public Land Régime in Mandated Territories—Refusal to Grant a Permit to Cut Trees in a Forest Situated on the Public Land—Responsibility of the French State.**

In re KARL AND TOTO SAMÉ.

France, Conseil d'Etat. July 3, 1931.

THE FACTS.—The present request to the Conseil d'Etat was in substance an action to establish the responsibility of the French State for an alleged illegal act of the Public Forestry Service in the Cameroons. Two natives, Karl and Toto Samé, who held an authorisation to exploit certain land, were, on October 24, 1924, refused a "permit to cut" by the French High Commissioner in the Cameroons. The natives requested the Conseil d'Etat to annul a decision of the Minister for the Colonies, dated September 22, 1925, by which he had refused to grant them the indemnity claimed by them as a result of the refusal of the permit. They alleged that the refusal amounted to an offence committed in the course of the performance of official duties. In his decision the Minister for the Colonies expressed the view that "the French State does not possess any right of property in the land in mandated territories" and that this view accorded with the Covenant of the League of Nations.

Held : that the request should be rejected. "If it is admitted that these public forests belong to the French State (a question of substance which should be referred for decision to the Minister for Foreign Affairs, who is alone competent to interpret the Treaty of Versailles), the record shows that the Commissioner of the Republic committed no offence in taking the steps complained of in his capacity as an agent of the French State. If it is admitted that these public forests belong to the territory of the Cameroons, the French State cannot be made responsible for acts committed by the Commissioner of the Republic as the agent for this territory."

[Report : *Dalloz,* 1931, Part 3, p. 36 ; *Sirey,* 1931, Part 3, p. 129, with a note by Ch. Rousseau ; *Revue du droit public,* 1931, pp. 785-795.]

NOTE.—See a detailed account of this case in the conclusions of Ettori, High Commissioner of the Government, reported in *Dalloz, Sirey,* and *Revue du droit public.*

The plaintiffs alleged that the public service had committed an offence in the course of the administration of the forests. The Conseil d'Etat could have rejected the request on the ground that the French State possessed neither public nor private domains in the Cameroons. The only domain in existence was that of the Cameroons. This principle was established by a Resolution of the Council of the League of Nations, dated June 9, 1926. For a previous decision concerning the mandated territories see *Annual Digest,* 1929-1930, Case No. 15. The following decisions of the Conseil d'Etat may be added to the case reported there : (1) territories under "A" Mandate : August 6, 1925, *In re Moundji, Recueil des arrêts du Conseil d'Etat,* 1925, p. 815 (competence of the Conseil d'Etat to decide cases arising out of the operation of the public services attached to the army of occupation in Syria) ; May 14, 1926, *In re Kherlakian, ibid.,* 1926, p. 496 (competence of the Conseil d'Etat to decide cases arising out of the operation of the French Intelligence Service in Syria) ; May 15, 1931, *In re Houberon, ibid,* 1931, p. 531, and *Dalloz hebdomadaire,* 1931, Part 3, p. 34 (lack of competence of the Conseil d'Etat to decide cases concerning the acts of the mandatory authority as the authority responsible for the local public services) ; (2) territories under "B" Mandate : Conseil d'Etat, March 28, 1924, *In re Woelfell, Recueil des arrêts du Conseil d'Etat,* 1924, p. 446 (non-applicability to acts occurring in a mandated territory of a document establishing a procedure for acts occurring in a colony) ; and Tribunal des Conflits, July 9, 1928, *Thomas* v. *Rouaux, ibid.,* 1928, p. 871 (application to territories under a "B" Mandate of the principle of the separation of the administrative from the judicial authority).

French Mandate Over the Cameroons—Ownership of the Forests on Public Land—Interpretation of Article 22 of the Covenant of the League of Nations—Exclusive Competence of the Minister for Foreign Affairs—Lack of Competence of the Minister for the Colonies to Interpret an International Treaty.

See Case No. 22 (*In re Karl and Toto Samé*).

V.—Territories under Joint or International Government

Case No. 23 **Condominium—Boundary Rivers—Joint Jurisdiction—Germany and Holland.**

DUTCH-PRUSSIAN CONDOMINIUM (1816) CASE.

Germany, Supreme Administrative Court. November 24, 1932.

THE FACTS.—The appellant ran a mill at a stream which formed the boundary between Germany and Holland. From this stream he drew water for the purposes of the mill; the water not so used he returned to the stream. The appellant applied for registration of these water rights in the Water Register, in accordance with the German Water Act. The District Committee refused the application on the ground that, under the Frontier Agreement between Prussia and Holland of June 26, 1816, water courses running between the two countries were owned by them jointly and that, accordingly, no right could be created which existed solely in Prussia. The miller appealed.

Held: that the appeal must be dismissed. The Agreement of 1816 created a joint ownership under international law, a so-called *condominium*, according to which both contracting States exercised a joint jurisdiction over frontier streams. This meant that the jurisdiction of each State was limited by that of the other State. Accordingly, there existed a joint and undivided jurisdiction over this portion of the stream. It followed that Prussia could not legislate unilaterally for the territory in question, seeing that the Prussian State did not enjoy unrestricted jurisdiction over it. The German Water Act was therefore not applicable to frontier streams which were subject to the joint jurisdiction of Prussia and the Netherlands.

[Report: *Reichs- und Preussisches Verwaltungsblatt*, Vol. 55 (1934), p. 528.]

NOTE.—The Court pointed out that, in the course of the parliamentary debates leading to the incorporation of the relevant Article in the Water Act, it was expressly stated that the special provisions of the Frontier Agreement could not be overridden unilaterally by a Prussian Act.

D.—RECOGNITION

[See also above, *Recognition of Acts of Foreign States and Governments* ; and below, Part IV, JURISDICTION : *Territorial*.]

ii.—Of Governments.

Recognition of Governments—Effects of Non-Recognition—Whether Depriving Subjects of Unrecognised Country of Right of Action—Position of Aliens. **Case No. 24**

RUSSIAN VOLUNTEER FLEET *v.* UNITED STATES.

United States, Supreme Court. February 24, 1931.

(Hughes, C.J. ; Holmes, Van Devanter, McReynolds, Brandeis, Sutherland, Butler, Stone, Roberts, JJ.)

THE FACTS.—This was an action brought against the United States in the Court of Claims by a Russian corporation to recover compensation for the requisition by the United States Shipping Board Emergency Fleet Corporation of contracts for the construction of two vessels. An Act of June 15, 1917, authorising the requisition, provided that the person entitled to compensation, in case the compensation awarded should be unsatisfactory, "shall be entitled to sue the United States" to recover "just compensation" (40 U.S. Stat. L. 182, 183). Section 155 of the United States Judicial Code provided that "aliens who are citizens or subjects of any government which accords to citizens of the United States the right to prosecute claims against such government in its courts, shall have the privilege of prosecuting claims against the United States in the Court of Claims, whereof such court, by reason of their subject matter and character, might take jurisdiction." (36 U.S. Stat. L. 1139.) The Court of Claims held (in 1929) that, since the United States had not recognised the Soviet Government of Russia, the petitioner was not entitled to maintain its suit under §155 of the Judicial Code. The action was dismissed for want of jurisdiction: *Russian Volunteer Fleet* v. *United States*, 68 Ct. Cl. 32. On *certiorari* to the United States Supreme Court,

Held: that the judgment must be reversed. The peti-

Case No. 24 *Contd.*

tioner's right to compensation was governed by the Act of June 15, 1917. That Act made no reference to §155 of the Judicial Code, with respect to alien suitors, and §155 could not be implied as establishing a condition precedent to recovery. The petitioner was an alien friend and as such was entitled to the protection of the Fifth Amendment of the United States Constitution prohibiting the taking of property for public use without just compensation. Delivering the Opinion of the Court, Chief Justice Hughes said: "As alien friends are embraced within the terms of the Fifth Amendment, it cannot be said that their property is subject to confiscation here because the property of our citizens may be confiscated in the alien's country. The provision that private property shall not be taken for public use without just compensation establishes a standard for our Government which the Constitution does not make dependent upon the standards of other governments. The Act of Congress should be interpreted in the light of its manifest purpose to give effect to the constitutional guaranty.[1]

"Nor do we regard it as an admissible construction of the Act of June 15, 1917, to hold that the Congress intended that the right of an alien friend to recover just compensation should be defeated or postponed because of the lack of recognition by the Government of the United States of the régime in his country. *A fortiori*, as the right to compensation for which the Act provided sprang into existence at the time of the taking, there is no ground for saying that the statute was not to apply, if at a later date, and before compensation was actually made, there should be a revolution in the country of the owner and the ensuing régime should not be recognized. The question as presented here is not one of a claim advanced by or on behalf of a foreign government or régime, but is simply one of compensating an owner of property taken by the United States." (282 U.S. 481, 492.) A condition could not be implied in the Act of June 15, 1917, which, to say the least, would raise a grave question as to its constitutional validity.

[Report: 68 Ct. Cl. 32; 282 U.S. 481].[2]

[1] This point does not seem to have been raised by the Court of Claims apparently this was a new point taken up by the Supreme Court itself.

[2] See Dickinson in *A.J.*, XXV (1931), pp. 214-221; *M.L.R.*, XXIX (1931), p. 1074; *Y.L.J.*, XL (1931), p. 1316.

Governments—Recognition of—Effects of Non-Recognition —Unrecognised Governments as Defendants—Succession of Governments—The Denikin Government in Russia in 1920. **Case No. 25**

VOEVODINE *v.* GOVERNMENT OF THE COMMANDER-IN-CHIEF OF THE ARMED FORCES IN THE SOUTH OF RUSSIA.

United States, Supreme Court of New York, Appellate Division. May 1, 1931.

THE FACTS.—The plaintiff, a resident and citizen of New York, sold goods to the Denikin Government, a *de facto* Government which existed for a short time in the southern part of European Russia, in opposition to the Soviet Government, until the Soviet Republic established authority over the area. The Denikin Government was not recognised by the United States as either a *de facto* or a *de jure* government. The plaintiff brought an action in a New York court alleging that he had not been paid for the goods sold and that, although the Denikin Government ceased to exist in or about 1920, certain assets belonging to it remained in the United States in the possession of its former agent. Claiming that there was danger that the funds would be dissipated, the plaintiff asked that a receiver be appointed for the property, that the agent be held accountable to the receiver and the creditors, and that the receiver should keep the property until a successor government should be recognised by the United States. The Denikin Government was not served and did not appear in this action.

On appeal to the Appellate Division of the Supreme Court of New York,

Held (*per* Sherman, J.): that the complaint did not state a cause of action. During the existence of the Denikin Government, which was assumed to have been a *de facto* government, no remedy existed against it in the courts of the United States, irrespective of whether or not it was recognised by the United States: *Wulfsohn* v. *Russian Socialist Federated Soviet Republic*, 234 N.Y. 372. A *de facto* government could not be sued without its consent; and when extinguished by conquest it became, so far as the question of its continued corporate existence was concerned, as if it had never existed: *Nankivel* v. *Omsk All Russian Government*, 237 N.Y. 150. If the Denikin Government had survived, therefore, the plaintiff could not have recovered a judgment against it. Its extinction did not give the plaintiff a better right. Moreover, the mere fact that property

Case No. 25 *Contd.*

belonging to the Government was in the United States gave the plaintiff no right to have it applied to the payment of his claim: *Twycross* v. *Dreyfus*, [1877] 5 Ch. 605. The Court did not accept the plaintiff's contention that this was a case analogous to the case of a dissolved corporation and that the property in question must be applied to satisfy the claims of creditors. The authorities cited concerned judgment creditors' actions or suits against the successor of a dissolved corporation or holders of its property. The analogy was misleading. Against a government, a creditor had only a moral and unenforceable claim, while against a corporation the action could be prosecuted to judgment. This suit could not be treated as a judgment creditor's action because the plaintiff was not then and could not become a judgment creditor.

Upon the overthrow of a *de facto* government another government replacing it would succeed to the representative right of the *de facto* government in all its property: *United States of America* v. *McRae, L.R.* [1869] 8 Eq. 69. The property in question remained to be taken over by a successor government, therefore, whenever claims thereto could be presented through actions in American courts by such government after it should have been recognised by the United States: *Russian Republic* v. *Cibrario*, 235 N.Y. 225.

[Report: 232 App. Div. 204; affirmed without opinion, 257 N.Y. 557.]

Case No. 26

Recognition—Consequences of—The Right to Sue—Status of the Trade Delegation of the U.S.S.R.

CIBRARIO *v.* RUSSIAN TRADE DELEGATION IN ITALY AND THE NATIONAL CITY BANK OF NEW YORK.

Italy, Court of Cassation. November 13, 1931.

THE FACTS.—The Cinematograph Department of the Russian Commissariat of Public Instruction had engaged Cibrario to supervise the purchase of cinematographic material and had paid one million dollars into the National City Bank of New York, empowering Cibrario to draw the sums necessary to pay the firms supplying the material. By means of false documents, Cibrario succeeded in getting the Bank to hand over to him 900,000 dollars. On his conviction for fraud by the American Courts, he fled to Italy and deposited some of the money with a bank in San Remo.

On October 7, 1926, the Trade Delegation of the Union of

Soviet Socialist Republics in Rome brought an action against Cibrario before the Italian Court at San Remo in order to recover the amount deposited with the Bank. The Court at San Remo, in a decision given on April 2, 1929, decided in favour of the defendant on the ground that the Soviet Trade Delegation was not entitled to sue as plaintiff. On appeal to the Court of Appeal of Genoa it was held, on May 6, 1930, that the Trade Delegation was entitled to sue. On further appeal before the Court of Cassation,

Held: that the decision of the Court of Appeal of Genoa must be affirmed. The Court said: "The Russian State in its present form (a main part of which, as is well known, consists in the carrying on of foreign trade exclusively as a function of the State by means of its own trade delegations endowed with diplomatic rights) has been recognised *de jure* by Italy by the following declaration in the Italo-Soviet Treaty of February 24, 1924:

> 'The power of each State is mutually recognised as the sole legal and sovereign power in the respective country, with all the consequences that thereby result to the other party according to the law of nations and international usage.'

"One of the consequences of recognition of the legal entity of a State admitted by international law is that that State may exercise, within the State which has recognised it, all the juridical activities which the law of the land allows. There is no doubt that, according to our existing laws, the State has the power of applying to the Courts through its own organs for the protection of any of its legitimate interests." As a result of the recognition of the Union of Soviet Socialist Republics by Italy, the Trade Delegation could not be denied the capacity to appear before Italian Courts in the name of the Union. The Delegation was the organ invested by Soviet legislation with the power to represent the Russian State in everything concerning foreign trade. The decision of the Court, derived from the application of general principles of international law to the case in point, found explicit support, moreover, in a provision of the Italo-Soviet Treaty of 1924 according to which Italy had undertaken to enable the Trade Delegation of the Union to exercise in Italian territory the functions entrusted to it by the Government of the Union.

[Report: *Giurisprudenza Torinese*, 1931, p. 1581; *Foro*

Case No. 26 *Contd.* *Italiano*, 1932, Part 1, p. 24. See also the note by Cavaglieri in *Rivista italiana di diritto internazionale privato e processuale*, 1931, p. 173.]

Case No. 27 **Recognition—Effects of Non-Recognition—Proof of Russian Nationality—"Soviet" and "Russian" Nationality—*Jus sanguinis*—Soviet Decrees and Non-Recognition of the Soviet Government.**

ICHLENEDJIAN AND OTHERS *v.* GREGORIAN.

Egypt, Mixed Court of Appeal of Alexandria. March 10, 1931.

THE FACTS.—This was an appeal from a decision of the Mixed Civil Tribunal of Alexandria, distributing the estate of Dame Hamaspiour Gregorian. The appellant complained that, instead of the law of Egypt (where the immovable property concerned was situated), the Imperial Law of Russia had been applied. It was also argued that Soviet law could not apply because Dame Gregorian was stateless, and accordingly the mixed tribunals were incompetent.

Held : that the appeal must be dismissed.

(1) The argument that all subjects of the former Russian Empire residing abroad either became foreign citizens or stateless, must be rejected, although it was clear that the deceased had not acquired Soviet nationality. "Whatever may have been the feudal theory of the Middle Ages it is clear that, in modern theory, allegiance is due to the King (in the case of the *ancien régime* the Czar) in his political capacity and not in his personal capacity, and this in spite of the absolutist character of the *ancien régime* in Russia. It follows from this that the destruction of the *ancien régime* cannot have the result of making the subjects of the Czar stateless. The sovereign power continues ; it merely reincarnates itself in a new body whether this be the Kerensky Government or the Soviet Government . . . and a Russian subject born under the old régime continues to owe his allegiance to the new government until the new government repudiates him, or the émigré finds a means of acquiring a new citizenship. It is not exact to speak of Soviet nationality. There is Russian nationality in respect of which to-day the Soviet Government exercises its authority, but it remains—what it has always been—Russian nationality. . . . By nationality is meant the political connections which exist between an individual and the sovereign power to whom he owes

his allegiance. These connections are fixed in different countries by different laws. . . . Russia, as to nationality, adopted in principle the Roman system of the *jus sanguinis*. In virtue of this principle, Dame Gregorian, born a Russian subject, remained a Russian subject though domiciled abroad." (At p. 72.)

(2) It could not be admitted that the Decree of the Soviet Government of 1924 denationalising certain Russian subjects abroad had any bearing on the question, for the Decree could not be considered by the Court.

(3) As the Soviet Government had not been recognised by Egypt the Imperial Law of Russia must be applied.

[Report: *Gazette des Tribunaux Mixtes d'Egypte*, XXIV (1933-1934), p. 71.]

NOTE.—And see *ibid.*, pp. 74-76. As to option of nationality note a decision of the Court of Appeal of March 5, 1931, holding that notice of option must be given to the State whose nationality is being repudiated: *ibid.*, p. 75. If nationality is changed during the proceedings it validates them, though at their commencement the tribunal was not competent: *ibid.*, pp. 78 and 103. And, as to recognition, compare a decision of March 20, 1933, by the Civil Tribunal of Alexandria, holding that the Soviet Government, though unrecognised by Egypt, could sue in its capacity as a "civil person," though not as a public authority: *ibid.*, p. 67.

Recognition of Governments—Effects of Non-Recognition—Incapacity to Appear as Plaintiff—Belgium and the U.S.S.R.—Commercial Representation of the U.S.S.R.—Whether Distinguishable from the U.S.S.R. **Case No. 28**

SOCIÉTÉ DESPA ET FILS *v.* U.S.S.R.

Belgium, Court of Appeal of Liège. February 20, 1931

THE FACTS.—The Commercial Tribunal of Verviers had entertained an action brought before it by the Union of Soviet Socialist Republics, on behalf of its commercial representation in Paris, against Société Despa et Fils, a Belgian firm, with regard to a contract for furnishing carried out by the firm. The Government of the U.S.S.R. was not recognised by Belgium. The defendants appealed to the Court of Appeal of Liège.

Held: that the appeal should be allowed, that the action was inadmissible, and that the costs in both actions should be borne by the U.S.S.R. "The depositions were made in the name of the U.S.S.R. in both instances. A foreign State has access to the Belgian Courts only if its Government has been officially

Case No. 28 *Contd.* recognised by the Belgian Government, which alone is competent for the purpose, it being a principle of public law that the power to grant recognition to another State belongs solely to the Executive and that the Courts can do no more than state the situation created by the action of the Government of their country (de Paepe, *Etude sur la compétence civile à l'égard des Etats étrangers*, p. 29, n. 5)." The Belgian Government had not recognised the Soviet Government. A refusal on the part of the Executive to recognise a foreign Government is tantamount to a denial of any juridical capacity to that Government (Court of Cassation, decision of March 3, 1930; see plea of the Procureur-Général of Brussels: *Belgique judiciaire*, 1930, cols. 273 *et seq.*).

The decision of the Court below was based on the view that it was the commercial representation of the U.S.S.R., located in Paris, which entered into the contract in question with the Société Despa et Fils and which asked the Belgian Courts in the present action to ensure that the conditions of the contract were observed. However, the Soviet Government itself had declared that its commercial representation in France was not distinguishable from the State of the U.S.S.R. Indeed, in the depositions made before the Court of Appeal of Paris (see decision of November 19, 1926: *Gazette du Palais*, 1927, No. 15) the U.S.S.R. pointed out that foreign trade was a monopoly of the State in Russia and was administered under the authority of a People's Commissar. Accordingly, "Russian commercial representation is part of the Soviet State itself. Only one industrial enterprise and one commercial enterprise exists in Soviet Russia, and that is the State itself."

[Report: *Pasicrisie*, II (1931), p. 108; *Clunet*, 59 (1932), p. 781.]

Non-Recognition—Effects of—Soviet Russia and Switzerland—Transfer to Russia of a Deceased Person's Estate.

See *In re Héritiers de Dame Pribiloff*, decided by the Swiss Federal Court on July 15, 1931, in which the Court ordered the transfer to the personal representatives in Russia of the estate of a person of Russian nationality who had resided in Switzerland and died there. At the time of the action Switzerland had not recognised the Government of the U.S.S.R. The Court said: "The questions as to where this property would be transferred later, and what part of it would return to Russia in the form of taxation or otherwise, notably by reason of the necessary conversion of foreign currency into roubles, are undoubtedly matters of interest to the personal representatives; however . . . these questions have no connection whatsoever with the delivery of the property and the right of succession."

[Report: *Entscheidungen des Schweizerischen Bundesgerichts*, 57 (II), p. 396.]

Recognition—Effect of Non-Recognition on Treaties—Suspension of Diplomatic Relations.

See Case No. 17 (*N. and M. Shipoff v. Elte*), and Case No. 16 (*Lowinsky v. Receiver in Bankruptcy of the Egyptisch-Türksche Handwerksigarettenfabriek "Jaka" Ltd.*).

E.—STATE SUCCESSION

I.—Succession to Rights

State Succession—Succession to Rights—Private Property Rights Confiscated by the Predecessor—Poland—Recovery of Independence. **Case No. 29**

ŁEMPICKI AND MORAWSKA *v.* POLISH TREASURY.

Poland, Supreme Court, First Division. January 26, 1932.

THE FACTS.—After the Polish insurrection of 1831 the Russian Government confiscated the estate of a former General in the Polish forces. After the establishment of the Polish State in 1918 the descendants of the General brought the present action against the Polish Treasury for the recovery of the estate which had been taken over by the Polish Government after the withdrawal of the Russian authorities. The District Court and the Court of Appeal decided for the plaintiffs. On appeal by the Attorney-General to the Supreme Court,

Held: that the plaintiffs were entitled to the estate. The Court said: "The duty to restore to the rightful owner, or to his successors, property confiscated by one of the partitioning Powers from a person who took part in the struggle for independence, is derived not from any law issued by the Polish State but from the fact that the Polish nation has recovered its independence and that consequently there has come about such a change in public and private law as to cause the revival of the rights and titles of the rightful owners of confiscated property. Those relations at private law which had been

Case No. 29 *Contd.* illegally created by the invaders and which are inconsistent with the present state of things, fall to the ground. Hence the Attorney-General's reference to the absence of a special statute in the matter is not well founded . . . ."

[Report: *Zb. O.S.N.*, I (1932), Part 1, No. 27, p. 45.]

NOTE.—See also *Bishop of Pinsk* v. *Gwircman*, decided on October 9, 1931, by the First Division of the Supreme Court (*Zb.O.S.N.*, I (1931), Part 2, No. 181, p. 64), where, however, the case was decided on the issue of the operation of a statute of limitations.

State Succession—Succession to Rights—Continuation of Possession.

See Case No. 233 (*Włodzimierz (City of) v. Polish Treasury*, Note).

State Succession—Succession to Rights.

See Case No. 43 (*Maricopa County Municipal Water Conservation District et Al. v. Southwest Cotton Company et Al.*).

II.—Succession with regard to Contractual and Other Obligations, and Concessions

Case No. 30 **State Succession—Succession to Obligations—Administrative Debts—Partial Succession—Bessarabia.**

VOZNEAC *v.* AUTONOMOUS ADMINISTRATION OF POSTS AND TELEGRAPHS.

Roumania, Court of Cassation, Third Division. June 22, 1931.

THE FACTS.—On January 9, 1918, the plaintiff paid in at the post office in Baltzi the sum of 2,304 roubles to be transmitted to an addressee in Chişinau. Both towns were in Bessarabia, which then formed part of Russia. The money never reached its destination. Later in 1918 Roumania annexed Bessarabia. Article 8 of the Treaty of Paris of October 28, 1920,[1] between Roumania and the Allied and Associated Powers provided that Roumania will assume, so far as Bessarabia is concerned, a proportionate part of the public debt and of other financial engagements of Russia to be determined by a special convention between Roumania and the Allied and Associated Powers. No such convention had been concluded. In 1928 the plaintiff brought an action against the Roumanian

[1] Hertslet's *Commercial Treaties*, Vol. XXIX, p. 1027.

Ministry of Communications claiming the amount sent in 1918. He was successful in the Courts of first and second instance. The autonomous Administration of Posts and Telegraphs, a department of the Ministry of Communications, appealed on the ground that it was not liable for the debts to individuals incurred by the former Russian administration of posts and telegraphs.

Held: that the appeal must be upheld. The Court accepted the contention of the appellant seeing that, in virtue of the annexation of Bessarabia by Roumania, the question at issue was not one of universal succession to the assets and liabilities of the former Russian State. This was a case of partial succession to be regulated by a special convention between the States concerned, as laid down in Article 8 of the Convention of Paris of October 1920. The plaintiff had not invoked the provisions of Article 8 of the above-mentioned Convention, the applicability of which to the present case was controversial, nor any other convention which would oblige the Roumanian State to take over the responsibility of the Russian State for debts to individuals. According to international doctrine and practice, these debts were the concern of the Russian State. The Roumanian Administration of Posts and Telegraphs was not liable for debts incurred by the former Russian State.[1]

[Report: *Jurisprudenţa română a Inaltei Curţi de Casaţie şi Justiţie*, 1932, pp. 36-38.]

State Succession—Succession to Obligations—Czechoslovakia and Hungary.

The view relied upon in the decision Boh. 4501 fin. (*Annual Digest*, 1927-1928, Case No. 58)—*i.e.*, that, since the date of the promulgation of Law No. 156 of June 23, 1926, tax-payers were deprived of the possibility of making against the Czechoslovak Treasury such financial claims as had accrued to them against the Treasury of the former Hungarian State in the period before the coming into existence of the Czechoslovak State in accordance with the legal provisions regarding the tax or duty concerned, except in cases provided for by the Law—was reaffirmed by the Supreme Administrative Court of Czechoslovakia in its decisions of September 10, 1932, No. 13,301 (Boh. 6332 fin.) and September 14, 1932, No. 13,870 (Boh. 6336 fin.).

For details of the interpretation of the Law of June 23, 1926

[1] The jurisprudence of the Roumanian Court of Cassation in regard to former State debts in Bessarabia has been consistent: see *Annual Digest*, 1929-1930, Cases Nos. 37 and 38.

Case No. 30 *Contd.* (*Annual Digest*, 1927-1928, p. 87, and *ibid.*, 1929-1930, p. 63), see the decision of the Supreme Administrative Court of Czechoslovakia of September 11, 1931, No. 13,231 (Boh. 9367 adm.).

III.—The Public Debt. Pensions

Case No. 31 **State Succession—Public Debt—Liability of German Colonies for Colonial Loans of Germany—Legal Status of Former German Colonies—Continuation of Corporate Character of the Colonies—Continuation of Germany's Guarantee of the Loans—Article 257 of the Treaty of Versailles—Effect of Changed Conditions on Guarantee for Loan.**

SCH. *v.* GERMANY.

Germany, Supreme Court for Civil Matters. April 14, 1932.

THE FACTS.—The plaintiff held bonds issued by the German Debt Administration in the years 1908, 1909 and 1913, for loans floated on behalf of the German Colonies. Interest and amortisation service of the loans had been guaranteed by the German Empire, the Colonies being the principal debtor. In the present action the plaintiff sued the German Reich on the guarantee. Article 257 (2) of the Treaty of Versailles provided that "all property and possessions belonging to the German Empire or to the German States situated in such territories shall be transferred with the territories to the Mandatory Power in its capacity as such and no payment shall be made nor any credit given to those Governments in consideration of this transfer." The other relevant provisions are conveniently stated in the *Held* below. The Court of Appeal found that Germany was not liable.

Held: that Germany was still liable as guarantor. The liability of the Colonies for the Colonial Loans issued on their behalf had not ceased by virtue either of Article 257 of the Treaty of Versailles or of the Hague Convention of January 20, 1930.

I. *Liability of the Colonies as the Principal Debtor.*—(*a*) In order to answer the question as to the guarantee it was first necessary to decide whether the liability of the principal debtor continued to exist. Under international law the effect of Article 257 (2) was that all debts incurred by the Colonies remained debts of the respective territories. The same applied to their liability arising from loans. It might be argued that Article 257 (1) ruled out this construction inasmuch as it provided that "neither the territory nor the Mandatory Power shall be charged with any portion of the debt of the German Empire or States." However, that Article did not refer to the liabilities of the Colonies. "The words of that provision are ambiguous, the English and French versions not being in harmony with each other. Whereas the former speaks of 'any portion of the debt of the German Empire or States', that is to say, of the debts of the German Empire or States, the latter uses the words 'aucune partie du service de la Dette de l'Empire ou des Etats Allemands', thus referring to the debt service of the German Empire or States. However, it does not seem necessary to attempt a reconciliation of the English and French texts, for neither of them covers the debts of the Colonies in their corporate capacity. At the same time it is impossible to make any distinction between local debts of the administration and so-called finance debts (loans), for these loans were issued on behalf of the Colonies, and the primary liability was by no means imposed on the Empire. Neither did the latter bind itself to undertake the debt service of the loan."

(*b*) Neither was the effect of the Note of the Allied Powers of June 16, 1919, such as to question in any way the liability of the Colonies for their loans. The Note read: "They [*viz.*, the Allied Powers] are of opinion that the Colonies should not bear any portion of the German debt, nor remain under any obligation to refund to Germany the expenses incurred by the Imperial Administration of the Protectorate." The Supreme Court said: "By this Note the Allied Powers, both on behalf of the territories as such and of the Mandatory Powers, declined to take over the local debts of the Colonial Administration. In spite of this the Court of Appeal rightly held that this refusal had not been expressed in Article 257 of the Treaty of Versailles and had not therefore become part of German law. The same applies to the obligations of the Colonies arising from loans."

(*c*) The liability of the Colonies was not impaired by Germany's waiver in Article III, B (a), of the Hague Convention of January 20, 1930, of "all claims respecting the loans issued by the former German Colonies." This waiver referred only to German claims under international law against the signatories of the Convention on account of loan liabilities, and not to claims of private creditors under the loan agreements. Thus the waiver could not remove by way of a convention the liability of the mandated territories.

Case No. 31 ***Contd.***

(*d*) The Treaty of Versailles did not deprive the Colonies of their corporate capacity. They had not ceased to have rights and obligations of their own. Only their character as *German* Colonies had been lost; they were no longer independent entities by German law.

II. *With regard to the Legal Status of the former German Colonies*, the Court said: "The German Colonies were neither themselves German States, not parts of the territory of the Empire. The latter exercised its sway over them, but they were not legally incorporated in it. The Supreme Court (*Seufferts Archiv, vol.* 52, No. 236) and the legal authorities regarded the Colonies as appurtenances of the Empire. By the Act of March 30, 1892, they were recognised as capable of having independent rights and obligations. It was thus that the notion of the "Colonial Fiscus" was created. The Act did not, however, confer upon the Colonies the status of member States of the Federal State. Under paragraph 1 their budget was to remain distinct from that of the Empire, and under paragraph 5 the assets of the respective territories were alone to be liable for debts arising from their administration,."[1]

III. *With regard to the Continuation of Germany's Guarantee:* "Germany claims that, even if the conclusion is reached that the principal debt has not been extinguished, she has ceased to be liable as surety by reason of the Colonies having been severed from the mother country. According to the defendant State's contention, it was a condition precedent of Germany's guaranteeing the loans that Empire and Colonies should be legally united or connected with each other ; at the material time nobody had envisaged the possibility of those territories being severed from the mother country. However, these considerations are incapable of negativing the liability as surety. It must be borne in mind that, for the Colonial Loans to be placed on the market on conditions equal or similar to those of the German loans proper, it was necessary for the Empire to furnish the creditors with a security additional to the sole principal liability of the Colonies. For this reason the Empire acted as surety for its Colonies. Had Germany guaranteed the loan only while the Colonies were united with her, this condition would probably have resulted in a greater discount of the bonds. For the danger of war could by no means be considered as

[1] See the comments on this point by Nostitz-Wallwitz in *Z. für a. ö. R. und V.*, IV (1934), p. 421. The decision reported here is in harmony with the decision of the Anglo-German Mixed Arbitral Tribunal in *Niger Company, Ltd.* v. *Etat Allemand : Recueil*, III, p. 232.

remote even by persons living in the years 1908, 1909 and 1913. Therefore any investor who purchased bonds on the conditions fixed by the Act of May 18, 1908 relied and, considering the business purpose of a guarantee, was entitled to rely, on the German guarantee in case the principal debtor became insolvent, at least as long as such principal debtor remained himself legally liable."[1]

[Report: *Entscheidungen des Reichsgerichts in Zivilsachen*, vol. 137, p. 1; *Juristische Wochenschrift*, 1932, p. 2799.]

State Succession—Public Debt—Treaty Obligation in Respect of—How Far Executory without Further Municipal Regulation. **Case No. 32**

KAISER-FERDINAND NORTH RAILWAY CASE.

Austria, Supreme Court. July 9, 1931.

THE FACTS.—In the present action the trustee for the protection of the rights of the holders of the 5 per cent. debentures of the Kaiser-Ferdinand North Railway sued the Austrian State for a declaration that the latter was bound to pay the debts to be taken over under Article 203 of the Treaty of St. Germain.

Held: that the action must be dismissed. The Austrian Republic was not the successor in title of the dual monarchy The obligation imposed by Article 203 must be construed as meaning that the taking over of the debts in question did not follow automatically from that article. The Court said: "It does not follow from the words 'shall take over' that Austria assumed direct obligations with regard to the debenture holders. Those words mean only that Austria is bound to take over the debts; but it is for Austria to declare that she has taken them over in accordance with an obligation under international law . . ." Though the debenture holders had become creditors of the Austrian Republic, their claims were barred until provision had been made for the putting into effect of the Treaty.

[Report : *Die Rechtsprechung*, 1931, p. 241.]

[1] See the comments by Nostitz-Wallwitz in *Z. für a. ö. R. und V.*, IV (1934), pp. 420 *et seq.* The decision departed from the views expressed in the earlier decision reported in *Entscheidungen des Reichsgerichts in Zivilsachen*, vol. 105, p. 260, which was criticised by a number of writers and was partly abandoned by the Supreme Court itself (*Entscheidungen des Reichsgerichts in Zivilsachen*, vol. 113, p. 285).

V.—Respect of Private Rights

Case No. 33

State Succession—Private Rights—Meaning of Acquired Rights—General and Particular International Law—Interference with Private Rights by Legislative Action—Non-Discrimination Against Aliens—Interpretation of Treaties—*Expressio unius est exclusio alterius*—Germano-Polish Convention of May 15, 1922, concerning Upper Silesia (so-called Geneva Convention)—Jurisdiction to Decree *restitutio in integrum.*

NIEDERSTRASSER *v.* POLISH STATE.

Upper Silesian Arbitral Tribunal. June 6, 1931.

(Kaeckenbeeck, President.)

THE FACTS.—The claimant was a mining engineer. In April 1927 an accident took place in the mine where he worked. Subsequently the Polish authorities cancelled his licence on the ground that the accident was due to his negligence, whereupon he was dismissed from his post. He now brought an action against the Polish State for the restitution of his licence and for compensation, relying upon Articles 4 and 5 of the Upper Silesian Convention between Poland and Germany of May 15, 1922.

Article 4 of the Convention provided as follows:

> § 1 (1): Sans préjudice des dispositions de l'article 256 du Traité de Paix de Versailles, l'Allemagne et la Pologne reconnaîtront et respecteront les droits de toute nature, et notamment les concessions et privilèges acquis avant le transfert de la souveraineté par des particuliers, des sociétés ou des personnes morales, dans leurs parties respectives du territoire plébiscité, et cela en conformité des lois relatives aux dits droits et des dispositions qui vont suivre.
>
> § 2 (3): Si des concessions ou des privilèges, autorisant ou concernant des installations, exploitations, établissements ou entreprises situés ou à situer sur le territoire plébiscité, ou ayant trait à un objet situé sur ledit territoire (concessions ou privilèges à incidence locale), ou bien si des driots subjectifs qui ne proviennent pas d'une concession, tels que des créances, dont ne fût-ce qu'un des lieux d' exécution mentionnés au paragraphe 269 du Code civil allemand se trouve dans le territoire plébiscité, sont

supprimés ou diminués par l'application de lois générales ou par d'autres dispositions, l'Etat qui applique ces lois ou prend ces dispositions sera tenu a l'indemnisation complète. Ce qui précède ne s'applique pas aux restrictions temporaires qui, d'après le droit en vigueur, doivent être tolérées par tout titulaire d'un droit. . . .

Article 5 provided as follows :

> La question de savoir si et dans quelle mesure une indemnité pour la suppression ou la diminution de droits acquis doit être payée par l'Etat, sera directement tranchée par le Tribunal arbitral sur plainte de l'ayant droit.

Held: that the claim must be dismissed. The possession of a mining engineer's licence did not fall within the category of rights in respect of which § 2 of Article 4 laid down the duty of compensation. The licence was neither a "concession" nor a "privilege" referred to in § 1 of Article 4. Neither did it fall within the list of occupations enumerated in § 2 (4). As the subsection did not state that the list was only by way of illustration, it must be regarded as exhaustive.

Neither was the claimant entitled to compensation on the ground of the general provision of Article 5 when read in conjunction with the general principles of international law and with § 1 of Article 4. Article 5 contained no independent provision of substantive law regarding cases in which compensation must be paid; it merely dealt with the jurisdiction of the Tribunal. Apart from the other detailed provisions of the Convention, § 1 of Article 4 provided for no obligation of compensation in case of interference with private rights. Paragraph 1 of Article 4 did not envisage all categories of rights. In particular, there was no doubt that it did not provide protection for "public rights relating to the organisation of the State". "It is true that general international law recognises the principle that private rights, acquired in accordance with the law of the ceding State, must not be arbitrarily taken away by the succeeding State. However, the successor State may, like the ceding State, take away or modify these rights by way of legislative action. Apart from legislation, international law does not permit arbitrary interference with private rights. If rights of aliens are interfered with in this manner without compensation, they can look for protection from their own State. The latter can then, if it deems it proper, demand satisfaction, in various forms, from the offending State. In doing this the foreign State cannot, in principle, demand for its subjects more

Case No. 33 *Contd.*

extensive rights than those enjoyed by nationals of the offending State. On the other hand, the nationals of the successor State, including those who have become its nationals as the result of cession, can have recourse only to the courts and administrative authorities of their own State and can ask for compensation or indemnity from the authorities only on the basis of the law of the land. For there is no rule of international law which lays down that nationals may claim from their own State compensation for the taking away of or interference with their acquired rights as the result of measures taken by the authorities of the State apart from legislation. This is so, if for no other reason, because international law is a law only between States. With regard to the nationals of the successor State international law imposes upon that State an obligation to respect private rights and not to interfere with them arbitrarily. But there is no question here of succession in the meaning of international law; in particular there is no question of compensation."

The above principles of international law could be modified by treaty, as was the case in Article 4 of the Geneva Convention. The duty of compensation laid down in Article 4, paragraph 2 (3), "goes much beyond the accepted principles of international law, inasmuch as it provides for full compensation also in cases of taking away or interference with rights by way of legislative measures of the acquiring State, which is a case of compensation alien to general international law. Accordingly, the protection of acquired rights in the Upper Silesian plebiscite area is very wide, but it does not go beyond the express provisions of the Geneva Convention." It was only in the cases expressly provided for by the Geneva Convention that the Tribunal was entitled to grant compensation. It was not competent, consistently with the terms of Article 5, to award anything else but compensation; it had no jurisdiction to decree a *restitutio in integrum* as demanded by the claimant.

[Report: *Schiedsgericht für Oberschlesien*, vol. II, No. 3/4, p. 156.]

NOTE.—It may be doubted whether the ruling of the Tribunal on such questions as the unrestricted right of the successor State to interfere with private rights by way of legislation or the absence of a duty of compensation in case of legislation which does not discriminate against aliens, is either based upon or will constitute a good precedent. Probably the decision could have been based on a narrower, but more acceptable, ground. The licence to exercise a profession is no less an acquired right than the possession of a concession. This is so, it is submitted, also in the meaning of the Geneva Convention. But any type of acquired right, even if protected by a clear provision of a treaty, may be limited or abolished for well-founded reasons of administrative or penal law. A concession, even if protected by treaty, is liable to be withdrawn if its owner conducts the business in a manner prohibited by law; the same applies to a licence to exercise a profession or occupation. But the reasonableness of the law and the good faith of the legislative or administrative authority is in such cases a proper subject for arbitral determination.

State Succession—Respect of Private Rights—Indirect Interference with Private Rights by Way of Taxation—Geneva Convention of May 15, 1922, between Germany and Poland. **Case No. 34**

KÜGELE *v.* POLISH STATE.

Upper Silesian Arbitral Tribunal. February 5, 1932.

(Kaeckenbeeck, President.)

THE FACTS.—For the relevant provisions of the Geneva Convention of May 15, 1922, between Poland and Germany see Case No. 33.

Prior to 1923 the claimant owned a brewery in Polish Upper Silesia. As the result of a series of licence fees successively imposed by the authorities, the business ceased to be remunerative, and he was eventually obliged to close it. He claimed compensation for the losses caused to him by the impositions prior to 1923, as well as by the resulting closing of the business.

Held: that the claim must be dismissed. The Tribunal said: "The increase of the licence fee was not in itself capable of taking away or impairing the rights of the plaintiff . . . The increase of the tax cannot be regarded as a taking away or impairment of the right to engage in a trade, for such taxation presupposes the engaging in the trade. It is true that taxation may render the trade less remunerative or altogether unremunerative. However, there is an essential difference between the maintenance of a certain rate of profit in an undertaking and the legal and factual possibility of continuing the undertaking. The trader may feel compelled to close his business because of the new tax. . . . But this does not mean that he has lost the right to engage in the trade. For had he paid the tax, he would be entitled to go on with his business."

[Report: *Schiedsgericht für Oberschlesien*, vol. III. No. 1, p. 24.]

NOTE.—For a somewhat similar reasoning, in a different type of

Case No. 34 Contd. case, see the Judgment of the Permanent Court of International Justice in the *Oscar Chinn* case, Series A/B, No. 63, at p. 88. But there is room for the view that an acquired right, protected by law, may become illusory and the object of a treaty defeated as the result of administrative action, including taxation, the reasonableness and justification of which is declared to be outside the jurisdiction of the Tribunal.

Case No. 35

State Succession—Private Rights—Respect of Acquired Rights—Rights of the Successor of the Protected Owner—Rights Acquired after Transfer of Sovereignty from the Original Owner.

UL LTD. *v.* POLISH STATE.

Upper Silesian Arbitral Tribunal. July 21, 1932.

(Kaeckenbeeck, President.)

THE FACTS.—For the relevant provisions of Article 4 of the Geneva Convention of May 15, 1922, between Poland and Germany see Case No. 33.

The plaintiffs were a limited company formed in 1923. They were the owners of a brewery which they were compelled to give up in 1926 in consequence of the introduction of the Polish State monopoly in alcoholic spirits. They claimed that as the result of that measure they had been deprived of their acquired right protected by the Convention. They had owned the business since 1893. They maintained that the formation of the company in 1923 was a purely formal device adopted with a view to transforming the firm into a family concern in the form of a company. The defendant asserted that as the company was formed after the transfer of sovereignty it was not protected by the Convention.

Held: that the claim must be dismissed. The Tribunal was not in a position to accept the plaintiff's contention that it would be contrary to the Treaty if the protection of vested rights ceased to operate as soon as there had taken place a change in the physical or juridical person who had acquired the rights in question prior to the change of sovereignty. The question, properly put, was not whether the protection given by Article 4 lost its effectiveness as the result of a change in the person of the owner of the right; the question was, in what circumstances did Article 4 afford protection? In the view of the Tribunal a right acquired after the transfer of sovereignty could not be regarded as acquired before the transfer for the mere reason that the predecessor in title acquired the right prior to the transfer of sovereignty. The Tribunal declined to attach importance to the view that the substance of the right protected by the Treaty would be materially impaired if it were accepted that it continued to exist only if there was no change in the person of the holder and that it ceased to be protected as soon as the original owner, who acquired it prior to the transfer of sovereignty, parted with it in favour of his successor in title. While considerations of what was equitable and right prompted the recognition of the duty to respect at least private rights acquired prior to the transfer of sovereignty, no such reasons militated in favour of international protection of rights acquired subsequently to the transfer of sovereignty. For if the State interfered with rights thus acquired, the original owner would suffer no loss. "There is no reason, necessarily following from legal principle, to protect internationally the right of the successor in title." Such right was not altogether without protection seeing that it enjoyed the ordinary protection of the law of the State.

[Report: *Schiedsgericht für Oberschlesien, Amtliche Sammlung von Entscheidungen*, vol. III. Nos. 2/3, p. 118.]

NOTE.—The Tribunal found that, in point of fact, the company formed in 1923 was not identical with the original owner and that the transfer of the undertaking to the company was therefore not a mere matter of form. It is not clear from the decision what would have been the attitude of the Tribunal if the two had been actually identical.

State Succession—Private Rights—Executory Decisions of Authorities in Annexed Territory Prior to Annexation. **Case No. 36**

JANINA MORTGAGES CASE.

Greece, Areopagus, 1931.

THE FACTS.—The point at issue was whether a decision ordering the execution of a mortgage, given during the Turkish régime, at Janina, which had since become part of Greece, was to be regarded as a foreign or as a Greek title. If the title was foreign, certain formalities were necessary, in accordance with the Greek Code of Civil Procedure, in order to make the rights which it conferred effective in Greece.

Held: that the decision must be regarded as a foreign title. "According to a generally recognised principle of international

Case No. 36 *Contd.*

law, whenever the execution of decisions or of other executory acts emanating from an authority in annexed territory prior to annexation, is requested in the territory of the annexing State, the title is regarded as a foreign one. This follows from the principle of non-retroactivity of annexation."

[Report: *Thémis*, vol. 42, p. 643.]

NOTE.—On the other hand, Greek Courts clearly recognise the continued validity of laws of the annexed territory, with the result that they need not be proved like a foreign law. See the decision of the Court of Patras, given in 1931 and reported in *Thémis*, vol. 43, p. 736, in the *Case of the Ionian Church*. See also *Clunet*, 54 (1927), p. 763; *ibid.*, 63 (1936), p. 455; and *Thémis*, vol. 47, p. 973.

Case No. 37

State Succession—Miscellaneous—Private Rights—Pre-War Debt—Changes in Currency—Payment by Roumanian Debtor in Roumanian Currency—Retorsion.

RIEBER *v.* KUTZER ET CIE. OF TESCHEN (CZECHOSLOVAKIA).

Roumania, Court of Cassation, Third Division.

February 20, 1931.

THE FACTS.—In 1914 the defendant, who was domiciled in Cernautzi (Bukovina, then part of Austria), contracted with a firm in Teschen (then in Austria), to purchase a quantity of paper, for which payment was to be made in Austro-Hungarian currency at the domicile of the vendor. Subsequently, Teschen became part of Czechoslovakia and Cernautzi became part of Roumania. The vendor claimed payment in Czechoslovak currency or, failing that, in Roumanian leis according to the rate of exchange based on the Czechoslovak crown. The plaintiff sought to discharge his debt by payment of a sum in leis equivalent to their value in Austro-Hungarian crowns[1] according to the official rate of exchange adopted by the Roumanian State when crowns were replaced by leis in the territory acquired under the Peace Settlement, namely, 2 crowns=1 leu. The plaintiff's claim was upheld by the Courts of first and second instance. The defendant appealed.

Held: that the appeal must be upheld. The question at issue between the parties could not be resolved on the basis of the Austrian Codes invoked before the Court . . . As there

[1] Since the unification of private law had not yet taken effect in Bukovina, which was a former Austrian province, the Austrian Codes were applicable.

was no national law applicable to this case and as it could not be decided on the basis of the Peace Treaty or subsequent conventions between Czechoslovakia and Roumania, the proper solution would be to adopt the principle that doubtful cases must be decided in favour of the debtor. Accordingly, the appellant was not bound to pay in Czechoslovak crowns, a foreign currency which did not exist at the time when the contract was concluded. He was entitled to discharge his debt in lei, his native currency, which not only existed at the time of the despatch of the invoices, but which at that time was practically equivalent to the Austro-Hungarian crown.

Moreover, this solution accorded also with the principle of retorsion seeing that the Czechoslovak Decree of April 1, 1919 (No. 167) prohibited Czechoslovak debtors from discharging in Czechoslovak crowns their obligations contracted in Austrian crowns up till February 26, 1919, in respect of creditors who, at that time, were regularly domiciled outside the Czechoslovak Republic and consequently also in respect of creditors who, at the same date, had their domicile in Bukovina. It followed therefore, in accordance with the principle of retorsion, that in regard to contracts concluded in Austria Bukovinian debtors were bound to pay their Czechoslovak creditors only in Roumanian currency at the rate of 2 crowns=1 leu.

[Report: *Jurisprudenţa română a Inaltei Curţi de Casaţie şi justiţie*, 1931, pp. 171-173.]

State Succession—Respect of Private Rights.

See Case No. 43 (*Maricopa County Municipal Water Conservation District et Al. v. Southwest Cotton Company et Al.*).

State Succession—Respect of Private Rights—Article 181 of the Treaty of Neuilly.

See Case No. 211 (*Greece v. Bulgaria: Article* 181 *of the Treaty of Neuilly, Preliminary Question*, Note).

State Succession—Effect on Private Rights—Cession of Territory—Power to Bind Inhabitants of Ceded Territory after Territory has Ceased to be under the Effective Authority of the Ceding State.

See Case No. 51 (*The Bathori*).

VII.—International Conventions

Case No. 38 **State Succession—Treaties—Changes in Condition of States —Federal States—How Far Succeeding to the Rights of State-Members—Prussia and Germany.**

FLENSBURGER DAMPFERCOMPAGNIE *v.* UNITED STATES.

United States, Court of Claims. February 8, 1932.

(Booth, C.J.; Green, Littleton, Williams, JJ.)

THE FACTS.—This was an action to recover tonnage duties and taxes levied on the plaintiffs, a corporation established under the laws of Prussia. The duties were collected upon the entry of the plaintiffs' vessels into the United States during the period from November 22, 1919, to November 9, 1921. The duties were assessed under Sections 4219 and 4225 of the Revised Statutes (46 U.S.C.A. §§121, 128). The plaintiffs' cause of action was based on Sections 4227 and 4229 of the Revised Statutes and the Treaty of 1828 between the United States and Prussia (8 U.S. Stat. L. 378). Section 4227 of the Revised Statutes provided that nothing in the chapter of which it was a part should be construed to impair any rights and privileges acquired by any foreign nation under the laws and treaties of the United States relative to the duty on tonnage of vessels (46 U.S.C.A. § 135). Section 4229 of the Revised Statutes, which was intended to enforce the Treaty of 1828 with Prussia, provided that no other or higher rate of duties should be imposed on vessels of Prussia than should be payable on vessels of the United States. The Treaty of 1828 contained substantially the same provision. On July 14, 1919, the War Trade Board section of the State Department, by bulletin 802, announced the issue of a general trade licence for trade with Germany. as permitted by the Trading with the Enemy Act, but the President did not formally declare the war at an end. Congress by its joint resolutions of March 3, 1921 (41 U.S. Stat. L. 1359), and July 2, 1921 (42 U.S. Stat. L. 105), declared the war at an end. The Government contended that Section 4229 of the Revised Statutes was obsolete and had been so since the formation of the German Empire in 1871.

Held (*per* Booth, C.J.): for the plaintiff. The Court said: "It is incontrovertible that subsequent to 1871 vessels from Prussia, Germany, flying the German flag, documented and manned under article 54 of the German Constitution, entered the ports of the United States and were not subjected to tonnage duties or taxes as sued for in this case. We have no doubt that in keeping with the established and long-continued policy of the United States with respect to reciprocal commercial relations, in so far as tonnage duties and taxes are concerned, the government construed section 4229 as applicable to Prussian vessels from Prussia, Germany. This policy was at no time interrupted in so far as here pertinent except during the period extending from the outbreak of the World War and the resumption of trade relations with Germany subsequent to July 14, 1919, following which time it was again resumed as of November 11, 1919. It is extremely difficult to hold that a statute given the effect accorded to section 4229 by the executive officers of the government charged with its administration for so long a period of time, was so construed and administered contrary to law. To say the least, to so hold exacts most convincing and 'cogent' reasons. . . . The government contemplated no such result, and in keeping with the spirit and intent of both the treaty and the statute gave effect to its provisions notwithstanding a change in the political status of one of the contracting parties mentioned in both the treaty and the statute. Congress did not see fit to repeal section 4229 or resort to section 4230 during this period, and assuredly if it had become obsolete, as contended for, the nations involved would have been alert to bring the matter to the attention of their respective public authorities. Contemporaneous history confirms, we think, that both the Governments of the United States and Germany were in accord in the belief that trade reciprocity, as in issue here, obtained and was conducted under and in virtue of both the treaty and the statute. There was no such change of sovereignty and status of subjects as in the cession by Spain to the United States of Puerto Rico and the Philippine Islands, or of the Virgin Islands by Denmark, or the acquisition by the United States of Hawaii. The rights previously secured by Prussia were treated and acknowledged as continuing under the régime of the German Empire, and vessels of Prussia were recognized as entitled to the exemption accorded them, without suggestion or intimation that a technical rule of construction forestalled the granted right under the statute. Reciprocity as to tonnage duties and taxes and provisions for its establishment and continuance are not essentially subject matters to be restricted to the letter of a law bringing it into existence, and we believe that where an ancient law extended it by express terms to a then existing segregated Kingdom, which later on became simply a constitu-

Case No. 38 *Contd.*

ent state of an Empire without being in any way calculated to change the status or character of the same with respect to commercial intercourse between the two countries, the law granting the right must stand until superseded by later statutes or treaties upon the same subject.

"From 1828 to July 14, 1919, Prussian vessels were exempted by the authorities of the United States, and it is conceded that subsequent to November 11, 1921, when the treaty of peace with Germany came into effect, reciprocity has continued. Therefore whatever of doubt may be engendered as to a defense now predicated upon the letter of section 4229, R.S., should be resolved in favor of its validity in conformity with a departmental construction of the act during this long period of time. . . .

"While a subsequent change of political status may operate to render ineffective a statutory provision in reference to the *status quo* existing on the date of its enactment, nevertheless it is obviously a delicate matter for a judicial tribunal to hold such a law invalid in the face of long-continued recognition of its validity as applicable to the changed conditions, and the failure of Congress to repeal the law involving important relations with a foreign government adds to the difficulty of so doing. The reciprocal trade relations established by the law continued and each nation involved recognized the legality of the procedure."

[Report: 59 F. (2d) 464; *A.J.*, XXVI (1932), p. 618.]

NOTE.—The Court attached importance to the fact that Section 4227 expressly exempted from its operation all treaty provisions with foreign States establishing different conditions of commercial intercourse. The Court said: "Therefore, it seems clear that any claim coming within the purview of Section 4227 necessarily arises out of and is dependent upon the treaty of 1828. United States *v.* Weld, 127 U.S. 51. The court, in other words, must resort to the treaty of 1828 and not the statute to ascertain the relative rights of the parties litigant. All that section 4227 accomplishes is to save acquired treaty rights from its operation. An existing unabrogated treaty is 'the supreme law of the land'."

VIII.—In Matters of Administration. Officials

State Succession—Legal Effect of Partition of Territory on Public Corporations—Succession in Title to *jura in rem* of Such Corporations. **Case No. 39**

POSEN SOCIETY CASE.

Germany, Court of Appeal of Berlin. October 6, 1932.

THE FACTS.—Before the World War a mortgage was registered on the defendant's property in favour of the Provinzial-Feuersozietät of Posen, a public corporation created by charter under Prussian law. Under the Treaty of Versailles the mortgaged property itself continued to be in Prussian territory, but most of the Province of Posen, together with the business and the greater part of the property of the mortgagee Society (which changed its name), was transferred to Poland. The remaining part of the immovable property of the Society became part of the Prussian Province of Grenzmark Posen—West Prussia, and was taken over by the Brandenburg Fire Society after an alteration of the latter's charter had been authorised by the Prussian Cabinet. Subsequently, the Society's business in so far as it lay in the Prussian Province was transferred to the newly incorporated Grenzmark Fire Society. In the present action the Polish Fire Society claimed rights arising from the mortgage as successors in title of the former Posen Society.

Held : that the action must be dismissed on the ground that the plaintiffs had no right to sue.

1. By virtue of the provisions of the Treaty of Versailles, the former Posen Fire Society had ceased to exist.

(*a*) Although Poland, in her territory, had kept the Society in existence under another name, this did not justify the contention that thereby the Polish Society could be regarded as identical with the former Prussian Corporation. "For Poland had only the power to maintain the Society in existence within her own territory, where she exercised jurisdiction. The contention that the Society thus continued by Poland continued to exist also in respect of that part of the Province of Posen which remained with Prussia and Germany does not commend itself to the Court. A Polish, *i.e.*, a foreign, public corporation could exercise Prussian-German powers of administration only by simultaneously infringing Prussian jurisdiction. Furthermore, whereas the Society's charter provides for the conduct of the business by the Province, and for the control of such

Case No. 39 *Contd.* business by the State, it is not conceivable how a foreign Province could conduct the business of a . . . Society on Prussian territory nor how a foreign State could be in a position to exercise control over such a Society."

(*b*) On the other hand, it would also be wrong to maintain that the former Posen Society continued to exist as a Prussian public corporation in respect of that part of the former Province of Posen which remained with Prussia. "The said Fire Society had been incorporated to function in the former Province of Posen. When this territory was broken up into two parts, which in future were to be under different jurisdictions, the object of the Society could no longer be carried out. Thus, inasmuch as the charter of incorporation had been granted only with regard to a particular territory, the Provincial Fire Society of Posen ceased to exist as a corporation as soon as the said territory was divided."

2. As to the effect on its rights of the extinction of the Society's corporate capacity, especially on its rights under private law, "the Court is of opinion that these rights are not dependent on the Provincial Fire Society of Posen existing as a corporated body. Consequently, it is out of the question for the mortgages and other private rights to be extinguished simultaneously with the loss of the Society's corporate character. Rather do the rights remain in force and constitute, in the words of the Supreme Court (*Entscheidungen des Reichsgerichts in Zivilsachen*, vol. 132, p. 342), a corporeal estate the succession to which is determined by statute, by international agreement, or by the application of general principles of law." With regard to the case at issue, the Court pointed out that neither the Treaty of Versailles nor any other international convention contained any provisions relevant to the matter, and that the succession must be ascertained in accordance with the following general principles of law.

"The first to be examined are the rules developed with regard to so-called State succession. It is not necessary to consider whether or not these rules are applicable to public corporations, for in no event would they extend beyond the borders of any ceded territory. Mortgages on property, like the property itself, are situate in one particular territory. They are therefore not affected by State succession unless they are situate within ceded territory. It follows that the State succession in question has not operated so as to cause the mortgage, forming the subject-matter of the present proceedings, to devolve upon the Polish Society." It could be said that as the defunct Society had been split up into two corporations which together owned all the property of the original Society, the Polish Society had acquired a proportionate part of the old Posen Society's assets. But that was not so. It must be admitted that such reasoning was not excluded by the fact that "thereby a foreign corporation would become entitled to rights under a German mortgage; for no rule of international law prohibits rights of a *private* nature to vest in a foreign State or public corporation."

However, if it were held that such proportionate right existed, it would mean, generally, that the Polish Society would be joint mortgagee of all the German properties concerned, and conversely, that the new Grenzmark Fire Society would enjoy a similar position in respect of all mortgages on Polish properties. "It is not necessary for the purposes of this decision to determine whether such joint rights exist with regard to property not necessarily belonging to one specific district (cf., concerning the liability for a debt of the Administration, *Entscheidungen des Reichsgerichts in Zivilsachen*, vol. 136, p. 339). However, different rules must needs apply to property which does pertain to a specific district. In such cases the jurisdiction over the territory where the property in question is situate is material for the decision as to who is entitled to it. The share in the assets of the extinct corporation is therefore to be determined by reference to the territories. This is also obviously the opinion of the Supreme Court in the decision cited above (*loc cit.*, at p. 344). Accordingly, the present mortgage must be held to belong to that part of the estate of the Provincial Fire Society of Posen which is situate in Prussia."

The mortgage had therefore passed to the Grenzmark Fire Society, inasmuch as that Society had taken over that part of the business of the Posen Society which was carried out in the territory left with Prussia.

To that extent the Grenzmark Fire Society was the successor in title of the former Posen Society.

[Report: *Juristische Wochenschrift*, 1932, p. 3819.]

NOTE.—This case, which is not, strictly speaking, a case of State succession, has been reported in some detail largely on account of its bearing on the effect of territorial changes on private rights. It will also be noted that the Court had recourse to rules of succession in international law in order to establish a general principle of law governing the matter.

Case No. 40 **State Succession—Effect of Partition of Territory on Liability for Private Debts of Administrative Authorities—Application of General Rules of International Law—Proportion of Distribution.**

RURAL DISTRICT COUNCIL OF GUTTENTAG *v.* P.

Germany, Supreme Court for Civil Matters. May 24, 1932.

THE FACTS.—On the partition of Upper Silesia between Germany and Poland, two-thirds of the former Upper Silesian Rural District of Lublinitz were ceded to Poland. The rest remained with Prussia and, together with some other Districts, was constituted as the new Rural District of Guttentag. In 1925 the "rump-District" of Lublinitz was sued by the personal representatives of a workman for damages on the ground that the workman had died as a result of eating contaminated meat supplied by the district slaughterhouse of Lublinitz. In those proceedings final judgment by default was given against the District, owing to the negligence, as was alleged, of the present defendant whom the District had briefed as advocate. In the present action the new District of Guttentag, as successor in title to the District of Lublinitz, sued the advocate for damages on the ground that, but for his negligent conduct of the case, the District would not have been held liable in the earlier proceedings.

Held (by the Supreme Court): that the judgment of the Court of Appeal must be quashed. Contrary to the Court of Appeal, which had held that the District of Guttentag, as successor of the District of Lublinitz, was liable for all the latter's debts, and contrary to the appellants' contention that they were not liable at all, the Supreme Court held that a proportionate liability existed. The Court said: "The appellants contend that the partition of the former District of Lublinitz had resulted in the latter's extinction and that no succession to public rights was possible unless created by special statute or ordered by the administrative authorities on the basis of a statutory authorisation. The Court does not feel able to accept this proposition. Though it is true that the former Prussian District of Lublinitz, by reason of its partition and the surrender of its greater part, has ceased to exist as a public corporation (*Entscheidungen des Reichsgerichts in Zivilsachen*, vol. 110, p. 315), . . . this could only have the effect of extinguishing those rights and obligations which were dependent on the continued existence of the District as such, that is to say, on the continuation of its corporate capacity. In no event do such obligations comprise debts of a private nature incurred by the District, such as the claim for damages of the personal representatives of L. [the deceased workman], based on Sections 31, 823 and 831 of the Civil Code. It was not contended that property owned by the former District had on its partition and on the consequent extinction of its corporate character, *ipso facto* become *bona vacantia*. Similarly that occurrence could not effect a termination of private claims vested in third persons. With regard to States it has been recognised as a general rule of constitutional law that in case of a change of jurisdiction private debts shall pass to the successor (cf. also *Entscheidungen des Reichsgerichts in Zivilsachen*, vol. 113, p. 281). Rights the existence of which does not depend on the continuation of corporate capacity and which thus remain extant, form a corporeal estate; the succession to that estate is regulated either by statute, or by international agreement, or, finally, by general principles of law. The latter phenomenon occurs particularly in the practice of international law in case of so-called State succession."

Neither statutes nor international conventions had been enacted or made with a view to regulating the succession in title to the former District of Lublinitz. Recourse must therefore be had to general principles of law accepted with regard to cases in which a public corporation becomes extinct and applied by international practice to cases of partititions of boroughs and districts on account of surrenders of territory. With reference to those principles the Court said: "After all, one-third of the old District remained under German jurisdiction. Therefore, although its capital, together with the organs of administration, were ceded, it cannot be said that the former corporation as such passed to Poland. Moreover, a general debt of the Administration was involved, arising from the alleged negligence of servants of the district slaughterhouse, a debt which was not essentially situate in one specific part of the territory. For this reason it is almost impossible to impose a sole liability on one specific part of it. Neither is there any sufficient legal basis for a joint liability of public corporations formed by combining individual divided parts of territory which has been split up. To hold that such joint liability existed might in certain circumstances lead to very unfair results which could not be met adequately by claims for compensation. . . . The most practical solution would seem to be a succession to parts of debts according to the proportion of the new distribution of

Case No. 40 *Contd.*

territory. The claim for compensation of the personal representatives of L. has been held to be a general debt of the Administration of the former District of Lublinitz; the debt was therefore owed by the whole territory. When this territory was broken up certain parts remained with the rump-District, and a proportionate part of the general debts of the Administration must be taken to have attached to it, so far as they related to the respective part of the former District."

The plaintiffs were, however, liable only in a small proportion, inasmuch as Poland received two-thirds of the territory of the District together with the seat of administration, as well as its assets. For the measure of distribution there must also be taken into account the revenue capacity of the individual parts of the District and the transfer to Poland of profit-bearing investments and institutions.

[Report: *Entscheidungen des Reichsgerichts in Zivilsachen*, vol. 136, pp. 339 *et seq.*: *Juristische Wochenschrift*, 1932, p. 2793. See also the comments by Nostitz-Wallwitz in *Z. für a. ö. R. und V.*, vol. IV (1934), p. 428.]

IX.—Binding Force of Laws and Judgments of Courts

Case No. 41

State Succession—Continuity of Laws—Acts Committed in Ceded Territory Prior to Cession.

CASE OF THE DEMOLISHED HOUSE IN KUŠEVJAL

Yugoslavia, Court of Cassation. November 18, 1931.

THE FACTS.—Kuševjal is a village situated in what was formerly Turkish territory in the Balkans. In 1911 the defendants demolished a house in that village and took away the building materials. In 1913 the district in question was ceded to Serbia, and thus formed part of the Kingdom of Yugoslavia. The defendants pleaded that the claim was barred by a statute of limitation. The period of limitation laid down in Article 939 of the Yugoslav Civil Code was three years with regard to torts and twenty-four years with regard to injury sustained as the result of a criminal offence. The question thus arose whether the criminal or tortious character of the act complained of was to be determined in accordance with the Turkish Penal Code, which was in force in the country when the act was performed, or in accordance with the Yugoslav Penal Code, which was in force in the country when the case was tried.

Held: that, notwithstanding the fact that the offence was committed at the time of Turkish sovereignty, it had to be judged according to the Yugoslav and not the Turkish laws.

[Report (incomplete): Ivanović, *Sudska praksa u* 1931 *godini sa Zbirkom načelnih odluka i mišljenja Opšte sednice Kasacionog suda od* 1931-33 *godine* (*Jurisprudence of Yugoslav Courts in* 1931, *with Collection of the Doctrinal Decisions and Opinions of the General Division of the Court of Cassation,* 1931-1933), No. 164, p. 201.]

State Succession—Respect of Private Rights—Continuation of Laws—Pension Rights. **Case No. 42**

STRUZEK *v.* DISTRICT APPEAL COMMITTEE FOR WAR CRIPPLES IN ŁÓDŹ

Poland, Supreme Administrative Court. December 1, 1931.

THE FACTS.—The plaintiff, who was resident in Polish Upper Silesia, served in the German Army during the World War. In 1917 the military medical authorities declared him to be unfit on account of a disease which existed before the military service but which had become aggravated owing to military service. He was declared to have lost 25 per cent. of his earning capacity owing to war service. It was stipulated that he must undergo another medical examination in 1918. A new German Law concerning pensions was issued on May 12, 1920, and a Polish Law was issued on March 18, 1921. A plebiscite was held in Upper Silesia on March 20, 1921. In 1922 Poland assumed sovereignty over that part assigned to it after the plebiscite. In 1926 the plaintiff was re-examined by the Polish military medical authorities under the Law of 1921 and was found to have suffered a 33 per cent. permanent disability, of which 10 per cent. was assigned to causes connected with his military service. This finding was approved by the defendant Committee in 1927. In the present action the plaintiff contended that Article 4 of the Polish-German Convention concerning Upper Silesia, concluded in Geneva on May 15, 1922, which guaranteed the respect of private rights, imposed upon Poland the obligation to respect the application of the German Law of May 12, 1920, which, he claimed, prohibited reconsideration of definitely assigned pension rights.

Case No. 42 *Contd.*

Held: that the action must be dismissed. "Neither generally binding principles nor any single rule of international law can be found which oblige a State which takes a territory under its sovereignty to take over at the same time laws which until then had been in force there. Such an obligation would, therefore, have to result in each case from special agreements concluded between the States in question. Such agreements, as forming special and exceptional law, must be interpreted most restrictively." Article 4 of the Geneva Convention dealt partly with strictly specified rights without mentioning war invalids' pensions, and partly with private rights based on the German Civil Code. The latter was not applicable to war pensions, which belonged to the domain of public law.

[Report: *Zb. W.N.T.A.*, IX. (1931), No. 462A, p. 369.]

Case No. 43

State Succession—Continuation of Laws—Succession to Rights—Respect of Private Rights—The State of Arizona and Mexican Law.

MARICOPA COUNTY MUNICIPAL WATER CONSERVATION DISTRICT NUMBER ONE *ET AL.* *v.* SOUTHWEST COTTON COMPANY *ET AL.*

United States, Supreme Court of Arizona. October 22, 1931.
(McAlister, C. J.; Ross, Lockwood, JJ.)

THE FACTS.—This was an action brought to restrain the defendants from storing and using certain surface waters of the Agua Fria River. The broad question involved was the law applicable to the relative rights of ownership and use of the subterranean waters of the State and of the surface waters. In particular, the Court had to determine whether the doctrine of prior appropriation, a doctrine not recognised by the common law of England, was applicable to percolating subterranean waters. The lower Court granted the injunction. On appeal,

Held: that the judgment must be reversed. The area which was now the State of Arizona was acquired from the Republic of Mexico in 1848 and 1853. At that time the United States succeeded to the sovereignty which was previously exercised by Mexico, with the same right to alter and amend existing laws, or establish new ones, as was previously held by Mexico: *Boquillas Co.* v. *St. David Ass'n*, 11 Ariz. 128; *Lux* v. *Haggin*, 69 Cal. 255. In the absence of affirmative action by the United States, or afterwards by the State of Arizona, the law existing in Arizona at the time of its acquisition must be presumed to continue unchanged: *Lux* v. *Haggin*, *supra*; *Clough* v. *Wing*, 2 Ariz. 371. The Court discussed the applicable principles of Mexican law and concluded that the doctrine of prior appropriation did not exist under Mexican law. It concluded, further, that at the time the territory of Arizona was acquired from Mexico, the United States and its agent, the Government of the territory of Arizona, succeeded to the right to dispose of and regulate the use of all waters of every nature, both surface and subterranean, in a dual capacity as sovereign and as proprietor of the public domain. This right, the Court said, was subject only to such vested rights to the use of specific waters as had been acquired, either formally from the Mexican Government, or impliedly as a result of local custom, and to the right of use of all percolating, subterranean waters underlying lands then in private hands by the owners of such lands. Reviewing the legislation passed since the acquisition of Arizona the Court concluded that as to percolating waters Arizona had adopted by statute the common law rules rather than the doctrine of prior appropriation.

[Report : 39 Ariz. 65.]

State Succession—Limits of—Continuity of Laws—Private Rights. **Case No. 44**

SPRINGS OF SAMOTHRACE CASE.

Greece, Court of Thrace. 1932.

THE FACTS.—The petitioner was the owner of certain land having water springs possessed of medicinal qualities. The land in question was situated in the Island of Samothrace, which was ceded by Turkey to Greece after the Balkan War. According to Turkish law the State possessed property in such springs, although it could grant to private persons the right of exploitation. According to Greek law the property in springs of that nature belonged to the owner of the land. The Greek State having now denied the petitioner the right of exploitation,

Held: for the petitioner. "The Greek State having become subrogated to Turkey with regard to the property in the springs, the Greek law in question is fully effective in the Island of Samothrace since its annexation."

[Report : *Thémis*, vol. 43, p. 426.]

State Succession—Continuance of Laws—Validity of. the German Constitution in Danzig—Separation of Danzig from the German Reich—Principle of Continuity of the Legal Order.

See the case decided by the High Court of Danzig on February 4, 1931: *Danziger Juristische Monatsschrift*, vol. 10 (1931), p. 124. In that case, which does not call for a detailed report, the Court held that the German Constitution of 1919 had legal force in Danzig although Danzig was at that time about to be separated from Germany by virtue of the Peace Treaty of Versailles. The Court said: "It is not permissible to argue that, in view of the impending separation of Danzig from the mother-country, the German Constitution had only a provisional effect in the territory of Danzig . . . . This follows from the principle of the continuity of the legal order according to which as a matter of principle there is a presumption in favour of the continued validity of legal provisions which were previously in force."

F.—SUCCESSION OF GOVERNMENTS

II.—Upon Termination of a Rebellion

Case No. 45 **Succession of Governments—Taking of Benefits—How Far Dependent upon Taking Over of Burdens—Ratification of Acts of Government Agents—Whether Partial Ratification Possible.**

CHINA (REPUBLIC OF) *v.* MERCHANTS' FIRE ASSURANCE CORPORATION OF NEW YORK.

United States, Circuit Court of Appeals, Ninth Circuit. May 8, 1931.

(Rudkin, Wilbur, Sawtelle, Circuit Judges.)

THE FACTS.—The Provisional Government of China, which had its capital at Peking and which was recognised by the United States, took out a policy of insurance with the defendant corporation upon the Telephone Exchange building at Wuchang. The building was destroyed by fire during the continuance of the Provisional Government. Thereafter the Nationalist Government took possession of the building and the policy and brought an action (No. 3004) upon the policy in the name of the Republic of China in the United States

Court for China. Shortly thereafter the present action (No. 3025) was instituted in the United States Court for China by a third Government at Peking, upon the same policy and loss, the Provisional Government having been displaced by the forces operating under Chang Tso Ling. Neither of the Governments which sued had been expressly recognised by the United States. The Trial Court concluded, however, that the United States had sufficiently recognised the Peking Government to justify the prosecution of the action by that Government. Consequently the action brought by the Nationlist Government, No. 3004, was dismissed. The Nationalist Government appealed to the United States Circuit Court of Appeals. In the meantime the United States recognised the Nationalist Government and, upon that ground, the Circuit Court of Appeals reversed the judgment of dismissal in Case No. 3004 (30 F. (2d) 278 ; *Annual Digest*, 1929-1930, Case No. 21). Meanwhile, the action brought by the Peking Government, No. 3025, was settled. As part of the settlement, judgment was entered in favour of the Peking Government, and upon payment of cash and the assignment of a claim to an agent of the Peking Government, satisfaction of judgment was entered. When Case No. 3004 was remanded for further proceedings by the Trial Court it was held therein that the question was *res judicata*, the judgment in No. 3025 being a bar to further prosecution of the claim.

The Nationalist Government then sought to annul the entry of satisfaction of judgment in Case No. 3025. It contended that its recognition by the United States related back to the beginning of the Nationalist Government, and, therefore, that at the time judgment was rendered and its satisfaction entered in Case No. 3025 the Nationalist Government was the only authority authorised to bring the action. It contended that the judgment was consequently its property, although it was secured by agents of the Peking Government. It was argued that payment of the judgment had been made to persons who were not authorised to represent the Republic of China, and that such payment should therefore be ignored and the satisfaction of judgment annulled. The United States Court for China refused to annul the entry of satisfaction of judgment.

On appeal,

Held (the judgment of the Court being delivered by Wilbur, J.) : that the order must be affirmed. The contention of the Nationalist Government was in conflict with the axiom that

Case No. 45 Contd.

he who takes a benefit must bear the corresponding burden. The Nationalist Government sought to appropriate the benefit of the judgment in favour of the Republic of China. It could not do so without assuming the corresponding burden, namely, the agreement under which the judgment was procured, and this agreement not only provided for entry of the judgment but also for its satisfaction. There seemed to have been no serious question that the money and the claim assigned in satisfaction of the judgment were available to the Nationalist Government. The principal complaint was that the insurance company transferred a claim against an insolvent bank in lieu of the corresponding obligation to pay money. However, this contention was based upon the erroneous theory that the judgment in case No. 3025 belonged to the Nationalist Government and that the appellant was not bound by the acts of the agents who procured that judgment, even though it ratified their acts to the extent of appropriating the fruits of their action in the form of a judgment. This conflicted with the rule that a principal who ratifies any portion of an unauthorised transaction of his agent must ratify the whole of it.

[Report : 49 F. (2d) 862.]

Succession of Governments—Actions Against Unrecognised Governments—Property of Unrecognised Governments—The Denikin Government in Russia in 1920.

See Case No. 25 (*Voevodine v. Government of the Commander-in-Chief of the Armed Forces in the South of Russia*).

G.—MISCELLANEOUS

Case No. 46

International Persons—Miscellaneous—Sovereign Order of Malta—Competence of Italian Courts with Regard to Internal Affairs Regulated by the Constitution of the Order.

See the case of *Sovereign Order of Malta* v. *Brunelli, Tacali and Others*, decided by the Italian Court of Cassation on December 17, 1931 : *Rivista italiana di diritto internazionale privato e processuale*, 1932, p. 31. This case, which does not require a detailed digest, arose out of the determination of the succession to the Recanati-Giustiniani benefice, which was subject to the jurisdiction of the Order of Malta and which had fallen vacant on the death of its incumbent. Of the various candidates the Order of Malta excluded some, who, it was contended, would otherwise have been eligible, on the ground that they lacked the prescribed requisites of nobility, morality and religious faith. Those excluded applied to the Italian Courts for a declaration that they had a right to be considered for the benefice and the enjoyment of the property attached thereto. The Court of Cassation *held* that the decision of the Court of Appeal of Venice on the matter must be reversed. The Italian Courts were not competent to review the decision of the Order with regard to the existence of the requirements of morality, etc. in the candidates for the benefice, but they had jurisdiction to ascertain who were qualified to stand as candidates for the benefice and from among whom the Order was at liberty to choose. The Court said: "The reliance placed by the appellant Order on the recognition of its character as a juridical person in international public law, which character was conferred on the Sovereign Order of Malta by the decisions of June 17, 1913, and February 18, 1916, does not seem sufficient to exclude the competence of the Italian Courts. This character may indeed confer special powers on the Order, corresponding to the needs of its autonomy; but it is necessary to examine what are the limits of those powers and how far they may be exercised exclusively. The examination of claims of eligibility for the benefice is the exclusive right of the Order, not so much because the property the use of which constitutes a perquisite of the incumbent, belongs to the Order, as because the qualifications of fitness expressly laid down by its constitution have been inserted by the Order itself." But "the question of qualification for the benefice arises, in the first place, in a private law relationship, such as is laid down in the Charter of Incorporation, and therefore constitutes for the interested person a subjective right the vesting of which, however, is subject to the judgment of the Order with regard to other requirements like those of nobility and morality."

State of the Vatican—Interpretation by Dutch Court of Concordat between the Holy See and a Third State—Letters Rogatory—Convention on Civil Procedure of July 17, 1905. **Case No. 47**

VAN BLARKOM C.S. *v.* ORDO FRATRUM MINORUM SANCTI FRANCISCI CAPUCINORUM.

Holland, District Court of Utrecht. November 30, 1932.

THE FACTS.—In proceedings between certain Dutch subjects and a religious Order established at Rome, it was found necessary, in accordance with Article 242 of the Dutch Code of

Case No. 47 *Contd.*

Civil Procedure, to interrogate the Governing Board of the Order on certain points in dispute. As no representative of the Order was able to come to Utrecht, the question was raised as to possible recourse to the Hague Convention on Civil Procedure of July 17, 1905, which provided, *inter alia*, for *commissions rogatoires* to be addressed by the tribunals of a contracting State to the judicial authorities of another. Not all of the Directors of the Board were domiciled in the State of the Vatican, some living at Rome, in Italian territory. Since, on the one hand, a commission to a Dutch consular officer at Rome was not possible in the circumstances of the case and since, on the other hand, the State of the Vatican was not a party to the Convention of 1905, the only practicable method seemed to be to commission the competent Italian tribunal to interrogate those members of the Board who were domiciled in Italian territory. The Court had now to decide whether this method was admissible having regard to the existing relations between Italy and the Pope, namely, the provisions of the article of the Concordat between Italy and the Holy See as summarised below.

Held: that the Concordat between Italy and the Holy See did not stand in the way of the proposed commission. In exempting from impediment, interrogation or annoyance all clergymen who, for reasons of professional business outside the Vatican territory, participate in the activities of the Holy See, the Concordat did not intend to cover the case of a director of a religious Order.

[Report: *Weekblad van het Recht*, No. 12689; *Nederlandsche Jurisprudentie*, 1933, p. 1264.]

PART III

STATE TERRITORY

A—IN GENERAL

I.—Nature of Territorial Sovereignty

Territory—Fictitious Parts of—Ships as State Territory—Jurisdiction—Application to Warships of Statutes of Member-States of Federal States—Warships as State Territory. **Case No. 48**

WARSHIP AS STATE TERRITORY (PRUSSIAN DECREE) CASE.

Germany, Prussian Supreme Administrative Court.
December 13, 1932.

THE FACTS.—Under Section 1 (1) of the Prussian Decree for the Temporary Regulation of the Trade Tax of November 23, 1923, trade tax was payable in respect of all trades which were carried on by keeping a place of business in Prussia. Section 1 (4) defined a place of business as any premises or establishment situated in a certain locality and used for the purposes of a trade. The appellant ran a ship's canteen on a German warship stationed at Kiel. He had been assessed for trade tax in respect of the running of the canteen, and he appealed against the assessment.

Held: that the appeal must be allowed. It was true that under international law warships were deemed to be parts of their State and were regarded as so-called moving territories. However, even if one were to hold that, according to that fiction, the warship was not only German Reich territory, but also at the same time territory of one of the Member-States of the Federal State, it did not follow that, by running a canteen on a warship, the appellant kept a place of business in Prussia. To fulfil the conditions of the Decree there must exist a fixed local centre, that is to say, a fixed, permanent connection with a geographically determinable point of the surface of the soil. This condition did not exist in respect of a warship, even where she was anchored or was otherwise temporarily connected with the territory of the State. "It makes no difference that when on the high seas warships (like merchant ships) are deemed to be parts of the home State.

Case No. 48 Contd.

The sole purpose of this fiction is to subject the acts occurring on board the ships to a given jurisdiction. It would be an exaggeration of the fiction to hold that a trade carried on on board a sea-going vessel was so carried on on fictitious land."

[Report: *Entscheidungen des Preussischen Oberverwaltungsgerichts*, vol. 90. p. 47.]

NOTE.—See also the decision of the Administrative Court of Baden of June 21, 1932 (*Entscheidungen der Gerichte und Verwaltungsbehörden aus dem Rechtsgebiet der inneren Verwaltung*, vol. 53, p. 535) where the Court laid down in clear terms the distinction between men-of-war and merchant vessels. The Court said: "According to recognised principles of constitutional and international law, national ships, after having left territorial waters and when on the high seas, are regarded as moving parts of the States whose flag they fly. It is only in respect of State-owned vessels that the principle prevails that they are subject to the jurisdiction of their State also in foreign territorial waters and rivers; as regards trading ships this only applies to ships while on the high seas, and to a certain extent while in coastal waters."

Territory—Parts of—Colonies—Status of German Colonies Before the World War.

See Case No. 31 (*Sch. v. Germany*, (II)).

Ships—Territorial Character of—The Law of the United States.

See Case No. 153 (*United States ex rel. Stapf v. Corsi, Commissioner of Immigration*).

Territory—Ships as State Territory—Ships in Foreign Territorial Waters.

See Case No. 93 (*Postal Packets (Braunschweig) Case*).

Territory—Ships—Territoriality of Ships.

See Case No. 91 (*United States v. Flores*).

II.—Acquisition of Territorial Sovereignty

ii.—Occupation. The Principle of Contiguity. Effect of Discovery.

Territory—Acquisition of Territorial Sovereignty—Continued and Peaceful Possession—Conditions of Occupation Creating Title—Absence of Adverse Claims—Extent of Occupation—Intention—Actual Exercise of Sovereignty—Relevancy of Legislation—Conquest and Abandonment—Treaties as Evidence of Undisputed Sovereignty—Meaning of Geographical Terms—Burden of Proof—Admissions in the Course of Diplomatic Negotiations—Treaties Containing Reservations as to a Disputed Right — Renunciation — Estoppel as the Result of Treaties—Declarations by a Foreign Minister—Binding Force of.

Case No. 49

PERMANENT COURT OF INTERNATIONAL JUSTICE.

LEGAL STATUS OF EASTERN GREENLAND.

Judgment of April 5, 1933.[1]

THE FACTS.—In 1380 the Kingdoms of Norway and Denmark were united under the same Crown. In the Treaty of Kiel of 1814 Norway, with the exception of Greenland, the Ferroe Islands and Iceland, was ceded to Sweden, and the Union thus came to an end.

The early settlements in Greenland, established about the XIth century, became tributary to the Kingdom of Norway in the XIIIth century. They disappeared about the XVth century. In 1721 a new colony was founded in Greenland by a Norwegian Company which received a concession for twenty-five years in respect "of the whole of Greenland," the King of Norway reserving for himself the "sovereignty, *absolutum dominium* and hereditary rights." In 1750 a concession was granted to a company at Copenhagen. About 1776 the Greenland trade became a monopoly of the State of Denmark.

During the XIXth and XXth centuries a number of Danish expeditions explored various parts of Greenland, and some settlements were founded. In the XXth century various Danish laws were passed relating to the administration of Greenland. In the various treaties concluded at that time with other States, Denmark expressly reserved Greenland from the

[1] The Court was composed as follows : Adatci (President) ; Guerrero (Vice-President) ; Rolin-Jaequemyns, Rostworowski, Fromageot, Anzilotti, Urrutia, Hurst, Schücking, Negulesco, Van Eysinga, Wang (Judges) ; Vogt and Zahle (Judges *ad hoc*).

Case No. 49 ***Contd.***

operation of these treaties. A number of Norwegian expeditions to Greenland were made after 1889.

As to the other facts relating to the history of the various stages of the occupation of Greenland and of the negotiations prior to the submission of the dispute to the Court, it is convenient to include them in the statement of the reasons underlying the decisions of the Court on the various points and submissions.

On July 10, 1931, the Norwegian Government informed the Danish Government and certain other interested Powers that it felt obliged to proceed to the occupation of certain territories in Eastern Greenland. On the following day the Danish Government, relying on the Optional Clause of Article 36 of the Statute of the Court, brought before the Court a suit against the Norwegian Government on the ground that the declaration of occupation of territories said to be subject to the sovereignty of Denmark, constituted a violation of the existing legal situation and was accordingly unlawful and invalid.

Denmark contended before the Court that :

(*a*) She had sovereignty over Greenland on the ground that her sovereignty over the island had existed for a long time, that she had exercised it peacefully and continuously, and that, until the present dispute, it had not been contested by any Power ;

(*b*) Norway had by various treaties recognised Danish sovereignty over Greenland as a whole and could not therefore dispute it ;

(*c*) Apart from these treaties, the Norwegian Minister for Foreign Affairs speaking in 1919 on behalf of his Government gave to the Danish Government a promise that Norway would not make any difficulties in the matter of the recognition of Danish sovereignty over the whole of Greenland.

The principal Norwegian contentions were :

(*a*) that the area covered by the declaration of occupation of July 10, 1931, was *terra nullius*; and

(*b*) that the attempts made by Denmark in 1915 and 1921 to obtain recognition of her position in Greenland was inconsistent with a claim to be already in possession of the sovereignty over all Greenland, and that she was therefore estopped from alleging a long established sovereignty over the whole island.

Held (Anzilotti, Judge, and Vogt, Judge *ad hoc*, dissenting) : that the Norwegian declaration of occupation of July 10, 1931, constituted a violation of the existing legal situation and was accordingly unlawful and invalid.

I. *Acquisition of Sovereignty by Continued and Peaceful Possession.*

(*a*) *Date of Existence of Sovereignty and its Infringement by Foreign Occupation.*—The date at which the Danish sovereignty must have existed in order to render invalid the occupation by Norway was the day on which the latter took place, *i.e.*, July 10, 1931.

(*b*) *Requirement of Continuity of Occupation.*—However, "it is not necessary that sovereignty over Greenland should have existed throughout the period during which the Danish Government maintains that it was in being. Even if the material submitted to the Court might be thought insufficient to establish the existence of that sovereignty during the earlier periods, this would not exclude a finding that it is sufficient to establish a valid title in the period immediately preceding the occupation" (at p. 45).

(*c*) *Conditions of Occupation Creating Title: Actual Display of Sovereignty: Intention: Absence of Adverse Claims.*—"A claim to sovereignty based not upon some particular act or title such as a treaty of cession but merely upon continued display of authority, involves two elements each of which must be shown to exist: the intention and will to act as sovereign, and some actual exercise or display of such authority.

"Another circumstance which must be taken into account by any tribunal which has to adjudicate upon a claim to sovereignty over a particular territory, is the extent to which the sovereignty is also claimed by some other Power. In most of the cases involving claims to territorial sovereignty which have come before an international tribunal, there have been two competing claims to the sovereignty, and the tribunal has had to decide which of the two is the stronger. One of the peculiar features of the present case is that up to 1931 there was no claim by any Power other than Denmark to the sovereignty over Greenland. Indeed, up till 1921, no Power disputed the Danish claim to sovereignty.

"It is impossible to read the records of the decisions in cases as to territorial sovereignty without observing that in many cases the tribunal has been satisfied with very little in the way of the actual exercise of sovereign rights, provided that the other State could not make out a superior claim. This is

Case No. 49 ***Contd.***

particularly true in the case of claims to sovereignty over areas in thinly populated or unsettled countries" (at pp. 45, 46).

(*d*) *Extent of Occupation.* (*i*) *Intention.*—The Danish rights were grounded in the rights acquired by Norway in the Xth-XIVth centuries. These rights were not limited to the two organised settlements established at that time. At that time "the modern notions as to territorial sovereignty had not come into being. It is unlikely that either the chiefs or the settlers in these colonies drew any sharp distinction between territory which was and territory which was not subject to them" (at p. 46). There was evidence that the jurisdiction of Norwegian kings was not limited to these settlements. After a temporary cessation of the occupation, further expeditions and acts of occupation took place in the XVIth century. These expeditions, "the efforts to assure respect on the part of foreign Powers for the King's rights there and the claim to exclude foreigners from the Greenland trade, all show that the King considered that in his dealings with Greenland he was dealing with a country with respect to which he had a special position superior to that of any other Power. . . . It must have covered the territory which is known as Greenland to-day, because the country was inhabited" (at p. 47).

(*ii*) *Actual Exercise of Sovereignty. Relevancy of Legislation.* As there were at this date no colonies or settlements in Greenland, the King's claims cannot have been limited to any particular places in the country.

"That the King's claims amounted merely to pretensions is clear, for he had no permanent contact with the country, he was exercising no authority there. The claims, however, were not disputed. No other Power was putting forward any claim to territorial sovereignty in Greenland, and in the absence of any competing claim the King's pretensions to be the sovereign of Greenland subsisted" (at pp. 47, 48).

While there was ample evidence as to the existence of the intention of the Norwegian kings to acquire sovereignty over the whole of Greenland as well as evidence of the actual exercise of such occupation, the question arose how far the latter conferred a valid title to sovereignty over the whole country. "The founding of the colonies was accompanied by the grant of a monopoly of the trade, and before long legislation was found to be necessary to protect and enforce the monopoly. In the earlier Ordinances of 1740-1751, issued at the time when Jacob Severin was the grantee of the monopoly, the prohibition of trading was restricted to the colonies, but those Ordinances also contained a prohibition of injurious treatment of the Greenlanders, and this was not limited to the colonies but operated in Greenland as a whole. Furthermore, the prohibition of trading was to apply not only in the existing colonies but in any future colonies which might be established. Legislation is one of the most obvious forms of the exercise of sovereign power, and it is clear that the operation of these enactments was not restricted to the limits of the colonies. It therefore follows that the sovereign right in virtue of which the enactments were issued cannot have been restricted to the limits of the colonies" (at p. 48).

As there was no claim to sovereignty by any other Power, and in view of the arctic and inaccessible character of the uncolonised parts of the country, the King of Denmark and Norway displayed during the period from the founding of the colonies in 1721 up to 1814 his authority to an extent sufficient to give his country a valid claim to sovereignty. His rights over Greenland were therefore not to be regarded as being limited to the colonised area.

(*iii*) *Exercise of Sovereignty in the Period immediately preceding the Outbreak of the Dispute.*—Apart from the history of the preceding periods the history of the ten years immediately preceding the Norwegian declaration of occupation showed to a sufficient extent the existence on the part of Denmark of "the two elements necessary to establish a valid title to sovereignty, namely: the intention and will to exercise such sovereignty and the manifestation of State activity" (at p. 63). This exercise of sovereignty consisted, *inter alia*, in legislation concerning navigation in the seas round Greenland, the regulation of fishing and hunting, the issue of permits to persons visiting the eastern coast of Greenland, and the conclusion of commercial agreements referring to Greenland.

II. *Conquest and Abandonment.*

The Court was unable to accept the Norwegian submission that Norwegian sovereignty was lost and Greenland became a *terra nullius* as the result of the disappearance, about 1500, o the first two Nordic settlements and their conquest by the Eskimos. "The word 'conquest' is not an appropriate phrase, even if it is assumed that it was fighting with the Eskimos which led to the downfall of the settlements. Conquest only operates as a cause of loss of sovereignty when there is war between two States and by reason of the defeat of one of them sovereignty over territory passes from the loser to the victorious

Case No. 49 ***Contd.***

State. The principle does not apply in a case where a settlement has been established in a distant country and its inhabitants are massacred by the aboriginal population. Nor is the fact of 'conquest' established. It is known now that the settlements must have disappeared at an early date, but at the time there seems to have been a belief that despite the loss of contact and the loss of knowledge of the whereabouts of the settlements one or both of them would again be discovered and found to contain the descendants of the early settlers.

"As regards voluntary abandonment, there is nothing to show any definite renunciation on the part of the kings of Norway or Denmark" (at p. 47).

III. *Treaties as Evidence of Undisputed Sovereignty.*

Denmark was entitled to adduce, as relevant evidence of the willingness of other States to recognise her sovereignty over Greenland, treaties with those States in which a stipulation was inserted to the effect that the convention shall not apply to Greenland. This applies, for instance, to such treaties as those concluded in 1826 with the United States which provided that "the present Convention shall not apply to the Northern possessions of His Majesty the King of Denmark, that is to say Iceland, the Faerö Islands and Greenland . . ." The Court could not accept the Norwegian contention that no importance could be attached to these conventions on the ground that at the time of their conclusion the Parties had no such questions in mind as whether Danish sovereignty was limited to the colonies or not, and whether the term "Greenland" meant more than the areas of actual occupation. "It is true that when they conclude a commercial convention, States are not dealing with such questions as the extent of their respective territories, but the usual object of a commercial convention is to give to each of the Parties facilities for trade and navigation in the territories of the other; consequently, the area within which such facilities are, or are not, accorded is a point of some importance. It is a question on which disputes may arise if there is any uncertainty. If the Parties were agreed that the treaty was not to apply in a particular area and the area is only designated by name, the natural conclusion is that no difference existed between them as to the extent of the area which that name covered" (at p. 52). Accordingly, "to the extent that these treaties constitute evidence of recognition of her sovereignty over Greenland in general, Denmark is entitled to rely upon them" (at p. 52).

IV. *Interpretation of Treaties. Meaning of Geographical Terms. Burden of Proof.*

The Court could not accept the Norwegian contention that both the treaties in question and the legislative and administrative acts of Denmark in the XVIIIth century relating to Greenland did not use that name in the geographical sense, but referred merely to such areas as were actually colonised. "This is a point as to which the burden of proof lies on Norway. The geographical meaning of the word 'Greenland', i.e., the name which is habitually used in maps to denominate the whole island, must be regarded as the ordinary meaning of the word. If it is alleged by one of the Parties that some unusual or exceptional meaning is to be attributed to it, it lies on that Party to establish its contention. In the opinion of the Court, Norway has not succeeded in establishing her contention. It is not sufficient for her to show that in many of these legislative and administrative acts action was only to be taken in the colonies. Most of them dealt with things which only happened in the colonies and not in the rest of the country. The fact that most of these acts were concerned with what happened in the colonies and that the colonies were all situated on the West coast is not by itself sufficient ground for holding that the authority in virtue of which the act was taken—whether legislative or administrative—was also restricted to the colonized area. Unless it was so restricted, it affords no ground for interpreting the word 'Greenland' in this restricted sense" (at p. 49). This was also the case in regard to the term 'Greenland' as used in the treaties. "The natural meaning of the term is its geographical meaning as shown in the maps. If it is argued on behalf of Norway that these treaties use the term 'Greenland' in some special sense, it is for her to establish it, and it is not decisive in this respect that the northern part of Greenland was still unknown" (at p. 52).

V. *Admissions and Estoppels.*

(*a*) *Admissions in the course of Diplomatic Negotiations.*—Contrary to the contention of Norway the Court could not attach decisive importance to the fact that in the course of the negotiations with the various Governments, intended to secure a formal recognition of Danish sovereignty, the Danish representative referred on occasion to their request for recognition of "extension of sovereignty". There could be no doubt that this expression when taken in itself is very difficult to reconcile with the Danish view, as put before the Court, that

Case No. 49 *Contd.*

the Danish Government was seeking a recognition of existing sovereignty and not consent to the acquisition of new sovereignty which did not as yet belong to her. However, "the Court has come to the conclusion that in judging the effect of these notes too much importance must not be attached to particular expressions here and there. The correspondence must be judged as a whole. One reason for this is that in some cases the notes were written by individual Danish diplomatic representatives, and, though no doubt they were based on the instructions these Ministers received, some variation must be expected and allowed for in the terms they used" (at p. 54). An examination of the relevant correspondence as a whole showed that in fact the Danish Government adopted uniformly the view that it possessed sovereignty over the uncolonised part of Greenland. Denmark was not therefore estopped from claiming that it possessed an old established sovereignty over all Greenland.

(*b*) *Admission by Concluding a Treaty Containing Reservations as to the Disputed Right.*—Contrary to the contention of Norway, "the conclusion of the 1924 Convention with Norway,. . though signed by that State on the footing that she maintained her point of view as to the territorial status of Eastern Greenland (*terra nullius*) and that the conclusion of the Convention did not prejudice her point of view, does not exclude the right of Denmark to maintain her point of view that she was entitled to and was in fact enjoying sovereignty over all Greenland, nor does it exclude her right to show that the elements which go to establish a valid claim to sovereignty were both present" (at p. 63).

(*c*) *Renunciation.*—The Court also considered the various international documents between 1814 and 1819 in connection with the termination of the Union between Denmark and Norway and found that "in consequence of the various undertakings resulting from the separation of Norway and Denmark and culminating in Article 9 of the Convention of September 1st, 1819, Norway has recognized Danish sovereignty over the whole of Greenland and consequently cannot proceed to the occupation of any part thereof" (at p. 68). (This aspect of the decision does not seem to raise any general question of law, but reference must be made to the consideration by the Court of the various drafts of the Treaty of 1819.)

(*d*) *Estoppel as the Result of Treaties.*—As the result of the conclusion of bilateral agreements with Denmark and of various multilateral agreements to which Denmark and Norway were parties, and in which Greenland was described as a Danish colony or as forming part of Denmark or in which Denmark was allowed to exclude Greenland from the operation of the agreement, "Norway reaffirmed that she recognized the whole of Greenland as Danish; and thereby she has debarred herself from contesting Danish sovereignty over the whole of Greenland, and, in consequence, from proceeding to occupy any part of it" (at pp. 68, 69).[1]

(*e*) *Estoppel as the result of a Declaration of the Foreign Minister.*—The Court attached decisive importance to a declaration made on July 22, 1919, by the Norwegian Minister for Foreign Affairs to the Danish Minister. In this declaration, recorded by him in a minute, the Norwegian Minister for Foreign Affairs "informed the Danish Minister that the Norwegian Government would not make any difficulties in the settlement of this question." The question as formulated in the abovementioned minute recording the statement of the Danish Minister was due to the anxiety of Denmark "to obtain the recognition of all the interested Powers of Denmark's sovereignty over the whole of Greenland," as well as a declaration that no objection would be raised against "the Danish Government extending their political and economic interests to the whole of Greenland." The same minute recorded a declaration on the part of Denmark that she had no interest in Spitzbergen (recognition of the sovereignty over which the Norwegian Government was trying to secure at that time) and an undertaking not to oppose the wishes of Norway in regard to the settlement of this question. The Court attached importance to the fact that Denmark regarded the Norwegian promise not to make any difficulty in the settlement of the Greenland question as an equivalent of her readiness not to oppose the Norwegian claim in regard to Spitzbergen.

The Court held that: (i) it was "beyond all dispute that a reply of this nature given by the Minister for Foreign Affairs on behalf of his Government in response to a request by the

[1] The Court referred, *inter alia*, to Article 5 of the Treaty of Commerce between Denmark and the United Kingdoms of Sweden and Norway of November 2, 1826, which read as follows: "The respective colonies of the two High Contracting Parties, including in the case of Denmark, Greenland, Iceland, and the Faroe Isles, shall be specially excepted from the provisions of the four preceding articles, which shall only be applicable to the Kingdom of Denmark, the Duchies of Slesvig, Holstein and Lauenbourg of the one part, and to the Kingdoms of Sweden and Norway, of the other part"; and to the Universal Postal Conventions of 1920, 1924, and 1929, which say that: "The following shall be considered as belonging to the Universal Postal Union: . . . (*c*) the Faroe Isles and Greenland, as being part of Denmark."

Case No. 49 ***Contd.***

diplomatic representative of a foreign Power, in regard to a question falling within his province, is binding upon the country to which the Minister belongs" (at p. 71); and (ii) that "as a result of the undertaking involved in the Ihlen declaration of July 22nd, 1919, Norway is under an obligation to refrain from contesting Danish sovereignty over Greenland as a whole, and *a fortiori* to refrain from occupying a part of Greenland" (at p. 73).

[Report: *P.C.I.J.*, Series A/B, No. 53.]

NOTE.—In his dissenting opinion Anzilotti, Judge, held in regard to V (*a*) that an examination of the diplomatic correspondence showed that in its negotiations with the Powers, Denmark deliberately asked not for recognition of an already existing sovereignty, but for recognition of the right to extend its sovereignty to the whole of Greenland (pp. 77-81). In regard to acquisition of sovereignty over Greenland as the result of actual occupation Judge Anzilotti held that, so far as the early claims to sovereignty—*i.e.*, prior to the interruption of the occupation in the sixteenth century—were concerned, there existed a "profound difference between the colonized regions of Greenland and the remainder thereof" (at p. 83); that a regular administration and judicial organisation existed only for certain colonies in the island; that these defects were of little importance not only because the requirements of international law were then smaller in the matter of actual exercise of sovereignty, but also because the claims to sovereignty put forward by Danish-Norwegian or Danish kings were at that time principally of a historical nature. However, subsequently "historical claims to dominion over whole regions—claims which had, formerly, played an important part in the allocation of territorial sovereignty—lost weight and were gradually abandoned even by the States which had relied upon them. International law established an ever closer connection between the existence of sovereignty and the effective exercise thereof, and States successfully disputed any claim not accompanied by such exercise" (at p. 84). The second occupation of the island since 1721 was not so comprehensive as to confer upon Denmark a title over the whole island in conformity with modern international law. The Norwegian declaration of July 10, 1931, referred to territories which were in effect *terra nullius*.

In regard to V(*e*) Judge Anzilotti (as well as the Norwegian Judge *ad hoc*: see p. 118[1]) agreed with the majority. He said: "No arbitral or judicial decision relating to the international competence of a Minister for Foreign Affairs has been brought to the knowledge of the Court; nor has this question been exhaustively treated by

[1] On this point, however, the Judge *ad hoc* held that the Foreign Minister's declaration was due to "a fundamental and excusable misapprehension," as to the nature of which see pp. 118, 119 and 71-73.

legal authorities. In my opinion, it must be recognised that the constant and general practice of States has been to invest the Minister for Foreign Affairs—the direct agent of the chief of the State—with authority to make statements on current affairs to foreign diplomatic representatives, and in particular to inform them as to the attitude which the government, in whose name he speaks, will adopt in a given question. Declarations of this kind are binding upon the State.

"As regards the question whether Norwegian constitutional law authorized the Minister for Foreign Affairs to make the declaration, that is a point which, in my opinion, does not concern the Danish Government: it was M. Ihlen's duty to refrain from giving his reply until he had obtained any assent that might be requisite under the Norwegian laws" (at pp. 91, 92). He therefore agreed that as "the Norwegian occupation was effected in violation of an undertaking validly assumed, it constitutes a violation of the existing legal situation, and it is therefore unlawful" (at p. 94). But he was not of the opinion that the Norwegian declaration was null and void: "A legal act is only non-existent if it lacks certain elements which are essential to its existence. Such would be the occupation of territory belonging to another State, because the status of a *terra nullius* is an essential factor to enable the occupation to serve as a means of acquiring territorial sovereignty. But this does not hold good in the case of the occupation of a *terra nullius* by a sovereign State in conformity with international law, merely because the occupying State had undertaken not to occupy it" (at p. 95). However, as the declaration of occupation was unlawful, it could not constitute a ground for the recognition of the Norwegian claim to sovereignty as demanded in the Norwegian counter-claim before the Court, "for an unlawful act cannot serve as a basis of an action at law" (at p. 95).

Territory—Acquisition of—Discovery—Proof of—Occupation—Requirement of Effectiveness—Extent of—Act of Berlin of 1885—Scope of—Duty of Notification—Abandonment. **Case No. 50**

CLIPPERTON ISLAND AWARD.

France and Mexico.

(Victor Emmanuel III, King of Italy, Sole Arbiter.)

January 28, 1931.

THE FACTS.—On November 17, 1858, Lieut. de Kerwéguen, of the French Navy, Commissioner of the French Government, while cruising half a mile off Clipperton Island drew up an instrument by which, in accordance with the instructions of the French Minister of Marine, he proclaimed French

Case No. 50 *Contd.*

sovereignty over the island. Geographical notes were taken; some members of the crew were landed; and after a second unsuccessful attempt to reach the shore, the vessel departed without leaving on the island any sign of French sovereignty. On December 8 of that year the French Consul at Honolulu published in the English journal, *The Polynesian*, the declaration of French sovereignty over Clipperton Island. Until 1897 no effective acts of French sovereignty over the island had been performed. In 1897 the French naval authorities, after learning that certain persons were collecting guano on behalf of an American company, asked the Government of the United States for an explanation, and the latter thereupon replied that it did not claim any right of sovereignty over the island. In December 1897 the island was occupied by Mexico, who considered that it had belonged to her for a long time. She contended that the island was discovered by the Spanish Navy, that by the law then in force as fixed by the Bull of Alexander VII it belonged to Spain, and that it passed to Mexico as the successor of Spain. A dispute followed between the French and Mexican Governments, and by an agreement signed on March 2, 1909, the question of the sovereignty over the island was submitted to arbitration by the King of Italy.

Held: that the sovereignty over Clipperton Island belonged to France as from November 17, 1858.

(1) *Proof of Discovery.*—It had not been proved that the island had been actually discovered by the Spanish navigators. Even admitting that the discovery had been made by Spanish subjects, it would be necessary, to establish the contention of Mexico, to prove that Spain not only had the right, as a State, to incorporate the island in her possessions, but also had effectively exercised that right. But that had not been proved. It was true that Mexico produced a geographical map printed from the archives of the Mexican Society of Geography and Statistics, where the island figured as comprised within the "Political and Military Governments of Spain in North America." However, the official character of the map could not be affirmed, seeing that it was not certain that it was drawn by order and under the supervision of the State.

(2) *Effect of Failure to Exercise Sovereignty.*—"Moreover, the proof of an historic right of Mexico's is not supported by any manifestation of her sovereignty over the island, a sovereignty never exercised until the expedition of 1897; and the mere conviction that this was territory belonging to Mexico, although general and of long standing, cannot be retained [*sic*]. Con-

sequently, there is ground to admit that, when in November, 1858, France proclaimed her sovereignty over Clipperton, that island was in the legal situation of *territorium nullius*, and, therefore, susceptible of occupation." (At. p. 393.)

(3) *The Requirement of Effective Occupation.*—There remained the question whether France proceeded to an effective occupation, satisfying the conditions required by international law for the validity of acquisition of territory by occupation.

The arbitrator must, in this question, attach importance to the regularity of the act by which France in 1858 made known in a clear and precise manner her intention to consider the island as her territory. As to the extent of the requirement of effectiveness the arbitrator said: "It is beyond doubt that by immemorial usage having the force of law, besides the *animus occupandi*, the actual, and not the nominal, taking of possession is a necessary condition of occupation. This taking of possession consists in the act, or series of acts, by which the occupying state reduces to its possession the territory in question and takes steps to exercise exclusive authority there. Strictly speaking, and in ordinary cases, that only takes place when the state establishes in the territory itself an organization capable of making its laws respected. But this step is, properly speaking, but a means of procedure to the taking of possession, and, therefore, is not identical with the latter. There may also be cases where it is unnecessary to have recourse to this method. Thus, if a territory, by virtue of the fact that it was completely uninhabitated, is, from the first moment when the occupying state makes its appearance there, at the absolute and undisputed disposition of that state, from that moment the taking of possession must be considered as accomplished, and the occupation is thereby completed. There is no reason to invoke the obligation contained in Art. 35 of the Act of Berlin of 1885 assuring to occupied territories the existence of an authority sufficient to cause acquired rights to be respected and, the case occurring, the liberty of commerce and of transit in the conditions upon which it may be stipulated. Since this Act of Berlin was subsequent to the French occupation here under consideration, concerns only territories on the coasts of Africa, and binds only the signatory states, of which Mexico is not one, in their mutual relations, it can have no weight in the present case. Besides, Art. 35, strictly speaking, has nothing to do with the taking of possession, but imposes an obligation which presupposes an occupation which has already taken place and is already valid." (At pp. 393-394.)

Case No. 50 *Contd.*

(*d*) *The Requirement of Notification.*—For the reasons stated above, the duty of notification as laid down in Article 34 of the Act of Berlin was not applicable to the present case. "There is good reason to think that the notoriety given to the act, by whatever means, sufficed at the time, and that France provoked that notoriety by publishing the said act in the manner above indicated." (At p. 394.)

(*e*) *Abandonment.*—There was no reason to suppose that France had subsequently lost her right by *derelictio.* "She never had the *animus* of abandoning the island, and the fact that she has not exercised her authority there in a positive manner does not imply the forfeiture of an acquisition already definitively perfected." (At p. 394.)

[Report : *A.J.*, XXVI (1932), p. 390.]

iii.—Cession. Conditional Cession. Plebiscite.

Case No. 51

Cession of Territory—Power to Bind Inhabitants of Ceded Territory After It Has Ceased to be Under the Effective Authority of the Ceding State.

The Bathori.

British Empire, Judicial Committee of the Privy Council. November 3, 1933.

The Facts.—See Case No. 230.

Held (by the Privy Council) : that the decision of the Prize Court must be affirmed. Their Lordships did not think it necessary to decide what was the status of Fiume at the date of the Treaty. In their view the Treaty of Trianon bound the people of Fiume irrespective of any future changes in the status of the city, and the terms of the Treaty were binding upon English Courts by virtue of the Treaty of Peace (Hungary) Act of 1921. "Whether the plaintiffs were or were not Hungarian nationals at the effective date of the Treaty, their Lordships have come to the conclusion that the clause in question plainly was intended to cover them. The Treaty was the treaty of peace between Hungary and the Allied Powers, and it appears reasonably clear that the intention of the parties was that for acts or omissions done to the property of Hungarian belligerents during the war those belligerents should have no redress whether they did or did not continue to be Hungarian nationals up to the date of the Treaty. Whether for acts done before the acquisition of new nationality the new State can or will exercise protection, or whether the former State can exercise protection, may be debatable; but in the circumstances attending a peace treaty it appears very natural that the former State should be required to renounce protection for its ex-nationals, and in the present Treaty it seems clear that Hungary did so act. This, however, only determined the question of construction. If the Treaty operated by international law only, the tribunal in Prize might well have had to determine how far Hungary's attempt to affect the rights of ex-nationals could be treated as effective. But for an English Court, whether in Prize or not, this question is precluded by the terms of the Treaty of Peace Act. The Orders in Council made under it are to have effect as if enacted in the Act. The Order provides that the scheduled sections of the Treaty are to have full force and effect as law. If, therefore, the clause in question bears the construction which has already been imputed to it, that construction must be enforced in British Courts as law."[1]

[Report: 47 *Lloyd's List Law Reports*, 123.]

Territory—Cession—Distinguished from Fixing of Boundaries—Creation of Private Title in the Territory After the Fixing of Boundaries.

See Case No. 55 (*San Lorenzo Title & Improvement Co.* v. *City Mortgage Co.; The Same* v. *Clardy et Al.; The Same* v. *Caples et Al.*).

v.—Conquest.

Territory—Acquisition of—Conquest—By Whom Effected.

See Case No. 49 (*Legal Status of Eastern Greenland*).

III.—Loss of Territorial Sovereignty

Territory—Loss of—Abandonment.

See Case No. 49 (*Legal Status of Eastern Greenland*).

Territory—Loss of—Abandonment—Presumption of.

See Case No. 50 (*Clipperton Island Award*).

[1] See also, for a learned discussion of the same question, the judgment of Lord Merrivale in the same case in the Admiralty Division at pp. 35-38 of [1933] P.

V.—Occupation of Foreign Territory in Time of Peace

Case No. 52 **Territory—Occupation of Foreign Territory in Time of Peace Pending a Plebiscite—The Law Applicable in the Occupied Territory—Tacna-Arica.**

De Wurts *v.* Wurts.

Peru, Supreme Court. July 11, 1932.

The Facts.—The plaintiff was a Chilean woman who sought a divorce from her German husband before the Courts of Peru, where both parties lived. They had been married in Tacna in 1917. Tacna and Arica had been part of Peru, and were taken over by Chile in 1884 under the Treaty of Ancón, which terminated the war between the two countries. Under the provisions of the Treaty Chile was to occupy the provinces for ten years, at the end of which a plebiscite was to be held to determine the sovereignty over these territories. No plebiscite ever took place, and Tacna and Arica remained under the control and occupation of Chile until the Treaty of Santiago of June 3, 1929, between Chile and Peru.[1] This Treaty divided the territory, with the result that Tacna returned to Peru.[2]

The Peruvian lower Courts held that the question of divorce depended upon the law of the marriage.[3] Peruvian law recognised the possibility of divorce, while Chilean law allowed no divorce. The trial Court granted a divorce in accordance with

[1] On this whole dispute see Dennis, *Tacna and Arica* (1931).

[2] See Dennis, *op. cit.*, p. 316; *League of Nations Treaty Series*, vol. 94, p. 401.

[3] The Court of Tacna here referred to Articles 11 and 13 of the Treaty of Montevideo of 1889 on International Civil Law. See Martens, *N.R.G.*, 2nd ser., vol. 18, p. 443.

The Treaty on International Civil Law received a remarkable application in *Takesita* v. *Heisiro Maeda*, decided on July 2, 1929: 35 *Anales Judiciales*, 78. This was a divorce action between two Japanese, who had been married in Japan. Although Japan was not a party to the Treaty on International Civil Law, made at Montevideo in 1889 between Peru, Argentina, Bolivia, Paraguay, and Uruguay, its rules were adopted on the ground that the Treaty "is the law of this State." This Treaty was also the basis for the decision in *Argentina American Films Corp.* v. *Empresa de Teatros y Cinemas Limitada de Lima*, decided on June 17, 1929: 16 *Revista del Foro*, 84, on the question of proof of law of the State of New York, although the United States was not a party to the Treaty.

Peruvian law. On appeal to the Court of Tacna, the judgment was reversed. On appeal to the Supreme Court,

Held: that the judgment of the Court of Tacna be reversed and that of the trial Court be affirmed. Chilean law did not apply to the marriage contracted in Tacna in 1917. The Court approved the dissenting opinion given by Cornego, J., in the Court of Tacna, according to which "there should be taken into account the fact that the reign of Chilean law in Tacna was precarious and based on force, and that it is not just that Peruvians who were obliged to perform their legal transactions according to that law should find themselves, when that state of force has ceased, still deprived of the benefits of a law which favours all other Peruvians."

[Report: 19 *Revista del Foro*, 304.]

VI.—International Leases and Grants in Perpetuity

Territory—Grants in Perpetuity—Panama Canal Zone—Applicability of Extradition Treaties Between Panama and the United States. **Case No. 53**

In re BURRIEL.

Panama, Supreme Court. June 20, 1931.

THE FACTS.—The petitioner was held for surrender to the Canal Zone, on a charge of causing harm by gross negligence there. He sought *habeas corpus* on the ground that he was a citizen of Panama, and that his case was covered by the Extradition Law[1] rather than by any extradition treaty with the United States. Under that Law citizens could not be surrendered, and extradition could not take place unless the punishment amounted to a year's imprisonment.

Held: that, while the petition must be rejected on other grounds, the Treaty with the United States was not applicable. The Court said: "Given the special conditions of the Canal Zone, which was granted by the Republic of Panama to the United States for special purposes, with 'all the rights, power and authority which the United States would possess and exercise if it were the sovereign of the territory,' the provisions of the existing extradition treaty[2] between the

[1] Law 44 of 1930.

[2] For the Extradition Treaty of 1904 see Malloy, *Treaties of the United States*, vol. 2 (1910), p. 1357.

Case No. 53 *Contd.*

United States and Panama, properly applied as between the two sovereign States, are in no way applicable in the reciprocal rendition of criminals between Panama and the Canal Zone, inasmuch as the latter does not form part of the territory of the United States of America."

[Report: 29 *Registro Judicial*, 605.]

VII.—Sovereignty over the Air

Case No. 54

Air Navigation—Status of Seaplanes—Alighting on the Sea.

FRENCH STATE *v.* C.

France, Tribunal of St. Nazaire. November 3, 1932.

THE FACTS.—The defendant came down in his seaplane a short distance out to sea (about 200 m.) off La Baule (France), steered to the shore, brought down the wheels and conducted the plane to the shore. He was prosecuted for having violated police regulations prohibiting landing (*atterrir*) or taking off outside a regularly established private aerodrome.

Held: that the regulations were not applicable. This was a case of "*amerrissage*" (bringing down a plane on the sea) which, in the case of a seaplane, was different from "*atterrissage*."

[Report: *Revue Aéronautique Internationale*, No. 6, p. 484.]

NOTE.—As in the case digested in *Annual Digest*, 1929-1930, Case No. 52, this is merely a decision bearing on a question of definition under a municipal statute. But, for the reasons stated in the note, *ibid.*, it is not without general interest.

B.—PARTS OF STATE TERRITORY

I.—Boundaries

I.—Land Boundaries.

Territory—Boundaries—Fixing of Boundaries as Distinguished from Cession of Territory—Nature of Possession of Territory After the Conclusion of the Treaty which Lays Down that the Territory Belongs to the Other State—Effect of Title Created with Regard to Land in the Territory in Question—Nature of Findings of Boundary Commission. **Case No. 55**

SAN LORENZO TITLE & IMPROVEMENT CO. *v.* CITY MORTGAGE CO.

THE SAME *v.* CLARDY *ET AL.*

THE SAME *v.* CAPLES *ET AL.*

United States, Court of Civil Appeals of Texas.

February 27, *March* 1, *March* 24, 1932

(Pelphrey, C.J. ; Jones, Caldwell, Special Associate Judges).

THE FACTS.—These three cases involved the title to lands on the Mexican border of the United States. The plaintiff claimed title under a deed of the lands in question, the deed having been executed by a Mexican Court on August 5, 1927. The defendants contended that at the time the deed was executed the lands in question were part of the United States, and that the Mexican Court had, therefore, no jurisdiction over them.

In determining the location of the boundary line between the United States and Mexico, the Court had to consider three treaties. The first, that of Guadelupe Hidalgo, concluded in 1848 (9 U.S. Stat. L. 922), provided that a part of the United States–Mexico boundary line should be the middle of the Rio Grande River. It was soon thereafter discovered that the boundary line was a shifting one, subject to change by erosion, accretion and avulsion. The Gadsden Treaty of 1884 (24 U.S. Stat. L. 1011, 1012) provided, as to avulsive changes, that "any other change, wrought by the force of the current . . . shall produce no change in the dividing line," and that the boundary line "shall continue to follow the middle of the original channel bed, even though this should become wholly dry or be obstructed by deposits." The result

Case No. 55 *Contd.*

of this Treaty was the creation of what are called "*bancos*" following an avulsive change in the river. A *banco* is a small tract of land on the opposite side of the river from the country to which it belongs. Such was the character of the land involved in this litigation. It was formed in 1898 and was called San Lorenzo Banco No. 302.

With a view to ending the inconvenience and misunderstandings caused by the existence of the *bancos*, a treaty was concluded in 1905 (35 U.S. Stat. L. 1863). In negotiations leading to the execution of the Treaty, it was proposed that the *bancos* should be ceded to the country on whose side of the Rio Grande they lay, but there was doubt as to the constitutional power of Mexico and the United States to cede portions of their territory. Consequently it was determined by the representatives of the two countries that the Treaty should be construed as fixing a disputed boundary and not as operating to cede territory. Article 1 of the Treaty provided that existing surveyed *bancos* (some 58 in number) should pass to the country on whose side of the Rio Grande they lay. An international boundary commission was created by the Treaty and in Article 2 it was provided that the Commission should be guided by the principle of the elimination of *bancos* established in Article 1. In Article 3 it was provided that, with regard to *bancos* as yet unsurveyed and those to come into existence, the Commission should, for the purpose of applying Articles 1 and 2, survey and mark the boundaries of the *bancos* to show the changes which had occurred. On March 21, 1930, the Boundary Commission classified the land in question as a *banco*. In Article 4 it was provided that "Property of all kinds situated on the said bancos shall be inviolably respected, and its present owners, their heirs and those who may subsequently acquire the property legally, shall enjoy as complete security with respect thereto as if it belonged to citizens of the country where situated."

In the first two cases, the trial Courts upheld demurrers to the complaints. In the third case the defendants' general demurrer was overruled, but the jury found for the defendants. On appeal,

Held: In *San Lorenzo Title & Improvement Co.* v. *City Mortgage Co.*, that the judgment should be affirmed. The Treaty of 1905 went into effect upon its signing: *Davis* v. *Police Jury*, 9 How. 280, 289. Since the San Lorenzo Banco No. 302 was formed in 1898 and the Treaty was signed on March

20, 1905, the Treaty of 1905 became operative on the latter date so far as San Lorenzo Banco No. 302 was concerned. At that time, therefore, sovereignty, dominion and jurisdiction over the *banco* passed from Mexico to the United States: *U.S.* v. *Reynes*, 9 How. 127. Whatever possession, if any, Mexico had of the *banco* after the Treaty was signed was of necessity a *de facto* possession, and a *de facto* possession in itself cannot confer the power of disposing of title. Although the international Boundary Commission was charged with the duty of designating the land involved as a *banco* and of surveying and marking it, the boundary was fixed by the Treaty itself prior to any action by the Commission. The Commission was merely a fact-finding body, engaged in marking out boundaries in accordance with existing treaties. Thus, although the Boundary Commission did not act in regard to San Lorenzo Banco No. 302 until 1930, the United States acquired jurisdiction over it when the Treaty of 1905 was signed.

[Report: 48 S.W. (2d) 310.]

Held: In *San Lorenzo Title & Improvement Co.* v. *Clardy et Al.*, that the judgment should be affirmed. The pleadings disclosed that the Constitution of Mexico prevented a cession of territory by its government. A construction that makes a treaty legal is to be preferred to one that makes it illegal. In accordance with this principle, and in cognisance of the diplomatic correspondence relating to the Treaty of 1905, it was concluded that the purpose of the Treaty was a readjustment of the boundary line and that it was not intended to operate as a cession of territory. Where territory is ceded, private property rights acquired prior to the cession are protected by the new sovereign. Where a disputed boundary line is finally ascertained or adjusted by agreement, however, grants made by a sovereign beyond the boundary are void, whether or not the sovereign had possession: *Coffee* v. *Grover*, 123 U.S. 1; *Kenedy Pasture Co.* v. *Texas*, 111 *Texas* 200. In such a case, the grants fail simply because of a want of title in the grantor. A *de facto* possession cannot supply the title. Consequently, no rights could arise out of the grant by Mexico unless it was protected by Article 4 of the Treaty of 1905 relating to the protection of property rights. This provision, however, was intended only to protect persons having existing property rights, and their successors, and not those who acquired grants subsequently to the Treaty. Even if it were conceded that the Treaty was one of cession, the *de jure* sovereignty over the existing *bancos* passed to the

Case No. 55 Contd.

respective countries at the time the Treaty was signed, although the *de facto* sovereignty could have remained in the ceding sovereign until the territory was actually delivered. In other words, Mexico could have retained possession of the San Lorenzo *banco* for strictly municipal purposes, *e.g.*, to preserve public order, for the settlement of disputes between individuals, and the like. Even under this construction, the appellant's contention could not prevail. The Treaty certainly conveyed to the United States the equitable title to all *bancos* on the north side of the river coming within its provisions, and thereafter Mexico had no power to grant land thereon: *Kenedy Pasture Co.* v. *Texas, supra; U.S.* v. *D'Auterive et Al.*, 10 How. 609. As to the international Boundary Commission, the Court concluded that it was merely a fact-finding body.

[Report: 48 S.W. (2d) 315.]

Held: In *San Lorenzo Title & Improvement Co.* v. *Caples et Al.*, that the judgment should be affirmed. No question of cession was involved. The boundary line was fixed by the Treaty of 1905; and after the promulgation of the Treaty the sovereignty retained by Mexico over the land in question was such as might be necessary for the government of the territory and police protection, but could not extend to the granting of titles or to any act which might prejudice the right of the United States in the territory thus acquired. The following cases were cited by the Court: *Kenedy Pasture Co.* v. *Texas*, 111 Tex. 200; *United States* v. *Reynes*, 9 How. 127; *Davis* v. *Police Jury*, 9 How. 280.

[Report: 48 S.W. (2d) 329.]

ii.—Water Boundaries.

Boundary Rivers—Condominium—Jurisdiction—Germany and Holland.

See Case No. 23 (*Dutch-Prussian Condominium* (1816) *Case*).

Boundaries—Water Boundaries—Gulfs—State of Florida and the Gulf of Mexico.

See Case No. 63 (*Lipscomb v. Gialourakis*).

II.—Rivers

iii.—International Rivers.

(*b*) Functions and Competence of International Commissions on International Rivers.

International Rivers—Jurisdiction on Rivers and in Harbours—Article 34 of the Rhine Navigation Convention of October 17, 1868—Construction of Treaties—Restrictive Interpretation. **Case No. 58**

Rhine Navigation Commission Case.

Germany, Court of Appeal of Karlsruhe. November 25, 1931.

The Facts.—The plaintiffs were owners of a barge which left Kehl harbour in tow of a tug. While still within the precincts of the harbour the barge was damaged as the result of the negligence of the master of the tug. An action for damages having been brought by the bargeowners against the owners of the tug, the defendants pleaded that the ordinary courts had no jurisdiction and that jurisdiction was vested in the Rhine Navigation Courts. They invoked Article 34 of the Rhine Navigation Convention, which provided as follows :

> "The Rhine Navigation Courts have jurisdiction :
>
> I. In criminal cases, for the investigation and punishment of all offences against the regulations concerning navigation and the river police.
>
> II. In civil cases, for the decision by way of summary procedure of claims : . . .
>
> (*c*) for injuries which ships and rafts shall have inflicted on their journey or while landing ; . . . "

Held (by the trial judge and the Court of Appeal) : that the defendants' plea failed. Article 34 of the Rhine Navigation Convention was not quite clear as to whether the Rhine Navigation Courts were competent to try cases arising in the open river only, or whether their jurisdiction extended also to Rhine harbours situate off the open river. The answer to that question depended on some general considerations as to the construction of the relevant provisions. The Court said : "The Rhine Navigation Convention is an international convention ; as such it is governed by the principles applicable to the construction of contracts. The intention of the parties

Case No. 56 ***Contd.***

at the time of the conclusion of the convention is therefore decisive. In construing international conventions, regard must be had to the peculiar nature of such agreements, and special importance is to be attached to the political motives and to the circumstances prevailing at the time when the agreement was made. In this respect account must be taken, in particular, of the competing claims of States and their consequent desire when entering into international conventions to keep their jurisdiction intact as far as possible. It follows, therefore, that international conventions must necessarily be construed narrowly where a waiver of jurisdiction is concerned. A wide construction, or an application of provisions by analogy, is admissible only when such procedure follows clearly from the meaning and purpose of the convention, which in turn are to be gathered from the intention of the parties. However, no such cogent reasons can be gathered either from the history or from the Rhine Navigation Convention itself."

The Court pointed out that, in the interest of shipping and of a developing traffic, international rivers like the Rhine called for a common administration and conservancy. This was so because any measures taken by one of the riparian States, or the non-repair by such State of a part of the river, must react unfavourably on shipping as a whole. The same reasons calling for common action applied to a uniform regulation of the police and to a uniform jurisdiction over the river. For measures taken by one riparian State might have repercussions on the entire shipping on the river, and might in certain circumstances make shipping extremely difficult. For these reasons, a uniform administration of justice was necessary in order to avoid any uncertainties as to the law applicable and as to the courts which should have jurisdiction in a particular case. Moreover, the line along the centre of the river bed was often at the same time the frontier between the States occupying its banks, and that line was invisible. In many cases it would therefore be difficult or even impossible to determine on whose territory a shipping accident or an offence against police regulations had occurred. A uniform jurisdiction was the only method of coping with such a situation. Also, shipping called for uniform legal principles applicable to the whole river. As no common law of the river existed, such principles could only be developed by the riparian States setting up common courts.

However, all these reasons for common regulation applied to the open river, and not to the harbours situate off the river, such as Kehl harbour. As regards harbours, the relevant law was certain and, therefore, such harbours could not be treated on the same footing as the open river. The history of the Rhine Navigation Convention showed that, owing to the desire of the riparian States to maintain their jurisdiction as far as possible, a common regulation had developed only gradually and not without difficulty. Such waiver of jurisdiction was conceded only where this was absolutely necessary in the interest of shipping on the Rhine. This was the only consideration determining the intention of the riparian States to waive jurisdiction. It could therefore be assumed that they did not intend to do so as regards the Rhine harbours, as in respect of them there existed no need for a waiver of their ordinary jurisdiction.

[Report: *Rechtsprechung auf dem Gebiete des Internationalen Privatrechts*, 1932, No. 133.]

iv.—The Utilisation of the Flow of Non-National and International Rivers.

Rivers—Diversion of Waters—Applicability of Rules of Municipal Law—Principles Applicable in Disputes Between Members of Federal States. **Case No. 57**

CONNECTICUT *v.* MASSACHUSETTS.

United States, Supreme Court. February 24, 1931.

(Hughes, C.J.; Holmes, Van Devanter, McReynolds, Brandeis, Sutherland, Butler, Stone, Roberts, JJ.)

THE FACTS.—This was an action brought by the State of Connecticut against the Commonwealth of Massachusetts to enjoin the latter from diverting waters from the watershed of rivers tributary to the Connecticut River to provide water for Boston and neighbouring cities and towns. Connecticut appeared as owner of riparian lands and of the bed of the river, and as *parens patriae*. The case was referred to a special master, who found that no substantial injury would presently result to Connecticut from the diversions by Massachusetts, and that Boston and the surrounding area were faced with a serious water shortage and needed a large quantity of additional water. The master consequently recommended that the action be dismissed.

On submission of the case to the United States Supreme Court, Connecticut argued that under the common law in

Case No. 57 *Contd.*

force in both States, each riparian owner had a vested right in the use of the flowing waters, unimpaired as to quantity, and that the taking of water by Massachusetts infringed vested property rights in Connecticut. It urged that the Court, following the law enforced by each of the States within its own boundaries, should grant an injunction against any diversion from the watersheds of the rivers in question.

Held: that the action must be dismissed. The governing rule was that this Court would not exert its extraordinary power to control the conduct of one State at the suit of another unless the threatened invasion of rights was of serious magnitude and was established by clear and convincing evidence: *New York* v. *New Jersey*, 256 U.S. 296, 309; *Missouri* v. *Illinois*, 200 U.S. 496, 521. Such circumstances were not present here.

Delivering the Opinion of the Court, Mr. Justice Butler said: "For the decision of suits between States, federal, state and international law are considered and applied by this Court as the exigencies of the particular case may require. The determination of the relative rights of contending States in respect of the use of streams flowing through them does not depend upon the same considerations and is not governed by the same rules of law that are applied in such States for the solution of similar questions of private right. *Kansas* v. *Colorado*, 185 U.S. 125, 146 . . . such disputes [between states] are to be settled on the basis of equality of right. But this is not to say that there must be an equal division of the waters of an interstate stream among the States through which it flows. It means that the principles of right and equity shall be applied having regard to the 'equal level or plane on which all the States stand, in point of power and right, under our constitutional system,' and that, upon a consideration of the pertinent laws of the contending States and all other relevant facts, this Court will determine what is an equitable apportionment of the use of such waters. *Wyoming* v. *Colorado*, 259 U.S. 419, 465, 470."

[Report: 282 U.S. 660; *A.J.*, XXVI (1932), p. 163[1].]

NOTE.—With regard to the specific question at issue the Court said: "The proposed taking of the waters of the Swift and Ware will not affect the present dam, works or production of power at King's Island. While the owning company has secured authority to build the higher dam, it has not resolved so to do. It is not found and there is nothing to show that it intends to construct any dam or works of a kind or capacity that, if now in use, would be

[1] See *M.L.R.*, XXIX (1931), p. 1104.

injuriously affected by such diversion. At most there is a mere possibility that at some undisclosed time the owner, were it not for the diversion, might construct additional works capable of using all of the flow of the river including the waters proposed to be taken by Massachusetts. Injunction will not issue in the absence of actual or presently threatened interference. The facts disclose no basis for relief in respect of that property. New York *v.* Illinois, 274 U.S. 488. New Jersey *v.* Sargent, 269 U.S. 328, 331, 338.

"Drinking and other domestic purposes are the highest uses of water. An ample supply of wholesome water is essential. Massachusetts, after elaborate research, decided to take the waters of the Ware and Swift rather than to rely on the sources in the eastern part of the Commonwealth where all are or are liable to become polluted."

III.—Territorial Waters

1.—Nature of the Maritime Belt.

Territorial Waters—Nature of—Whether Part of State Territory. **Case No. 58**

The Vauclin.

(*Cie. Générale Transatlantique* v. *Pacce.*)

Algeria, Court of Appeal of Algiers. December 9, 1931.

The Facts.—This was a claim for salvage money on account of assistance rendered to the *SS. Vauclin*, belonging to the Cie. Générale Transatlantique, in the territorial waters of Algeria, off the port of Philippville. The action was brought before the Court of that place. The defendant Company maintained that the Court was not competent. The Court agreed with the defendants. On appeal,

Held: that the Court of Philippville was not competent and that the Company could only be sued before the Court of its domicile. The Court of Appeal said: "Territorial waters are subject to the measures of police and safety of the State (*pouvoir de police et de sûreté de l'Etat*), but they are not part of the French or colonial territory and therefore do not come within the territorial jurisdiction of any French Court."

[Report: *Le Droit maritime français*, vol. X, p. 102.]

Note.—Compare the decision of the Court of Algiers of March 20, 1913, reported in *Revue Internationale de Droit Maritime*, vol. XXX, p. 324, and affirmed by the Court of Cassation on November 26, 1918, *Proux* v. *Courcoux*, *ibid.*, vol. XXXI, p. 327, and *Dalloz*, 1923,

Case No. 58 Contd. Part I, p. 103. For a criticism of this doctrine see the notes by Gidel, *Le droit international public de la mer*, vol. III (1935), *La mer territoriale et la zone contiguë*, p. 176, and by Niboyet in *Revue critique de droit international*, 1935, pp. 159-161.

Case No. 59 **Maritime Belt—Whether Part of the State Contiguous thereto.**

UNITED STATES *v.* ZILVER.

United States, District Court, E.D. New York. January 26, 1932.

(Galston, District Judge.)

THE FACTS.—This was an action in equity brought pursuant to Section 15 of the Naturalisation Act of 1906 (8 U.S.C.A. § 405) to revoke a certificate of citizenship alleged to have been illegally issued to the defendant. Section 382 of Title 8, U.S.C.A., provided in part: "Absence from the United States for a continuous period of one year or more during the period immediately preceding the date of filing the petition for citizenship for which continuous residence is required as a condition precedent to admission to citizenship shall break the continuity of such residence" (as amended on March 2, 1929, c. 536, § 6 (b), 45 U.S. Stat. L. 1513). The Government alleged that the defendant had been absent from the United States from August 11, 1928, to August 12, 1929, in violation of the statute, and was therefore not entitled to a certificate of citizenship. The defendant contended that he came within the three-mile territorial limit of the United States before midnight, August 11, 1929.

Held: that the action should be dismissed. Although the vessel upon which the defendant returned to the United States did not arrive in Seattle until 3.42 p.m., August 12, 1929, it appeared from the testimony that the vessel was within the three-mile territorial limit of the United States by midnight, August 11, 1929. Therefore the defendant was not absent from the United States as a matter of law for one year, for there could be no doubt that the maritime belt is to be considered part of the country contiguous thereto: *Manchester* v. *Massachusetts*, 139 U.S. 240; *Cunard SS. Co.* v. *Mellon*, 262 U.S. 100.

[Report: 55 F. (2d) 250.]

ii.—Breadth of the Maritime Belt.

Territorial Waters—Extent of—Swedish Claims—Fishing Rights—Bays. **Case No. 60**

THE HEINRICH AUGUSTIN.

Sweden, Supreme Court. November 14, 1927.

THE FACTS.—On January 20, 1925, the trawler *Heinrich Augustin*, registered in Germany, was seized for alleged illegal trawling within Swedish territorial waters. The seizure took place about one and a half miles outside of the line drawn from Halland's Väderö's lighthouse to Tylö lighthouse at the entrance to Laholm Bay. Laholm Bay is slightly over twelve miles wide.

It was contended for the prosecution that historically and by reason of the Fishery Decree of May 5, 1871, Swedish jurisdiction extended over a maritime belt of one geographical mile or four nautical miles calculated from the line of low water or from the shores of coast-lying islands which are not constantly submerged. This contention was supported by reference to numerous decrees since the latter half of the eighteenth century, various statements to foreign Powers, Swedish protests against violations of this limit during the World War, etc. The defendant maintained that the original Swedish limit of territorial waters had been three miles, which accorded with international practice, the four-mile limit dating only from the Norwegian rule of 1869; that the Halland's Väderö-Tylö line was first adopted in 1899 in the Swedish Convention with Denmark; and that during the War Sweden had practically adopted a ten-mile limit in regard to bays. For these reasons it was contended that the base line should be drawn between the points where the Bay ceased to have the characteristic formations of a bay, which in the case of Laholm Bay would be considerably within the points insisted upon by the prosecution. Accordingly, the seizure of the trawler, it was asserted, did not take place within Swedish territorial waters.

Held (by the Court of Halmstad): that "the region in question must be considered as Swedish waters." The Court said that whilst the arguments of both sides had failed to give any definite indication as to how the limit of Swedish territorial waters at Laholm Bay was determined formerly according to Swedish law, the fact that in the Convention between Sweden and Denmark a special concession was made

Case No. 60 *Contd.*

to empower Danish fishermen to fish within the four-mile limit claimed by Sweden in the present case, must be taken as strong support for the assumption that prior to the Convention Sweden had maintained that view. "The fact that Denmark, who is Sweden's closest neighbour in regard to the fishing waters in question and at the time of the convention was undoubtedly more than any other foreign Power interested in keeping Laholm Bay open for fishing, accepted the above stipulations, without doubt gives strong support to the assumption that the Swedish Crown even before the convention maintained the conception in regard to the extension of Swedish territorial waters which was embodied in the convention.

"Furthermore, inasmuch as it has not been proven that the Crown at any later date has failed to uphold the same view, it may be considered as clearly demonstrated that the Crown for a considerable period has treated as Swedish fishing waters the whole Bay of Laholm within a line drawn between Halland's Väderö lighthouse and Tylö lighthouse and in addition a region situated within one geographical mile outside of this boundary."

Held (by the Court of Appeal): that the reasoning and decision of the lower Court must be affirmed.

Held (by the Supreme Court, upholding the decisions of the lower Courts): that "on the grounds established at the court of first instance, the place where the apprehension of the trawler took place must be considered as being within Swedish territorial waters. . . ."

[Report: *A.J.*, XXIV (1930), p. 776.]

NOTE.—This case was reported in *Annual Digest*, 1925-1926, Case No. 92. The present digest is included as illustrating from a different angle the point decided by the Court. For a detailed account of this case, together with a summary of the legal argument submitted at its various stages, see Bellquist in *A.J.*, XXIV (1930), pp. 776-783, on which the present digest is based.

Case No. 61

Bays—Territorial Waters—Limits of—Fisheries—Iceland—Statement of German Ministry of Defence—How Far Binding Upon German Courts.

THE SENATOR SCHRÖDER.

Germany, Hamburg Maritime Court (*Seeamt*). *June* 3, 1932.

THE FACTS.—In this case, the circumstances of which do not appear clearly from the report, the Court had to decide whether the captain of a German steam fishing boat, the *Senator Schröder*, was guilty of illegal fishing in Icelandic waters. The *Senator Schröder* was arrested by the Icelandic fishery cruiser *Aigir* on October 26, 1931, and it is not clear whether the present judgment was concerned with the question of the civil or the criminal liability of the captain.

The Icelandic Government by a decree of November 5, 1928, had replaced the former fishery limit by a new limit three sea miles from a line drawn between the extremities of bays on the coast.

In the locality where the incident arose, the fishery limit as formerly drawn ran at a distance of three sea miles from a line connecting Reynisdrangar and Kötlutangi, such line having been accepted as the territorial limit (*Landesgrenze*) in the previous Danish charts. Under the new decree the fishery limit had been set three miles from a line connecting the projecting points Portland and Kötlutangi. There was therefore a discrepancy between the old and the new fishery limits.

Subsequent to the decree of November 5, 1928, the Icelandic Supreme Court had pronounced in three cases—concerning two German trawlers (the *Capella* and the *Georg Robbert*) and one English trawler—that the decree of November 5, 1928, was not binding on foreign ships on the ground that the limits of sovereignty could not be changed by the unilateral action of a government, but only by international agreement. The three steamships were therefore acquitted after it had been established that they had fished within the new limit but outside the old one. The Icelandic Government associated itself with the opinion of the Supreme Court, and this was made known by means of the Danish "Information for Mariners" of July 29, 1931. This was followed by a corresponding announcement in the German "Information for Mariners" of August 8, 1931.

Held: that the captain was not responsible. It appeared from the announcement of August 8, 1931, that Germany recognised only the old limit. "In general, under international law a line running at a distance of three sea miles along the coast is accepted as the limit of sovereignty, and this coincides with the fishery limit. It is not recognised in international law that this line must be drawn in a different way when bays are found, although this is recognised in particular international treaties, as, for instance, in the International Treaty concerning the Regulation of Fisheries in the North Sea. This Treaty, however, is not relevant in the present case since it is valid only for the North Sea, and Iceland lies outside the northerly limit

Case No. 61 ***Contd.***

of the North Sea (61°).[1] . . . The German Government is therefore justified and, in the interest of German sea fisheries, had a genuine interest in opposing this method of drawing the limits and in demanding for German sea fisheries the application of the former three-mile limit only. . . ."

"According to information supplied by the Minister for Defence, no international agreement has yet been reached on the question what is to be regarded as a bay. Until this question is cleared up, there is therefore nothing to be said from the point of view of the Admiralty against the action of Iceland in considering the indentation between Reynisdrangar and Kötlutangi as a bay, as happened in the establishment of the old limit, and in connecting these two points by a line and drawing the fishery limit parallel to this line at a distance of three sea miles. The Maritime Court cannot associate itself with this attitude, since its duty is to answer the question as to the guilt of Captain Z. ; it cannot decide that the captain is guilty because the question which is here at issue has not yet been cleared up. As the question is still open, the natural deduction to make would be that no fault should be imputed to Captain Z. The Maritime Court is, however, unanimously of the opinion that this slight deviation from the straight line of the coast between Reynisdrangar and Kötlutangi, which over a length of eight sea miles attains a depth of only one sea mile, cannot be regarded as a bay, either in the geographical sense or in that of international law ; that therefore the drawing of the connecting line, and the old fishery limit calculated from that line, is not justified in this instance ; and that the fishery limit must rather follow the course of the coast at a distance of three miles. If the old limit drawn by Iceland were valid, Captain Z. would in fact have been just inside that limit. If, on the other hand, the limit runs in such a way as the Maritime Court considers right, he was at no time in a prohibited place in his ship."

[Report : *Hanseatische Rechts- und Gerichtszeitschrift*, Part B, November 5, 1932.]

[1] The Court pointed out that a similar Treaty concerning the determination of bays in drawing the limit of sovereignty was concluded between Iceland, Denmark and England on July 24, 1901, but that, as Germany did not accede to this Treaty, the Icelandic Government was not justified in enforcing against Germany the method of drawing the limit agreed to in this Treaty.

Territorial Waters—Breadth of Maritime Belt—The Law of Cuba—Collision with a British Vessel—Relevance of Treaty Concluded with the United States. **Case No. 62**

The Hallmoor.

Cuba, Audencia de la Habana. February 11, 1932.

The Facts.—This was an action by the owners of a Cuban vessel against the owners of the *Hallmoor*, a British vessel, on account of damage suffered in a collision between the two vessels. The relevant Cuban statutes are referred to below. The trial Court held that it lacked jurisdiction, since the collision took place outside Cuban territorial waters. On appeal,

Held: that Cuban Courts had jurisdiction. The collision occurred within Cuban territorial waters. The only applicable legislation laying down limits of Cuban territorial waters was a Spanish law of May 7, 1880, which referred to "the littoral sea, or the maritime zone which girds the coasts or frontiers of the Spanish dominion, in all the breadth determined by international law."[1] However, there was no general agreement in international law as to the breadth of territorial waters.

Delivering the opinion of the Court, Fernandez, J., said: "Within the sphere of international law, the Republic of Cuba is not bound to England by any treaty governing territorial waters. Although it made with the United States the Treaty of 4 March, 1926,[2] whose chief purpose on the part of the United States was to obtain greater effectiveness for its Volstead Act by preventing smuggling, in which Treaty it accepted three miles as the extent of territorial waters and expressed the intention of maintaining this limit, the obligatory force of that Treaty cannot extend to another purpose not expressed in the Treaty and to the benefit of other nations who are not signatories to it. . . .

"Since 1901, there have been in force in Cuba the present Customs Rules, in Art. 74 of which the extent of Cuban

[1] Article 1 of *Ley de 7 de mayo, sobre uso y dominio de las aguas del mar y sus playas*, 61 *Boletin de la Revista General de legislacion y jurisprudencia* (1880), 55. This Spanish law was made applicable to Cuba by a royal decree of January 9, 1891, and remained in effect after the proclamation of the independence of the Republic of Cuba.

[2] United States Treaty Series, No. 738; also printed in *A.J.*, XX (1926), Suppl., p. 136. Article 1 of the Treaty provided as follows: "The high contracting parties declare that it is their firm intention to uphold the principle that three marine miles extending from the coast line outwards and measured from low-water mark constitute the proper limits of territorial waters."

Case No. 62 *Contd.*

territorial sea is fixed at 12 miles or 4 leagues from the coast." The first section of that article provided that, in order to assure the collection of amounts due, the Customs Service shall keep the necessary watch over the coasts from the moment a boat enters the jurisdictional waters of the Island of Cuba. The second section provided expressly that the jurisdictional waters of Cuba extend to four leagues from the coast or from the keys [shoals or rocks] adjacent thereto. Article 244 of the Rules imposed on the officials of the Coast Guard the duty to visit vessels which came to the waters of the Island or within four leagues of the coast, if bound for the Island. "In the face of these clear provisions, it cannot be claimed, in order to restrict the decisive effect they have for the matter in point, that the provision is made solely for customs purposes." If that had been the purpose in enacting the first paragraph of Article 74, the legislator would have expressly fixed the limit of the territorial sea for these purposes; it would not have referred to the general notion of jurisdictional waters, which means those which the State uses for all purposes derived from its sovereignty, and then established clearly in a separate section the width of those jurisdictional waters.

Since the collision took place within twelve miles of the shore, it took place within what the Court considered to be Cuban territorial waters. The case therefore fell within the jurisdiction of the Cuban Courts.

[Report: *Repertorio Judicial*, 1933, 35.]

VI.—Bays

Case No. 63

Gulfs—Jurisdiction in—Extent of—Boundary Lines—State of Florida and Gulf of Mexico.

LIPSCOMB *v.* GIALOURAKIS.

United States, Supreme Court of Florida, Division B.

March 12, 1931.

(Buford, C.J.; Whitfield, Ellis, Terrell, Brown, JJ., and Hutchinson, Circuit Judge.)

THE FACTS.—This was an action to secure the release of the defendants, who had been indicted for violations of Florida statutes regulating sponge fishing. Section 8087, Comp. Gen. Laws of Florida, 1927, prohibited the maintenance and use of diving suits, helmets or other apparatus used by deep-sea divers for the purpose of taking commercial sponges from the Gulf of Mexico, the Straits of Florida or other waters within the territorial jurisdiction of Florida. According to the indictment the violations of the statutes in question took place in the waters of the Gulf of Mexico, within the jurisdiction of Taylor county, and within the territorial limits of the State of Florida. The boundary of Florida, along the Gulf of Mexico, is defined by Article 1 of the Florida Constitution as a line three leagues from the mainland. The boundary lines of Taylor county are defined by statute as running "to the Gulf of Mexico" and "along the Gulf of Mexico" : Comp. Gen. Laws of Fla. 1927, § 27. The defendants contended that the indictment showed on its face that the offence was not committed within the jurisdiction of Taylor county. The defendants were discharged on writs of *habeas corpus*. On appeal,

Held (*per* Buford, C.J.) : that the judgment must be reversed. Article 1 of the Florida Constitution extended the boundary of Florida, along the Gulf of Mexico, to a distance three leagues from the mainland. Section 1 of Article 8 of the Constitution provided as follows : " The State shall be divided into political divisions to be called counties." It was apparent from this section that all of the State of Florida was required to be divided into counties and it must be held, therefore, that counties bordering on the Gulf of Mexico included that area within the Gulf adjacent to the upland and out to the State boundary line. Unless otherwise provided by statute, the rule applying to territorial boundaries of riparian rights should be applied in locating county boundary lines. Upon reaching the high water mark, the line is extended into the water at right angles with the shore line. The words " to the Gulf of Mexico " in the statute defining the bounds of Taylor county must be construed to mean to the boundary line of the State of Florida, in the Gulf of Mexico. Since the State of Florida could exercise its sovereign powers over the waters of the Gulf of Mexico within the boundary lines of the State, three leagues from the shore, and since Taylor county extended to the State boundary line, the accused was correctly charged with an offence committed within the jurisdiction of Taylor county within the jurisdiction of the State of Florida.

[Report : 101 Fla. 1130.]

Bays—Base Line—Territorial Waters—Swedish Claims.

See Case No. 60 (*The Heinrich Augustin*).

X.—State Servitudes

Case No. 64 **State Servitudes—Status of Foreign Officials in National Territory—Poland and the Free City of Danzig.**

POLISH OFFICIALS IN DANZIG CASE.

Danzig, High Court. April 9, 1932.

THE FACTS.—This was an action for damages against the principal Polish customs official at the Customs House at Danzig. The plaintiff, who carried on a wholesale fruit business in Danzig, alleged that in February 1931 she had exported a car-load of apples to Lodz (Poland); that on arrival at their destination they were wrongfully seized by the Polish customs officer on the ground that the goods were of German origin and therefore subject to the duty imposed upon imports from Germany into Poland; and that, although she succeeded in regaining possession of the goods, she suffered, as a consequence of the seizure, a loss of Zl. 3,580. She contended that the goods were shipped directly from Rotterdam (Holland) by sea without touching German territory, and that the customs official at Danzig who had caused the goods to be seized at Lodz was responsible for the loss.

The defendant was an official stationed at Danzig by virtue of Article 14 of the Treaty between Poland and Danzig of November 9, 1920 (the so-called Treaty of Paris). That article provided as follows: " The territory of the Free City represents, in respect of customs, an administrative unit which is entrusted to officials of the Free City working under the general supervision of the Polish Central Customs Administration; the Polish Government shall participate in the supervision of the customs service by the appointment of Polish inspectors to be attached to the Danzig staff." The defendant was not a member of the Polish diplomatic service in Danzig. He admitted that he did not belong to the category of persons invested with diplomatic character referred to in Section 18 and 19 of the Danzig Law concerning the Jurisdiction of the Courts. However, he contested the competence of the Danzig Courts and claimed complete personal immunity on the ground that, according to general principles of international law, officials who were working abroad pursuant to State servitudes of a public law character were immune from jurisdiction and that the agreements between Poland and Danzig confirmed this general principle of international law. Accordingly, he contended, officials of the Polish Republic enjoyed immunity from the jurisdiction of Danzig Courts, in particular in the case of an action based on a claim for damages arising out of their official activities.

Held : that the Court had jurisdiction. There was no reason whatsoever to assume that a foreign official on duty in Danzig who did not come within Sections 18 and 19 of the Law referred to above should be able to claim immunity from any action arising in connection with his official function. There was nothing in the existing agreements between Poland and Danzig which altered the position in this respect.[1] In interpreting paragraph 4 of the Agreement of May 17, 1922, the Court held that it was not intended to accord to Polish officials employed in the territory of Danzig any exemption whatsoever from the jurisdiction of the Danzig Courts. The Court said: " The High Commissioner [for Danzig] laid down expressly that all persons of Polish nationality [employed in Danzig], apart from diplomatic representatives, shall be subject to the laws and the jurisdiction of the Free City of Danzig. Since Poland did not claim immunity from Danzig jurisdiction for any other category of persons, this rule undoubtedly applied to Polish officials employed in Danzig. Consequently, any concessions granted by Danzig in any subsequent agreement, based on this decision, and concluded with a view to giving further satisfaction to Polish claims, must be interpreted restrictively as they represent limitations on the legal status of Danzig as recognised by the High Commissioner." The Court rejected the view that the subjection of Polish officials to the jurisdiction of Danzig Courts would interfere with the efficient fulfilment of their functions.[2]

[Report: *Danziger Juristische Monatsschrift*, vol. 11 (1932), p. 52; *Zeitschrift für Ostrecht*, vol. 4 (1932), p. 899, with a note by Wainlever, *ibid.*, p. 902.]

[1] The Court discussed here at some length the history of the dispute which arose between the Free City and Poland with regard to the legal position of these officials. The dispute was submitted to the High Commissioner for Danzig, against whose ruling both parties appealed to the Council of the League of Nations. The Council, at its session of May 13, 1922, recommended negotiations with a view to achieving a final settlement. In pursuance of this recommendation an agreement was entered into on May 17, 1922, and both parties withdrew their appeal.

[2] The Court referred to the Agreement between Luxembourg and the German Reich of June 11, 1872 (*R G B* 1, p. 330), Section 4, paragraph 3, of which reads as follows: "All officials of the railway (under German administration) are subject to the railway disciplinary authorities and the regulations as regards discipline; as regards any other matters, however, they are subject to the laws and authorities of the country in which they reside and in which they perform their functions."

C.—MISCELLANEOUS

State Territory—Miscellaneous—Injurious Use of Territory —Injury to Property in One State as the Result of Drifting of Fumes From Another.

See the Report of the International Joint Commission between the United States and Canada of February 28, 1931, on the question of injury to property in the State of Washington by reason of the drifting of .fumes from the smelter of the Consolidated Mining and Smelting Company of Canada in Trail, British Columbia. In that Report, which contains no discussion of legal issues, the Commission determined the amount of damages, approved remedial works to be installed by the Company to eliminate the damage, and provided for the settlement of any future damage: *A.J.*, XXV (1931), p. 540. For further conventional regulation of the matter see the Convention of April 15, 1935, between the United States and Canada: U.S. Treaty Series, No. 983; *A.J.*, XXX (1936), Suppl., p. 163.

PART IV

JURISDICTION

A.—JURISDICTION IN GENERAL. TERRITORIAL AND PERSONAL

I.—Territorial

i.—Over Territory in General and Persons and Property Situated Therein.

[See also Part II, *Recognition of Acts of Foreign States and Governments*, and *Recognition of Foreign States and Governments*.]

Jurisdiction—Over Non-Resident Aliens with Regard to Property Within the Jurisdiction—Double Taxation. **Case No. 65**

BURNET, COMMISSIONER OF INTERNAL REVENUE, *v.* BROOKS *ET AL.*, EXECUTORS.

United States, Supreme Court. March 13, 1933.

(Hughes, C.J.; Van Devanter, McReynolds, Brandeis, Sutherland, Butler, Stone, Roberts, Cardozo, JJ.)

THE FACTS.—This was an action brought to contest the ruling of the Commissioner of Internal Revenue in including certain property in the gross estate of the decedent. The decedent was a British subject resident in Cuba. He was not engaged in business in the United States. The property in question consisted of stocks and bonds issued by both domestic and foreign corporations, bonds of foreign governments, bonds of a domestic municipality and a balance of a cash deposit. The stock certificates and bonds were in New York City in the possession of the decedent's agents, who collected the income and placed it to the credit of the decedent in a New York bank. None of the securities was pledged or held for any indebtedness. The Board of Tax Appeals decided that the property should not be included in the decedent's gross estate for the purpose of the Federal Estate Tax: 22 B.T.A. 71. The decision was affirmed by the Circuit Court of Appeals: 60 F. (2d) 890. On *certiorari* to the United States Supreme Court,

Held: that the judgment must be reversed. The property in question was included in the terms of the statute, which provided

Case No. 65 *Contd.*

that in the case of a non-resident of the United States that part of the gross estate was to be returned and valued "which at the time of his death is situated in the United States": Revenue Act of 1924, c. 234, 43 U.S. Stat. L. 253, 303-307.

It had been contended that the reference in the statute to *situs* must, as to intangibles, be taken to incorporate the principle of *mobilia sequuntur personam*. But when the statute was passed it was well established that the taxing power could reach such securities on the ground that they had a *situs* where they were physically located. It could not be assumed that Congress was legislating in disregard of existing doctrine, nor with a view to decisions as to State power which were not rendered until several years later. See *Farmers' Loan & Trust Co.* v. *Minnesota*, 280 U.S. 204, 209.

A question was raised as to the power of the United States to impose the tax. Apart from any self-imposed constitutional restriction, the property was within the jurisdiction of the United States—that is, it was property within the reach of the power which the United States by virtue of its sovereignty could exercise as against other nations and their subjects without violating any established principle of international law: *Winans* v. *Attorney-General, L.R.* [1910] A.C. 27; *Disconto-Gesellschaft* v. *U.S. Steel Corp.*, 267 U.S. 22.

"As jurisdiction [in this matter] may exist in more than one government, that is, jurisdiction based on distinct grounds—the citizenship of the owner, his domicile, the source of income, the *situs* of the property—efforts have been made to preclude multiple taxation through the negotiation of appropriate international conventions. These endeavours, however, have proceeded upon express or implied recognition, and not in denial, of the sovereign taxing power as exerted by governments in the exercise of jurisdiction upon any of these grounds."

[Report: 288 U.S. 378[1]; *A.J.*, XXVII (1933), p. 766.]

[1] See *Columbia Law Review*, 33 (1933), p. 925; *Cornell Law Quarterly*, vol. 18, p. 74; *H.L.R.*, 46 (1932-1933), p. 524; *ibid.*, 47 (1933-1934), p. 307; *Yale Law Journal*, 42 (1932-1933), p. 1277.

Jurisdiction—Acts Done Outside the Jurisdiction but Producing Effects Within It—Extradition—Meaning of the Term "Fugitive." **Case No. 66**

Ex parte HAMMOND.

United States, Circuit Court of Appeals, Ninth Circuit.

June 24, 1932.

(Wilbur, Sawtelle, Circuit Judges; Norcross, District Judge.)

THE FACTS.—This was an action to prevent the extradition of the petitioner, who was charged by the Canadian Government with obtaining money by false pretences from the Regal Petroleum Company at Calgary, Canada. The petitioner's agent, acting for him and in his name, drew a draft on the Bank of Montreal at Calgary to be charged to the account of the Regal Petroleum Company. The draft was deposited to the petitioner's credit in the Western National Bank at Los Angeles, California. The draft was forwarded to Calgary, Canada, by correspondents of the Western National Bank, and was presented to and paid by the Bank of Montreal, which charged it to the account of the Regal Petroleum Company. The petitioner contended that since the draft was deposited with his Los Angeles bank and was credited to his account there, the offence of obtaining money by false pretences was completed in California, and that jurisdiction over the alleged crime was in the State of California. He further contended that he was not within the terms of the applicable Treaty with Great Britain (the Webster-Ashburton Treaty, concluded on August 9, 1842; 8 U.S. Stat. L. 572; and the Supplementary Extradition Treaty proclaimed on April 22, 1901, Article 1, Part 2: 32 U.S. Stat. L. 1864), for the reason that he was not a fugitive from Canada, seeing that he made the false pretences at Chicago, Illinois, after he had left Canada, and had never returned there. The District Court refused the writ. On appeal,

Held (*per* Wilbur, J.): that the order appealed from should be affirmed. Canada had jurisdiction over the offence. The evidence was sufficient to justify the Commissioner's conclusion that the draft was deposited in the Los Angeles bank for collection. In that event the banks collecting the draft in Calgary, Canada, were acting as agents for the appellant: *Spooner* v. *Bank*, 144 Ga. 745; *White* v. *National Bank*, 102 U.S. 658. It had been held that the offence of obtaining money under false pretences was committed if and when and where the victim parted with his money as a result of the false

Case No. 66 *Contd.*

pretences: *People* v. *Chapman*, 55 Cal. App. 192, 196; *State* v. *Shaeffer*, 89 Mo. 271. Acts done outside a jurisdiction, but intended to produce and producing detrimental effects within it, justified a State in punishing the offender if the State should succeed in getting him within its power: *Strassheim* v. *Daily*, 221 U.S. 280. Article 10 of the Treaty in question provided that persons who were charged with the commission of certain specified offences in the jurisdiction of one of the parties to the Treaty and who sought asylum, or should be found, in the territories of the other, could be extradited. The provision was clearly not limited to fugitives, but applied to any person within the jurisdiction of either nation who had committed an extraditable offence within the jurisdiction of the other. Although the title and preamble of the Treaty, and the proclamation putting it into effect, used the term "fugitives," the express language of Article 10 was controlling.

[Report: 59 F. (2d) 683.]

Case No. 67

Jurisdiction—Offences Consummated Outside State Territory but Begun Within the Territory—Offences Partly Committed Within the Jurisdiction.

PEOPLE *v.* CHASE.

United States, Superior Court of California, Appellate Division, Los Angeles County. June 25, 1931.

(McLucas, P.J.; Bishop, Shaw, JJ.)

THE FACTS.—This was a criminal prosecution brought against the defendants for violation of Section 318 of the California Penal Code, which read in part as follows: "Whoever, through invitation or device, prevails upon any person to visit any room, building, or other places kept for the purpose of gambling or prostitution, is guilty of a misdemeanor." The defendants were charged with prevailing upon numerous persons to visit a ship, the *Johanna Smith*, upon which gambling took place. The ship was anchored off the coast of California. The defendants claimed that since the *Johanna Smith* was anchored on the high seas the offence alleged was beyond the jurisdiction of the State Court. The defendants were found guilty and appealed from an order refusing a new trial.

Held: that the judgment must be affirmed. It was clear that the offence defined in Section 318 was only complete when the invitation or device mentioned in the section was successful, that is, when the person solicited actually visited the gambling place. Nevertheless, the gist of the offence was the giving of the invitation or the use of the device, and hence the crime was committed where this was done. It was sufficient if that place was within the jurisdiction of the Court. The jurisdiction was not affected by the location of the place visited by the other person : see *State* v. *Stickney*, 118 Minn. 64. Since the invitations were given in the State of California, the State had jurisdiction over the offence.

Even if this conclusion were wrong and the offence under Section 318 were consummated at the place visited, nevertheless the acts of invitation, etc., constituted a part of the offence and the Court would have jurisdiction under Section 27 of the Penal Code. This section provided : "The following persons are liable to punishment under the laws of this state : 1. All persons who commit, in whole or in part, any crime within this state." Even if the *Johanna Smith* were on the high seas, the offence could be prosecuted in the United States under this section since the invitation was given there : *People* v. *Botkin*, 132 Cal. 231 ; *People* v. *Chapman*, 55 Cal. App. 192, 197. It did not matter that there might be no law on the high seas by which the transaction in question was made a crime : *People* v. *Staples*, 91 Cal. 23, 29.

[Report : 117 Cal. App. 775.]

Jurisdiction—Crimes Originating Abroad—Place Where the Intention to Commit a Crime was Formed—Concurrent Jurisdiction of the Place Where the Crime was Executed. **Case No. 68**

STATE *v.* NAHOUM.

United States, Supreme Court of Louisiana. February 2, 1931.

(O'Neill, C.J.; Overton, Land, St. Paul, Rogers, Brunot, JJ.)

THE FACTS.—This was a criminal prosecution brought against the defendant for embezzling funds of the West Coast Trading Co., S.A., a Mexican corporation. The money involved constituted the proceeds of a sale of rice by the Company to a New Orleans broker, and was actually received by the defendant in New Orleans, Louisiana. The defendant contended that since the intent to embezzle the funds was formed while he was in Mexico, Louisiana had no jurisdiction over the offence. The defendant was convicted. On appeal,

Case No. 68 *Contd.*

Held: that the conviction must be affirmed. An embezzler could be prosecuted at the place where his intention to commit the crime was formed: *State* v. *Sullivan*, 49 La. Ann. 197. But this was not the sole place where the venue could be laid and jurisdiction existed also where the money was converted: 16 C.J. 189.

[Report: 172 La. 83.]

Case No. 69

Jurisdiction—Extraterritorial Operation of Legislation—Dissolution of Corporations Having No Branches Outside the Jurisdiction—Whether to be Recognised by Foreign Courts—Dissolution of Russian Corporations—Continuity of States—Russian Empire and Soviet Russia.

LAZARD BROTHERS & CO. *v.* MIDLAND BANK, LTD.

England, House of Lords. November 28, 1932.

(Lords Buckmaster, Blanesburgh, Warrington of Clyffe, Russell of Killowen, and Wright.)

THE FACTS.—Lazard Brothers & Co. had in 1930 obtained judgment by default for a considerable sum of money against the Moscow Industrial Bank, alleged to be a Russian company. They also obtained a garnishee order against the Midland Bank attaching money alleged to be due from that bank to the Moscow Industrial Bank. Upon appeal to the Court of Appeal[1] both the judgment by default and the garnishee order founded on it were set aside on the grounds that: (1) the Moscow Industrial Bank had ceased to exist as a juristic person in 1930, so that the judgment by default and the garnishee order founded on it were null and of no effect; (2) in any case the judgment against the Moscow Industrial Bank could not be allowed to stand since service of notice of the writ in the action had been irregular in that the procedure applicable to service in a foreign country had not been followed.

Held: that the judgment of the Court of Appeal (which reversed an order of Roche, J., making absolute a garnishee order *nisi* against the respondents) must be affirmed. The Court found, on the evidence of the Russian law, that the Moscow Industrial Bank, which never had any branches in England, ceased to exist as the result of various Russian legislative measures taken since 1919. *Per* Lord Wright, as to

[1] *L.R.* [1932] 1 K.B. 617 (C.A.).

(1) above: "English Courts have long since recognized as juristic persons corporations established by foreign law in virtue of the fact of their creation and continuance under and by that law. . . . But as the creation depends on the act of the foreign state which created them, the annulment of the act of creation by the same power will involve the dissolution and non-existence of the corporation in the eyes of English law. The will of the sovereign authority which created it can also destroy it. English law will equally recognize the one, as the other, fact." (At p. 297.)

As to (2): "No reference is made [in the contention of the appellants pointing to the impossibility of service in Russia] to the procedure under Order XI, r. 8, which by order of the Lord Chancellor, dated March 21, 1906, was applied to the "Russian Empire": that order [which provided for action through diplomatic channels in case of impossibility of service] has never been cancelled: it originally referred to the territorial jurisdiction of what was up to 1917 the Russian Empire but is now the Union of Soviet Republics. This internal change in the system of government, when once the new Government is recognized by this country, has no effect on the external status of Russia *quoad* this country as a personality in International Law. The identity of the State remains the same for international purposes: the change from monarchy to republic does not, in general, abrogate treaties or conventions, any more than loss of or increase in territory. The order of the Lord Chancellor accordingly still applies to Russia and could and should have been invoked for the purpose of effecting service there."

[Report: *L.R.* [1933] A.C. 289; [1932] 49 *T.L.R.* 94.]

NOTE.—I. The Court distinguished the present case from *Russian Commercial and Industrial Bank* v. *Comptoir d'Escompte de Mulhouse*, *L.R.* [1925] A.C. 112; *Annual Digest*, 1925-1926. But it admitted that the view which it took in that case and in other cases of the effect of Russian decrees on the existence abroad of Russian corporations "has now to be reconsidered in the light of new evidence and of the historical evolution of ten years."

II. A foreign corporation which has ceased to exist as a juristic person in the country of its incorporation cannot bring or defend an action in a British Court, even if a branch exists in England, under separate management, which purports to carry on business. (*Russian and English Bank* v. *Baring Brothers & Co., Ltd.*, *L.R.* [1932] 1 Ch. 435.) It may, however, be wound up as an unregistered company under Section 338 of the Companies Act, 1929. (*In re Russian and English Bank*, *L.R.* [1932] 1 Ch. 663.) The Court may, on application of the liquidator, vest by order all the property of

Case No. 69 *Contd.* the company in the liquidator in his official name, and it is in this name only that further actions to recover assets and debts due may be conducted. (*Russian and English Bank* v. *Baring Brothers*, C.A. [1935] 1 Ch. 120.)

Case No. 70 **Jurisdiction—Territorial—Effect of Decrees of Foreign Government Purporting to Monopolise Certain Kinds of Economic Activity, to Dissolve Existing Companies, and to Nationalise Their Property.**

COMMERCIAL AND INDUSTRIAL BANK OF RUSSIA

v. AKTIEBOLAGET GÖTEBORGS BANK.

Sweden, Supreme Court. June 26, 1931.

THE FACTS.—By Decrees issued in December 1917 and January 1918, different Russian Government authorities ordered, *inter alia*, that the banking business should be a State monopoly, that all existing banking companies and bankers' offices should be amalgamated with the National Bank, that the National Bank should take over all the assets and liabilities of the enterprises which had to liquidate, that all funds of the private banks should by complete confiscation pass into the hands of the National Bank, and that all shares in the banking companies should be annulled. The Decrees were carried into effect in Russia, and in April 1918 the Commissariat for the National Bank declared the administrations of the private banks abolished as from April 1, 1918. In 1924 the Swedish Government recognised the Soviet Union.

The plaintiff company had been incorporated in Russia in 1889. Since in December 1917 the Bolsheviks had taken possession of the company's assets in Petrograd, some of the members of the former board of administration established themselves in Kiev, where the company had a branch office, and later on, as the dominion of the Bolsheviks was extended, at other places in Russia. In 1920 the Board decided to transfer the management of the business to Paris, where another branch existed. In 1921 the company was registered with the Court of Commerce in Paris as having its seat in Petrograd and a branch in Paris. The Board continued the business, eventually mainly for the purpose of winding it up.

In 1928 the plaintiff company instituted proceedings before the Court of Stockholm to recover the balance of an account with the Swedish company.

Held: that judgment must be given for the plaintiff company. The decision of the Supreme Court was based in all essentials on the same reasoning as in Case No. 61 reported in *Annual Digest*, 1929-1930 (*Forsikringsaktieselskapet Norske Atlas* v. *Sundén-Cullberg*).

[Report : *Nytt Juridiskt Arkiv*, 1931, p. 351.]

Jurisdiction—Territorial—Effect of Decrees of Foreign Governments. **Case No. 71**

RUDITZKY *v.* AKTIEBOLAGET SVENSKA HANDELSBANKEN.

Sweden, Supreme Court. March 26, 1932.

THE FACTS.—A Norwegian firm, which during the World War bought large quantities of hemp from Mayer Ruditzky, a Russian merchant, brother of the plaintiff, had through a Norwegian bank given the defendant, a Swedish bank, an order to open a reimbursement credit for the firm with the Banque de Commerce de Sibérie, a Russian bank which acted as Mayer Ruditzky's banker. As the goods arrived at a certain place in Sweden, the price was to be placed by the Swedish bank at the disposal of the Russian bank. In pursuance of this transaction the Norwegian firm paid over to the Swedish bank several sums of money, and the Swedish bank credited these amounts to the Russian bank in its account with the Swedish bank. The Russian bank was informed of the entries. The sums, however, were not paid out to the Russian bank ; nor, it seemed, were they paid by that bank to Mayer Ruditzky. As to the Decrees issued by the Soviet authorities with regard to the banking business in Russia, see Case No. 70.

The plaintiff as holder of the rights not only of his brother, but also of the Norwegian bank and the Norwegian firm, claimed, in an action brought before the Court of Stockholm, the amount credited to the Russian bank to his account. The Court of Stockholm dismissed the claim.

Held (by the Svea Court of Appeal and the Supreme Court, reversing the judgment of the Court of first instance) : that judgment must be given in favour of the plaintiff in view of the fact that two persons in Paris who had pretended to act as members of the Board of Administration of the Russian Bank had consented to the payment of the sum to the plaintiff and that no other claim had been made for the sum during the period of prescription which had otherwise elapsed. The Supreme Court once more had the opportunity to make the same statements of

Case No. 71 Contd. law as to the effect of the Russian Decrees as in the preceding case and the earlier cases referred to in the report.

[Report : *Nytt Juridiskt Arkiv*, 1932, p. 217.]

NOTE.—See also *Münchener Rückversicherungs-Gesellschaft Aktiengesellschaft* v. *Brand-Och Livforsaleringsaktiebolaget Skåne*, decided on March 26, 1932, by the Swedish Supreme Court: *Nytt Juridiskt Arkiv*, 1932, p. 225. The plaintiff company owned 43 per cent. of all the shares in an insurance company, Pomoschtch, incorporated in Russia in 1888. Pomoschtch—which, after the revolution in 1917, like other Russian insurance companies, had been nationalised and subjected to confiscation as regards its Russian assets (see *Annual Digest*, 1929-1930, Case No. 61)—had re-insured certain risks in Skåne. By these transactions Pomoschtch became the creditor of Skåne for a certain amount. The plaintiff company instituted proceedings against Skåne before the Court of Malmö to obtain judgment first for 43 per cent. of the balance and later—relying on a deed of transfer signed by the former manager of Pomoschtch—for the whole balance. The Court of Malmö dismissed the claim. The Court of Appeal and the Supreme Court both gave judgment for the plaintiff company.

Case No. 72 **Recognition of Acts of Foreign States—Divorce Decrees—Absence of Special Convention.**

KADLER *v.* KADLER.

Poland, Supreme Court, Third Division (*Court* 1).

February 5, 1931.

THE FACTS.—The parties were married in Warsaw in a Catholic church in 1901. In 1903 they went to a place now in the territory of Soviet Russia. In 1911 the wife returned to the territory now forming part of Poland. In 1921 her husband obtained a divorce under Soviet law from the Soviet authorities. In 1923 he returned to Poland. In 1928 the plaintiff sued him for alimony due to her as his wife. The defendant pleaded the divorce. The two lower Courts decided in favour of the plaintiff. The Supreme Court upheld the decision and

Held : for the plaintiff. The Court said : "Between the Polish Republic and the Union of Socialist Soviet Republics no convention has as yet been concluded in the matter of mutual recognition of divorce decrees of either State by the other State. Hence the Polish Republic has no legal obligation arising from any treaty to recognize decisions of Soviet Courts in the matter of divorce in cases in which at least one of the parties, as in the present case, is undoubtedly a Polish citizen, even if the decision of the Soviet Court is in accordance with the law prevailing in the place where the decision was given."

[Report : *O.S.P.*, X (1931), No. 419, p. 406.]

Jurisdiction—Enforcement of Foreign Sovereign Rights—Claims for Court Fees—Action to Recover Court Fees. **Case No. 73**

COURT FEES (DANZIG) CASE.

Danzig, County Court. November 18, 1932.

THE FACTS.—This was an action instituted by the Polish State against a person resident in Danzig, to recover the Court fees of an action decided by a Polish Court.

Held : that the action must be dismissed. The claim was not one based on private law. Court fees were public taxes. "They are levied in pursuance of the sovereign rights of the State. In accordance with the principles of international law, a foreign State may not employ the organs of another State for the execution of its foreign sovereign rights, for instance, to enforce payment of its public charges. Exceptions may be provided for by treaties between States." There was no such treaty between Poland and Danzig.

[Report : *Danziger Juristische Monatsschrift*, vol. 12 (1933), p. 13.]

Jurisdiction—Extraterritorial Effect of—Garnishee Order for Claims Against a Foreign Debtor Arising from a Mortgage Situate in Germany. **Case No. 74**

GARNISHEE ORDER CASE.

Germany, District Court III of Berlin. May 27, 1931.

THE FACTS.—The appellant was a judgment creditor and applied for a garnishee order. He sought to attach a claim which the debtor had on a mortgage registered in Germany on German property against a third debtor residing abroad. The local Court refused the application on the ground that the garnishee order would, in the circumstances of the case, constitute an infringement of the jurisdiction of a foreign State. On appeal,

Held : that the application must be granted. It was true

Case No. 74 ***Contd.*** that the Court of Appeal of Berlin, in its decision of April 5, 1929 (*Juristische Wochenschrift*, 1929, p. 2360, No. 1), laid down that the prohibition to pay, in connection with a garnishee order, where the third debtor resided abroad, was directed against foreign property and that such attachment constituted an infringement of foreign jurisdiction which was contrary to international law. However, that decision was not applicable to the facts of the present case. The present application was brought with regard to a mortgage on German property, for which a German venue existed under Article 24 of the Code of Civil Procedure. In a previous decision (Order of June 4, 1929, 8 W. 4798/29), the Court of Appeal of Berlin expressed doubts as to the practicability of serving garnishee orders or writs of attachment abroad. However, this Court felt compelled to depart from the former decisions on the matter. But the impracticability of service was immaterial for the determination of the question whether or not the order as such was lawful. Accordingly, the Court to which application was made was not entitled to examine the question of practicability. This was to be determined at a later stage of the proceedings by the authority whose duty it was to arrange for service in the territory of the foreign State.

[Report: *Rechtsprechung auf dem Gebiete des Internationalen Privatrechts*, 1931, No. 144.]

NOTE.—See also the decision of the Court of Appeal of Karlsruhe of October 15, 1931, in which it was held that a German court is entitled to issue a writ of execution against a debtor who is resident abroad, if such writ can be served on the debtor on German territory. This might happen where the debtor owned real property in Germany, and therefore visited Germany at certain intervals, or where he had authorised a person resident in Germany to receive payments on his behalf. However, a foreign authority could not be requested to serve the writ of execution on the debtor so as to make it fully effective, just as no German authority would be allowed to grant a corresponding foreign request to that effect. To do so would constitute an inadmissible infringement of foreign territorial jurisdiction: *Juristische Wochenschrift*, 1932, p. 667. See also the decision of the District Court of Königsberg of November 2, 1931. In that case the debtors were resident in the Free City of Danzig. The local Court of that State had begun proceedings for an arrangement with the creditors with a view to avoiding the debtors' bankruptcy. The creditors had a judgment debt in Germany against the debtors, and on the strength of it attempted to attach goods belonging to the debtors and warehoused in Germany. On account of the Danzig arrangement proceedings the sheriff refused to effect the attachment. The lower Court ordered him to proceed with the attachment of the goods situate in Germany. He appealed. The appeal was dismissed. The Court said : "The fact of proceedings for an arrangement pending against the debtors in the Danzig Free City does not prevent a creditor who does not take part in them from suing out a writ of execution in respect of assets of the debtor situate in Germany. For compromise proceedings abroad are of no effect in Germany unless a special international convention has been concluded between the respective States. No such convention exists between Germany and the Danzig Free City" : *Juristische Wochenschrift*, 1932, p. 207.

Jurisdiction—Extraterritorial Effect of—Application of National Statutes—Principle of Territoriality. **Case No. 75**

TERRITORIALITY PRINCIPLE (GERMAN LABOUR LAWS) CASE.

Germany, Supreme Labour Court. July 1, 1931.

THE FACTS.—This case arose out of the dismissal of a German workman who had been employed by the syndicate of German undertakings charged by Germany with the performance of reparation works in France to be executed under the Treaty of Versailles. He sued the syndicate. The plaintiff had been employed in a workshop in France, having been placed there under a Statute dealing with persons severely injured during the War. He contended that the dismissal was illegal, inasmuch as the conditions set up by the Statute concerning the Employment of Persons Severely Injured during the War had not been complied with. His action for continued payment of his wages was dismissed by the Lower Court on the ground that, owing to the territoriality principle, the Statute in question applied only to service agreements existing in Germany. It was immaterial that the syndicate consisted of German undertakings, for the territoriality principle permitted the application of the Statute solely within the borders of the State which had enacted it. Such Statutes were not applicable beyond those limits, irrespective of the nationality of the parties. The plaintiff appealed.

Held : that the appeal must be dismissed. The Court followed the Lower Court in holding that the Act concerning the Employment of Persons Severely Injured during the War was not applicable to the plaintiff's service agreement. The Court said : "The provisions of this Act partake of the nature of public law. Their source is the power of the State over its own subjects, and they cannot therefore be applied to foreign contracts, for such application depends on the jurisdictional powers of the State. These cannot extend beyond its frontiers. The principle that rules of public law are applicable only within the territory of the legislating State obtains also where such rules affect private relations between German nationals. Accordingly, the Supreme Labour Court, in its decision No. 7/31 of April 1, 1931 (*Entscheidungen des Reichsarbeitsgerichts*, vol. 8, p.195), held that the provision of § 96 of the Act concerning Workmen's Councils in Industrial and Trading Companies and Firms, for the protection of workmen and employees from dismissal, was not applicable to foreign service agreements."

[Report: *Entscheidungen des Reichsarbeitsgerichts*, vol. 9, p. 40.]

NOTE.—See also the decision of the Supreme Labour Court, *ibid.*, vol. 8, p. 195, which was quoted in the judgment reported above. In that case the application of the Act concerning Workmen's Councils in Industrial and Trading Companies and Firms was refused for similar reasons. With regard to the territoriality principle see also the decision of the Court of Appeal of Dresden of October 25, 1932 (reported in *Rechtsprechung auf dem Gebiete des Internationalen Privatrechts*, 1933, No. 57), where the application of the Russian Decree concerning the Law of Inheritance of April 27, 1918, was in issue. The Court pointed out that the Russian Decree in question was governed by the territoriality principle and that Russia did not claim its application abroad. This appeared clearly from several circulars of the People's Commissars of Foreign Affairs and of Justice. Thus in the circular issued on April 12, 1922, it was said: "The property legislation contained in the decrees of the Soviet Government regulates matters concerning property only for the territory of the R.S.F.S.R. Property situate out of the R.S.F.S.R. is in no way connected with the Republic, and foreign countries cannot apply Russian law to them, even if such property is owned by Russian citizens."

Case No. 76 **Jurisdiction — Principle of Territoriality — Bankruptcy Proceedings Abroad.**

In re DUTCH TRUSTEE IN BANKRUPTCY.

Germany, Court of Appeal of Cologne. December 9, 1931.

THE FACTS.—A Dutch trustee in bankruptcy brought an action to recover assets belonging to the debtor and situate in Germany.

Held: that the action must be dismissed. " The Dutch trustee in bankruptcy is not entitled to bring the present action, for the bankruptcy proceedings were brought in Holland and the attachment consequent on them is of no effect in Germany. When examining the effect of bankruptcy proceedings abroad on the debtor's property in this country, it must be borne in mind that bankruptcy proceedings constitute a compulsory measure by the State. Thus every bankruptcy involves the exercise of the executive power of the State . . . Now, it is a rule of both constitutional and international law that a State can exercise its jurisdiction only within its territory. For this reason international bankruptcy law provides that the effect of bankruptcy shall be limited to the territory of the State where a receiving order is made (so-called principle of territoriality) . . . " The Court pointed out that the provisions of German bankruptcy law concerning the effect of a foreign receiving order were identical with the rules of international law. The principle of territoriality was expressly embodied in § 237 of the German Bankruptcy Act. According to that provision, German assets belonging to a debtor against whom a receiving order has been made abroad, could be attached on behalf of individual creditors irrespective of the foreign bankruptcy proceedings.

[Report: *Rechtsprechung auf dem Gebiete des Internationalen Privatrechts*, 1932, No. 161.]

NOTE.—See similar decisions of the Court of Appeal of Munich of November 29, 1931 (*Rechtsprechung auf dem Gebiete des internationalen Privatrechts*, 1932, No. 160), and of the District Court of Königsberg of November 2, 1931 (*Juristische Wochenschrift*, 1932, p. 207). The judgment of the Court of Appeal of Brunswick of April 1, 1932 (*Rechtsprechung*, etc., 1932, No. 162) dealt with the case of a Belgian trustee in bankruptcy who took the place of the original party to an action pending in a German court. The Court pointed out that such succession was in harmony with the territoriality principle, seeing that the amount and the nature of the German debtor's liability was, as a rule, independent of the fact that the trustee in bankruptcy took up the plaintiff's action.

Jurisdiction—Death Duties Due to a Foreign State—Enforceability of. **Case No. 77**

LAMBERTINI *v.* MAUVRODIS.

Italy, Court of Appeal of Genoa. January 5, 1932.

THE FACTS.—The Minister Plenipotentiary of Greece, on

Case No. 77 Contd.

behalf of his Government, applied for an order that Signora Lambertini should pay to the Greek Treasury the death duties due on the death of her husband, a Greek subject, at Genoa in January 1929.

Held: that the application must be rejected. The Court said: "The action cannot be allowed because the [Greek] Government would thus be enabled to exercise an essential and fundamental function of sovereignty, in the form of the imposition and collection of taxes, within the territory of the [Italian] State. It is indisputable that the imposition and collection of taxes, which presupposes the power of command and compulsion, falls within the category of essential powers of sovereignty which can only be exercised within the boundaries of the State. In order that a foreign State may be able to impose and collect taxes or duties in Italy, there must be in existence either a particular law or a convention having the force of law. It does not appear either that any law of this kind has been promulgated, or that any such convention has been made between the Government of Greece and that of Italy giving the Greek State the right, not only of levying, but also of demanding under compulsion, taxes on property in Italy."

[Report: *Rivista*, 1932, p. 432; *Rivista italiana di diritto internazionale privato e processuale*, 1932, p. 61.]

Case No. 78

Jurisdiction — Extraterritorial Effect of — Russian Nationality Decrees—Effect of Treaty of Peace Transferring Russian State Property in Lithuania to the Lithuanian State.

LITHUANIAN MINISTRY OF THE INTERIOR *v.* ASOV-DON COMPANY.

Lithuania, Supreme Court. December 21, 1931.

THE FACTS.—This case turned on the interpretation of Article X of the Peace Treaty between Lithuania and Soviet Russia of July 12, 1920,[1] by virtue of which certain categories of Russian property situated in Lithuania were transferred to the latter. In the present action the Lithuanian Minister for the Interior asked for a declaration that, as the result of that provision, certain land belonging to the defendants, the Asov-Don Commercial Bank, a Russian company dissolved in consequence of Soviet legislation, was the property of Lithuania. It was contended on behalf of the defendants that the Russian

[1] *L.N.T.S.*, vol. III (2), p. 106.

decrees had no effect in Lithuania and that the Soviet Government could not therefore transfer to Lithuania property which that Government never possessed. The District Court decided in favour of the Ministry of the Interior. On appeal before the Supreme Court,

Held : that the appeal must be dismissed. The terms of the Treaty were clear. The question of the extraterritorial effect of Russian legislation was not relevant seeing that the decrees in question did not nationalise the property of Russian companies ; they nationalised the companies as such. The banks were liquidated and amalgamated with the State Bank, which took over the property and the debts of the liquidated banks. This was a further reason why the property of these banks must now be regarded as the property of the Russian State.

[Unreported.]

Jurisdiction—Aliens Abroad—Duty of Aliens to Appear as Witnesses—Aliens Subpœnaed Within the Jurisdiction.

See Case No. 141 (*Jurisdiction* (*Foreign Witnesses*) *Case*).

ii.—Criminal Jurisdiction over Foreigners.

Jurisdiction—Criminal Jurisdiction Over Foreigners for Crimes Committed Abroad—Protective Jurisdiction. **Case No. 79**

In re GONZÁLEZ.

Mexico, Supreme Court. July 21, 1932.

THE FACTS.—This was an appeal from a judgment of the Federal District Judge, which had refused González relief against a sentence of imprisonment passed on him by the Superior Court of Campeche (one of the member-States of the United States of Mexico). González was a Spanish national who, as the agent of a Mexican, one Salorio, had wrongfully retained the shipping documents on a consignment of logwood. The offence was committed in the United States. González was arrested and brought before the State Courts of Campeche, on a charge of "abuse of confidence," under the State laws of Campeche. On appeal to the Federal Supreme Court,

Held : that the judgment of the Federal District Judge must be reversed on the issue of jurisdiction. The crime with which González was charged was within the federal jurisdiction, and

Case No. 79 *Contd.*

not within the jurisdiction of the State of Campeche.[1] On the more general question of jurisdiction, the Court had no doubt that the Federal Courts would have jurisdiction. This was a crime committed by an alien outside the territory of the Mexican Republic and affecting the legal interests of a Mexican citizen. The penal law of a State was applicable to crimes committed in any place and by any person, provided that they attacked property or legal interests of that State or of its citizens. Mexican legislation had adopted the principle according to which "the State has the right and the duty to defend, by the application of penal laws, all its internal legal interests; the determining criterion, in this case, is the nationality of the property or legal interest which has been injured by the criminal act done abroad."[2]

[Report: 35 *Semanario Judicial* (5th ep.), 1500.]

Jurisdiction—Over Foreign Vessels—Jurisdiction of Municipal Courts with Regard to Seizures Effected in Violation of Treaties.

See Case No. 1 (*The Mazel Tov*).

[1] On the question whether the State or federal law was applicable, the Court based its decision in favour of the federal law on the following reasoning: "The fact of punishing a criminal act committed outside the country presupposes the exercise of the sovereignty of the State as against another State. . . . Accordingly, in the case of crimes committed by known persons who, like González, are aliens, and which are consummated outside the national territory, no other law can be applicable than the Federal Penal Code. It makes no difference whether the victim of the crime resides in Campeche or in another State of the Republic. For, as against foreign States, sovereignty belongs exclusively to the Mexican Nation."

[2] The Mexican Federal Penal Code of 1929, in force at the time of this decision, provided, in Article 6, as follows:

"Crimes committed abroad by a Mexican against Mexicans, or against aliens, or by an alien against Mexicans, can be punished in the Republic according to its laws, if the following requirements are met:

"I. That the accused is in the Republic, having come either voluntarily or as the result of extradition; II. that, if the victim is an alien, there is a complaint by the proper party; III. that the accused has not been definitively tried in the country where he committed the crime; or, if he has been so tried, that he has not been acquitted, pardoned, or had his sentence extinguished by lapse of time; IV. that the offence with which he is charged has the character of a crime in the country where it was committed as well as in the Republic [of Mexico]; and, V. that, according to the laws of Mexico, the crime involves a penalty of more than one year's imprisonment."

(These principles have also been adopted in the Mexican Federal Penal Code of 1931 (Article 4).)

It will be noted that similar Mexican legislation underlay the *Cutting* controversy between Mexico and the United States: see *United States Foreign Relations* (1887), pp. 751 *et seq.*; Moore, *Digest*, II, p. 228.

iii.—Over Ports and National Waters.

[See also Part III, *Territorial Waters*.]

Jurisdiction—Over Foreign Vessels in Ports—Torts Committed on Board a Foreign Vessel—American Seaman on German Vessel in a United States Port. **Case No. 80**

URAVIC *v.* JARKA CO.

United States, Supreme Court. January 5, 1931.

(Hughes, C.J.; Holmes, Van Devanter, McReynolds, Brandeis, Sutherland, Butler, Stone, Roberts, JJ.)

THE FACTS.—This was an action brought in a Court of the State of New York to recover damages for causing the death of Anton Uravic, an intestate American citizen, employed as a stevedore by the defendant, a Delaware corporation. At the time of receiving the injury that caused his death, Uravic was helping to unload a vessel flying the German flag, in the harbour of New York. He was on the vessel at the time and was injured through the negligence of a fellow-workman.

The Jones Act of 1915, §33 (C. 153, as amended by the Act of June 5, 1920, c. 250, §33, 41 U.S. Stat. L. 988, 1007; U.S. Code, Title 46, §688), gives an action at common law to the personal representative of any seaman suffering death in the course of employment, and makes applicable all statutes of the United States conferring or regulating such right of action in the case of railway employees. R. S. §4612, U.S. Code, Tit. 46, §713, defines a seaman as "every person (apprentices excepted) who shall be employed or engaged to serve in any capacity on board . . ." In the case of injury to a railway employee, the negligence of a fellow servant is not a defence: Act of April 22, 1908, c. 149, §1, 35 U.S. Stat. L. 65, U.S. Code, Tit. 45, §51. The defendant contended that §33 of the Jones Act of 1915 did not apply to a stevedore working on a foreign vessel. The action was dismissed. The decision was affirmed by the Court of Appeals, 252 N.Y. 530. On *certiorari* to the United States Supreme Court,

Held: that the judgment must be reversed. It had been decided that stevedores came within §33 of the Jones Act of 1915: *International Stevedoring Co.* v. *Haverty*, 272 U.S. 50. The general language of the statute, giving the right to "any seaman," applied to stevedores working on foreign vessels. The jurisdiction and authority of Congress were unquestionable:

Case No. 80 *Contd.* *Cunard Steamship Co.* v. *Mellon*, 262 U.S. 101, 124. It was argued that the statute would clearly not apply to a seaman on a foreign vessel. It would be a sufficient answer that, while §33 gave the rights of seamen to stevedores, it did not mean that they were to be regarded as seamen on the particular vessel upon which for the moment they happened to be at work. They were simply given the rights of seamen and, as they were American workmen, they had the rights of American seamen as well on German as on American ships.

Furthermore, the case concerned the conduct of persons within the jurisdiction affecting the safety of other persons within the jurisdiction. There would seem to be no reason for the United States to adopt a different rule for people subject to its authority merely because they were on a private vessel registered abroad. Crimes committed upon such private vessels were punishable by the territorial jurisdiction: *Wildenhus's* Case, 120 U.S. 1; *Patterson* v. *Bark Eudora*, 190 U.S. 169, 177. There was no reason to limit the liability for torts committed upon such vessels when they went beyond the scope of discipline and private matters that did not interest the territorial power.

[Report: 282 U.S. 234.][1]

Case No. 81 **Jurisdiction in Territorial Waters—Entry in Distress—Meaning of the Expression "Stress of Weather"—Application of the Anglo-American Convention of 1818—Interpretation of Treaties by Reference to Circumstances at the Time of the Conclusion of the Treaty.**

THE MAY v. THE KING.

Canada, Supreme Court. April 28, 1931.

THE FACTS.—By Sect. 10 of the Canadian Customs and Fisheries Protection Act, 1927, it was provided as follows:

> "Every fishing ship, vessel or boat which is foreign, or not navigated according to the laws of Great Britain or of Canada, which,
>
> (*a*) not being thereto permitted by any treaty or convention, or by any law of Great Britain, or of Canada for the time being in force, has been found fishing or preparing to fish, or to have been fishing in British waters

[1] See *Columbia Law Review*, xxxi (1931), p. 505; *Cornell Law Quarterly*, vol. XVI, p. 371.

within three marine miles of any of the coasts, bays, creeks or harbours of Canada, or in or upon the inland waters of Canada;

(*b*) has entered such waters for any purpose not permitted by treaty or convention, or by any law of Great Britain or of Canada for the time being in force .... shall .... be forfeited."

Sect. 1 of the same statute made an exception for the case of entry in distress. By Article 1 of the Convention of 1818 the United States renounced any right to take fish "within three marine miles of any of the coasts, bays, creeks, or harbours of His Britannic Majesty's dominions in America, ... Provided, however, that the American fishermen shall be admitted to enter such bays or harbours for the purpose of shelter ..."

The *May*, a fishing vessel of American registry, had been arrested by a Canadian patrol launch when at anchor within three miles of the coast of British Columbia. The contentions of the appellant are stated below.

Held (*per* Lamont, J., affirming the judgment of the Exchequer Court): that the vessel was forfeit. The evidence failed to disclose a case of distress, so that Sect. 1 of the Customs Act did not apply. The "stress of weather" on which the appellants relied was the necessity to seek shelter to repair the engine, namely, to renew the packing of the oil pump which had become worn, thus causing the pump to leak. The leaking resulted in a waste of oil, but it did not affect the usefulness of the pump and did not render navigation dangerous. The Court said: "It is common ground that this section, although primarily enacted as a customs provision for the protection of the revenue, does, by the exception contained in the words "unless from stress of weather or other unavoidable cause" give effect to a principle of international law recognized by both countries, namely, that vessels of one nation will be excused for entering the territory of another if there is an actual necessity for their so doing. It is a well recognized principle, both in this country and in the United States, that the jurisdiction of a nation is exclusive and absolute within its own territory, of which its territorial waters within three marine miles from shore are as clearly a part as the land. All exceptions, therefore, to the full and complete power of a nation within its own territory must be traced to the consent of the nation itself given as a general rule by treaty, convention or statute. From this it follows that each nation has the absolute right to prescribe the conditions upon which the vessels of

Case No. 81 *Contd.*

another nation will be permitted to enter its territorial waters. What we have to do, therefore, is to ascertain what conditions have been prescribed, to define the limits thereof, and then see if the facts, as disclosed by the evidence, bring the "May" within these limits." After quoting from the judgments in *The Eleanor* (1809), Edwards' Admiralty Reports 135 (at pp. 159-161), *The Diana*, 7 Wallace 354 (at p. 360), and *The New York*, 3 Wheaton 59 (at p. 68), the Court said: "A perusal of the above authorities leads to the conclusion that an entry by a foreign vessel into Canadian waters cannot be justified on the ground of "stress of weather" unless the weather is such as to produce in the mind of a reasonably competent and skilful master, possessing courage and firmness, a well grounded *bona fide* apprehension that if he remains outside the territorial waters he will put in jeopardy his vessel and cargo. In every case the questions whether the master fairly and honestly on reasonable ground believed it necessary to take shelter, and whether he exercised reasonable skill, competence and courage in the circumstances, are questions of fact for the tribunal whose duty it is to find the facts."[1]

Upon the question of the application of the Convention of 1818 the Court held that that Convention was only applicable to the Atlantic coast of Canada, since the sovereignty of Great Britain over the present Pacific coast of Canada was disputed by the United States until the conclusion of the Oregon Boundary Treaty of 1846.

[Report: [1931], *Canada Supreme Court Reports*, 374; [1931] 3 *Dominion Law Reports*, 15.]

NOTE.—Upon evidence of similar facts the same decision was given in *The Ship "Queen City" and Others* v. *The King*: [1931] *Canada Supreme Court Reports*, 387; [1931] 3 *Dominion Law Reports*, 147. For comment on these cases see Laing in *A.J.*, XXVI (1932), p. 374.

[1] It was contended for the appellant that even if the term "stress of weather" was held to mean an uncontrollable necessity when applied to merchant ships, it should not be given that meaning when applied to fishing vessels, as fishermen were "wards of civilization and entitled to favourable treatment." The Court said: "The statute makes no such distinction and I am unable to see any good reason why fishing vessels should not comply with the statute. The owners or operators of these vessels carry on their business for profit and, in this case, in competition with Canadian fishermen. They should, therefore, be held to a strict observance of the conditions which the statute prescribes for their entry into Canadian waters."

Hot Pursuit—Illegal Fishing—Jurisdiction Over Foreign Vessels Within Territorial Waters. **Case No. 81a**

For an affirmation of the right of hot pursuit in the case of a foreign vessel engaged in illegal fishing and captured thirteen miles off the French coast after having been sighted in and pursued from French territorial waters, see the decision of the Court of Appeal of Bastia, Corsica, of September 22, 1931, in the case of the trawler *Buccari : Le Droit maritime français*, vol. 10, p. 98. See also *ibid.*, p. 442, and *Z. für a. ö. R. und V.*, III (1932-1933), Part II, p. 266, for a decision, to the same effect, of the Tribunal Correctionnel de Bastia of June 18, 1931. In that case the Court pointed out, in answer to the argument that French Courts had no jurisdiction over foreign commercial vessels with regard to what happened on board, that it came within the exception admitted by the defendants themselves, namely, that the offence in question interested the whole fishing population of Bastia, who felt keenly that illegal methods of fishing were highly damaging to their livelihood.

Jurisdiction—Over Foreign Vessels in National Ports.

See Case No. 91 (*United States* v. *Flores*).

Jurisdiction—Over Foreign Vessels Within Territorial Waters.

See Case No. 81a (*The Buccari*).

iv.—At the Maritime Frontier. Hovering Laws.

[See also below, C. *High Seas.*]

Jurisdiction—Outside Territorial Waters—Anti-Smuggling Legislation—British Practice—Enforcement of Legislation Contrary to International Law. **Case No. 82**

CROFT *v.* DUNPHY.

British Empire, Judicial Committee of the Privy Council, on appeal from the Supreme Court of Canada.

(Lords Tomlin, Thankerton, Macmillan, Wright, and Sir George Lowndes.)

July 28, 1932.

THE FACTS.—Sections 151 (1) and 207 (1) of the Customs Act of Canada, 1927, authorised the boarding of a vessel

Case No. 82 *Contd.*

"hovering" in the territorial waters of Canada and the seizure of the vessel and cargo if dutiable goods were found on board. The territorial waters of Canada were defined for the purposes of the Act by Sect. 151 (7) as being "waters forming part of the territory of the Dominion of Canada and the waters adjacent to the Dominion within three marine miles thereof in case of any vessel and within twelve marine miles thereof in the case of any vessel registered in Canada." The respondent's schooner, of Canadian registration, was seized under these sections of the Act when at a distance of 11½ miles from the coast. In this action against the appellant, the customs officer who effected the seizure, it was contended that the seizure was illegal, on the sole ground that the Dominion Parliament had no power to enact legislation purporting to operate to a distance of twelve miles from the coast of Canada. The Supreme Court of Canada, reversing the decision of the trial judge, by a majority held that the legislation was *ultra vires*, having regard to its extraterritorial effect.

Held: that the legislation was valid and that the judgment of the Supreme Court of Canada must be reversed.

Per Lord Macmillan, delivering the judgment of the Board: "It may be accepted as a general principle that states can legislate effectively only for their own territories. To what distance seaward the territory of a state is to be taken as extending is a question of international law upon which their Lordships do not deem it necessary or proper to pronounce. But whatever be the limits of territorial waters in the international sense, it has long been recognized that for certain purposes, notably those of police, revenue, public health and fisheries, a state may enact laws affecting the seas surrounding its coasts to a distance seaward which exceeds the ordinary limits of its territory. [Reference was here made to the judgment of Lord Stowell in *The Le Louis*,[1] and to the writings of Sir Travers Twiss, Halleck, Hall, Phillimore and Wheaton.] Legislation of the Imperial Parliament, even in contravention of generally acknowledged principles of international law, is binding upon and must be enforced by the Courts of this country, for in these Courts the legislation of the Imperial Parliament cannot be challenged as *ultra vires*: per Lord Justice-General Dunedin in *Mortensen* v. *Peters*.[2] It may be that legislation of the Dominion Parliament may be challenged as *ultra vires* on the ground that it is contrary to the principles

[1] (1817) 2 Dod. Adm. 210, 245.
[2] (1906) 8 F. (J.C.) 93, 101.

of international law, but that must be because it must be assumed that the British North America Act has not conferred power on the Dominion Parliament to legislate contrary to these principles. In the present case, however, there is no question of international law involved, for legislation of the kind here challenged is recognized as legitimate by international law, and in any event the provision impugned has no application to foreign vessels. The sole question is whether the Imperial Parliament, in conferring upon Canada, as it admittedly has done, full power to enact customs legislation, bestowed or withheld the power to enact the provisions now challenged." The British "Hovering Acts," now repealed, but in force at the date of the British North America Act, were recalled,[1] and the Board concluded that it could not be conceived that the Imperial Parliament had meant to withhold from the Dominion Parliament the power "to enact provisions similar in scope to those which had long been an integral part of Imperial customs legislation and which presumably were regarded as necessary to its efficacy."

[Report : *L.R.* [1933] A.C. 156.]

NOTE.—There can be no doubt, after the Statute of Westminster,

[1] The learned Lord here surveyed the history of British anti-smuggling legislation. He said : "Now from early times the customs legislation of the Imperial Parliament has contained anti-smuggling provisions authorizing the seizure of vessels having dutiable goods on board when found "hovering" off the coast within distances substantially in excess of the ordinary territorial limits. So far back as 1768 there is to be found in the statute 9 Geo. 3, c. 9, s. 22, legislation authorizing the forfeiture of dutiable goods found in vessels "hovering" within two marine leagues of the shore. There are numerous subsequent enactments of a similar character, and legislation of this nature has been extended as far as to twenty-four miles from the coast. So familiar indeed are such provisions in the history of British customs legislation that the series of measures embodying them have come to be known compendiously as the "Hovering Acts." Although these Acts have now all been repealed, the Customs Consolidation Act of 1876, by s. 179, authorized the forfeiture of any ship belonging wholly or in part to British subjects, or having half the persons on board subjects of Her Majesty, if found with prohibited goods on board within three leagues of the coast of the United Kingdom. In the case of other vessels not British the limit is fixed at one league from the coast. The previous Imperial Act of 1853 (16 & 17 Vict. c. 107), which was in force when the British North America Act was passed, dealt, in s. 212, with even greater distances from the coast. It is not without interest to note as a matter of history that the risk of illicit trade between the French island of St. Pierre and His Majesty's North American possessions was the subject of special legislation in a statute of 1763, 4 Geo. 3, c. 15, by s. 35 of which any British ship "hovering" within two leagues of St. Pierre and Miquelon might be seized and forfeited.

"It will thus be seen that when the Imperial Parliament in 1867 conferred on the Parliament of Canada full power to legislate regarding customs, it had long been the practice to include in Imperial statutes relating to this branch of law executive provisions to take effect outside ordinary territorial limits. The measures against "hovering" were no doubt enacted by the Imperial Parliament because they were deemed necessary to render anti-smuggling legislation effective." (At pp. 165, 166.)

Case No. 82 *Contd.* 1931, Sect. 3, that the Parliament of a Dominion has full power to make laws having extraterritorial operation. It was unnecessary to decide in this case whether the Statute of Westminster had retrospective effect.

vii.—Exemptions from and Restrictions upon Territorial Jurisdiction.

(*a*) Foreign States

[See also Part II, *Acts of Sovereignty and Transactions of a Private Character.*]

Case No. 83 **Jurisdiction—Immunity from—Foreign States—Implied Waiver by Bringing an Action—Extent of Implied Waiver—Liens—Waiver of Immunity and Execution of Judgment.**

Mexico *v.* Rask.

United States, District Court of Appeal of California, Fourth Appellate District. October 29, 1931.

(Marks, Barnard, Jennings, JJ.)

The Facts.—This was an action before a Californian Court by the United States of Mexico to recover possession of a patrol boat from the defendant. The boat was used for patrol purposes along the Pacific Coast of Mexico in connection with the enforcement of the Mexican customs and revenue laws. A bond was furnished by a surety and the boat was delivered to the plaintiff pending the trial. The defendant was a shipwright. The boat had been delivered to him in California, by an authorised officer of the Mexican Government, for a general overhaul and repair. The defendant contended that by virtue of an unpaid balance due for labour and materials he had a lien on the boat entitling him to possession until the sum owing should be paid. Upon the ground of sovereign immunity from suit, the plaintiff's attorneys objected to the jurisdiction of the Court to consider the defence of a lien and to render an affirmative judgment against the plaintiff. It was further contended that the lien asserted was maritime in nature and could be enforced only in a court of admiralty. The Trial Court directed that the patrol boat be returned to the defendant or, if it could not be returned, that the defendant recover from the United States of Mexico the unpaid balance due for labour and materials and costs. The bond of the surety was ordered to be delivered to the defendant.

On appeal to the California District Court of Appeal,

Held (by Marks, J.): that the judgment must be affirmed. It was true that an action against a foreign Government would not be entertained in any Court in the United States without the consent, express or implied, of the Government against which the action was brought: *Oliver American Trading Co. Inc.* v. *Government of the United States of Mexico,* 5 Fed. (2d) 659. Nor could a warship or commercial vessel belonging to a foreign Government be taken from the possession of that Government, without its consent, by an action *in rem*: *The Schooner Exchange* v. *M'Faddon,* 7 Cranch 116; *Berizzi Bros. Co.* v. *The Pesaro,* 271 U.S. 562; *The Parlement Belge,* L.R. 5 P. D. 197. However, where a foreign Government filed an action in a federal or State Court of the United States, it submitted to the jurisdiction of the Court. That submission included jurisdiction to hear a defence and, in a proper case, to grant affirmative relief against the Government, within the claim asserted, or concerning the property in controversy: *The Siren,* 7 Wall. 152; *The Gloria,* 286 Fed. 188; *People of Porto Rico* v. *Bonocio Ramos,* 232 U.S. 627; *The Newbattle, L.R.* 10 P. D. 33.

Furthermore, the claim of sovereign immunity could not be made by a private attorney without a showing of authority to represent the United States of Mexico in making the claim: *The Pesaro,* 255 U.S. 216; *Ex Parte Muir,* 254 U.S. 522; *Lyders* v. *Lund,* 32 F. (2d) 308; *The Gul Djemal,* 264 U.S. 90.

The lien asserted was not maritime in nature. Article 3, section 2, of the United States Constitution extended the judicial power of the United States to "all cases of admiralty and maritime jurisdiction." By statute, the jurisdiction of federal Courts was declared to extend to "all civil causes of admiralty and maritime jurisdiction, saving to suitors in all cases the right of a common law remedy where the common law is competent to give it." (42 U.S. Stat. L. 635.) Consequently the State Courts could enforce remedies *in personam* in maritime causes, but not remedies *in rem*: *Knapp, Stout & Co.* v. *McCaffrey* 177 U.S. 638, 644; *The Hine* v. *Trevor,* 4 Wall. 555. That a non-maritime lien, dependent upon possession, existed in favour of a shipwright who furnished labour and materials used in the repair of a vessel, was well settled. See *Pendergast* v. *The Kalorama,* 10 Wall. 204. By Section 3051 of the Civil Code, this common law lien had been written into the statute law of California. It followed, therefore, that the Courts of California had jurisdiction in this case.

It was not necessary to determine whether the defendant could take the boat in question from the possession of the Mexican Government on an execution issued on his judgment in the Court below. The decision in the case of *Dexter and*

Case No. 83 *Contd.*

Carpenter v. *Kunglig Jarnvagsstyrelsen*, 43 F. (2d) 705, was authority adverse to the validity of such a course of action. It was held in that case that the bringing of an action by a foreign Government or its agency in the Courts of the United States was a consent to the rendering of a judgment against it, but not a consent to a levy of execution upon its property in the United States in satisfaction of the judgment. Possibly the plaintiff's remedy was now limited to the surety, who was a resident of the United States.

[Report : 118 Cal. App. 21.]

Case No. 84

Jurisdiction—Immunity of Foreign States—Member-States of a Federal State—The United States of Brazil—The State of Céara—Loans Issued in France—Competence of French Courts.

CÉARA (STATE OF) *v.* D'ARCHER DE MONTGASCON.

France, Court of Appeal of Paris, First Chamber. June 11, 1931.

Court of Cassation, Civil Chamber, October 24, 1932.

THE FACTS.—The State of Céara, a part of the Federal Republic of Brazil, issued a loan in France in respect of which, by a decision in default of the Civil Tribunal of the Seine, dated February 24, 1927, it was ordered to pay 500 gold francs to M. d'Archer de Montgascon for every State bond presented for repayment. The State of Céara opposed this decision on the ground that, being a State, it was not subject to the jurisdiction of French Courts. The Court, in a second judgment dated July 11, 1929, declared itself to be competent on the ground that the State of Céara had "neither diplomatic representation nor the capacity to negotiate with foreign States" and that, "lacking, so far as foreign relations were concerned, a separate and independent political personality, it could not claim immunity from jurisdiction which is one of the privileges of sovereignty." The State of Céara appealed against this judgment to the Court of Appeal of Paris.

Held (by the Court of Appeal of Paris) : that the decision of the Tribunal of the Seine must be confirmed. "The State of Céara is only one of the former provinces which were united in the United States of Brazil ; in virtue of its autonomy it is an administrative unit with its own rights, which it exercises freely within the internal framework of the federation ; it has no international existence. The Federal State alone possesses the undivided sovereign power by reason of which it is entitled to immunity from jurisdiction.

[Report : *Gazette des Tribunaux*, July 19, 1931.]

On further appeal,

Held (by the Court of Cassation) : that the appeal of the State of Céara must be dismissed : jurisdictional immunity "in so far as its relations with other countries are concerned, can only be validly invoked by a State with a separate personality in international public law. A reference to the Brazilian Constitution shows that this is not the case with the State of Céara. Whatever its status within the sovereign Confederation of the United States of Brazil, of which it is a part, it has no diplomatic representation and no personality of its own in international political relations."

[Report : *Dalloz*, 1933, Part 1, p. 196, with a note by Gros ; *Gazette des Tribunaux*, December 7, 1932.]

NOTE.—French Courts have always held that the principle of immunity from jurisdiction cannot apply in cases involving public decentralised authorities, *e.g.*, member-States of a Federal State, provinces, departments, municipalities, etc. (Court of Appeal of Paris, July 19, 1894, *In re Ville de Genève*, a case concerning the succession of the Duke of Brunswick : *Dalloz*, 1894, Part 2, p. 513 ; Court of Cassation, July 1, 1895, the same case : *Sirey*, 1896, Part 1, p. 225 ; Court of Appeal of Colmar, June 27, 1928, *State of Céara* v. *Dorr* : *Clunet*, vol. 56 (1929), p. 1040, *Annual Digest*, 1927-1928, Case No. 21.) For a criticism of this doctrine see the note by Pillet in *Sirey*, 1896, Part 1, p. 226 ; Weiss, *Droit international privé*, vol. 5, p. 94 ; Niboyet, *Manuel de droit international privé* (2nd ed., 1928), No. 802 bis, and "Les immunités de juridiction en France des Etats étrangers engagés dans des transactions privées," in *R.G.*, vol. 43 (1936), pp. 525-545. See also the note by Gros on the conditions for securing immunity from jurisdiction. As to international private law on the matter, see the decision of the Court of Cassation, Civil Chamber, of May 31, 1932, *French State* v. *Veuve Carathédory*: *Dalloz*, 1933, Part 1, p. 169, with a note by Professor Crémieu.

Case No. 85 **Jurisdiction—Immunity from—Jurisdiction *ratione loci* and *ratione materiae*—Exemption of Foreign States from Provisions of Municipal Law as to Jurisdiction *ratione loci*—Attachment of Property of Foreign States—Jurisdiction Over Foreign States—Acts of a Public Character—Jurisdiction in Respect of Acts Covered by an Agreement Between a Government and a Private Party.**

BRASSEUR AND ASSOCIATES *v.* THE REPUBLIC OF GREECE.

Belgium, Civil Tribunal of Antwerp. July 8, 1932.

Court of Appeal of Brussels. May 24, 1933.

THE FACTS.—On October 27, 1890, the Turkish Government granted to the Deutsche Bank a concession for the construction and operation of a railway to link Salonica with Monastir. The concession stipulated that the Turkish Government should have the right to repurchase the railway at any time after October 28, 1920. On February 5, 1891, a private company, known as the Salonica-Monastir Railway Company, was formed to exploit the concession. In 1893 the Company floated a loan comprising 120,000 bonds. Some of these bonds were taken up by certain Belgian subjects, Mahieu, Bastin, Brasseur and Associates, the plaintiffs in the present case. In 1910 the shares of the Company became the property of the Compagnie de Chemins de Fer Orientaux. After the Balkan Wars, the railway lay almost entirely within the new frontiers of Greece. On October 17, 1925, an agreement was concluded between the Company and the Greek State whereby the latter agreed to indemnify the Company against the loss suffered down to the time of the agreement and to exercise the right of repurchase stipulated in the original concession ; at the same time the Greek State undertook to assure the service on the bonds previously issued, subject to the reservation of any rights acquired under the Peace Treaties. In return the Company renounced all its rights over the line in favour of the Greek State. On the same day the Greek State repurchased from the Compagnie de Chemins de Fer Orientaux almost all the shares in the Salonica-Monastir Railway Company held by the latter. On July 19, 1928, the Greek Government, in accordance with the provisions of the Treaty of Versailles for the sequestration of enemy property (Article 297 (*j*)), issued a Decree cancelling 80,000 of the bonds which it had taken over in 1925. On May 8, 1931, certain Belgian owners of some of these bonds (Mahieu, Bastin Brasseur and Associates), authorized by the

President of the Tribunal of Antwerp, carried out acts of attachment against two Belgian companies, "La Société Commerciale de Belgique" and "La Société Nationale de Crédit à l'Industrie," with which certain sums had been deposited to the account of the Greek State as security for the performance of contracts made by these companies with regard to public works.

The holders of the bonds of the Salonica-Monastir Railway Company then brought an action against the Greek State before the Tribunal of Antwerp in order: (1) to secure recognition of the legality of the acts of attachment with regard to the sums in the hands of the Belgian companies which, according to the plaintiffs, were owing to them by the Greek State on account of coupons, due for payment, of the bonds of the Salonica-Monastir Railway Company held by them; and (2) to obtain a decision against the defendant State for payment of the total sum due to the plaintiffs on the above-mentioned bonds. The Greek Government pleaded to the jurisdiction of the Court on grounds which are summarised below.

Held: (1) With regard to the contention that the Tribunal had no jurisdiction *ratione loci*; that the objection could not be admitted. The Greek plea was based on the contention that the obligation of which the plaintiffs sought to secure performance was neither contracted in Belgium nor to be performed there. It could be admitted that the normal basis for the competence of the Court was lacking. However, the Court had jurisdiction with regard to aliens under Article 53 of the Belgian Law on Competence of March 25, 1876, whereby, in the absence of another basis of jurisdiction as contemplated by that Law, the plaintiff had the right to bring his action before the Court in the place where he was domiciled or resident. The Court could not admit the plea of the defendant State that the Belgian Law in question referred only to private persons and not to foreign States.

2. With regard to the contention that the Tribunal had no jurisdiction *ratione materiæ*, the Tribunal rejected that contention inasmuch as the agreement of 1925 between the Company and the Greek Government had reference to compensation for losses suffered as the result of seizure during military operations and other similar acts of a public character. " While the seizure of the railway line during military operations and the decision to exercise the right to repurchase mentioned above were undoubtedly acts performed by the defendant State as a public person by virtue of the '*imperium*' which belongs

Case No. 85 ***Contd.*** to it within the limits of its political mission, the position was different with regard to the agreement, which gave rise to reciprocal rights and obligations for the settlement with the aforementioned Company of the financial consequences of the acts in question." It followed that the stipulation whereby the defendant State undertook the performance of the obligations in question was within the domain of private law according to which the foreign State became subject to the jurisdiction of the Belgian Courts.

On the other hand, the Tribunal had no jurisdiction inasmuch as the defendant State, while in general recognising the binding force of that stipulation, contended that in the present case it was released from any obligation because it had sequestrated as enemy property the bonds held by the plaintiffs, in accordance with the Treaty of Versailles. "This step, which in the opinion of the defendant State was based on Article 287 (*j*) of the Treaty of Versailles, was taken by a State in the exercise of its sovereignty .... The Tribunal could not, therefore, pass judgment on the legality of the principle underlying this step ... without exceeding its powers and attacking the independence enjoyed by the defendant State on the same terms as Belgium."

Furthermore, it was not possible to infer from the facts of the case that "the defendant State had explicitly or even impliedly renounced with regard to the said sums its rights under international custom which, with certain exceptions in the modern law of civilised States irrelevant to the present case, recognised the immunity of the property of a foreign State from measures of forceful execution such as attachment ... Changes in such matters could usefully be made only through agreements and the subsequent growth of an international jurisdiction. Moreover, countries with a large volume of international trade, for whom respect for international law was a vital interest, could afford less than other States to have recourse to unilateral action in this domain."

Held, accordingly: that the Tribunal was competent *ratione loci*, but that it had no jurisdiction by reason of the subject matter. The plaintiffs were ordered to pay the full costs of the action.

On appeal,

Held (by the Court of Appeal of Brussels): (*a*) *As to the Attachment of the Property of the Greek State*: that the decision of the Court below must be upheld in so far as it had declared the acts of attachment null and void. The Court held that the acts of attachment had been authorised and executed upon a foreign sovereign State which, like the Belgian State, could not be subjected to measures of forceful execution ; that the principles of public international law which recognised the equality of States made any other decision impossible ; that in this connection it was not permissible to attempt to make a distinction between public and private acts of the debtor State or to seek to determine whether the latter in serving its own interests had acted by reason of its public authority (*jure imperii*) or as a civil person (*jure gestionis*) ; that it could not accept the plea that, in the first stage of the proceedings, the attachment was merely a conservatory measure and became an act of forceful execution only after its legality had been upheld by a court ; that the principle of immunity applied also to conservatory attachment (see decision of the Court of Brussels of June 27, 1921 : *Belgique judiciare*, 1922, col. 210), and affected the process of attachment even in its first phase, which was in fact the beginning of the course of forceful execution ; that the claim of the Greek Republic to immunity from acts of execution was justified, and the plaintiffs' plea that in the present case the Greek State had renounced the right of immunity assured to it by international custom, was inadmissible ; that, while a foreign State might consent to the performance of an act of attachment against it by its creditor in a specific case, such consent could not be presumed, although it might be given tacitly ; and that the two facts from which the plaintiffs sought to deduce the consent of the Greek State were inconclusive for the purpose. For these reasons the Court upheld the decision of the Court of first instance that the acts of attachment were null and void.

(*b*) *Jurisdiction on the Merits.*—(i) The Court confirmed the decision of the Court below, declining to assume jurisdiction inasmuch as the plaintiffs (the holders of the bonds) contended that the refusal of the Greek State to pay to them the sums claimed should be declared invalid on the ground that the governmental decrees of June 25 and July 19, 1928, on which Greece relied, were illegal.

The Court of Appeal held "that the Greek State was immune from Belgian jurisdiction in respect of governmental acts performed by it in its capacity as a public authority acting *jure imperii;* that the Cabinet of the Greek Republic approved, on June 25, 1928, the cancellation of the bonds of the Salonica-Monastir Railway 3 per cent Loan of 1893 which were in th

Case No. 85 *Contd.*

possession of Germans in 1917; that on June 19, 1928, the Greek Minister of Finance issued a decree, in virtue of the Greek Law No. 1073 of 1917 and of the provisions of the Treaty of Versailles, cancelling the bonds of the Loan of the Salonica-Monastir Railway Company in the possession of Germans at the outbreak of or during the World War; that the above-mentioned decree stated that, according to the information at the disposal of the Public Accounts Office of Greece, there were about 80,000 of these bonds; that the decree had the character of a political act and the Belgian Courts were not competent to enquire into its legality; that the plaintiffs' plea that the Court, before declaring its incompetence, should have examined the ministerial decree to discover whether it was in conformity with the provisions of the Treaty of Versailles upon which it was based, could not be admitted; and that the Belgian Courts were not competent to hear claims arising out of the political action of a foreign Government or to interfere by such methods in the exercise of its sovereignty (Court of Cassation, January 9, 1911: *Pasicrisie*, 1911, 178)."

(ii) On the other hand, the Court of Appeal amended the decision of the Court below in so far as the plaintiffs asserted that the refusal of the Greek State to pay the sums claimed should be declared invalid on the ground that their bonds were not amongst the 80,000 bonds cancelled by the ministerial decree of July 19, 1928. The Court held that it was competent to hear the action in this limited form, but before giving its decision requested the parties to submit further arguments on the following points:

a. Was the burden of proof on the Greek State to show that the bonds of the plaintiffs were amongst the 80,000 cancelled bonds or upon the plaintiffs to show that their bonds were not amongst the cancelled block?

b. How could either of the parties prove its allegation?

So far as these aspects of the matter were concerned, the plaintiffs no longer questioned the legality of the two decrees invoked by the Greek State, but confined themselves to maintaining that their bonds did not fall within the scope of these measures. The action of the Greek State in arguing that the plaintiffs' claim was unfounded because their bonds were amongst the 80,000 cancelled bonds, was not that of a political authority, but was merely the expression of a view as to the application of a general order to a particular case and as to the existence or non-existence of a debt for which it was liable *jure gestionis*. The Greek State "was thereby acting like any private person who was called upon to pay a sum claimed in virtue of a bond entitling the holder to payment and who considered that he was under no obligation to pay the sum and defended the action brought against him."

[Report: *Clunet*, 59 (1932), p. 1088; *Pasicrisie*, 1933, II. p. 197.]

Jurisdiction—Immunity from—Foreign States—Private Activities of Foreign States—Russian Trade Delegation in Italy. **Case No. 86**

SLOMNITZKY *v.* TRADE DELEGATION OF THE U.S.S.R. IN ITALY.

Italy, Court of Appeal of Milan. January 23, 1932.

THE FACTS.—Slomnitzky, a Russian subject, was engaged on December 15, 1925, as an employee of the Soviet Trade Delegation in Milan. On February 24, 1926, he was dismissed without notice and without compensation. He applied to the Italian Courts for an order against the Soviet Delegation for payment of compensation in lieu of notice and on account of loss of seniority.

Held: that the application must be granted. The Court adhered to the opinion prevailing in Italy according to which foreign States could be subjected to Italian jurisdiction in matters concerning their activities within the sphere of private law. The Court found that the activity of the Soviet Trade Delegation was of that nature. It based its decision on the following grounds:

1. With regard to the principle that a foreign State, in its private law activities, is subject to the Italian jurisdiction, the Court said: "When a State acts in the territory of another State as a person of public law, as an international person, in short, as a sovereign entity, it is agreed that it cannot be subjected to the jurisdiction of the State whose hospitality it enjoys. The well-known maxim *par in parem non habet jurisdictionem* applies. It is open to question, however, whether a corporation in the domain of public law can be held to exist in the case of a State performing acts in the territory of another State . . . which are indistinguishable from those carried on by any physical or juridical person, national or foreign. . . . Italian and Belgian jurisprudence, which has always denied almost completely the immunity of a foreign State summoned before the Courts in respect of acts done by it

Case No. 86 *Contd.* as a subject of private law, has now been joined by that of other countries such as Roumania, Egypt, Sweden, Switzerland and France."

2. With regard to the nature of the activity carried on by the Trade Delegation of the U.S.S.R., the Court said: "A distinction of the first importance must be made between acts which imply, and derive from, the exercise of the sovereign power, and those which derive from the exercise of private powers. . . . By the Treaty of February 7, 1924, Italy recognised that the Russian Government considers foreign trade to be a State undertaking, and agreed by Article 3 to facilitate the exercise of that function, but she did not on her part thereby endow the undertaking of trade with the dignity and quality of sovereignty. Therefore, in the opinion of this Court, it follows that Italy is in no way bound by that Treaty to grant to the Russian Trade Delegation immunity from jurisdiction in respect of acts, such as the carrying on of trade, done by it in the sphere of private law in this country."

3. As to the character of the Russian Trade Delegation, the Court said: "There is no doubt that, under the terms of the above-mentioned Article 3, it forms an integral part of the plenipotentiary delegation which enjoys the rights of inviolability and the other privileges and exemptions granted to members of the diplomatic missions, including the right to use a cipher. But the immunity granted by the Treaty to the personnel of the Trade Delegation and to the members of the Council of the Delegation is one matter, while the immunity from jurisdiction of that Delegation in respect of acts which it may do in Italy and which may be considered as belonging to the realm of private law . . . is another matter."

[Report: *Rivista italiana di diritto internazionale privato e processuale*, 1932, p. 64.]

Case No. 87 **Jurisdiction—Immunity from—Foreign States—Action against the U.S.S.R.—International Public Loans.**

DE FROE *v.* THE RUSSIAN STATE, NOW STYLED "THE UNION OF SOVIET SOCIALIST REPUBLICS."

Holland, District Court of Amsterdam. January 11, 1932.

THE FACTS—The plaintiff, as administrator of an estate, brought an action against the Russian State, now "The Union of Soviet Socialist Republics," claiming the principal and interest of a debenture of the Russian consolidated public loan of 1880, 6th issue. The bond was drawn for repayment in May 1917, and therefore before the Russian revolution of 1917. The defendant State did not appear.

Held : that the Court had no jurisdiction. "Article 13 (*a*) of the Law of May 15, 1829, embodying general provisions concerning legislation, supplemented in 1917,[1] explicitly enacts that the jurisdiction of the Courts is restricted by the exceptions recognised by the Law of Nations. Although there is no unanimity on the question whether, in principle, a sovereign State may be subjected against its will to the jurisdiction of a tribunal of another State for *acta gestionis*,[2] it is nevertheless almost universally taken for granted, though on different grounds, that no such subjection is possible in the case of a claim in regard to State loans raised by public subscription."

[Report : *Weekblad van het Recht*, No. 12453, with comment by J. H. W. Verzijl.]

NOTE.—This decision is in accordance with the resolution of the Institut de droit international of 1891 (Hamburg session), contained in Article 5 of the *Projet de règlement international sur la compétence des tribunaux dans les procès contre les Etats souverains ou chefs d'Etat étrangers* : "Ne sont pas recevables . . . les actions concernant les dettes de l'Etat étranger contractées par souscription publique," and with the judgment of the Brussels Court of Appeal of November 22, 1907 (*Clunet*, 35 (1908), p. 210). See also Weiss, "Compétence ou incompétence des tribunaux à l'égard des Etats étrangers," in *Recueil des cours de l'Académie de droit international*, 1 (1923), pp. 289 *et seq.* ; Fischer Williams, "Le droit international et les obligations financières qui naissent d'un contrat," *ibid.*, pp. 521 *et seq.* ; Bosch, *De Staatsschulden in het internationaal recht* (1929), pp. 94 *et seq.*

The question whether or not foreign States may be sued in Dutch Courts in respect of *acta gestionis* has not yet been definitely settled. For an answer in the affirmative see : District Court of Amsterdam, July 14, 1921 (*Nederlandsche Jurisprudentie*, 1921, p. 849) ; in the negative : District Court of Dordrecht, July 11, 1923 (*Weekblad van het Recht*, No. 11088 ; *Nederlandsche Jurisprudentie*, 1924, p. 344 ; *Annual Digest*, 1923-1924, Case No. 69 ; *Bulletin de l'Institut Intermédiaire International*, vol. X, pp. 2 *et seq.*, with comment by Dr. G. van Slooten Azn).

[1] See concerning this Law *Annual Digest*, 1919-1922, Case No. 84.

[2] Acts of a private law nature.

Case No. 88 **Jurisdiction—Immunity from—Foreign State Undertakings—Criteria of a State Undertaking—Administration of the Undertaking by the Minister of Transport—Profit and Loss Figures in the State Budget.**

POLISH STATE RAILWAYS CASE.

Danzig, County Court (*Landgericht*). *November* 10, 1931.

THE FACTS.—This was an action for damages against the undertaking known as "Polish State Railways," arising out of a transport accident between the stations of Wreschen and Pelplin (both in Poland). The defendants (the undertaking) contended that the Danzig Court had no jurisdiction on the ground that it was a State enterprise and therefore entitled to immunity from the jurisdiction of Danzig Courts. The plaintiffs maintained that in view of the changes in the constitution of the company, the details of which are conveniently reproduced below, the "Polish State Railways" ceased to be an undertaking of a foreign State.

Held: for the defendants. The Court was bound to apply the accepted rule of international law according to which "foreign States are exempt from the jurisdiction of a national Court except in cases concerning property situated in the national territory and in cases of voluntary submission to jurisdiction." It was true that in pursuance of a decree of the President of the Polish State of September 24, 1926, the Polish State railways had been transformed into an undertaking known as "Polish State Railways." But the character of the Polish State railways had not thereby been affected, and they could not be regarded as a private company. They remained a "*statio fisci*." This followed from their legal character, as established by the presidential decree of September 24, 1926. According to this decree the "Polish State Railways" had become an independent company for the administration of the State railways, registered in the Companies' Register and endowed with legal personality. The funds of the State railways had been transferred in trust to the new enterprise and had become a separate fund. The undertaking had its own annual budget and had to provide for its own expenditure. However, in virtue of Article 12, paragraph 4, of the decree, the net profit or the net deficit appeared in the State budget, and under Article 16, paragraph 1, of the same decree the Minister of Transport directly administered the undertaking. It appeared from these two clauses that the undertaking,

"The Polish State Railways," was run by the State on its own account. For this reason the undertaking preserved its character as a "*statio fisci.*" The purely formal transformation did not affect its legal status.

[Report: *Danziger Juristische Monatsschrift*, vol. XI (1932), p. 63.]

States—Immunity from Jurisdiction—Receiving Orders with Regard to Funds in Which a Foreign State Has a Legal Interest. **Case No. 89**

GALLOPIN *v.* WINSOR *ET AL.*

United States, Supreme Court of New York, Appellate Division. July 1931.

(Finch, P.J.; McAvoy, Martin, O'Malley, Sherman, JJ.).

THE FACTS.—This was an appeal from an order of the Supreme Court granting the plaintiff's motion for appointment of receivers and for an injunction. It appeared that the Government of Mexico was a necessary party in interest in the fund proposed to be impounded by the receiving order.

Held: that the order should be reversed. Since Mexico was a sovereign State and could not be made a party without its consent, there was no jurisdiction to appoint receivers of its funds or to issue an injunction against the disposition thereof.

[Report: 234 App. Div. 601.]

Jurisdiction—Foreign States—Acts of a Public Law and Private Law Nature—Consular Premises.

See Case No. 187 (*Consular Premises (Greece) Case*).

Immunity from Jurisdiction—Unrecognised Governments—Property of—The Denikin Government in Russia in 1920.

See Case No. 25 (*Voevodine* v. *Government of the Commander-in-Chief of the Armed Forces in the South of Russia*).

(*d*) Foreign Armed Forces.

Case No. 90 **Extraterritoriality of Armed Forces—British Forces in Egypt—Customary International Law.**

Amrane *v.* John.

Egypt, Civil Tribunal of Alexandria. January 14, 1932.

The Facts.—In June 1929 a member of a British military force in Egypt ran over the plaintiff and caused her injuries in respect of which she presented a claim to the British Commander-in-Chief. By a letter of January 1930 she was informed that a military court had enquired into the matter and had decided that the chauffeur of the vehicle in question had not been to blame, and that no compensation would be paid. The plaintiff then brought this action against Colonel E. S. John, the British Commander.

Held : that the action failed because : (1) the accident was caused by a British soldier leading a "camion militaire," but it was not he, but the Commander, who was being sued, and the latter was, in effect, a representative of the British Government ; (2) although there was no written agreement between Egypt and Great Britain regulating the immunity of troops from local jurisdiction,[1] yet international law recognised such immunity. "It is not necessary here to consider whether in principle a distinction may be drawn between actions arising out of private acts and those arising out of the exercise of public authority, because, in the present case, it is not disputed that the act in question falls into the latter category."

[Report : *Gazette des Tribunaux Mixtes d'Egypte*, XXIV (1933-1934), p. 108.]

[1] See now the Convention annexed to the Anglo-Egyptian Treaty of August 1936 : *U.K. Treaty Series*, No. 6 (1937), Cmd. 5360, p. 23.

II.—Personal

i.—Over Subjects in respect of Crimes Committed Abroad.

Jurisdiction—Over Nationals in Respect of Crimes Committed Abroad—The Law of Mexico.

See *In re Espiridón Ozuna*, decided by the Mexican Supreme Court on October 23, 1930: 30 *Semanario Judicial* (5th ep.), 1088.

ii.—Over Nationals Abroad or on the High Seas and their Property Situated Abroad.

Jurisdiction—Territorial Principle—Jurisdiction Over Nationals With Regard to Crimes Committed on National Vessel Within Territorial Limits of a Foreign State—Territoriality of Ships—Jurisdiction Over Foreign Vessels in National Ports. **Case No. 91**

UNITED STATES *v.* FLORES.

United States, Supreme Court. April 10, 1933.

(Hughes, C.J.; Van Devanter, McReynolds, Brandeis, Sutherland, Butler, Stone, Roberts, Cardozo, JJ.)

THE FACTS.—This was a criminal prosecution brought in the United States District Court against the defendant, an American citizen, on the charge of having committed murder aboard an American ship in foreign territorial waters. At the time of the offence charged the ship was at anchor in the Port of Matadi, which is subject to Belgian sovereignty, and which lies two hundred and fifty miles inland from the mouth of the Congo River. The ship was unloading, being attached to the shore by cables.

Sections 273 and 275 of the United States Criminal Code define murder and fix the punishment. Section 272 makes punishable offences defined by other Sections of the Criminal Code, *inter alia*, "when committed upon the high seas, or on any other waters within the admiralty and maritime jurisdiction of the United States and out of the jurisdiction of any particular

Case No. 91 Contd.

state . . . on board any vessel belonging in whole or in part to the United States or any citizen thereof."

Section 8 of Article I of the United States Constitution grants to Congress the power "to define and punish piracies and felonies committed on the high seas, and offenses against the law of nations." Section 2 of Article III provides that the judicial power of the United States shall extend "to all cases of admiralty and maritime jurisdiction." The District Court sustained a demurrer to the indictment on the ground that the Court was without jurisdiction to try the offence charged: *United States* v. *Flores*, 3 Fed. Supp. 134. On appeal to the United States Supreme Court,

Held (*per* Stone, J.): that the judgment must be reversed. After reviewing the history of the adoption of the Constitution, the Court concluded that Section 8 of Article I of the Constitution was not intended to be a limitation on the legislative and judicial power granted by Section 2 of Article III. To construe the former clause as a limitation on the latter would be to deny the power to define and punish crimes of less gravity than felonies committed on vessels of the United States while on the high seas and crimes of every grade when committed on them in foreign territorial waters.

The grant of admiralty jurisdiction contained in Section 2 of Article III must be construed to extend to offences committed aboard an American vessel in foreign territorial waters. *United States* v. *Rodgers*, 150 U.S. 249, 265, is authority for this proposition. British Courts have consistently held that jurisdiction follows British ships into the territorial jurisdiction of foreign sovereigns: *Queen* v. *Carr & Wilson*, 10 Q. B. D. 76; *Queen* v. *Anderson*, L.R. 1 Crown Cases Reversed 161; *Rex* v. *Allen*, 1 Moody C. C. 494. The jurisdiction was not affected by the fact that at the time of the offence the ship was at a point remote from the sea. *United States* v. *Rodgers*, *supra*, applies to this point also, for there the offence was committed in a foreign territorial jurisdiction upon water beyond the ebb and flow of the tide.

It was argued that Section 272 of the Criminal Code, punishing offences on United States vessels "when committed within the admiralty and maritime jurisdiction of the United States," did not extend to offences committed in foreign territorial waters. Although criminal statutes of the United States were not by implication given an extraterritorial effect, that principle was not applicable to a merchant vessel, which for purposes of jurisdiction of the Courts of its own country must be deemed to be a part of the territory of that sovereignty and not to lose that character in foreign waters.

A related question, not presented here, may arise when jurisdiction over an offence committed on a foreign vessel is asserted by the State in whose waters it was lying at the time of its commission. The position of the United States has been that at least in the case of major crimes, affecting the peace and tranquility of the port, the jurisdiction asserted by the sovereign of the port must prevail over the vessel: *Wildenhus's Case*, 120 U.S. 1. This doctrine did not impinge upon the doctrine that the United States may define and punish offences committed by its own citizens on its own vessels while in foreign waters where the local sovereign has not asserted its jurisdiction.

[Report: 289 U.S. 137; *A.J.*, XXVII (1933), p. 569.][1]

Jurisdiction—Over Nationals Abroad—Consular Functions With Regard to Nationals Abroad—How Far Dependent Upon Express Treaty Provisions. **Case No. 92**

BLACKMER *v.* UNITED STATES.

United States, Supreme Court. February 15, 1932.

(Hughes, C.J.; Van Devanter, McReynolds, Brandeis, Sutherland, Butler, Stone, JJ.)

THE FACTS.—Harry M. Blackmer, a citizen of the United States resident in Paris, France, was adjudged guilty of contempt of the Supreme Court of the District of Columbia for failure to respond to two subpœnas, served upon him in France, requiring him to appear as a witness on behalf of the United States at a criminal trial in that Court. The hearing of the contempt charge was held in the absence of the defendant, and fines were imposed to be satisfied out of property of Blackmer which had been seized by order of the Court. The subpœnas were issued and served, and the proceedings to punish for contempt were taken, under the provisions of the Act of July 3, 1926 (44 U.S. Stat. L. 835). That Act provided that whenever the attendance at the trial of a criminal case of a witness abroad, who is a citizen of the United States or domiciled therein, is desired by the United States, the judge of the Court in which the action is pending may order a subpœna to be issued, to be addressed to a consul of the United States and to be

[1] See *H.L.R.*, 46 (1932-1933), p. 1338; *Virginia Law Review*, vol. XIX, p. 873.

Case No. 92 *Contd.*

served by him personally upon the witness with a tender of travelling expenses. Upon proof of such service and default, the Court could make an order requiring the witness to show cause why he should not be punished for contempt, and the witness's property could be seized and held to satisfy a judgment. Provision was made for personal service of the order. If the witness was adjudged guilty of contempt, a fine could be imposed.

Blackmer contended that the statute violated the due process clause of the Fifth Amendment to the United States Constitution, on the grounds, *inter alia*, that: (1) the Act did not provide a valid method of acquiring judicial jurisdiction to render a personal judgment against the defendant and judgment against his property; (2) Congress had no power to authorise United States consuls to serve process except as permitted by treaty. On *certiorari* to the Supreme Court,

Held: that the decrees must be affirmed. (1) By virtue of the obligations of citizenship, the United States retained its authority over the petitioner, and he was bound by its laws, made applicable to him in a foreign country: *Cook* v. *Tait*, 265 U.S. 47, 54, 56; *United States* v. *Bowman*, 260 U.S. 94, 102. The United States possessed the power, inherent in sovereignty, to require the return to the United States of a citizen resident abroad, whenever the public interest required it, and to penalise him in case of refusal. Compare *Bartue and the Duchess of Suffolk's Case*, 2 Dyer's Rep. 176b; *Knowles* v. *Luce*, Moore 109. With regard to such an exercise of authority there was no question of international law, but solely a question of the purpose of the municipal law which established the duties of the citizen in relation to his own government.

(2) "The question of the validity of the provision for actual service of the subpœna in a foreign country is one that arises solely between the Government of the United States and the citizen. The mere giving of such a notice to the citizen in the foreign country of the requirement of his government that he shall return is in no sense an invasion of any right of the foreign government; and the citizen has no standing to invoke any such supposed right. While consular privileges in foreign countries are the appropriate subjects of treaties,[1] it does not follow that every act of a consul, as, *e.g.*, in communicating with citizens of his own country, must be predicated upon a special provision

"[1] Cf. Dainese *v.* Hale, 91 U.S. 13, 15, 16; In re Ross, 140 U.S. 453, 462, 463. See, also, U.S.C., Tit. 22, secs. 71 *et seq.*; Hyde, *op. cit.*, [*International Law*, vol. I] sec. 488, pp. 828-832."

of a treaty. The intercourse of friendly nations, permitting travel and residence of the citizens of each in the territory of the other, presupposes and facilitates such communications. In selecting the consul for the service of the subpœna, the Congress merely prescribed a method deemed to assure the desired result but in no sense essential. The consul was not directed to perform any function involving consular privileges or depending upon any treaty relating to them, but simply to act as any designated person might act for the Government in conveying to the citizen the actual notice of the requirement of his attendance. The point raised by the petitioner with respect to the provision for the service of the subpœna abroad is without merit."

[Report: 284 U.S. 421; *A.J.*, XXVI (1932), p. 611.]

NOTE.—See also *A.J.*, XXV (1931), p. 723; *ibid.*, XXVI (1932), p. 351; *M.L.R.*, XXX (1931-1932), pp. 137, 968.

Jurisdiction—Applicability of National Statutes—Ships in Foreign Coastal Waters. **Case No. 93**

POSTAL PACKETS (BRAUNSCHWEIG) CASE.

Germany, Court of Appeal of Braunschweig. June 27, 1932.

THE FACTS.—The plaintiff had posted two packets at the German post office at Braunschweig (Germany) for carriage to Singapore. The post office delivered them to the North-German Lloyd, who carried them on the SS. *Elberfeld*. When off the Spanish coast, but within Spanish territorial waters, the ship went aground, and both ship and cargo, including the two packets, were lost. The plaintiff sued the German post office for compensation. He based his claim on the relevant German Statute passed in 1871 (the Reich Post Act).

Held: that the action must be dismissed. The packets were lost at a place which, according to constitutional and international law, was within the jurisdiction of Spain. It was immaterial that the packets were carried on a German ship. This would have been relevant had the ship been on the high seas when the accident occurred; for in such a case a ship is by international law deemed to be part of the State to which it belongs. According to the principle of territoriality, which governed also German law, only such provisions of German law could be taken into consideration with regard to the defendants' liability as contemplated an extraterritorial application, or in

Case No. 93 *Contd.* regard to which such application was provided for by constitutional or international law. This was not the case with regard to the Statute of 1871.

[Report: *Rechtsprechung auf dem Gebiete des Internationalen Privatrechts*, 1932, No. 54.]

B.—EXTRATERRITORIAL JURISDICTION

I.—Consular Jurisdiction. Régime of Capitulations. Mixed Courts. Jurisdiction and Organisation

Case No. 94 **Jurisdiction of Mixed Tribunals—Treaties as Part of Public Order—Nullity of Clauses in Contracts Derogating from Competence of Mixed Jurisdictions.**

ISCAKI *v.* MUTUAL LIFE INSURANCE COMPANY OF NEW YORK.

DE BERLIN *v.* HOIRS FABIO EMINENTE.

J. SHALLAM & SONS AND OTHERS *v.* COMPAGNIE UNIVERSELLE DU CANAL DE SUEZ.

Egypt, Mixed Court of Appeal of Alexandria.

May 25 *and June* 18, 1931.

THE FACTS.—These cases concerned several companies who, in the first two cases, were being sued in respect of contracts of life insurance made, or to be carried out, in Egypt, and in the third case, in respect of dividends payable by the company. In all three cases the jurisdiction of the mixed tribunals was disputed on grounds stated below.

Held, in all three cases: that the mixed tribunals were competent notwithstanding, with regard to the first two cases, express clauses in the contracts withdrawing them from the jurisdiction of the mixed tribunals in favour of a foreign tribunal; and notwithstanding, with regard to the third case, an express clause in the company's charter giving jurisdiction, in respect of internal disputes, to a foreign arbitral tribunal. It made no difference, with regard to the first two cases, that the companies involved had their headquarters abroad, or even, with regard to one, had no agency or representation in Egypt. The principles governing the competence of the mixed tribunals were laid down by international treaty and formed part of the régime of public order. Consequently any attempt to confer jurisdiction on a foreign tribunal by such clauses must necessarily fail, and the clauses must be declared null and void.

[Report: *Clunet*, 59 (1932), p. 202; *Gazette des Tribunaux Mixtes d'Egypte*, XXIII (1932-1933), pp. 231 and 302.]

NOTE.—As to earlier proceedings in the same matter in January 1931, see *ibid.*, XXI (1930-1931), p. 91. And see, particularly, the conclusions of the Procureur-General, *ibid.*, XXIII (1932-1933), pp. 231-237, who at p. 233 submits the argument that "international treaties bind the individual subjects of the governments parties to them, and these treaties would be altogether illusory if these individuals could, so to speak, make special capitulations having the result of maintaining a right of recourse to their own national tribunals, a right already renounced by their governments on their behalf." To the same effect, on different facts, see a decision of the same Court, given on March 3, 1931: *ibid.*, XXIV (1933-1934), p. 128.

Rights of Foreigners in Egypt—Applicability of Press Laws—Police Measures—Consent of Capitulatory Powers. **Case No. 95**

PROTOPAPAS *v.* MINISTRY OF FINANCE AND OF THE INTERIOR.

Egypt, Civil Tribunal of Cairo. December 21, 1931.

THE FACTS.—This was an action by a foreigner for damages caused by the suppression of a newspaper, owned by him, in virtue of a law which, he contended, did not apply to him. It was argued by the Administration that the act involved was a police measure falling within the Minister's discretion, and outside judicial review.

Held: that by the Laws of 1889 and 1911 police regulations did not apply to foreigners unless the prior approval of the Court of Appeal was obtained, and the consent of the Capitulatory Powers. Neither had been obtained in the present case, and the action must therefore succeed.

[Report: *Gazette des Tribunaux Mixtes d'Egypte*, XXII (1931-1932), p. 351.]

NOTE.—Monopoly services operated by the State, *e.g.*, telephones, do not fall within this rule, and impositions made in pursuance of such powers do not require such assents: decision of the Civil Tribunal of Cairo of April 25, 1932, *ibid.*, p. 357. There is a power of judicial review over administrative acts violating the rights of foreigners: *ibid.*, pp. 361-363.

Case No. 96

Jurisdiction of Mixed Tribunals—As Constituting Part of Public Order—Consular Certificates as Proof of Nationality.

VIEROS *v.* SALEH AND OTHERS.

Egypt, Mixed Court of Appeal of Alexandria. April 21, 1932.

THE FACTS.—This was an appeal from a judgment of the Civil Tribunal of Mansourah declaring that a judgment obtained by the appellant against Saleh in a local tribunal was ineffective, and setting it aside on the ground that Saleh was an Italian citizen. A certificate was produced showing that Saleh was registered at the Italian Consulate as one born and domiciled at Musarata, but the appellant submitted that this certificate was not conclusive and that proof of regular registration, in accordance with the Italo-Egyptian Agreement of 1923, ought be given. The appellant further argued that Saleh had not raised the plea of incompetence before the local tribunal.

Held : that the appeal must be dismissed. The incompetence of local courts in respect of foreigners was a principle of public order. Consequently, the fact that a foreigner allowed himself to be sued in a local court and defended himself there without protest, did not validate the judgment. With regard to proof of Saleh's nationality, the principle must be applied that consular certificates which were not contested by the local authorities nor contradicted by other evidence before the Court, were sufficient proof of nationality.

[Report : *Clunet*, 60 (1933), p. 448 ; *Gazette des Tribunaux Mixtes d'Egypte*, XXIV (1933-1934), p. 75.]

NOTE.—To the same effect, on proof of nationality, see the decision of May 26, 1932, in *Esther Zagdoun* v. *Marie Zagdoun and Others* : *Clunet*, 60 (1933), p. 202 ; *Gazette des Tribunaux Mixtes d'Egypte*, XXIV (1933-1934), p. 153.

Capitulations—Mixed Tribunals of Egypt—Whether International Tribunals—Relation to Diplomatic Protection—Responsibility of Egypt for Acts of Mixed Tribunals—Criminal Proceedings by Native Courts Against Persons Acquiring the Nationality of the Capitulatory Power Since the Beginning of the Proceedings.

See Case No. 98 (*Salem Case : United States and Egypt*).

C.—HIGH SEAS

II.—Jurisdiction on the High Seas

i.—For Ensuring the Safety of Traffic. Collisions. Salvage.

Jurisdiction—High Seas—Collision of Ships of Different Nationalities—Cause and Effect of the Offence—Territoriality of Ships. **Case No. 97**

AFRICAN STEAMSHIP CO. (def.) *v.* OLDENBURG-PORTUGIESCHE DAMPFSCHIFFS-REEDEREI (pl.).

Germany, Supreme Court for Civil Matters. November 12, 1932.

THE FACTS.—This was an action for damages brought by a German shipowner against an English company after their ships had collided on the high seas through the fault of the defendants' vessel. The defendants contended that English law governed the case, and that, under that law, their liability was limited to a certain amount. The Court below found for the plaintiff.

Held (by the Supreme Court): that the defendants' appeal must be dismissed. Although the error which caused the collision had been made on board the defendants' vessel, the tort, which was the basis of the claim for damages, was not completed until the very moment of the actual collision. Accordingly it was also committed on board the German ship. Where a tort is committed in such a manner that the tortfeasor's action "takes place in *one* territory, but the damage is sustained in *another* territory, then *both* places are, in law, places where the tort has been committed. The same applies to a collision on the high seas between ships of different nationalities. Such ships are regarded as parts of their home State. Any act done on board such vessels is governed by the same rules as obtain in respect of acts done in the actual territory of the home State. If, as happened in the present case, the negligent acts causing the collision took place on board the British vessel, but the damage was suffered on board the German one, then both ships must be regarded as being *loci delicti commissi*. The tort was thus committed in both English and German territory." In such circumstances the law of both countries applied to the case, and the plaintiffs

Case No. 97 Contd. were entitled to base their claim on German law. The Court declined to follow the decision of the Reichsgericht, printed in *Entscheidungen des Reichsgerichts in Zivilsachen*, vol. 74, p. 46, according to which the nationality of the ship at fault was alone material.

[Report: *Entscheidungen des Reichsgerichts in Zivilsachen*, vol. 138, p. 243.[1]]

[1] The decision of the Court of Appeal, the *Oberlandesgericht* of Hamburg, of February 19, 1932, is reported in *Rechtsprechung auf dem Gebiete des Internationalen Privatrechts*, 1932, No. 59.

PART V

STATE RESPONSIBILITY

B.—NATURE AND KINDS OF STATE RESPONSIBILITY

I.—In General. Absolute Responsibility and Responsibility Based on Fault

State Responsibility—In General—Effect of Limitation of Sovereignty—Responsibility of Egypt for Acts of Mixed Courts.

See Case No. 98 (*Salem Case : United States and Egypt*).

State Responsibility—Legal Consequences of—Breach of "Unilateral" or "Unequal" Treaties.

See Case No. 98 (*Salem Case : United States and Egypt*).

State Responsibility—Consequences of—Action in National Emergency—Whether Relieving of Duty of Compensation.

See Case No. 229 (*Royal Holland Lloyd* v. *United States* (*d*)).

State Responsibility—In General—Abuse of Rights.

See Case No. 202 (*Case of the Free Zones of Upper Savoy and the District of Gex,* Note II.)

State Responsibility—In General—Fault as a Condition of Liability—Error in Judgment.

See Case No. 229 (*Royal Holland Lloyd* v. *United States* (*b*)).

VI.—For Wrongs Unconnected with Contractual Obligations

i.—Acts and Omissions of State Organs and Officials.

(*a*) Denial of Justice. Exhaustion of Legal Remedies.

Case No. 98 **State Responsibility—Denial of Justice—State Responsibility and Limitations of Sovereignty—Responsibility of Egypt for the Mixed Courts—Nationality of Claims—Right of Espousal—Interpretation of Arbitration Agreement—Grammatical and Historical Interpretation—Preparatory Work—Examination of Right of Citizenship by the Tribunal —Question of Fraud—Naturalisation and Loss of Original Nationality—Principal of Effective Nationality—Right of a State to Invoke Claimant's Nationality of a Third State as a Bar to Proceedings—Exhaustion of Legal Remedies—Competence of Arbitral Tribunals to Enquire into the Question—Diplomatic Protection and Jurisdiction of Mixed Courts—Compensation for Breach of a "Unilateral" Treaty—Denial of Justice Through Alleged Faulty Judicial Procedure—Criminal Proceedings by Native Courts Against Persons Who Have Acquired the Nationality of a Capitulatory Power Since the Beginning of the Proceedings—Effect of Loss of Diplomatic Protection—Denial of Justice as the Result of Absence of Impartiality—Evidence—Admissibility of Sworn Affidavits.**

Salem Case.

United States and Egypt.

(Simons, Nielsen, Badawi Pasha.)

June 8, 1932.

The Facts.—This was a claim by the United States against Egypt on behalf of George J. Salem, who was born in Egypt and who subsequently became an American citizen by naturalisation. Salem was born in 1883 of a father of Persian nationality. In 1903 he went to the United States, and in 1908 became an American citizen. In 1909 he returned to Egypt. He returned to the United States in 1911 in order to have his passport renewed and to preserve his rights as an American citizen. He then again returned to Egypt. In 1913 he was implicated in criminal proceedings, and in reply to an enquiry by the

Egyptian authorities the State Department at Washington stated that a presumption of expatriation under the Act of 1907 had arisen against Salem and that he was no longer an American citizen. Subsequently, however, the Department of State reversed its decision and informed the Egyptian Government accordingly. In 1914 Salem again went to the United States in order to have his passport renewed, and then once more returned to Egypt. Owing to the War he could not return to the United States, and when in 1915 and 1917 he was involved once more in criminal proceedings, the American Agent informed the Egyptian Government that Salem was not registered at the Agency as an American citizen and that he was not entitled to American protection. In 1918 Salem was once more prosecuted for forgery in connection with the inheritance from his father, who died a Persian subject. In this connection he deposited certain documents with the prosecuting authorities. In 1919 Salem obtained from the Egyptian authorities a passport to enable him to go to England to patent an invention. He travelled through Paris and there obtained an American Emergency Passport. When once more in the United States he was successful in obtaining a regular American passport. He then applied for discontinuance of the judicial proceedings by the Egyptian authorities on the ground that he was an American citizen. In 1921 the Egyptian Court of Appeal finally declared that it had no jurisdiction. At the same time Salem made unsuccessful attempts to recover from the Egyptian authorities the documents which he had deposited with them and which, in his view, showed his innocence. In 1922 the American Consul instituted an investigation against Salem in connection with the criminal charge pending against him. The result of the investigation was a complete exoneration of the accused. Thereupon Salem brought before the Mixed Court at Cairo an action against the Egyptian Government for damages sustained owing to the criminal proceedings taken against him and the retention of his documents. The Court held that the action against the Government was inadmissible. The Mixed Court of Appeal confirmed that judgment, not for the reason that the action was inadmissible, but on the ground that the Court at Cairo had no legal jurisdiction whatsoever.

Salem then continued through diplomatic channels his efforts to obtain compensation. On January 20, 1931, the Governments of Egypt and the United States concluded an arbitration agreement in which they submitted for a decision by a special arbitral tribunal the following two questions :

Case No. 98 ***Contd.***

(*a*) Is the Egyptian Government, under the principles of law and equity, liable in damages to the Government of the United States on account of the treatment accorded to the American citizen, George J. Salem ?

(*b*) In case the Tribunal finds that such liability exists, what sum should the Egyptian Government in justice pay to the Government of the United States in full settlement of such damages ?

Held (Nielson, arbitrator, dissenting) : that the Egyptian Government was not liable.

(1) *The Nationality of the Claim. The Right of Espousal. Interpretation of the Arbitration Agreement. Grammatical and Historical Interpretation. Preparatory Work.*—The Egyptian Government contended that as Salem acquired American citizenship by fraud, the American Government was not entitled to raise on his behalf claims for violation of his rights of citizenship by the Egyptian authorities.

Paragraph 1 referred expressly to the claim of the United States against the Egyptian Government arising out of treatment accorded to George J. Salem, *an American citizen.* That phrase was repeated in another paragraph of the Agreement. According to the obvious grammatical construction of these sentences Salem was indicated to be an American citizen and ought to be acknowledged as such by both parties. On a strictly grammatical interpretation the Arbitral Tribunal was not entitled to doubt this fact. However, the grammatical construction was not the only possible one. The sentences of both paragraphs could also be read to mean that by the words "American citizen" the juridical basis for the claim for damages was indicated, and, as the claim was disputed between the parties in its entirety, the investigation of the validity of this basis would also fall under the jurisdiction given by them to the Arbitral Tribunal. "That an arbitral tribunal is authorised to interpret the arbitration agreement (*compromis*) whereunder it is constituted, has been contested in certain cases, but the prevailing opinion in international practice acknowledges their right to do so. Such interpretation is, however, only admissible if the wording of the compromise allows of several meanings of which none can be recognised as the clear will and purpose of the parties. In this case the arbitral tribunal has to investigate which meaning agrees with what has been the joint will of the parties when they concluded the compromise. Now in order to ascertain the joint will of the parties, an arbitral tribunal is likewise entitled, according to the predominating international practice, to refer to the discussions and negotiations which led to the compromise." (At pp. 25, 26.)[1] These negotiations as examined by the Tribunal showed that the article in question ought to be interpreted "not in accordance with the limited grammatical construction but in a broad sense (sensu lato)" (at p. 31).

(2) *Examination of the Right of Citizenship by the Tribunal. The Question of Fraud.*—In view of the above, the Tribunal was entitled to examine whether Salem had obtained the renewal of American citizenship by fraudulent methods. "The Arbitral Tribunal is, therefore, entitled to examine whether the American citizenship of Salem really exists. Such examination is not impeded by the principle of International Law that every state is, generally speaking, sovereign in deciding the question as to which persons it will regard as its subjects, because the bestowal of citizenship is a manifestation of its international independence. In fact as soon as the question of nationality is in dispute between two Sovereign Powers, it cannot be exclusively decided in accordance with the national law of one of these Powers. In the present case it should be ascertained whether one of the Powers, by bestowing the citizenship against general principles of International Law, has interfered with the right of the other power, or if the bestowal of the citizenship is vitiated because it has been obtained by fraud. In order to decide the question of fraud it will be necessary to examine if the false representations with which the nationality of a certain Power has been acquired refer to those points on which according to the law of that Power the acquisition of nationality is essentially dependent." (At p. 31.) The Tribunal then examined the relevant American enactments and found that no fraud on the part of Salem had taken place. The Tribunal pointed out that "an Arbitral Tribunal should use the greatest caution, when giving a decision that the nationality which is claimed and acknowledged as valid by a Sovereign Power has been acquired by fraud" and that "each doubt in this respect should be interpreted in favour of the validity of the act of naturalisation" (at p. 34).

(3) *Naturalisation and Loss of Original Nationality. The Principle of Effective Nationality.*—The Tribunal then considered the question whether the Egyptian Government could

[1] Nielsen, arbitrator, while not questioning the admissibility, in proper cases, of preparatory work, invoked, in his dissenting opinion, the rule that there is no need for interpretation when the treaty is clear, and also the rule *expressio unius est exclusio alterius* (at pp. 63-65).

Case No. 98 ***Contd.***

oppose to Salem's naturalisation the fact that he had acquired American nationality without the consent of the Egyptian Government, which meant that he had never lost Egyptian nationality. This followed from the rules of the Turkish Law of 1869 which was then in force in Egypt. These rules had not ceased to be applied until the time when an Egyptian Nationality Law was promulgated. That was in turn based on the same principles as the Turkish Law. "The Turkish law which makes the acquisition of foreign nationality dependent on the permission of the Government is internationally not to be objected to. It is indeed generally admitted that every person of age is entitled to choose his nationality. This rule, however, only means that the State which he leaves cannot reclaim him from the State the nationality of which he acquires, and that the State of origin shall not be entitled to contest the other State's right to bestow nationality on an immigrant. But the above-mentioned principle does not prevent the State of origin making by its national legislation the loss of its nationality dependent on a special permission of its Government, which means that it may treat the emigrant again as its national as soon as he returns into its territory" (at p. 35).[1] Accordingly, the Egyptian Government could successfully oppose the American claim if they could produce evidence that Salem was an Egyptian subject and that he had acquired American nationality without the express consent of the Egyptian Government. However, the Tribunal found as a matter of fact that Salem never possessed Egyptian nationality and that he was a Persian subject at the time of his naturalisation in the United States.

(4) *The Right of a State to Invoke the Claimant's Nationality of a Third State as a Bar to Proceedings.*—Although the Tribunal

[1] The Tribunal rejected, *obiter*, the validity of the principle of effective nationality. It said: "the Arbitral Tribunal cannot admit that where such a return occurs the State of Origin be entitled by International Law to maintain that its claim is more important in justice than the claim of the new state. The principle of the so-called 'effective nationality,' referred to by the Egyptian Government, does not seem to be sufficiently established in International Law. It was used in the famous Canevaro case; but the decision of the Arbitral Tribunal appointed at that time has remained isolated. In spite of the Canevaro case, the practice of several Governments, for instance, the German, is that if two Powers are both entitled by International Law to treat a person as their national, neither of these Powers can raise a claim against the other in the name of such person (cf. Borchard l.c. p. 588)" (at p. 35). [As this point was decided *obiter*, it is perhaps unnecessary to emphasise that the principle of effective nationality has been recognised in a series of arbitral decisions since the *Canevaro* case and in the Hague Convention of 1930 on Certain Principles relating to Conflicts of Nationality Laws.]

found that Salem was a Persian national at the time of his naturalisation, it was not open to the Egyptian Government to invoke against the United States the eventual continuation of the Persian nationality of Salem, "the rule of International Law being that in a case of dual nationality a third Power is not entitled to contest the claim of one of the two Powers whose national is interested in the case by referring to the nationality of the other Power (cf. Mackenzie v. Germany, 1922, Opinions of the Mixed Claims Commission, U.S. and Germany, p. 628)" (at p. 37).

(5) *Exhaustion of Legal Remedies. Competence of Arbitral Tribunals to Enquire into the Question.*—The Tribunal could not accept the view of the United States that the Egyptian Government was not entitled to invoke the alleged fact that Salem had not exhausted the legal remedies in Egypt on the ground that the Arbitration Agreement conferred upon the Tribunal jurisdiction only as regards the claim for damages. "International Arbitral Tribunals have repeatedly acknowledged that the conclusion of an arbitration agreement involves no abandonment of the claim to exhaust all legal means; for instance, see the decision given March 19, 1925, by the American-British Arbitral Tribunal, instituted in accordance with the agreement of August 18, 1910, in the dispute of the Canadian claims to refund paid customs duties, in *Nielsen*: American and British Claims Arbitration, p. 347 ff." (at p. 38). The Tribunal then examined the Egyptian contention that the claimant had not exhausted the legal remedies available in Egypt and found, on the facts, that that contention was not well founded.

(6) *Diplomatic Protection and Jurisdiction of Mixed Courts.*—The Tribunal, in the exercise of its equitable jurisdiction, was prepared to accept the Egyptian contention that the jurisdiction of the Mixed Courts in Egypt excluded redress by way of diplomatic protection.[1] This was so, although the Tribunal was not prepared to accept in its entirety the contention of the Egyptian Government to the effect that the Mixed Courts were

[1] The competence of the Mixed Courts of Egypt to pass judgment on claims of foreigners against the Egyptian Government was based on Paragraphs 10 and 11 of the "*Règlement d'Organisation judiciaire pour les Procès Mixtes en Egypte*" agreed upon between Egypt and the Capitulatory Powers. Under Paragraph 10 all actions between the Egyptian Government and foreigners belonged to the jurisdiction of these Courts. Paragraph 11 (3) provided that the Mixed Courts "are not entitled to construe an act of administration or delay its execution but they are competent to decide on injuries done by such acts to acquired rights of a foreigner recognized by treaties, laws or conventions."

Case No. 98 *Contd.*

to be regarded as international arbitral tribunals, and that, therefore, no further arbitration proceedings could be opened against the decision of these courts. It must be admitted that the Mixed Courts had not an exclusively national character. They were, with regard to their organisation and to the laws which they had to apply, the result of agreements concluded with the Capitulatory Powers. Also, they had an international character in the sense that the majority of their members, in accordance with these agreements, were foreigners. Experts of the Egyptian Mixed Jurisdiction, among them official representatives of the American Government, had emphasised the international character of the Mixed Courts.[1]

However, the Tribunal could not formally accept the view that these Courts were international courts. The judges of the Mixed Courts were appointed by the Khedive and subsequently by the King of Egypt. They received their salaries from the funds of the Egyptian Government. The law according to which the Mixed Courts gave their decisions, as well as their rules of organisation, were issued as national Laws. The decisions of the Mixed Courts of Egypt were not international decisions ; they were issued in the name of the King of Egypt. At the same time, the Tribunal could not disregard the fact that the Capitulatory Powers, in concluding the conventions concerning the institution of the Mixed Courts, had abandoned the diplomatic settlement of claims of their subjects in favour of the national jurisdiction of the Mixed Courts in all cases in which these subjects could bring an action against the Egyptian Government before this mixed jurisdiction.

It appeared that the Powers regarded the mixed jurisdiction, instituted with their consent and partly composed of judges of their respective nationalities, as a substitute or compensation for their former right to raise through the diplomatic channel claims for damages on account of the treatment of their subjects in Egypt.

"It must therefore be assumed that on transferring the competence for such claims to the Mixed Courts both parties, the Capitulatory Powers and Egypt, took upon themselves a certain risk : the Capitulatory Powers took the risk that the Mixed Courts can decide against them without their having the opportunity to keep open the diplomatic way for settling the claims of their nationals and the Egyptian Government took the risk that the Mixed Courts would consider the foreign

[1] See Brinton, *The Mixed Courts of Egypt* (1930), p. 18, n. 12.

interests before Egyptian interests, the foreign judges being in a majority, and that they often would decide for that reason against the Government." (At p. 45.)

For these reasons the Tribunal was, in principle, inclined to accept the general contention of the Egyptian Government as to the exclusion of diplomatic redress in respect of claims adjudicated by the Mixed Courts.

However, that principle did not wholly apply in the present case because: (*a*) it was to some extent overridden by the powers conferred upon the Tribunal in the Arbitration Agreement; (*b*) while it covered the question of the damages due to Salem, it was irrelevant to that part of the claim of the United States which arose out of the alleged violation of the treaty rights of the United States as a Capitulatory Power. That claim was not a private one taken up by the Government. It was a claim as between Government and Government, and as such outside the jurisdiction of the Mixed Courts.

(7) *Compensation for a Breach of a "Unilateral" Treaty.*—The Tribunal could not accept the contention of the Egyptian Government that pecuniary compensation as claimed by the United States was inadmissible on the ground that the treaty on which the allegedly violated capitulation rights of the United States were based, namely, the Treaty of 1830 with Turkey, granted to the United States unilateral rights and that, according to international law, no claim for money in respect of violation of such a one-sided agreement could be entertained. "The Arbitral Tribunal cannot acknowledge the existence of such an international rule; it will always depend upon the circumstances whether compensation in money can be claimed in respect of the violation of a valid treaty, even if it be unilateral. This treaty, however, cannot be described as a purely unilateral agreement. If, according to paragraph 5 of the treaty of 1830, Turkey grants to the United States the exclusive right to issue criminal sentences regarding their subjects on Turkish territory by consular jurisdiction, the Government of the United States undertakes at the same time the obligation to exercise their jurisdiction up to the same standard of efficiency as the native jurisdiction and consequently to employ all the necessary personal and material means required for that purpose." (At p. 46.)

(8) *Denial of Justice through Alleged Faulty Judicial Procedure.*—The Tribunal could not accept the contention of the United States that there had taken place a denial of justice through faulty judicial procedure on account of the fact that,

Case No. 98 *Contd.*

according to Egyptian law, the public prosecutor who was charged with the investigation was likewise entitled to open the trial, thus combining in his person the rôle of accuser, investigating magistrate and judge deciding on the opening of the trial. The United States relied upon principles of the common law according to which a special jury other than that judging the crime is entrusted with the decision whether the accused shall be brought to trial or not. However, "in the different codes of criminal procedure in force among civilised nations, this sort of guarantee is not so general that another method of preparing the trial could be designated as being below the standard of International Law. The system whereby the trial is preceded by an investigation executed by a judge is under most codes of procedure an exception, and only carried out when grave crimes are at stake ; generally the investigation is left to the Parquet[1] so that the accusing and the investigating magistrate coincide. It is true that even under the law of countries where the rules of criminal procedure are based on the French system, the result of the investigation is mostly examined by a judge before the trial is opened, but every lawyer conversant with the so-called continental system of criminal procedure knows well that the examination of the file, in the case of minor delinquencies, is more or less formal." (At p. 50.)

(9) *Criminal Proceedings by Native Courts against Persons who have Acquired the Nationality of a Capitulatory Power Since the Beginning of the Proceedings.*—The Tribunal could not admit the claim of the United States on account of proceedings being taken by the Egyptian courts against a national of a Capitulatory Power. The Tribunal was obliged to attach importance to the fact that twice, in 1915 and 1917, the Diplomatic Agent of the United States in Cairo informed the Egyptian authorities that Salem was no longer entitled to American protection because a presumption of expatriation had arisen against him. According to Egyptian law, the courts were bound to continue the criminal proceedings legally opened against a person even if that person acquired a foreign nationality during the proceedings. This rule was in accordance with the principles of international law and with the jurisdiction of the Egyptian Mixed Courts.[2]

[1] The Public Prosecutor.

[2] The Tribunal referred here to de Wée, *La compétence des Juridictions Mixtes d'Egypte* (1929), pp. 183, 184, and to the decision of the Mixed Court of Appeal of February 12, 1903 (*Bulletin*, XV, p. 143), where it was said : "a change of nationality occurring in the course of an action cannot have the effect of divesting a jurisdiction legally vested at the introduction of the claim."

(10) *Effect of Loss of Diplomatic Protection.*—The United States could not maintain against Egypt that according to the law of the United States the loss of the title to diplomatic protection was independent of the loss of standing under American consular jurisdiction. "If an American who has lost the right to claim diplomatic protection by his Government commits a crime in Egypt and the American Consular Jurisdiction refuses to prosecute him, it is self-evident that the territorial jurisdiction recovers the competence to prosecute him; the criminal proceedings directed against such a person by the national courts cannot, therefore, be contested under International Law." (At p. 53.)

(11) *Denial of Justice. Absence of Impartiality.*—The Tribunal could not, on the facts before it, accept the contention of the United States that Salem suffered a denial of justice on the ground that the prosecuting authorities and the courts were unfavourably inclined towards him. It was possible that the Mixed Court at Cairo made a mistake in applying the relevant paragraph (776) of the *Code Civil Mixte*, and that the Mixed Court of Appeal at Alexandria, in dismissing the claim as not well-founded in spite of the fact that this part of the case had not been pleaded, used terms which went beyond its intended meaning. Such errors in judgment could not be regarded as a denial or a warping of justice in the sense of international law. As a rule, the validity of judgments issued by competent law courts must be acknowledged. "In consequence, International Law has from the beginning conceived under the notion of 'denial of justice' forming a basis of political claims only exorbitant cases of judicial injustice. Absolute denial of justice; inexcusable delay of proceedings; obvious discrimination of foreigners against natives; palpable and malicious inequity of a judgment—these are the cases which, one after another, have been included under the notion of 'denial of justice.' If American theory and practice seems inclined to extend this notion, the Arbitral Tribunal cannot follow this example . . . . *As a rule,*[1] a foreigner must acknowledge as applicable to himself the kind of justice instituted in the country in which he has chosen his residence, including all deficiencies of such jurisdiction, imperfect as it is like every other human work." (At p. 58.)

(12) *State Responsibility and Limitations of Sovereignty.*—In any case, the responsibility of the Egyptian Government for

[1] The italics are the Editor's. Without the suggested emphasis on the italicised words, the statement in this sentence may prove to be misleading.

Case No. 98 *Contd.*

the acts and omissions of the Mixed Courts was less extensive than that for purely Egyptian courts. The jurisdiction of the Mixed Courts was instituted and continued not only through the will of the Egyptian State, but also by conventions concluded with the Capitulatory Powers. Both parties, by executing these conventions, sacrificed part of their sovereignty. The Capitulatory Powers gave up a part of their jurisdictional prerogative on Egyptian territory by waiving the civil jurisdiction of their consuls. The Egyptian Government gave up a part of its sovereignty by undertaking to accept in civil cases, especially in cases of alleged violation of rights of foreigners on the part of Egyptian authorities, the jurisdiction of a court composed of a majority of foreigners. "If the Mixed Courts are at fault the Egyptian Government is unable to prevent the repetition of such faults ; they can neither remove the judges nor punish them by disciplinary action—this action is reserved to the Mixed Court of Appeal—nor can they modify the laws in accordance with which the court is composed and has to decide its cases . . . The responsibility of a state can only go as far as its sovereignty in the same measure as the latter is restricted, that is to say, as the State cannot act in a free and independent manner, the liability of the State must also be restricted. Consequently, the alleged denial of justice committed by the Mixed Courts cannot be brought forward as a cause of complaint against Egypt either to support the claim made in the name of George Salem or to prove the alleged violation of the treaty rights of the United States." (At p. 59.)[1]

(13) *Evidence. Admissibility of Sworn Affidavits.*—With regard to the admissibility of the sworn affidavits of Salem relating to his treatment by the Egyptian prosecuting authorities, the Tribunal said : "the presentation of such affidavits sworn by parties or representatives of parties, *viz.*, by persons who are interested in the issue of the dispute, are in accordance with the regular practice of International Law. The pro-

[1] But see here the following passage from the Dissenting Opinion of Nielsen, arbitrator : "Agreements originally providing for the establishment of the extraterritorial courts may well be said, of course, to have effected a limitation on Egyptian sovereignty. Obviously, therefore, Egypt was not and is not now responsible for the extraterritorial courts. But the Mixed Courts were not established to create any such limitation on sovereignty, but obviously for the reverse purpose, that is, in a measure to restore sovereign rights. And since by agreement with the capitulatory Powers Egypt to some extent decreased the limitation on the exercise of sovereign Powers by subjecting foreigners to the jurisdiction of a domestic judiciary, there is, in my opinion, responsibility for that domestic judiciary." (At p. 99.)

ceedings before international arbitral tribunals are essentially confined to written evidence because those tribunals have no jurisdiction to force witnesses to appear and testify before them ; the non-admittance of affidavits would therefore rob International Arbitration of a very important means of procuring evidence. It is, however, left to the discretion of the Arbitral Tribunal to judge how far they will give weight to such sworn affidavits." (At p. 51.)

[Report : *Printed Award*, Cairo, Government Press, 1932 (the references are to this report) ; *Revue de droit international* (Paris), XI (1933), pp. 768-816. See also as to this case Assabghy, *ibid.*, pp. 70-132 ; Siotto Pintor in *L'Egypte contemporaine, Revue de la Société Royale d'Economie Politique, de Statistique et de Législation*, Vol. XXIV, pp. 547-571 ; Arminjon in *Clunet*, 60 (1933), pp. 785-811.]

Denial of Justice—Meaning of—Acts of Non-Judicial Authorities—Whether Constituting Denial of Justice—Effect on Calvo Clause. **Case No. 99**

In re THE INTEROCEANIC RAILWAY OF MEXICO LIMITED, THE MEXICAN EASTERN RAILWAY COMPANY LIMITED, AND THE MEXICAN SOUTHERN RAILWAY LIMITED.

Great Britain and Mexico : Claims Commission.

(Zimmerman, Stoker, Flores.)

June 18, 1931.

THE FACTS.—This was a series of claims arising out of various acts of interference by Mexican revolutionary forces with the activities of the claimant Companies, destruction of and damage done to their stock, and requisitions of their property. The concessionary contracts of these Companies included an Article embodying in comprehensive terms the so-called Calvo Clause.[1] The Commission adhered to the

[1] That Article provided : "The Company shall always be a Mexican Company, even though any or all its members shall be aliens, and it shall be subject exclusively to the jurisdiction of the courts of the Republic of Mexico in all matters whose cause and right of action shall arise within the territory of said Republic. The said Company and all aliens and the successors of such aliens having any interest in its business, whether as shareholders, employees or in any other capacity, shall be considered as Mexican in everything relating to said Company. They shall never be entitled to assert, in regard to any titles and business connected with the Company, any rights of alienage under any pretext whatsoever. They shall only have such rights and means of asserting them as the laws of the Republic grant to Mexicans, and Foreign Diplomatic Agents may, consequently, not intervene in any matter whatsoever."

Case No. 99 *Contd.*

rule enunciated in the *Mexican Union Railway* case,[1] where the Calvo Clause was incorporated in almost identical terms, and declared that it had no jurisdiction to entertain the claims. It found on the facts before it that the claimants had not exhausted the available local remedies; that it could not, therefore, be said that there had taken place a denial of justice; and that there could consequently be no room for invoking the exceptions laid down in the *Mexican Union Railway* case.

At the same time the Commission considered the contention of Mexico that there could be no room in the present case for denial of justice, seeing that no act or omission of a judicial organ was the subject of the complaint. The acts in question were those of the Minister of Finance.

Held: that the Mexican contention must be rejected. The Commission could not "concur in the view that the judicial authorities can only be the ones [who can become guilty of a denial or undue delay of justice], in other words, that only the courts can be made responsible for international delinquency of this description. They are undoubtedly aware that denial of justice or its undue delay will, in a majority of cases, be an act or an omission of a tribunal, but cases in which administrative, or rather non-judicial authorities, can be blamed for such acts or omissions are equally existent.

"If an alien is arrested by the police on a false charge, his strongest desire will be to be put upon his trial without delay, in order to prove his innocence. But if the authorities in whose power he happens to be prevent him from being led before a court, if they bar him access to a tribunal, this must certainly be characterized as a denial of justice or as an undue delay of justice, the responsibility for which does not rest with the courts or with any judicial authority, but with the non-judicial officials, who deprived the alien of his liberty.

"If an alien, having won a lawsuit and being desirous of seeing the judgment executed, addresses himself to those non-judicial authorities upon whom, in most countries, execution of the judgments of civil courts is incumbent, and they either refuse to assist him, or postpone their action indefinitely, the alien in question is certainly entitled to complain of denial or undue delay of justice, although the responsibility cannot be laid at the door of the tribunal that sustained his action.

"If a foreigner, in the pursuit of his private interests, needs a document, which can only be delivered by one of the admin-

[1] *Decisions and Opinions of the Commissioners*, 1931, p. 157.

istrative authorities in the country where he transacts his affairs, and if this document is improperly withheld or delivered too late to be of any use, this will again constitute the same breach of international law, without any judicial authority being blameable.

"The Commission deem that these examples, which could be supplemented by many others, show that non-judicial authorities also can be guilty of a denial or undue delay of justice, and if it could, in the case now before them, be shown that such authorities had been guilty of that international delinquency, they would not hesitate to declare themselves competent in spite of the claimants having agreed to a Calvo Clause." (At pp. 126, 127.)

[Report : *Decisions and Opinions of the Commissioners*, 1933, p. 118.]

Denial of Justice—Undue Delay of Justice—Meaning of—Effect on Calvo Clause. **Case No. 100**

In re EL ORO MINING AND RAILWAY COMPANY (LIMITED).

Great Britain and Mexico : Claims Commission.

(Zimmerman, Stoker, Flores.)

June 18, 1931.

THE FACTS.—This was a claim for compensation for the transport of troops and goods on behalf of Mexican revolutionary and federal forces, for work done and material supplied to these forces, and for losses suffered at their hands in the years 1910-1920. The Company, which was a British one, received in 1897 a concession which embodied the so-called Calvo Clause in terms almost identical with those in the *Mexican Union Railway* case. However, in the *Interoceanic Railway of Mexico* case (Case No. 99) the Commission held that the effects of that Clause must be disregarded if the claimant has been the victim of a breach of international law such as denial of justice or undue delay of justice. In the present case, for reasons which appear below, the Commission

Held : that there had taken place an undue delay of justice, that the Calvo Clause was therefore inapplicable, and that the Commission had jurisdiction. The Commission said : "Nine years have elapsed since the Company applied to the Court to which the law directed it, and during all those years

Case No. 100 ***Contd.***

no justice has been done. There has been no hearing; there has been no award. Not the slightest indication has been given that the claimant might expect the compensation to which it considered itself entitled, or even that it might be granted the opportunity of pleading its cause before that Court.

"The Commission will not attempt to lay down with precision just within what period a tribunal may be expected to render judgment. This will depend upon several circumstances, foremost amongst them upon the volume of the work involved by a thorough examination of the case, in other words upon the magnitude of the latter. It will often be difficult to define the time limit between a careful and conscientious study and investigation, on the one hand, and procrastination, undue postponement, negligence and lack of despatch on the other. The Commission have, in their Decision No. 53 (Interoceanic Railway), laid down their opinion that a court with which a claim for an enormous amount had been filed in November 1929 could not be blamed for undue delay if it had not administered justice by June 1931. It is obvious that such a grave reproach can only be directed against a judicial authority upon evidence of the most convincing nature.

"But it is equally obvious that a period of nine years by far exceeds the limit of the most liberal allowance that may be made. Even those cases of the very highest importance and of a most complicated character can well be decided within such an excessively long time. A claimant who has not, during so many years, received any word or sign that his claim is being dealt with is entitled to the belief that his interests are receiving no attention, and to despair of obtaining justice.

"In the opinion of the Commission, the amount of work incumbent upon the Court, and the multitude of lawsuits with which they are confronted, may explain, but not excuse the delay. If this number is so enormous as to occasion an arrear of nine years, the conclusion can be no other than that the judicial machinery is defective, and that the organisation of its jurisdiction is not in proper proportion to the task it has to fulfil. A very obvious delay of justice originating in the overburdening with work of Courts insufficient in number is in effect equivalent to that undue delay of justice which the Commission have, in their Decision No. 21 [the *Mexican Union Railway* case] accepted as justifying claimants in applying to their own Governments, in spite of having signed a Calvo Clause." (At p. 150.)

[Report : *Decisions and Opinions of the Commissioners*, 1933, p. 141.]

State Responsibility—Denial of Justice—Executive Inaction —Burden of Proof. **Case No. 101**

In re GILL.

Great Britain and Mexico : Claims Commission.

(Zimmerman, Stoker, Flores.)

May 19, 1931.

THE FACTS.— In this case Great Britain claimed damages on behalf of a British subject on account of injuries suffered as the result of an assault and robbery committed by some men belonging to the Mexican revolutionary forces. The basis of the claim was the alleged failure of the Mexican authorities to apprehend and to punish the offenders.

Held (unanimously), on the evidence : that Mexico was responsible. The Commission affirmed the view expressed in a former case (*Mexico City Bombardment Claims* case)[1] in the following terms : "In a great many cases it will be extremely difficult to establish beyond any doubt the omission or the absence of suppressive or punitive measures. The Commission realises that the evidence of negative facts can hardly ever be taken in an absolutely convincing manner. But a strong *prima facie* evidence can be assumed to exist in these cases, in which first the British Agent will be able to make it acceptable that the facts were known to the competent authorities, either because they were of public notoriety or because they were brought to their knowledge in due time ; and second the Mexican Agent does not show any evidence as to action taken by the authorities." (At pp. 87, 88.) The same view was expressed by the Commission in a subsequent case (*Bowerman* case) to the effect that "whenever an event causing loss or damage is proved to have been brought to the knowledge of the Mexican authorities or is of such public notoriety that it must be assumed that they have knowledge of it, and it is not shown by the Mexican Agent that the authorities took any steps to suppress the acts or to punish those responsible for the same, the Commission is at liberty to assume that strong *prima facie* evidence exists of a fault on the part of the authori-

[1] *Annual Digest*, 1929-1930, Case No. 100.

Case No. 101 ***Contd.*** ties." (At p. 88.) In the present case the Commission said: "The majority fully realise that there may be a number of cases, in which absence of action is not due to negligence or omission, but to the impossibility of taking immediate and decisive measures, in which every Government may temporarily find themselves, when confronted with a situation of a very sudden nature. They are also aware that authorities cannot be blamed for omission or negligence, when the action taken by them has not resulted in the *entire* suppression of the insurrections . . . or has not led to the punishment of *all* the individuals responsible. In those cases no responsibility will be admitted. But in this case nothing of the kind has been alleged. The highest authorities in the country were officially acquainted with what had occurred. They stated that they were touched by the account. They added that they had, as regarded compensation, to consider that the precedent might have grave consequences, but the Mexican Agent has not shown a single proof that any action to inquire, suppress or prosecute was taken, although Sultepec is within easy distance of the Capital. Evidence to that effect, would, when existant, be at the disposal of said Agent, to whom the Archives of the Republic of the various States and of the Municipalities are available for this purpose." (At pp. 88, 89.)

[Report: *Decisions and Opinions of the Commissioners*, 1933, p. 85.]

NOTE.—See also the *Buena Tierra Mining Company* case, *ibid.*, p. 259; the *Kidd* case, *ibid.*, p. 36; and the *Bartlett* case, *ibid.*, p. 51.

Calvo Clause—Effect of Denial of Justice.

See Case No. 99 (*In re The Interoceanic Railway of Mexico Limited, and Others*).

State Responsibility—Exhaustion of Legal Remedies—Competence of International Tribunals to Enquire into the Question.

See Case No. 98 (*Salem Case: United States and Egypt*, 5).

(*b*) EXECUTIVE ACTION OR INACTION.

State Responsibility—Executive Action or Inaction—Principles of International Law With Regard to Responsibility for Arrest, Detention or Deportation of Aliens—Amount of Damages for Unjustified Detention—Responsibility for Act of Consul Acting on Behalf of a Foreign Consul—Evidence—Burden of Proof—Rights of Foreign Troops in Occupied Territory—Interpretation of Arbitration Agreement—Error in the Agreement. **Case No. 102**

CHEVREAU CASE.

France and Great Britain.

Beichmann, Arbitrator.[1]

June 9, 1931.

THE FACTS.—At the beginning of 1918 a British military force was sent from Bagdad with orders to encamp on the edge of the Caspian Sea, in Persian territory, with a view to preventing German and Turkish forces from entering Mesopotamia or Persia. This was done with the permission of the Persian Government, which consented to the sending of a military force to the zone of influence accorded by her to Great Britain by the Agreement of 1907. The force, which was a small one, encountered hostility on the part of some local political chiefs, and its advance and communications were seriously threatened by enemy spies and agents. A number of spies, or alleged spies, were arrested. They included a French citizen, Julien Chevreau, who before the War lived for a time in Germany and England and subsequently became a language teacher at Moscow. During the War he went to Persia. He was arrested on August 8, 1918; he was then taken to Bagdad, where on September 24, 1918, he was admitted to hospital. At the beginning of December he was put in the camp for Turkish prisoners of war. His case was then taken up by the French authorities and in January 1919 he was sent back to France.

France claimed damages on account of unjustified arrest and detention and maltreatment during detention.

Held: that Great Britain was liable in damages for the failure to make proper investigation after the arrest, but that she was not liable for the arrest as such.

[1] The Arbitrator had the assistance of the offices and of the personnel of the International Bureau of the Permanent Court of Arbitration.

Case No. 102 ***Contd.***

(1) *Rights of Foreign Troops in Occupied Territory.*—"The British forces in Persia had the right to take the measures necessary to protect themselves against the acts of the civilian population which were of a kind harmful to their operations or favourable to the enemy, a right which in general, according to international law, belongs to belligerent forces occupying enemy territory." (At pp. 159, 160.)

(2) *Principles of International Law with Regard to Responsibility for Arrest, Detention or Deportation of Aliens.*—The Arbitrator laid down the following general principles:

"(1) The arbitrary arrest, detention or deportation of a foreigner may give rise to a claim in international law. But the claim is not justified if these measures were taken in good faith and upon reasonable suspicion, especially if a zone of military operations is involved.

"(2) In cases of arrest, suspicions must be verified by a serious inquiry, and the arrested person given an opportunity to defend himself against the suspicions directed against him, and particularly to communicate with the consul of his country if he requests it. If there is no inquiry, or if it is unnecessarily delayed, or, in general, if the detention is unnecessarily prolonged, there is ground for a claim.

"(3) The detained person must be treated in a manner fitting his station, and which conforms to the standard habitually practised among civilized nations. If this rule is not observed, there is ground for a claim." (At p. 160.)

(3) *Unjustified Detention.*—While on the facts before him the Arbitrator found that there was a *prima facie* reason for the arrest of Chevreau and that there was no maltreatment *during detention,* he found that the British authorities failed, after the arrest, to hold an enquiry as to the accuracy of the charges on which he had been arrested. "It was the duty of the British authorities to initiate without delay an inquiry in which M. Chevreau, informed of the suspicions lodged against him and of the acts charged to him, might have furnished explanations of these acts and defended himself against the charges of which he was the object. They should also have allowed him to get in touch with his consul if he had so requested." (At p. 167.) The failure of the British authorities to fulfil these duties justified an award of damages.

(4) *Interpretation of the Arbitration Agreement. Error in the Agreement.*—Although the *compromis* entrusted the Arbitrator with the consideration of the question of the damage suffered during the detention in Persia, the Arbitrator held, in view of

the fact that during the proceedings both Parties discussed the circumstances of the detention in Bagdad, that it was not their intention to limit the task of the Arbitrator in that way. "It was in consequence of a material error that, in the *compromis*, the parties expressed themselves in terms which, taken literally, appear to limit the Arbitrator's examination to that period only in which M. Chevreau was detained in Persia. In fact, it is hard to understand the reasons for such a limitation." (At p. 176.)

(5) *Amount of Damages for Unjustified Detention.*—In deciding the question of damages the Arbitrator considered the conclusion adopted by Plumley, Umpire, in the Venezuelan Arbitrations in 1903, to the effect that the sum of $100 a day was the proper sum. He said that "the computation of damages according to a certain daily rate is but a practical means of avoiding an arbitrary assessment. In principle, it is a question of determining, according to the individual circumstances of each case, the global sum which would give equitable compensation for the moral or material injury suffered.

"It would not be in accordance with this principle to determine the indemnity to be allowed by simply calculating the number of days taken into consideration and applying to them a rate of assessment which might be considered as equitable in the conditions which existed in America. This rate is, in the opinion of the Arbitrator, too high for the conditions which, at the time in question in the present case, were prevalent in Europe and Persia." (At p. 177.) On the other hand, the Arbitrator considered that the time of Chevreau's stay in hospital and the period of negotiations between the British and French authorities, including the preparations for Chevreau's return, must be included.

(6) *Responsibility for Act of Consul Acting on Behalf of a Foreign Consul.*—Great Britain was not responsible for the loss of Chevreau's books and notebooks sent to the Vice-Consul of Great Britain in his capacity as representative of the French Consulate. "The British Government could not be held responsible for a negligence of which its consul, acting as the representative of the consulate of another nation, might have been guilty" (at p. 179).

(7) *Evidence. Burden of Proof.*—The Arbitrator did not accept the contention of the French Government that, as the case was submitted to arbitration by virtue of a special agreement, there was no plaintiff or defendant, and that accordingly the rules as to the apportionment of the burden of proof as

Case No. 102 *Contd.*

between plaintiff and defendant did not apply. It was true that the *compromis* referred to the duty of "determining to the satisfaction of the Arbitrator the authenticity of all points of fact offered to establish or disprove responsibility." But that provision was not intended to exclude the ordinary rules of proof. It only showed that there could also be a duty to prove the existence of the facts alleged in order to deny responsibility. The Arbitrator pointed out that the Order relied upon by France and issued on August 15, 1929, by the Permanent Court of International Justice (*Territorial Jurisdiction of the International Commission of the Oder*) referred only to a question of procedure and not to questions bearing on the burden of proof.[1]

[Report : *A.J.*, XXVII (1933), p. 153.[2]]

Case No. 103

State Responsibility—Executive Action—Responsibility for Damage Done to the Property of Aliens in the Course of Suppression of Rebellion.

In re HEYN, WISLICENUS AND SCHMIDT.

German-Mexican Claims Commission. January 11, 1930.

Decisions Nos. 1, 2 *and* 3.

THE FACTS.—These were claims on behalf of certain German nationals in respect of damage caused to their property by the forces of the legitimate Madero Government during the bombardment of the *Ciudadela* in Mexico City in February 1913. The *Ciudadela* had been occupied by insurgents and the forces of the Madero Government were attempting to dislodge them. The Claims Convention between Germany and Mexico provided that Mexico should be liable *ex gratia* for damage caused by the acts of certain forces including "the forces of a Government *de jure* or *de facto*."

Held (by Cruchaga, Presiding Commissioner, for the Commission) : that the claims must be disallowed. A Government could not be held liable for acts committed in the exercise of its duty to maintain law and order. "If the protection of nationals and foreigners by the territorial sovereign constitutes

[1] In that Order the Court decided that in a case submitted by special agreement a Party cannot confine itself to making oral submissions with regard to only one of the questions put before the Court. (*P.C.I.J.*, Series A, No. 23 ; Series E, No. 6, p. 217.)

[2] The records of the written proceedings before the Arbitrator have been deposited and are available in the Squire Law Library, Cambridge.

a primary obligation, the failure to comply with which results in international responsibility, it follows that it is neither just nor equitable to punish a government which complies with it, nor to limit its authority to undertake legitimate acts of repression which may result in damage or loss to resident foreigners whom it must protect from insurrections just as much as its own nationals."

[Unreported].

State Responsibility—Executive Action—Detention of Neutral Ships.

See Case No. 229 (*Royal Holland Lloyd* v. *United States* (*b*)).

(*c*) CONNECTED WITH LEGISLATION.

State Responsibility—State Legislation as a Cause of International Responsibility—State Legislation and International Obligations—Constitutional Provisions and State Responsibility—Free City of Danzig.

Case No. 104

PERMANENT COURT OF INTERNATIONAL JUSTICE.

TREATMENT OF POLISH NATIONALS AND OTHER PERSONS OF POLISH ORIGIN OR SPEECH IN THE DANZIG TERRITORY.

Advisory Opinion of February 4, 1932[1].

THE FACTS.—On May 22, 1931, the Council of the League of Nations adopted a Resolution requesting the Court to give an Advisory Opinion on two questions, of which the first was as follows :

> "Is the question of the treatment of Polish nationals and other persons of Polish origin or speech in the territory of the Free City of Danzig to be decided solely by reference to Article 104(5) of the Treaty of Versailles and Article 33, paragraph 1, of the Convention of Paris (and any other treaty provisions in force which may be applicable), or also by reference to the Constitution of the Free City; and is the Polish Government accordingly entitled to submit to the organs of the League of Nations, by the method provided for in Article 103 of the Treaty of Versailles and Article 39 of the Convention of Paris, disputes concerning the application to the above-mentioned persons of the provisions of the Danzig Constitution and other laws of Danzig ?"

[1] The Court was composed as follows : Adatci (President) ; Guerrero (Vice-President) ; Baron Rolin-Jaequemyns, Count Rostworowski, Fromageot, Altamira, Anzilotti, Urrutia, Sir Cecil Hurst, Schücking, van Eysinga, Wang (Judges) ; Bruns (Judge *ad hoc*).

Case No. 104 *Contd.*

Article 104 (5) of the Treaty of Versailles read as follows:

"The Principal Allied and Associated Powers undertake to negotiate a treaty between the Polish Government and the Free City of Danzig, which shall come into force at the same time as the establishment of the said Free City, with the following objects:

. . . .

"(5) to provide against any discrimination within the Free City to the detriment of citizens of Poland and other persons of Polish origin or speech."

Article 33 of the Convention of Paris between Poland and Danzig read as follows:

"The Free City of Danzig undertakes to apply to racial, religious and linguistic minorities provisions similar to those which are applied by Poland on Polish territory in execution of Chapter I of the Treaty concluded at Versailles on June 28th, 1919, between Poland and the Principal Allied and Associated Powers, to provide, in particular, against any discrimination, in legislation or in the conduct of the administration, to the detriment of nationals of Poland and other persons of Polish origin or speech, in accordance with Article 104, paragraph 5, of the Treaty of Versailles.

"The provisions of Articles 14 to 19 of the Treaty concluded at Versailles between the Principal Allied and Associated Powers and Poland on June 28th, 1919, as also the provisions of Article 89 of the Treaty of Versailles with Germany, shall equally apply to the Free City of Danzig."

The relevant paragraph (2) of Article 103 of the Treaty of Versailles provided as follows:

"The High Commissioner will also be entrusted with the duty of dealing in the first instance with all differences arising between Poland and the Free City of Danzig in regard to this Treaty, or any arrangements or agreements made thereunder."

Article 39 of the Convention of Paris laid down as follows:

"Any differences arising between Poland and the Free City of Danzig in regard to the present Treaty or to any subsequent agreements, arrangements or conventions, or to any matter affecting the relations between Poland and the Free City, shall be submitted by one or the other

Party to the decision of the High Commissioner, who shall, if he deem it necessary, refer the matter to the Council of the League of Nations."

A controversy subsequently arose between Poland and Danzig as to what extent a dispute concerning the application of the Danzig Constitution and other laws of Danzig to Polish nationals and other persons of Polish origin or speech, had to fulfil the conditions laid down in Article 39, namely, (*a*) to be a difference "arising between Poland and the Free City," and (*b*) to affect the relations between Poland and the Free City. Poland contended that the legal status of Danzig was *sui generis ;* that the guarantee of the League and the respect of the Treaty rights of Poland constituted an inseparable element of the legal status of Danzig ; that the usual distinction between matters of a domestic and of an international character did not hold good in the present case ; and that as a result Poland was entitled to submit to the organs of the League in conformity with Article 103 of the Treaty of Versailles and Article 39 of the Paris Convention disputes with Danzig arising out of the very enactment of certain laws by Danzig without regard to their application in violation of her treaties with Poland.

Held (Guerrero, Count Rostworowski, Fromageot and Urrutia, Judges, dissenting) : that the Polish contention must be rejected. "The treatment of Polish nationals and other persons of Polish origin or speech in the territory of the Free City of Danzig must, as between Poland and the Free City, be decided solely by reference to Article 104 : 5 of the Treaty of Versailles and Article 33, paragraph 1, of the Convention of Paris (as also, if necessary, by reference to other treaty provisions in force or rules of ordinary international law) and not by reference to the Constitution of the Free City, with the result that the Polish Government cannot submit to the organs of the League of Nations disputes concerning the application to the aforesaid persons of the Danzig Constitution and other laws of Danzig by the method provided for in Article 103 of the Treaty of Versailles and Article 39 of the Convention of Paris except in the case of disputes concerning the violation, as a result of such application, of an international obligation of Danzig towards Poland arising either from treaty provisions in force between them or from ordinary international law" (at p. 42).

The fact that the legal status of Danzig was *sui generis* did not authorise the Court to depart from the ordinary rules

Case No. 104 *Contd.*

governing relations between States and to establish new rules for the relations between Poland and Danzig. "The general principles of international law apply to Danzig subject, however, to the treaty provisions binding upon the Free City and to decisions taken by the organs of the League under these provisions. The peculiar character of the Danzig Constitution, as has been said above, affects only the relations between Danzig and the League. A violation or an erroneous application of the Constitution by Danzig is, therefore, so far as international relations are concerned, a matter solely between the League, as guarantor, and Danzig. With regard to Poland, the Danzig Constitution, despite its peculiarities, is and remains the Constitution of a foreign State. Any grievance which Poland may allege against the Free City arising out of the application by the latter of its Constitution as such cannot therefore give rise between Poland and the Free City of Danzig to differences in regard to a matter affecting the relations between Poland and the Free City within the meaning of Article 39 of the Convention of Paris; differences submitted to the High Commissioner under these conditions cannot therefore be entertained by him.

"It should however be observed that, while on the one hand, according to generally accepted principles, a State cannot rely, as against another State, on the provisions of the latter's Constitution, but only on international law and international obligations duly accepted, on the other hand and conversely, a State cannot adduce as against another State its own Constitution with a view to evading obligations incumbent upon it under international law or treaties in force. Applying these principles to the present case, it results that the question of the treatment of Polish nationals or other persons of Polish origin or speech must be settled exclusively on the bases of the rules of international law and the treaty provisions in force between Poland and Danzig.

"The application of the Danzig Constitution may however result in the violation of an international obligation incumbent on Danzig towards Poland, whether under treaty stipulations or under general international law, as for instance in the case of a denial of justice in the generally accepted sense of that term in international law. On this point, the Court refers to its Advisory Opinion No. 15; in this Opinion—which deals with the jurisdiction of the Danzig Courts in regard to pecuniary claims against the Polish Administration of Danzig railway officials who have passed into the Polish service—the Court, whilst upholding this jurisdiction, adds that this conclusion does not affect the right conferred on Poland by Article 39 of the Convention of Paris to resort to the international procedure provided for in that article, if, for instance, a decision of the Danzig Courts should conflict either with the general principles of international law or with the rules governing the relations between Poland and Danzig. However, in cases of such a nature, it is not the Constitution and other laws, as such, but the international obligation that gives rise to the responsibility of the Free City. This is in conformity with the general principle of the international responsibility of States and with the decision given by the Court in the case concerning certain German interests in Polish Upper Silesia (Judgment No. 7) and is, moreover, admitted by the Government of the Free City in its written statement submitted to the Court. Should such a case arise, Poland would undoubtedly be entitled to submit it to the organs of the League under Article 103 of the Treaty of Versailles and Article 39 of the Convention of Paris." (At pp. 23-25.)

[Report : *P.C.I.J.*, Series A/B, No. 44.]

(*e*) PLEA OF NON-DISCRIMINATION AGAINST FOREIGNERS.

Plea of Non-Discrimination—Operation of Treaties.

See Case No. 2 (*Re Arrow River & Tributaries Slide & Boom Co. Ltd.*).

VII.—For Acts and Omissions of Revolutionary or *de facto* Governments

State Responsibility—*De facto* and Revolutionary Governments—Responsibility for Acts of. **Case No. 105**

In re PATTON.

Great Britain and Mexico : Claims Commission.

(Zimmerman, Stoker, Flores.)

July 8, 1931.

This was a claim on behalf of the heir of a British subject for losses suffered as the result of a robbery committed by soldiers belonging to a Mexican revolutionary force. The Commission dismissed the claim on the ground that no negligence on the part

Case No. 105 *Contd.*

of the authorities had been proved. But in principle the Commission affirmed the responsibility of a State for acts and omissions of a *de facto* authority with regard to normal aspects of administration. The Commission said: "Even when a country passes through a period of anarchy, even when an established and recognised Government is not in existence, the permanent machinery of the public service continues its activity. The Commission share the view expressed in this regard in Decision No. 39 of the General Claims Commission between Mexico and the United States of America [*Annual Digest*, 1925-1926, Case No. 170] . . . They might add that the Police continued to function, that it continued to regulate traffic in the capital, to investigate crimes and to arrest criminals, as also that the Courts continued to administer justice. This means that public authorities that were obliged to watch over and to protect life and property continued to exist, although it is not denied that the performance of those duties will often have been very difficult in those disturbed times of civil war." (At p. 218.)

[Report: *Decisions and Opinions of the Commissioners*, 1933, p. 215.]

Case No. 106

State Responsibility—Acts of Revolutionary *de facto* Governments—Considerations to be Taken into Account by an Equity Tribunal.

STOLL CASE.

German-Mexican Claims Commission. February 18, 1930.

Decision No. 47.

THE FACTS.—This was a claim on behalf of a German national in respect of damage suffered during the Mexican revolutionary period at the hands of the forces of General Huerta. Huerta had come into power through the deposition and execution of President Madero.[1] The Claims Convention between Germany and Mexico provided that Mexico should be liable *ex gratia* for damage caused by the acts of certain forces, including "the forces of a Government *de jure* or *de facto*." Although Huerta had been in undisputed control of the capital and of a considerable portion of the country, and although his Government had been recognised *de jure* by a number of European States, including Germany, it was con-

[1] For the history of the Mexican revolution see Gruening, *Mexico and Its Heritage* (1928), and Feller, *The Mexican Claims Commission* (1935), pp. 155 *et seq.*

tended by the Mexican Agent that Mexico could not be held liable under the Convention for the acts of his forces. It was maintained that since Huerta had seized power through usurpation and murder, he was not the head of a Government, but merely the "holder of power." His Government could not be a *de jure* Government, which is one coming into power in accordance with the Constitution and having the support of the nation. Nor could it be a *de facto* Government, which is a régime which ripens into a *de jure* Government.

Held (by Cruchaga, Presiding Commissioner, the German Commissioner dissenting) : that the claim must be disallowed in so far as it was based on acts of Huerta forces. The Presiding Commissioner said : "The German-Mexican Convention of March 16, 1925, marked the fulfilment of the generous offer of the Mexican nation to make reparation, *ex gratia*, for the damage caused to foreigners during a certain period and by certain kinds of forces which participated in the revolution. This offer was made by the head of the Constitutionalist Army, Venustiano Carranza, at the very moment when, with the support of the Mexican people, he fought the Huertist usurpation of power. It does not appear to me to be just or equitable to hold responsible for the acts of a spurious administration created with all the vices condemned by public law, the very people which repudiated it on the battlefield and which, through its legitimate representatives, has refused to recognise the validity of the acts of Victoriano Huerta and his satellites.

"A commission of equity cannot, by its decisions, legitimise the system of military uprisings which has so greatly retarded democratic progress in a majority of American countries. Nor can it condone the violation of political morality as a means of assuming representative power in a republic. On the contrary, it should condemn such acts as violative of the high principles on which our civilisation is based." [1]

[Unreported.]

[1] But see, for a contrary view, the opinion of Verzijl, Presiding Commissioner, in the *Georges Pinson* case, decided by the French-Mexican Claims Commission on October 19, 1928 : *Jurisprudence de la Commission franco-mexicaine des réclamations*, at p. 106 ; *Annual Digest*, 1927-1928, Case No. 159. See also the *Hopkins* case, decided on March 31, 1926, by the United States-Mexican General Claims Commission : *Annual Digest*, 1927-1928, Case No. 170. The French, British and Spanish Claims Conventions with Mexico (which were originally couched in the same terms as the German-Mexican Convention) were amended in 1930 and 1931 to the effect that the Commissions shall have no jurisdiction over damage caused by the forces of Huerta.

C.—CLAIMS

I.—In General

Claims—Nature of Claims Against Foreign States in Pursuance of Diplomatic Protection of Nationals Abroad.

See Case No. 120 (*Gschwind v. Swiss Confederation*).

Claims—Necessity of an Actual Decision as a Basis for a Claim for Compensation—Insufficiency of Oral Ruling.

See Case No. 205 (*The Kronprins Gustaf Adolf; The Pacific. United States and Sweden*).

Waiver—Conditions of a Valid Renunciation of Rights.

See Case No. 205 (*The Kronprins Gustaf Adolf; The Pacific. United States and Sweden*).

II.—Nationality of Claims

Case No. 107 **Claims—Nationality of—Claims by Insurance Companies in Respect of Losses Suffered by Nationals of the Defendant State.**

In re The Eagle Star and British Dominions Insurance Company (Limited) and Excess Insurance Company (Limited).

Great Britain and Mexico: Claims Commission.

(Zimmerman, Stoker, Flores.)

April 23, 1931.

The Facts.—This was a claim on behalf of certain insurance companies of British nationality for amounts paid by them to a Mexican subject in respect of goods insured with the companies and looted by, apparently, armed revolutionary forces.

Held: that the Commission had no jurisdiction. There was a substantial difference between the position of insurers and that of other claimants, although they were in a similar position in so far as the losses suffered by both of them could be traced to certain events. But there the similarity ended. "Other claimants—assuming that the facts are proved—have suffered losses directly, unexpectedly and unwillingly. Insurers suffer losses indirectly as a consequence of a contract, into which they have entered voluntarily, professionally, in the normal and ordinary course of their business and in consideration of certain payments. They suffer losses not in the first place and just because certain events have occurred, but because, in their legitimate desire to subserve their own financial interests, they have undertaken to run the risk of those events.

"It seems difficult to look at Insurers in the same light as at other claimants. They who, as a professional act and with a view to make profit, undertake risks, to which other persons are exposed, who in order to cover those risks, stipulate for the payment of certain sums of money, balanced in the course of a long experience in proportion to the extent of the danger incurred, who direct an entire organisation based on the existence of risks, which would be useless in the case of their absence, and who are finally able to assume such chances and to calculate such premiums as will ultimately result in a profit on the whole volume of their transactions, cannot be regarded as entitled to compensation on the same footing as persons to whom the occurrences which gave rise to the claim were an unforeseen calamity.

"The professional character, in which Insurers apply for compensation, makes it more difficult to determine the amount of the loss than in the case of other claimants. Very often this amount will not be equal to the amount paid by them to the insured party, because it will be dependent upon the premiums received. It will also be dependent upon another circumstance. It is universally known that Insurers are working on a vast system of reinsurance, by which they, on the one hand, take over part of the risks insured by other Companies, while, on the other hand, they cede part of their own contracts to those other Companies. As a consequence of this system the surface over which the risks are really spread is often very extensive. It may not be confined to the Companies of one country, but may be international. For this reason it is quite possible that, although the insurance contract was signed and the amount paid by a British Company, the ultimate loss was divided over many corporations, of which one or more may have another nationality. Consequently the decision on the nationality of the claim from its inception until now does not depend solely upon the nationality of the Insurer claiming, but would also require an investigation of the reinsurance

Case No. 107 Contd. contracts, subdividing the profits and losses from the original insurance.

"The view may be taken—as is laid down in several codes—that the Insurer is, by the payment of the insurance money, subrogated to the right of the Insured, and that he is entitled to such compensation as was due to the latter, but at the same time it is evident that he can never exert any rights that did not belong to the Insured." (At pp. 34, 35.)

In the present case the insured party was a Mexican firm not entitled to claim compensation from their Government under the terms of the Convention. If the Commission were to declare itself competent to adjudicate upon this claim, it would grant to the insurance companies a right which the firm that suffered the loss did not have. The result would be to lay upon the Mexican Government a liability towards another Government which would not have arisen had not the firm in question entered into a contract to which the Mexican Government was not a party. This would not be a just or even a reasonable application of the Convention.

[Report: *Decisions and Opinions of the Commissioners*, 1933, p. 32.]

Case No. 108 **Claims—Nationality of—Partnerships—Distinction Between Nationality of Partnerships and Nationality of Partners.**

In re Messrs. D. J. and D. Spillane and Company.

Great Britain and Mexico: Claims Commission.

(Zimmerman, Stoker, Flores.)

May 13, 1931.

The Facts.—In this case the claim, which was in respect of some forced loans and requisitions by Mexican revolutionary authorities, was put forward on behalf of a partnership of the two brothers Spillane, both British subjects. The Mexican Government objected to the jurisdiction of the Commission on the ground that although the two brothers were of British nationality, no proof had been adduced to show that the firm was a British partnership.

Held: that the partnership of Messrs. D. J. and D. Spillane and Company, having been formed under Mexican law and being domiciled and working in Mexico, possessed Mexican nationality. For this reason the claim in the name of the partnership could not be put forward under the Special Claims Convention. However, as the deeds produced before the Commission showed that the two brothers were the sole partners of the firm and that they were already so at the time the losses were sustained, the Commission held that their interest was equivalent to the total capital of the partnership. Accordingly, while holding that they were not competent to take cognisance of the claim as long as it was preferred on behalf of the partnership, the Commission declared that a claim filed in the name of the partners individually would be taken into consideration.

[Report : *Decisions and Opinions of the Commissioners*, 1933, p. 72.]

Claims—Nationality of—Partnership—Holding of 50 per cent. of Partnership Capital. **Case No. 109**

In re STEVENS AND GIBB.

Great Britain and Mexico : Claims Commission.

(Zimmerman, Stoker, Flores.)

June 30, 1931.

THE FACTS.—This was a claim on behalf of Messrs. Stevens and Gibb, both British subjects, in respect of losses suffered by them as partners owning a ranch in the State of Puebla, in Mexico. With regard to the latter named, the claim was put forward on behalf of Mrs. Gibb. In the course of the Oral Argument the Mexican Agent drew attention to the fact that in Gibb's will his wife was not named either as heir or executrix. The British Agent thereupon withdrew the claim with regard to Gibb. As to Stevens, the Mexican Agent contended that the Commission had no jurisdiction on the ground that at the time of the occurrence Stevens did not hold more than 50%, but only just 50%, of the capital of the partnership, and also because there had been no allotment as required by Article 3 of the Convention of November 19, 1926.[1]

[1] That Article provided, *inter alia*, as follows : "In view of certain special conditions in which some British concerns are placed in such societies which do not possess that nationality it is agreed that it will not be necessary that the interest above mentioned shall pertain to one single individual, but it will suffice that it pertains jointly to various British subjects, provided that the British claimant or claimants shall present to the Commission an allotment to the said claimant or claimants of the proportional part of such losses or damages pertaining to the claimant or claimants in such partnership, company or association."

Case No. 109 Contd.

Held: that the Commission had jurisdiction. "In their reading of article 3 of the Convention, and particularly of the words "*in which British subjects have or have had an interest exceeding fifty per cent,*" it is evident that in order to entitle a British subject to appear before the Commission for losses suffered by a non-British partnership, it is sufficient that British subjects should, at the time of the events on which the claim is based, have had an interest exceeding 50%. Any other interpretation would lead to the unwarrantable result that one of the British partners could, after suffering the loss, be deprived of his right to claim, through a transfer by another partner of his own interest, to a subject of another State. This cannot, in the view of the Commission, have been the intention of the Convention . . . Neither can they concur in the view that the claim cannot be taken into consideration, because no allotment of the proportional part of the losses of the partnership has been presented. They can find for the provision requiring such allotment no other ground than a justifiable desire that Mexico should not, after once having been obligated to pay compensation to British subjects, whose interests in a non-British Company, Partnership or Association exceeded fifty per cent., be again confronted by an integral claim on the part of the Company, Partnership or Association itself. In order to safeguard the respondent Government against this eventuality, the Convention stipulates that the joint interest be reduced, by means of an allotment, by the proportional part of the losses, for which British partners or shareholders claim. But in the present claim the firm, according to article 14 of the Deed of Partnership, has been dissolved through the death of one of the partners. The partnership no longer exists and it is therefore impossible to obtain the allotment. By those same facts the eventual possibility of a claim by the partnership of the amounts already awarded to a partner, is excluded. The reason for producing an allotment has therefore disappeared." (At pp. 192, 193.)

[Report: *Decisions and Opinions of the Commissioners*, 1933, p. 191.]

NOTE.—See also, to the same effect, the *Adams* case, decided by the same Commission on July 3, 1931: *ibid.*, p. 199.

Claims—Nationality of—Continuous Nationality of the Claimant State Until the Time of Presentation and Award—Hague Codification Conference—Bases of Discussion—Answer of the British Government. **Case No. 110**

In re ESCHAUZIER.

Great Britain and Mexico : Claims Commission.

(Zimmerman, Stoker, Flores.)

June 24, 1931.

THE FACTS.—The damage in respect of which the present claim was brought was suffered at the hands of Mexican revolutionary forces by William Eschauzier, a British subject, who died in October 1920, having appointed his brother Francis Eschauzier, also a British subject, executor and sole heir. The latter died in 1924, leaving a will appointing his wife as executrix and sole heir. After the claim had been filed, she became an American citizen by marriage.

Held : that the Commission had no jurisdiction. A long course of arbitral decisions had established that a claim, in order to constitute a proper subject matter of an international award, must have remained continuously in the hands of a citizen of the claimant Government until the time of its presentation. However, the principle of nationality of claims went further than that.[1] "When it is certain and known to the tribunal, that a change of nationality has taken place prior to the date of the award, it would hardly be just to obligate the respondent Government to pay compensation to a citizen of a country other than that with which it entered into a convention." (At p. 180.) The most recent developments of international law seem to go in the direction of attaching great

[1] The Commission summarised as follows the argument in favour of making the time of presentation the decisive test : "It might be argued that international jurisdiction would be rendered considerably more complicated if the tribunal had to take into account changes supervening during the period between the filing of the claim and the date of the award. Those changes may be numerous and may even annul one another. Naturalisations may be applied for, and obtained, and may be voluntarily lost. Marriages may be concluded and dissolved. In a majority of cases, changes in identity or nationality will escape the knowledge of the tribunal, and often of the Agents as well. It will be extremely difficult, even when possible, to ascertain whether at the time of the decision all personal elements continue to be identical to those which existed when the claim was presented. Jurisdiction would undoubtedly be simplified if the date of filing were accepted as decisive, without any of the events that may very frequently occur subsequently to that date, having to be traced up to the date of rendering judgment." (At p. 180.)

Case No. 110 *Contd.* value to the conditions existing at the time of the award. The Commission referred, as supporting that principle, to point XIII of the Bases of Discussion for the Conference for the Codification of International Law, drawn up by the Preparatory Committee, as well as to the answer of the British Government with regard to this question. "In the light of such weighty documents on the subject, the Commission do not feel at liberty to ignore the fact that the claimant no longer possesses the British nationality." (At p. 182.)

[Report : *Decisions and Opinions of the Commissioners*, 1933, p. 177.]

Claims—Nationality of—Change of Nationality of Claim as the Result of an Amendment of the Claim.

See Case No. 219 (*In re Laue y Cia., in Liquidation*).

Claims—Nationality of—Right of Espousal—Competence of Tribunals.

See Case No. 98 (*Salem Case : United States and Egypt,* (1)).

Nationality of Claims—Right of a State to Invoke the Claimant's Nationality of a Third State as a Bar to Proceedings.

See Case No. 98 (*Salem Case : United States and Egypt*).

IV.—State Control over Private Claims

Case No. 111 **State Responsibility—The Calvo Clause—Conditions of Admissibility—Requirement of Clear and Unambiguous Terms—The Calvo Clause in Contracts to Which the Defendant Government is Not a Party—Whether It May be Invoked by the Government.**

In re MACNEILL.

Great Britain and Mexico : Claims Commission.

(Zimmerman, Stoker, Flores.)

April 10, 1931.

THE FACTS.—This was a claim put forward on behalf of the owner of a system of tramways in the State of Colima (Mexico) for compensation for the requisition by the Constitutionalist Army during the years 1914-1916 of animals, fodder and passenger and freight vans. It was contended by Mexico that the Commission had no jurisdiction in view of the so-called Calvo Clause in the original contract which provided, in Article 7, as follows: "The concessionaries, or the Company which they organize, may transfer their rights to another Company or to an individual with the approval of the Corporation, under the precise condition that the business will preserve its Mexican character and without rights of foreigners, even if it may be sustained by foreign capital."

Held: that the Commission had jurisdiction. The case was not analogous to the *Mexican Union Railway* case decided by the Commission in February 1930 (*Annual Digest*, 1929-1930, Case No. 129). The decision in that case was dictated by the clear and detailed provisions of the clause in question. This was not the position in the present case seeing that the wording of Article 7 was vague and obscure. The fact that the undertaking was to preserve its character as a Mexican company was not an obstacle to an appeal to the British Government in case the capital were British. There remained only the words "and have no rights of alienage." The term "rights of alienage" could not be found in the municipal laws of Mexico or Great Britain nor in any acknowledged rule of international law, nor in judgments of international tribunals. It was an expression which as yet did not allow of a clear and well-defined interpretation. Accordingly, the Commission was unable to understand what were the precise rights waived by the concessionaire. For this reason they could not accept a similarity between this clause and the clause inserted in the concession dealt with in the *Mexican Union Railway* case. "The majority holds the view that a so-called Calvo Clause to be respected in international jurisprudence, must be drafted in such a way as not to allow any doubt as to the intentions of both parties. The Commission cannot see that this has been done in art. 7 of the Concession." (At p. 24.)

Moreover, the clause inserted in Article 7 formed part of a contract between a concessionaire and the municipal corporation of the town of Colima, a local authority. Although this contract had been approved by the Congress of the State of Colima, it was not a deed to which Mexico was a party. "It is the opinion of the Commissioners that provisions affecting citizenship, the rights of foreigners, naturalization, etc., to be valid before an international tribunal, must emanate from treaties, the national legislation, decrees of the National

Case No. 111 ***Contd.*** Government, or deeds signed by or on behalf of such a Government. They cannot be regarded as valid, when they are stipulated by a local corporation, which is not entitled to dispose of such vital matters as the right of a concessionaire to appeal to his Government." (At p. 24.)

The fact that that Article was part of a contract to which the Mexican Government was not a party, constituted another very important discrepancy between the present case and the claim of the Mexican Union Railway, which had contracted with the same Government against which the claim was directed. "Here the Government had nothing to do with the concession. For the Government the contract was *res inter alios acta*. From the Government is claimed compensation not for the non-observance of the contract, but for losses outside any contractual relation. The majority of the Commissioners fail to see how the Government can derive rights from this contract to which they were not a party." (At pp. 24, 25.)

[Report: *Decisions and Opinions of the Commissioners*, 1933, p. 21.]

Claims—State Control Over—Termination of Jurisdiction of Arbitral Tribunals—Effect of.

See Case No. 190 (*X. v. Germany*).

Calvo Clause—Effects of Undue Denial of Justice.

See Case No. 100 (*In re El Oro Mining and Railway Company*).

Claims—Diplomatic Protection—Relation to Jurisdiction of Mixed Tribunals—Effect of Loss of Diplomatic Protection—Distinguished from Loss of Nationality.

See Case No. 98 (*Salem Case: United States and Egypt*).

E.—DAMAGES (MEASURE OF DAMAGES)

I.—Award of Damages in General. Grounds for Awarding Damages

Measure of Damages—Basis of Computation—Annuity. **Case No. 112**

In re CLAPHAM.

Great Britain and Mexico : Claims Commission.

(Zimmerman, Stoker, Flores.)

June 9, 1931.

THE FACTS.—This was a claim on behalf of a British subject who, as the result of unauthorised action by a group of Mexican revolutionary soldiers, was injured and had to have his leg amputated. In considering the measure of damages to be awarded, the Commission

Held : that the Mexican Government must pay as compensation the amount which would be necessary to purchase an annuity in accordance with principles which the Commission laid down as follows : "There can be no doubt that the loss of a foot must very seriously impair the earning capacity of a man carrying on the profession of Electrical and Mechanical Engineer. It is more than likely that such an injury will, for more than one kind of work, place him in an inferior position as compared with able-bodied applicants, that there will be many periods during which he will not be able to obtain employment, and that he will often have to be satisfied with a smaller remuneration than a man enjoying complete physical fitness.

"It seems just and equitable therefore that an award be granted him, that will set off, by means of an annuity, the lifelong injury which was the result of the wound.

"The Commission have found no guidance in any law or decree for the determination of the annuity, the less so as in nearly all other cases the annuity begins very soon after the accident, whereas in this case sixteen years and probably more will have elapsed before any payment can follow.

"The Commission, also taking into account the station in life of the claimant, thinks an annuity of $2,000 pesos Mexican gold fair and reasonable, and as, in order to purchase such

Case No. 112 *Contd.* annuity a man of the age of Mr. Clapham will have to pay about $20,000 pesos Mexican gold, they fix the award at that figure." (At p. 162.)

[Report: *Decisions and Opinions of the Commissioners*, 1933, p. 159.]

Case No. 113 **Measure of Damages—General Assessment—Question of Currency.**

In re WATSON.

Great Britain and Mexico: Claims Commission.

(Zimmerman, Stoker, Flores.)

May 19, 1931.

THE FACTS.—This was a claim in respect of acts of plunder and extortion committed by a body of Mexican revolutionary forces on a British subject, a farmer in the Mexican State of Sinaloa.

After having found that the claim was well founded the Commission said:

(*a*) *With respect to the Measure of Damages.*—"While it will hardly ever be practicable to reach complete exactitude in the determining of the volume of the losses, it will not be less difficult to arrive at an absolutely perfect estimate of their amount. The value of beans and cattle will of course depend upon their quality, and upon the current prices in the markets where their owner may be able to sell them. Those prices will be affected by the economic situation of the period, the rate of exchange for the national currency, by the possibilities of transport and exportation, and by the degree of stability and tranquillity prevailing at the time of the marketing.

"The Commission do not feel themselves able to weigh all these factors separately and exactly after seventeen years have elapsed. But they feel justified in declaring that sufficient proof has been shown to adopt as fair and reasonable an amount of 8,000 pesos, Mexican national gold." (At pp. 94, 95.)

(*b*) *Question of Currency of the Award.*—With regard to the currency in which their awards would be expressed in the future, the Commission laid down the following rule: "It seems arbitrary to let such currency be dependent upon what is asked in the claim. There is no reason why gold pesos should be awarded in one case, silver pesos in another, Pounds

Sterling in a third, and United States dollars in a fourth. The Commission, having also regard to article 9 of the Convention,[1] are of the opinion that the awards can be based upon no other money than the national and legal money of the State to be held liable for the payment. Awards will, for that reason, in future be made in Mexican national gold." (At p. 95.)

[Report : *Decisions and Opinions of the Commissioners*, 1933, p. 92.]

NOTE.—See, on the other hand, *In re Urmston*, decided by the same Commission on August 6, 1931, where the latter rejected a claim for the deterioration of the value of property on the ground, *inter alia*, that it was a phenomenon which was probably common to all landed property in Mexico during the revolutionary period. "It resulted from various circumstances and measures, but it is not a loss which can, at least not in the case now under consideration, be ascribed to any specific acts of revolutionary or other armed forces. Neither is it possible to determine the amount of the depreciation, nor to examine whether it has, partly at least, been compensated for by a subsequent rise in value." (*Ibid.*, p. 337.)

Damages—Measure of—Nervous Shock—Medical Treatment. **Case No. 114**

In re MCNEILL.

Great Britain and Mexico : Claims Commission.

(Zimmerman, Stoker, Flores.)

May 19, 1931.

In this case, which was a case of wrongful imprisonment and extortion by Mexican revolutionary forces, the Commission based the award of damages on the facts that the treatment of the claimant caused a serious derangement of his nervous system, that a considerable time elapsed before this breakdown was overcome to a sufficient extent to enable him to resume work, and that the patient incurred heavy expenses in order to conquer his physical depression.

The Commission took the view that "the compensation to be awarded to the claimant must take into account his station

[1] That Article provided as follows : "The form in which the Mexican Government shall pay the indemnities shall be determined by both Governments after the work of the Commission has been brought to a close. The payments shall be made in gold or in money of equivalent value and shall be made to the British Government by the Mexican Government."

Case No. 114 *Contd.* in life and be in just proportion to the extent and to the serious nature of the personal injury which he sustained." (At pp. 100, 101.)

[Report : *Decisions and Opinions of the Commissioners*, 1933, p. 96.]

Damages—Award of—Computation—Unjustified Detention.

See Case No. 102 (*Chevreau Case*).

II.—Indirect Damage and Damages for Loss of Profits

Case No. 115 **State Responsibility—Indirect Damage—Damage Caused Indirectly to Aliens as the Result of Measures Adopted With Regard to Nationals—Unjustified Enrichment.**

THE UNITED STATES OF AMERICA ON BEHALF OF DICKSON CAR WHEEL COMPANY

v

THE UNITED MEXICAN STATES.

United States and Mexico : Special Claims Commission.

(Alfaro, MacGregor, Nielsen.)

July 1931.

THE FACTS.—In April 1912 the National Railways Company of Mexico made a contract with the Dickson Car Wheel Company by which the latter undertook to deliver some car wheels. These deliveries were made in December 1913 and January 1914. In December 1914 the Mexican Constitutionalist Government took possession of the National Railways; in 1925 the railways were returned to private management. During that period the Dickson Company repeatedly addressed itself to the National Railways Company requesting payment, but received the answer that owing to the seizure of the railways the Company received no revenue whatever and was for the time being unable to meet its obligations. Before the Commission the United States contended that Mexico was internationally responsible for the obligation contracted by the Railways Company. The claim was based on the following three contentions : (1) that, since the seizure of the railways, the Company ceased to have an independent existence and that the Government succeeded to its rights and obligations; (2) that the Government was responsible on account of unjustified enrichment inasmuch as it made use of the material delivered to the Railways Company; (3) that the Government was responsible for the loss which, by seizing the railways, it indirectly caused to the Dickson Company.

Held (by the majority of the Commission, Nielsen, Commissioner, dissenting): that the claim must be rejected.

(1) *Succession to Rights and Obligations.*—The National Railways Company had disappeared as a legal entity, and it was therefore impossible to hold that the Government had succeeded to the rights and obligations contracted by it prior to the seizure. (The Commission distinguished, in some detail, the present case from those of the *Home Insurance Company* (*Opinions of Commissioners*, 1927, p. 51) and the *Illinois Central Railroad Company* (*ibid.*, p. 15).)

(2) *Unjustified Enrichment.*—The Commission said: "The interpretation of the theory of unjust enrichment has encountered serious difficulties in its practical application in municipal law. There is no doubt that at the present time that theory is accepted and applied generally by the countries of the world, even in the absence of a specific law, but the difficulty rests in fixing the limits within which it can and must be applied . . . It is obvious that the theory of unjust enrichment as such has not yet been transplanted to the field of International Law as this is of a juridical order distinct from local or private law."[1] "It is necessary to establish the international illegality of the causative act, and that the injury suffered by the national of the claimant country be the result of that act." (At pp. 184, 185.) The Commission then pointed out that in any case the theory of unjust enrichment was not applicable to the present case on certain grounds peculiar to the passing of property under Mexican law, and also because, in 1925, the Mexican Government returned the railways and agreed to pay for the damage caused by the use of them.

(3) *Damage Indirectly Caused to an Alien.*—In order to create international liability the act of the Mexican Government in seizing the railways had to combine two elements: an unlawful international act and a loss or injury suffered by a national of the claimant State. Neither of these conditions was fulfilled

[1] *Sed quaere.* See *Zillerszpic* v. (*Polish*) *Treasury* (*Annual Digest*, 1927-1928, Case No. 55); *Lena Goldfields Arbitration* (*ibid.*, 1929-1930, Case No. 1); *Cie. des Chemins de Fer du Nord* v. *German State* (*ibid.*, Case No. 294). [Ed.]

Case No. 115 ***Contd.***

in the present case. The Commission formulated the following principles applicable to the case before it:

"I. A State does not incur international responsibility from the fact that a subject of the claimant State suffers damage as a corollary or result of an injury which the defendant State has inflicted upon one of its own nationals or upon an individual of a nationality other than that of the claimant country, with whom the claimant is united by ties of relationship.

"II. A State does not incur international responsibility from the fact that an individual or company of the nationality of another State suffers a pecuniary injury as the corollary or result of an injury which the defendant State has inflicted upon an individual or company irrespective of nationality when the relations between the former and the latter are of a contractual nature."[1]

With regard to the liability of the State for incidental losses suffered by aliens as the result of the adoption of measures with regard to nationals, the Commission said: "The damage that might have been suffered by the claimant company is not definite, but is of a provisional character. Even if it had not been able to collect its credit with the National Railways

[1] The majority of the Commission reached that conclusion on the basis of wider considerations as to the position of the individual in international law. The Commission said: "The relation of rights and obligations created between two States upon the commission by one of them of an act in violation of International Law, arises only among those States subject to the international juridical system. There does not exist, in that system, any relation of responsibility between the transgressing State and the injured individual for the reason that the latter is not subject to international law. The injury inflicted upon an individual, a national of the claimant State, which implies a violation of the obligations imposed by International Law upon each member of the Community of Nations, constitutes an act internationally unlawful, because it signifies an offense against the State to which the individual is united by the bond of nationality. The only juridical relation, therefore, which authorizes a State to exact from another the performance of conduct prescribed by International Law with respect to individuals is the bond of nationality. This is the link existing between that law and individuals and through it alone are individuals enabled to invoke the protection of a State and the latter empowered to intervene on their behalf.

"A State, for example, does not commit an international delinquency in inflicting an injury upon an individual lacking nationality, and consequently, no State is empowered to intervene or complain on his behalf either before or after the injury." (At pp. 187, 188.) The Commission discussed in support of its view cases of injury suffered by persons linked by family relations to persons of another nationality who have been the victims of an injurious act of another State: *Lusitania Death Claims* cases (United States and Germany, Mixed Claims Commission, *Administrative Decisions and Opinions*, pp. 198, 209); *Banca* case (Ralston, *Venezuelan Arbitrations of* 1903 (1904), p. 172); *Life Insurance* cases decided by Judge Parker in the German-American Claims Commission (*Consolidated Edition of Decisions*, p. 137). Detailed reference was also made to Borchard in *A.J.*, XX (1926), p. 70.

Company because for several years this company had been in a special condition, such condition was created by the fact that the Government of Mexico had to take over the management of the lines in order to face an emergency which put in serious danger the social order and even the independence of that Nation. Considering the matter even from this viewpoint, there would be no international responsibility on the part of the Government of Mexico for this act. States have always resorted to extraordinary measures to save themselves from imminent dangers and the injuries to foreigners resulting from these measures do not generally afford a basis for claim. Moratoriums imposed upon National Banks are measures of this character, and there is no precedent showing that international indemnities have been awarded on this ground. The foreigner, residing in a country which, by reason of natural, social or international calamities is obliged to adopt those measures, must suffer the natural detriment to his affairs, without any remedy, since Governments, as expressed by a distinguished jurist, are not insurers against every event." (At pp. 192, 193.)

[Report: *Opinions of Commissioners*, October 1930 to July 1931, p. 175.]

NOTE.—And see *ibid.*, pp. 193-206, for the Dissenting Opinion of Nielsen, Commissioner, who was of the view that Mexico was responsible for the acts of her authorities causing a *direct* injury, namely, the destruction of property rights of an American citizen.

Damages—Measure of—Remoteness of Damage.

See Case No. 229 (*Royal Holland Lloyd* v. *United States* (*e*)).

F.—INTEREST

I.—In General

Interest—Award of—In Cases of Agreements to Compensate *ex gratia*. **Case No. 116**

In re GRIESE.

German-Mexican Claims Commission. January 17, 1930.

Decision No. 8.

THE FACTS.—This was a claim on behalf of a German national in respect of damage caused by revolutionary forces.

Case No. 116 *Contd.* The Claims Convention of March 16, 1925, provided for the payment of compensation for damage due to certain specified causes. It provided, further, that the Commissioners should decide in accordance with the principles of equity, since it was "the desire of Mexico *ex gratia* fully to compensate the injured parties" and that it was therefore "to be sufficient that it be established that the alleged damage actually took place and was due to one of the causes enumerated in the Convention for Mexico to feel moved *ex gratia* to afford such compensation." The Convention made no provision for the payment of interest on awards. Nevertheless, the German Agent contended that interest should be paid by Mexico.

Held : that the claimant should recover the amount of the damage, but that no interest should be awarded. The German Commissioner took the view that no interest could be awarded in cases in which the liability of Mexico was *ex gratia*, but that it could be awarded in the case of claims based on international law. The Presiding Commissioner took the view that interest might be awarded whenever the Commission should consider it equitable. Neither of these Commissioners considered that interest should be awarded in the present case. The Mexican Commissioner dissented.[1]

[Unreported.]

II.—Rate of Interest. Compound Interest

Interest—Award of—Rate of Interest—*Dies a quo—Dies ad quem.*

See Case No. 229 (*Royal Holland Lloyd* v. *United States*, (*f*) *and* (*g*)).

[1] The German Commissioner said : "I am disposed to agree with the thesis of the Mexican Agent that an indemnity based solely on a promise *ex gratia* cannot bear interest without an express declaration by Mexico to this effect. The silence of the Convention must, therefore, in my view, be interpreted to the effect that interest should not be awarded by our Commission with respect to this class of indemnities. The other part of the thesis of the Mexican Agent is without doubt erroneous. It is not true that all the indemnities with which our Commission deals are *ex gratia*, that is, spontaneous and gratuitous. On the contrary, many of them are based on the general principles of international law. There is no reason to consider that Mexico is exempt from the payment of interest in cases in which its responsibility is based on international law, and in such cases international law or the practice of previous international tribunals has established rules for the payment of interest." Probably the dissent of the Mexican Commissioner amounts to an *obiter* suggestion that interest could in no case be awarded.

For a discussion of the practice of other Commissions, see Feller, *The Mexican Claims Commissions* (1936), pp. 308-312.

G.—MISCELLANEOUS

State Responsibility—Miscellaneous—Occupation of House by Military Forces—Payment of Rent—Whether Constituting Contractual Relation as Distinguished from Compulsory Occupation. **Case No. 117**

In re HOWARD.

Great Britain and Mexico : Claims Commission.

(Zimmerman, Stoker, Flores).

March 26, 1931.

THE FACTS.—This was a claim for the difference in the rental value of, and for damage caused to, a house of which revolutionary forces in Mexico took possession in July 1914 and of which the plaintiff was deprived until July 1918. During the period of occupation the plaintiff received rent at the rate of 15 pesos a month, while the rental value of the house as stated in the Memorial was 80 pesos. The Mexican Government submitted that as the plaintiff received a rent, the claim arose out of contract and did not therefore fall within the competence of the Commission, which had jurisdiction to consider damage caused as the result of revolutionary troubles.

Held : that independently of the question whether the Commission was competent to take cognisance of claims arising out of contractual relations, it had jurisdiction in the present case. "There could not be assumed free will on the side of the owner. His house was occupied by authorities, civil or military, and he had no other choice than to cede it to them. The fact that now and then he received a certain amount from some of those who were in actual possession, does not change the compulsory character of the occupation nor convert it into a contract of lease. It seems only natural that claimant accepted what those in power were disposed to pay. It is not shown that he declared himself satisfied with these payments, nor that he has ever waived his right to claim for indemnification as soon as this might prove possible." (At p. 16.)

[Report : *Decisions and Opinions of the Commissioners*, 1933, p. 15.]

PERMANENT COURT OF INTERNATIONAL JUSTICE.

State Responsibility—International Debts—Set-Off.

For a case of a set-off of a debt owed by one State to another see the Advisory Opinion of the Permanent Court of International Justice given on March 8, 1932,[1] on the *Interpretation of the Greco-Bulgarian Agreement of December 9th*, 1927 (*Caphandaris-Molloff Agreement*) : *P.C.I.J.*, Series A/B, No. 45. The matter dealt with by the Court did not raise issues of general importance and is therefore not reported in this volume.

State Responsibility—Miscellaneous—Unjustified Enrichment.

See Case No. 115 (*United States of America on behalf of Dickson Car Wheel Company* v. *United Mexican States*).

State Responsibility—Miscellaneous—Responsibility for Act of Consul Acting on Behalf of a Foreign Consul.

See Case No. 102 (*Chevreau Case*).

[1] The Court was composed as follows : Adatci (President) ; Guerrero (Vice-President) ; Baron Rolin-Jaequemyns, Count Rostworowski, Fromageot, Altamira, Anzilotti, Urrutia, Sir Cecil Hurst, Schücking, van Eysinga, Wang (Judges) ; Caloyanni and Papazoff (Judges *ad hoc*).

PART VI

THE INDIVIDUAL IN INTERNATIONAL LAW

A.—IN GENERAL

I.—Position of Individuals in International Law

[See also Part I, INTERNATIONAL LAW IN GENERAL : v. *Relation to Municipal Law ;* and Part VIII, TREATIES : ix. *Operation and Enforcement of Treaties.*]

Individuals—Position in International Law—How far Benefiting Directly under a Treaty regardless of Municipal Legislation—The Crown as Trustee or Agent for the Subject. **Case No. 118**

CIVILIAN WAR CLAIMANTS ASSOCIATION LTD. *v.* THE KING.

British House of Lords. November 19, 1931.

(Lords Buckmaster, Warrington of Clyffe, Atkin, Tomlin, and Macmillan.)

THE FACTS.—The suppliants were a company formed to obtain compensation for civilians who had suffered loss or damage in person or property from German air raids, bombardment, sinking of ships, and other causes during the war, 1914-1918, and were assignees of the claims of a large number of individual claimants who had suffered damage from these causes. At the end of the War, by the Treaty of Versailles, Germany accepted responsibility for herself and her allies for causing all the loss and damage to which the Allied and Associated Governments and their nationals had been subjected (Article 231), and undertook to make compensation for all damage done to the civilian population of the Allied and Associated Powers and to their property (Article 232). The amount of the damage was to be determined by a Reparation Commission (Article 233). The findings of this Commission were to be notified to the German Government as representing the extent of that Government's obligations (Article 233).

The suppliants brought a Petition of Right against the Crown and claimed :

(1) That the damage to the claimants was included in the total claims against Germany submitted to the Repara-

Case No. 118 ***Contd.***

tion Commission by the Crown and in the assessment of the claims of this country against Germany notified by the Commission to the German Government ;

(2) That the Crown had received from Germany payments under the Treaty of Versailles (including payments in respect of the sums due under Articles 231 and 232) and that Germany had made these payments on the understanding that these claimants would be paid out of these moneys ;

(3) That, even if the making of a treaty was a high prerogative in respect of which the Crown could not act as trustee or agent for any British subject, His Majesty's prerogative was limited to the performance of the provisions of the Treaty, and the moneys received from Germany (or part thereof) were moneys held and received for and on behalf of the claimants who were the persons referred to in Article 232, and the Crown held the moneys as agent or trustee for the claimants.

The suppliants also relied on various statements made by Ministers of the Crown, leading them to believe that money would be obtained from Germany to compensate them, and on invitations to register their claims with the Foreign Claims Office and the Reparation Claims Office.

Held, by Roche, J., in the Court of first instance :

(1) That it was a general principle of English law that, in all that related to the making and performance of a treaty with another Sovereign, the Crown was acting under its prerogative, and could not be an agent or trustee for any person whatsoever. It was not possible to distinguish the position of the Crown in making the treaty and in disposing of the proceeds of the treaty (*Rustomjee* v. *The Queen*, (1876) 1 Q.B.D. 487 ; 2 Q.B.D. 69 (C.A.)) ;

(2) That, under this principle, the Crown, in concluding the Treaty of Versailles and in carrying it out and receiving payments from Germany under it, did not act as agent or trustee for any individual British subjects, and did not hold any moneys received by it as agent or trustee, whatever might be the grounds on which the payments had been claimed from Germany, or the provisions of the Treaty under which the payments were made ;

(3) That this principle applied, except in so far as the position was altered in any particular case by Act of Parliament or

Orders or Regulations made under the authority of any Act of Parliament (*Baron de Bode* v. *The Queen*, 13 Q.B. 364; 3 H.L.C. 449);

(4) That, although the relations of the Crown and individual British creditors, in respect of debts recovered through the Ex-Enemy Debts Clearing House, were governed by the provisions of the Treaty of Peace Act, 1920, and Orders in Council made thereunder, in a manner which might create an exception to the general principle stated above, there was no Act or Statutory Order which applied to the claims of the suppliants or to the moneys recovered from Germany in respect of their claims so as to prevent the application of the general Common Law principle;

(5) That consequently the Crown held the moneys recovered from Germany under the Peace Treaty under its prerogative and was under a duty to administer such moneys according to the advice of its ministers. The administration of such moneys was a matter for Parliament, and not for courts of law. The suppliants could not establish any claim to such moneys enforceable in a court of law.

On appeal, both the Court of Appeal and the House of Lords decided in favour of the respondent on substantially the same grounds as Roche, J. Lord Buckmaster held, *inter alia*:

(1) That there was no evidence whatever of any acceptance of trusteeship or agency by the Crown;

(2) That the persons whose claims were made were not considered by Germany in making the payment at all. The terms of the Treaty were that Germany should pay the sum necessary to satisfy the claims of various people, and it was left to the governments themselves, as between them and their nationals, to determine how the money was to be distributed.

Per Lord Atkin: " . . . when the Crown is negotiating with another Sovereign a treaty, it is inconsistent with its sovereign position that it should be acting as agent for the nationals of the sovereign State, unless indeed the Crown chooses expressly to declare that it is acting as agent. There is nothing, so far as I know, to prevent the Crown acting as agent or trustee if it chooses deliberately to do so. In the circumstances of this case there appears to me to be nothing which indicates that the Crown expressly assumed the position of agent or trustee, and I think the circumstances negative the idea that the Crown ever did intend to occupy that position and negative any circumstance from which the law might impose upon it the position either of agent or trustee."

[Report: 46 *T.L.R.* 581 (Roche, J.); 47 *T.L.R.* 102 (C.A.); *L.R.*, [1932] A.C. 14 (H. of L.).]

Case No. 119 **Individuals—Position in International Law—Benefits Stipulated for Individuals in Treaties—How far Conferring Direct Rights upon Individuals—Governments as Trustees of Individuals—Relation of Treaties to Municipal Law—Necessity of Municipal Legislation—Interpretation of Treaties—The English Doctrine of Equity of Redemption in Treaties.**

ADMINISTRATOR OF GERMAN PROPERTY *v.* KNOOP.

England, High Court of Justice (*Chancery Division*).

November 21, 22, 23, *December* 19, 1932.

THE FACTS.—In accordance with Article 297 of the Treaty of Versailles which reserved to the Allied Powers the right to liquidate the property of German nationals within their territories at the date of the Treaty, Article 1 (xvi) of the Treaty of Peace Order, 1919, made under the Treaty of Peace Act, 1919, created certain charges on all such property of German nationals. In this case the plaintiff, the Administrator of German Property, claimed a declaration that certain moneys in the United Kingdom, held by trustees of a will proved in 1871, on behalf of four beneficiaries of German nationality, were subject to these charges. The defendants contended, *inter alia*, that in so far as these charges continued to exist they ought to be released pursuant to the terms of the London Agreement, concluded in 1929 between the British and German Governments. Article I of this Agreement provided: "The Government of the United Kingdom will . . . release and where necessary re-transfer to the original German owners . . . the property rights and interests originally belonging to them and now subject to the charge created in pursuance of the Treaty of Versailles where such property was not already liquid, liquidated or finally disposed of at the date of the coming into force of the agreement." This Agreement, they contended, was entered into by the German Government as agent and trustee for the defendants (and other German nationals in the same position) as principals, who were therefore entitled to rely on it. The case of *Fenton Textile Association, Ltd.* v. *Krassin and Others* [(1921) 38 *T.L.R.* 259] was referred to as authority for the proposition that the Court could look at and give effect to any treaty which did not offend against the law of the land or require it to be altered.

Held (by Maugham, J.): for the plaintiff.

(1) "The London Agreement . . . has not been, so far as related to anything with which this Court is concerned, the subject of an English statute, and the agreement is, therefore, not one on which reliance can be placed in this Court as justifying a property claim."

(2) As to the proposition that in negotiating the London Agreement the German Government was acting as agent and trustee on behalf of its nationals, the general principles applicable, except perhaps in a very few exceptional cases, were laid down in *Civilian War Claimants Association* v. *The King*[1] [Case No. 118] and *Rustomjee* v. *The Queen*[2]—"the relation of trustee or agent which is alleged to subsist between a Sovereign Power and the subjects of that Sovereign Power in the negotiation and conclusion of a treaty is one which cannot exist in any State like ours and, I may add, in any State like that which now exists in Germany." There might, of course, have been an express declaration of agency, but none was discoverable in this case, nor could one be implied. "I may perhaps observe for myself that if one Sovereign Power enters into an agreement or treaty with another on the terms that the former agrees to release or to transfer to the nationals of the latter valuable rights, while the latter agrees to make payments of value to the former, [3] there would seem to be the strongest possible ground for not laying hold of expressions here and there for the purpose of arriving at the conclusion that, whether or not the one Sovereign Power complies with its obligations, the other Sovereign Power is bound to pay to the nationals of that other Sovereign Power the sums which are mentioned or referred to."

(3) In accordance with the view expressed in *Josef Invald Aktiengesellschaft* v. *Pfeiffer*, (1927) 43 *T.L.R.* 399; 44 *T.L.R.* 352, the Court held that the effect of the charge created by the Treaty and the Order in Council was to divest the property from the persons otherwise entitled to it and give the Administrator the right to retain and liquidate it without any right of redemption on the part of such persons and that a conveyance or transfer would be necessary to restore the property to them. " . . . It would be extraordinary if the English doctrine

[1] *L.R.*, [1932] A.C. 14.

[2] (1876), 1 Q.B.D. 487; 2 Q.B.D. 69.

[3] This refers to the Agreement concluded with Germany at the Hague Conference in 1929 for the final settlement of the reparations problem, ratified, together with the London Agreement, in May 1930.

Case No. 119 *Contd.* equity of redemption was to be found in such a treaty, because it is well known to most people who have ever had anything to do with French or Continental Laws that those laws do not contain any such doctrine as that of trusts or anything resembling the English doctrine of equity of redemption."

[Report: *L.R.* [1933] Ch. 439.]

Case No. 120 **Position of Individuals in International Law—Aliens—Protection by the Home State—Nature of the Legal Relation between the Home State and the National in Whose Favour Diplomatic Protection is Exercised—Discretion of the Political Department—Claim against the State on account of Inadequate Protection—Nature of the Claim against the Foreign State.**

GSCHWIND *v.* SWISS CONFEDERATION.

Switzerland, Federal Court. October 14, 1932.

THE FACTS.—Gschwind, a Swiss national, had since 1899 owned an export house for cotton and textile machinery in Manchester, with a branch at St. Gallen (Switzerland). During the World War the British authorities took certain measures, in connection with the general regulation of trade with neutral countries, as the result of which Gschwind suffered damage to his business. He sued the British Government for compensation, but his action was for the greater part dismissed in 1927 by the decision of the English War Claims Compensation Court. He thereupon requested the Swiss Federal Council to put forward his claim for compensation against the British Government through diplomatic channels. After having had a number of meetings with the Swiss Legation in London, Gschwind's English solicitor drafted a "memorandum" which the Legation submitted to the British Government for "favourable consideration." Subsequently, the British Government intimated to the Swiss Minister that they were not in a position to entertain the claim for compensation inasmuch as, contrary to the Swiss contention, no violation of the Commercial and Establishment Treaty of 1855 between the United Kingdom and Switzerland had taken place. The British Government's reply was then communicated to Gschwind, who thereupon applied for a renewed submission to the British Government of his claims, accompanied by fresh evidence. After further examination the Federal Political Department decided not to take any further diplomatic steps with the British Government. Thereupon Gschwind filed an action for damages against the Swiss Confederation in the Federal Court. He contended that a "legal relationship" analogous to that of agency had been created between himself and the Federal Political Department, and that in executing this quasi-contractual duty the Department had failed to exercise due care.

Held: that the action must be dismissed. Between the plaintiff and the defendant, the Swiss Confederation, there was neither an agency nor any other contractual relationship. Such a relation would be necessary to give rise to an obligation on the part of the Confederation to pay damages for improper performance of a duty undertaken in circumstances like the present.

"The granting of diplomatic protection in respect of injuries inflicted upon nationals by authorities or servants of a foreign State in disregard of rules of international law is not merely a right, under international law, of the home State as against the foreign State. From the point of view of internal constitutional law, diplomatic protection is also an administrative duty generally towards the nationals who have suffered injury. In so far as diplomatic protection can be combined with other State interests, it is a duty incumbent on the organ in charge of the foreign affairs of the country, viz. the Federal Council and the Political Department respectively. It is a duty established in the interest of the nation as a whole, which is entitled to expect that foreign countries will treat its citizens in accordance with international law. Such protection is part of the administration of the State. All citizens are entitled to it under equal conditions and in the same way. However, the acts of the public authority in this matter must be governed by objective rules of general application. Therefore, if a Swiss subject alleges that he has suffered damage as the result of a breach of international law, and applies to the Federal Council for intercession with the foreign State and for steps to be taken with a view to obtaining compensation, such application can only have the object of drawing the attention of the federal authority to the case and of inducing it to examine the matter. The steps to be taken are not determined by the request of the applicant, but by the substantive law governing the duties of the competent authority in such matters. The fact that he has been injured in breach of international law does not confer upon the citizen a right to assistance by the Confederation in a manner desired by him. This cannot be so, simply for the reason that the competent authority cannot be guided only by the interests of the injured individual; it has to consider, simultaneously and

Case No. 120 *Contd.*

primarily, the general interest of the State and the possible reactions of such proposed steps on the political and other relations with the foreign State. Now what is true with regard to initiating diplomatic protection is equally true of the scope and continuation of the measures taken in cases in which the foreign Government adopts a negative attitude. The same considerations prevail here as in the case of the commencement of the proceedings. If in the light of these considerations further diplomatic action appears inexpedient, then this must influence decisively the attitude of the intervening authority. The appreciation of these various considerations presupposes an exact knowledge of the political situation and of the relations for the time being with the foreign State. Accordingly, the discretion of the political authority in charge of Swiss international relations must be unfettered and final (see Article 102, No. 2, of the Swiss Constitution)." It was true that the plaintiff had received a communication from the political federal authorities declaring their willingness to take steps in his favour. However, such "promise is merely a declaration by the competent authorities that they are prepared to do what it is their duty to do under the existing law; it is an intimation of the proposed official steps. It is impossible to construe that communication as the creation of a contractual relationship with the applicant, a relationship in the nature of an agency imposing on the Confederation a duty to protect the interests of the principal by enforcing his claims against a foreign State. Apart from the substantive reasons against such an interpretation, its adoption would not, from the practical point of view, be beneficial to the person asking for protection. For it would necessarily lead the federal authority to decline to take steps against a foreign government, even in cases in which they would otherwise have been prepared to act, in order not to be forced by such a promise into a legal relationship which must ultimately be untenable in view of their duty to take into consideration general interests other than those of the injured individual.[1]

[1] The Court distinguished the present case from *Re Bächli*, dated March 1, 1927 (unreported) and *Re Wäffler* (*Entscheidungen des Schweizerischen Bundesgerichts*, 55 (II), p. 107. In these cases a Swiss legation abroad received advances from Swiss subjects in order to assist compatriots who had become destitute in consequence of revolutionary disorders in the foreign State concerned. The legation also accepted valuables by way of deposit. The Court said: "It may be admitted that in those cases contractual relationships—a loan and a deposit under public law—were held to exist between the Confederation and the lender and depositor respectively. But this does not mean that a similar relationship has been created by the mere 'promise' to take steps against a foreign government in the interest of a national who suffered injury contrary to international law. . . ."

"The argument based on agency or quasi-agency is incompatible with the terms of the request addressed by the Confederation to the foreign State. In the applications dated February 28, 1927, October 3, 1927, and February 22, 1928, respectively, the plaintiff requested the Political Department to apply to the British Government on the ground that British authorities and officials had infringed, to the plaintiff's detriment, provisions of the Swiss-English Commercial and Establishment Treaty and thus had committed a breach of the principle of international law "*pacta sunt servanda.*" The intervention requested by the plaintiff could be based only on some such principle of international law. The infringement of private rights alone could not have afforded sufficient ground for intervention. For a State which intervenes with a foreign State on account of a breach of international law—whether of a convention or of a recognised principle of customary international law—and claims reparation therefor, asserts (as has already been decided in *Entscheidungen des Schweizerischen Bundesgerichts*, 52 (II), pp. 235 *et seq.*,[1] particularly at p. 259, in the case of an intervention connected with a frontier incident) a claim appertaining to the State and arising out of the non-performance of the convention entered into with the foreign State or the disregard of the consideration due to it under the recognised customary law governing international relations. It makes no difference that the State in effect acts in the interest of individual nationals in cases in which the breach of international law has at the same time resulted in injury to their property. In the latter case the individual may be in a position to sue the foreign State in its own courts, provided that the municipal law of that State permits such actions. This was in fact what the plaintiff did in respect of part of his claim before the English War Claims Compensation Court. The simultaneous breach of international law can, in principle, give rise not to claims made by the individual directly affected, but only by the State whose national he is. It must be admitted that, contrary to the view which was formerly universally adopted in international law and which seems to be predominant even at the present day, some modern writers attribute legal capacity under international law not only to States, but also to individuals (cf. Politis, *Les Nouvelles Tendances du Droit International* (1927), pp. 55 *et seq.*; Knubben in Stier-Somlo, *Handbuch des Völkerrechts* (1928), pp. 487 *et seq.*). However, even these writers admit that those cases constitute

[1] *Heirs of Oswald* v. *Swiss Government*, *Annual Digest*, 1925-1926, Case No. 180.

Case No. 120 *Contd.*

exceptions, and that a special international convention is necessary (*e.g.*, Articles 297 and following of the Peace Treaty of Versailles, 1919, concerning the right of nationals of the ratifying Powers to appear before Mixed Arbitral Tribunals) in order to confer upon individuals international rights of their own: see principally Knubben, *loc. cit.*, p. 496. The plaintiff does not contend that a convention of this nature exists in the present case. He has not even attempted to put forward against Great Britain a claim based on international law (*e.g.*, by bringing a claim before an international arbitral tribunal). That being so, no relationship of agency can arise where a State, by intervening with a foreign government on account of a breach of international law, asserts a right appertaining to it, or where such State decides to intervene and notifies the national concerned of this fact. It also follows that the competent State authority must be able to make decisions independently of the wishes of the injured national, both as to whether diplomatic protection shall take place at all and as to how far it shall be pursued, for instance, by invoking arbitration in case of a negative attitude of the foreign State."

[Report: *Entscheidungen des Schweizerischen Bundesgerichts*, 58 (II), p. 463.]

NOTE.—See also *Pig-Exporting Co. of Kőbánya* v. *Hungarian State Treasury*, decided by the Hungarian Supreme Court on March 31, 1932 (No. P. IV. 4188/1930). In that case the authorities of the Czechoslovak Republic refused to allow the plaintiff to import pigs. He claimed damages from the Hungarian Treasury on the ground that the Czechoslovak action was based on a commercial and veterinary convention entered into between Hungary and Czechoslovakia. The Supreme Court dismissed the claim. The Court said: "An international contract is the expression of the constitutional sovereign will of the Hungarian State. The Treasury cannot be made responsible for any such measure even if it causes prejudice to all or some Hungarian citizens." [Report: *Grill Uj Döntvénytâra*, XXV, Case No. 744.]

Individuals—Effect of Treaties—Jurisdiction of Mixed Courts.

See Case No. 94 (*Iscaki* v. *Mutual Life Insurance Company of New York*; *De Berlin* v. *Hoirs Fabio Eminente*; *J. Shallam & Sons* v. *Compagnie Universelle du Canal de Suez*).

Individuals—Agreements with Foreign Governments—Visa.

See Case No. 139 (*Frisina* v. *Egyptian Government*).

Individuals—Effect of Treaties—International Unions—Telegraphic Convention of 1875—Interpretation of Article 3 of the Convention—Immunity of Private Companies Acting under Sovereign Authorisation.

See Case No. 217a (*Elias and Abdou Noujaim* v. *Eastern Telegraph Co.*).

B.—NATIONALITY

I.—In General. Proof of Nationality

Nationality—In General—Recognition of Acts of Foreign States as to Acquisition and Loss of Nationality.

See Case No. 15 (*Ettinger* v. *Ministry of the Interior*).

Nationality—The Term "National"—Meaning of—How Far Applicable to Companies.

See Case No. 147 (*Foreign Companies (Acquisition of Property) Case*).

Nationality—Proof of—Consular Certificates. **Case No. 121**

KLEMP CASE.

German-Mexican Claims Commission. April 11, 1927.

Interlocutory Resolution.

THE FACTS.—The claim of an alleged German national for damages having been submitted to the Commission, the Mexican Agent contended that there was not sufficient proof of the nationality of the claimant. The only proof submitted was a certificate executed by a German Consul in Mexico stating that the claimant was born in Mexico, that he had been inscribed in the Register of the German Legation, and that he had always preserved his German nationality.

Held (by Cruchaga, Presiding Commissioner, for the Commission) : that the Mexican contention was right. A consular certificate could not be considered as sufficient proof of nationality. The President said : "Consular certificates of registration establish nationality only for purposes of statistics ; of complying with the laws of compulsory military service ; of

Case No. 121 ***Contd.***

payment of taxes upon income from an estate which a national, resident abroad, may have in his own country; of acquisitions of property, inheritances or legacies; or of pensions and maintenances, etc.

"Such consular certificates of registration are of a domestic nature as *prima facie* proof of nationality. They can serve and be utilised, in an emergency, to establish the presumption that the bearer has the right to protection, as in the case of arbitrary acts of the local police or molestation to the person or property, if the local law authorises such protection. But they are not sufficient evidence of nationality in claims against the State for alleged damage or injury, especially when these claims are prosecuted before a mixed commission or international arbitral tribunal whose initial duty it is to consider the true nationality of the claimant. . . .

"To grant to the Consul the absolute power of weighing and deciding upon the documentary evidence submitted by an applicant for registration, would be tantamount to creating him a judge to determine the right to submit claims to an international mixed commission. This would mean trespassing upon the essential duty of the commission to ascertain the nationality of the claimants, on which the very right to claim before it is based.

"The duty of the commission to establish, by itself, the nationality of the claimants, before granting or denying them the right to initiate their actions, cannot, by reason of its very nature, be delegated. It would be a delegation of such primary power and duty to compel the commission to recognise as irrebutable or sufficient, the mere record of consular registration.

"The preceding conclusions become still more evident if we take into consideration the difficulties that are presented by cases of dual nationality or of conflicts of nationality, arising from the doctrines of *jus soli* and *jus sanguinis*. If the consular registration is sufficient proof of nationality, it would follow that the registree, in spite of having double nationality, is a national of the country with which he is registered, thus preventing any attempt which the other country might make to have him considered as its own national. In cases of dual nationality, the consular certificate would be decisive for the question of the proper nationality and, if the criterion taken by the Consul is that imposed by the principle of *jus sanguinis*, the criterion imposed by the principle of *jus soli* would thereby be ignored. The Consul would in this way decide, without possibility of appeal, a question in which the sovereignty of two countries is involved. In effect, for example, a child of a German born in Mexico, is, according to German Law, a German, and could be entered in the German consular registers in Mexico; but this same child, born in Mexico of a German father, is a Mexican, and the certificate of registration as a German would have no weight with the Mexican authorities. . . .

"Germany, a country which has adopted the principle of *jus sanguinis*, regards as a German the son of a German, even when the child is born on alien territory, birth in Germany being no criterion for the acquisition of German nationality.

"The certificate which is presented in this case records that the claimant, Klemp, born in Bochum (Germany), is entered in the Consular Register. The fact of his having been born on German territory does not impress upon him the character of a German national. It therefore follows that the very document invoked as exclusive proof of the nationality of the claimant, shows that it is not proven pursuant to German Law."

[Report: *A.J.*, XXIV (1930), p. 610.]

Proof of Nationality—Exchange of Notes—Binding Effect. **Case No. 122**

SOCIÉTÉ DE BIENFAISANCE GRECQUE-ORTHODOXE SYRIENNE D'ALEXANDRIE *v.* G. J. SIAG AND OTHERS.

Egypt, Civil Tribunal of Alexandria. May 26, 1932.

THE FACTS.—In this action the plaintiff association claimed an interest in the immovable property of the late Joseph Hanna Siag, under a holographic will made in May 1891. Among other arguments it was contended by the defendants that the deceased had died a Turkish, and not a Russian, subject, and that in the determination of rights of succession to his property the mixed tribunals were incompetent. The plaintiff association, in reply, argued that the deceased's Russian nationality had been frequently recognised by the Egyptian Government, and produced a letter from the Ministry for Foreign Affairs, dated 1924, explaining that the Egyptian Government had in 1915 addressed enquiries to the diplomatic representative of Russia concerning the deceased's nationality; that it had been confirmed that he had been registered as a Russian national by the Russian Consulate and was still claimed by the Russian Government as a subject; and that the Egyptian Ministry had then informed the diplomatic representative of Russia that it had given instructions to the

Case No. 122 *Contd.* local authorities that the deceased's wife must be treated as a Russian national.

Held: that this exchange of notes between the Egyptian and Russian Governments was conclusively binding on the Tribunal, and that the Russian nationality of the deceased could no longer be questioned, for "the judicial authority is incompetent to question the regularity of an act of sovereignty emanating from two governments in the plenitude of their powers."

[Report: *Gazette des Tribunaux Mixtes d'Egypte*, XXIV (1933-1934), p. 86.]

NOTE.—In March 1932, the Mixed Court of Appeal upheld in principle, but subject to exceptions which applied in the instant case, the rule laid down in earlier decisions that the mixed tribunals are incompetent in disputes between local subjects and subjects of States detached from the former Ottoman Empire by the Treaty of Lausanne: *ibid.*, pp. 70 and 109. The whole question is fully discussed in a decision of the full Court of Appeal given on May 2, 1929: *ibid.*, XXI, (1930-1931), p. 87.

Case No. 123 **Proof of Nationality—Consular Certificates—Conflict of Evidence.**

BOUBEZ *v.* DAME EDRA SABBAGH BEY.

Egypt, Mixed Court of Appeal of Alexandria.

February 17, 1932.

THE FACTS.—The defendant claimed Spanish protection, and, in the Court below, produced a certificate from the Spanish Consul; but, in the Court of Appeal, a certificate from the Egyptian Government was produced, in which it was ordered that she be treated as an Egyptian. The competence of the mixed courts was put in issue.

Held: that, although a certificate of a consul was sufficient proof of foreign nationality where no proof of Egyptian nationality was offered, yet, where foreign nationality was contested, precise proof of the mode of its acquisition was required. The Court would not relinquish either to consuls or to the Egyptian Government the legal decision of such questions "unless the rule in virtue of which nationality is claimed arises out of an international agreement which the Governments interested are alone competent to interpret."

[Report: *Clunet*, 60 (1933), p. 445; *Gazette des Tribunaux Mixtes d'Egypte*, XXIV (1933-1934), p. 79.]

NOTE.—As to the effect of such a diplomatic agreement in a case of disputed nationality see Case No. 122 above.

II.—Acquisition of Nationality. Nationality as Affected by Changes of Sovereignty

Nationality—Acquisition of—Compulsory Acquisition of Nationality—Whether Countenanced by International Law. **Case No. 124**

In re RAU.

German-Mexican Claims Commission. January 14, 1930.

Decision No. 51.

THE FACTS.—This was a claim on behalf of an alleged German national in respect of damage caused to his property by revolutionary forces. The Mexican Agent objected to the jurisdiction of the Commission on the ground that, by purchasing real property in Mexico, the claimant had acquired Mexican nationality under Article 30 of the Mexican Constitution of 1857. Article 30 provided that "aliens who acquire immovable property in the Republic or have Mexican children, provided they do not express the wish to preserve their nationality," should be Mexican nationals. In answer to this contention the German Agent pointed out that a Mexican Law of 1886 provided that Mexican nationality was not automatically acquired, but that the alien was required to fulfil certain formalities in order to become a Mexican. The Mexican Agent thereupon contended that the Law of 1886 was unconstitutional.

Held (by Cruchaga, Presiding Commissioner, for the Commission): that the Commission had jurisdiction. The Commission had no power to pass on the constitutionality of Mexican laws. The Law of 1886 must be considered as interpreting the Constitution so as not to confer Mexican nationality automatically. Such an interpretation was in accordance with international law, which does not permit compulsory change of nationality.[1]

[Unreported.]

[1] See, to the same effect, the case of *Occelli*, decided by the Italian-Mexican Claims Commission, Decision No. 67 (unreported); and the case of *Barcena* decided by the Spanish-Mexican Claims Commission, Decision No 11 (unreported).

Case No. 125 **Nationality—Acquisition of—Commencement of—Declaration of Intention to Become a Citizen.**

JOHNSON *v.* NICKOLOFF *ET AL.*

United States, Circuit Court of Appeals, Ninth Circuit.

October 19, 1931.

(Wilbur, Sawtelle, Circuit Judges; James, District Judge.)

THE FACTS.—The appellant filed a motion for leave to prosecute an appeal *in forma pauperis* under the Act of June 27, 1922, c. 246, 42 U.S. Stat. L. 666 (28 U.S.C.A. § 832). This statute expressly limited the parties entitled to take advantage of its provisions to "any citizen of the United States entitled to commence any suit or action, civil or criminal, in any court of the United States." The appellant claimed to be a citizen of the United States by reason of having filed a declaration of intention to become a citizen on July 15, 1931, and because he had resided in Alaska for twenty years.

Held: that the motion should be denied. The benefits of the statute extend only to citizens: *Volk* v. *B. F. Sturtevant Co.*, 99 Fed. 532; *The Memphian*, 245 Fed. 484; *The Bennington*, 10 F. (2d) 799. The appellant was not a citizen, since a person does not become a citizen of the United States until the procedure of naturalisation has been fully complied with and an order divesting him of his former nationality and making him a citizen has been signed by a judge of a Court having jurisdiction: 26 *Op. Attys. Gen.* 611.

[Report: 52 F. (2d) 1074.]

Case No. 126 **Nationality—Re-acquisition of—Re-acquisition of Italian Citizenship by Residence in the Kingdom—Effect of Declaration of Desire to Retain the Acquired Citizenship.**

MARESCA *v.* BALSAMO.

Italy, Court of Cassation. May 29, 1931.

THE FACTS.—See *Annual Digest*, 1929-1930, Case No. 132. Maresca, an Italian citizen by birth, was naturalised as a citizen of the United States of America in 1915. He returned to Italy in 1923 and died there on June 17, 1926. In his will, dated March 31, 1924, he clearly showed his desire still to be regarded as an American citizen. The question of his nationality then became relevant in an action concerning his estate. According to Italian law an Italian naturalised abroad resumes his Italian citizenship after two years' continuous residence in Italy.

Held: that Maresca died an Italian citizen. The fact that he wished to retain American citizenship was immaterial. The status of citizen was not one which could be left to the free and unfettered choice of the individual, seeing that it was a matter of vital political interest. Freedom of choice could be recognised "only within the limits imposed by such interests, tantamount as they are to the defence of nationality. Thus the citizen cannot break that relationship by an act of will, except by government dispensation, unless, at the same time, he transfers his residence abroad. . . . The public element is similarly involved in the regulation of the re-acquisition of nationality. Even though foreign citizenship has been obtained, the original citizenship revives as soon as residence in the Kingdom has been continued for two years. Given this state of fact, the result follows automatically, with or without the knowledge of the person concerned. The re-acquisition of the original citizenship places the person concerned in the same status as that in which he was prior to the loss of citizenship. He can again cause his dependence on the original political unit to cease, but, *mutatis mutandis*, only on the same conditions as before, *i.e.*, by proving the acquisition of foreign citizenship. . . ."

[Report: *Foro italiano*, 1932, p. 904.]

NOTE.—See also, to the same effect, *Alessio* v. *Delù*, decided by the Court of Appeal of Turin on April 8, 1932: *Giurisprudenza Torinese*, 1932, p. 589. And see the judgment of the Court of Appeal of Naples of April 22, 1932: *Monitore dei Tribunali*, 1932, p. 576.

Nationality—Acquisition of—Acquisition of Citizenship through Performance of Military Service—Nature of Military Service in Question. **Case No. 127**

KAHN *v.* PODESTÀ OF MILAN.

Italy, Court of Milan. July 13, 1931.

THE FACTS.—Kahn, born in Milan on May 16, 1908, of a French father, was enrolled on the conscription lists on January 24, 1928. In the years 1928, 1929 and 1930 he asked for and obtained postponement of actual performance of military service on the ground of being a student. On May 8, 1930, he made an application for French citizenship and asked for recognition of French nationality.

Case No. 127 Contd. *Held*: that Kahn could not be considered a French citizen. "Article 6 of the Civil Code speaks of the acquisition of citizenship by those who have served or are serving in the national forces on land or sea or who have otherwise fulfilled the obligations of military conscription without claiming exemption from it on the ground of being a foreigner. Article 3 of the Law of 1912 refers in general terms to the performance of military service. For the fulfilment of the condition laid down by law in the Civil Code and in the law in force, the actual performance of military service is not necessary; it is sufficient that the obligations of conscription have been in some way complied with, even by mere attendance for medical inspection, provided that the person in question does not ask for exemption from military service on the ground of being a foreigner." In the present case Kahn, by asking for postponement of military service on the ground of being a student, rather showed directly a desire to serve with the national forces.

[Report: *Rivista*, 1932, p. 564.]

Nationality—Acquisition of—Validity of—Examination by International Tribunals.

See Case No. 98 (*Salem Case: United States and Egypt* (2)).

Nationality—Acquisition and Loss of—Effect as against Third States—Treaties—Effect on Third Parties—Effect on Russia of the Minorities Treaty of 1919—Interpretation of Treaties—Filling of Gaps by Construction—Russo-Polish Peace Treaty of March 15, 1921.

See Case No. 201 (*Minorities Treaty (Russian Subjects) Case*).

V.—Naturalisation

Case No. 128 **Nationality—Naturalisation—Retention of Former Nationality—Operation of Brazilian "Tacit Naturalisation" Laws.**

DE PAULI *v.* MINATA MARIA STELLA.

Brazil, Federal Supreme Court. July 18, 1932.

THE FACTS.—This case involved the operation of the Brazilian "tacit naturalisation" laws.[1] The plaintiff was a

[1] Art. 69 of the Brazilian Constitution of 1891 provided as follows: "The following are Brazilian citizens: ***5. Foreigners, residents of Brazil, who hold real estate in Brazil and who are married to Brazilian women or have Brazilian children, unless they have declared their intention to retain their original nationality." See Flournoy and Hudson, *A Collection of Nationality Laws* (1929), pp. 47-48.

woman of Italian birth, who had separated from her husband (also of Italian birth). She brought this action to annul a sale of her husband's property to two of his sons by a former marriage. Under Brazilian law,[1] the property of a married couple was governed by their national law. If their national law was Brazilian law, there was community of property and the wife could annul the sale in question.[2] If their national law was Italian, there was no community of property, and the sale was valid without the wife's consent.[3] The husband had come to Brazil, bought real property there, and had a daughter born (of the former marriage) in Brazil in 1890. In 1894 he married the plaintiff. In 1910 he bought the property in question. At the time of the marriage, husband and wife described themselves in the documents as "natives of Italy."[4] The Supreme Court of São Paulo upheld judgment for the plaintiff, on the ground that she was a Brazilian. On appeal by the defendants to the Federal Supreme Court,

Held: that the appeal must be dismissed. Since the husband already owned some realty and had a daughter born in Brazil in 1890, he was Brazilian at the time of his marriage unless he elected to retain his Italian nationality.[5] Some positive act on his part was necessary to retain his former nationality and to prevent him from being naturalised. There was no proof of such acts. The fact that they called themselves "natives of Italy"[4] was not proof of intention to retain Italian nationality. This was so although in another case such proof had been found in a description of the parties to the marriage as "of Italian nationality."[6]

[Report: 17 *Revista de Jurisprudencia Brasileira*, 319.]

NOTE.—See also *Rodrigues* v. *Nila Moreira* (September 11, 1930), 99 *Revista de Direito*, 507, where it was held that in the case of marriage between a Brazilian woman and a Portuguese husband, the marital property was governed by Brazilian law, seeing that the wife had not lost her Brazilian nationality of birth.

Naturalisation—Loss of Former Nationality—Conflict of Nationality.

See Case No. 98 (*Salem Case: United States and Egypt*, (3)).

[1] See the Brazilian Civil Code, Introduction, Art. 8. And see Clovis Bevilaqua, *Codigo Civil dos Estados Unidos do Brasil Commentado*, I, 123 (3rd ed., 1927).

[2] See the Brazilian Civil Code, Articles 258 and 259.

[3] See the Italian Civil Code, Art. 1433.

[4] "*naturaes da Italia.*"

[5] See footnote 1 on p. 254, *ante*.

[6] "*de nacionalidade italiana.*"

VI.—Expatriation. Loss of Nationality

Case No. 129 **Nationality—Loss of—Married Women—Burden of Proof—Presumptions—The Law of the United States.**

In re HANSEN *v.* CORSON CONSTRUCTION CO.; STATE INDUSTRIAL BOARD, RESPONDENT.

United States, Supreme Court of New York, Appellate Division. October 9, 1931.

(Van Kirk, P.J.; Hinman, Hill, Rhodes, Whitmeyer, JJ.)

THE FACTS.—This was an action commenced by the appellants before the State Industrial Board to commute a workmen's compensation award made to Louise Hansen, the widow of a deceased employee. Section 17 of the Workmen's Compensation Law provided that compensation to aliens shall be the same in amount as provided for residents and that "the Commission may, at its option, or upon the application of the insurance carrier, shall, commute all future installments of compensation to be paid to such aliens, by paying or causing to be paid to them one-half of the commuted amount of such future installments of compensation as determined by the Commission." The sole question involved was whether or not the widow was an alien. Her husband was admitted to citizenship on April 11, 1904. He married the claimant in the United States on August 26, 1913, she at that time being a citizen of Norway. In 1916 the claimant left the United States and thereafter resided continuously in Norway. The deceased remained a citizen of the United States until his death in 1929. The Industrial Board refused the application. On appeal,

Held: that the award should be affirmed. The burden was on the appellants to prove that the claimant was an alien, and that burden had not been discharged. Section 10 of title 8, U.S.C., the former statute as continued in force for the purpose of this case, provided that "any woman who is now or may hereafter be married to a citizen of the United States, and who might herself be lawfully naturalized, shall be deemed a citizen." It also provided that "any foreign woman who acquires American citizenship by marriage to an American shall be assumed to retain the same after the termination of the marital relation if she continue to reside in the United States, unless she makes formal renunciation thereof before a court having jurisdiction to naturalize aliens, or if she resides abroad, she may retain her citizenship by registering as such before a United States Consul within one year after the termination of such marital relation." The appellants had not proved that the claimant was an alien. The record failed to show whether or not the claimant appeared before a consul. Thus the appellants had not the benefit of the presumption which might arise if it were shown that the claimant had failed to register.

[Report: 233 App. Div. 326.]

Nationality—Loss of—Statelessness—Married Women—General Principles of Law—Unity of the Family. **Case No. 130**

NATIONALITY OF MARRIED WOMEN (DANZIG) CASE.

Danzig, High Court. November 30, 1932.

THE FACTS.—This was an appeal from a decision of the County Court dismissing a petition for divorce owing to lack of jurisdiction.

The parties contracted a marriage before the Registrar at Hamburg (Germany) on July 27, 1920. The plaintiff, the husband, was an Argentine national and the defendant at the time of her marriage was of German nationality. Having regard to the provisions of the Danzig Code of Civil Procedure, the jurisdiction of the Court depended upon the answer to the question whether the defendant was an alien or not. She claimed that by virtue of her marriage with an Argentine citizen she had acquired Argentine nationality. The Court examined whether or not she possessed Argentine nationality (*a*) by virtue of the law of Argentina or (*b*) by virtue of a general principle of law.

Held: that the defendant was not an alien within the meaning of Section 606, paragraph 4, of the Danzig Code of Civil Procedure. According to that clause an alien was a person who possessed the nationality of a foreign state; a stateless person was not an alien within the meaning of that provision. The defendant was not in a position to claim any nationality whatsoever and was accordingly to be regarded as stateless. The Court arrived at this conclusion on the following grounds:

(*a*) Through her marriage with an alien, the defendant had lost her German nationality. She did not, however, acquire at the same time Argentine nationality because Argentine law did not recognise marriage as a title for the acquisition of Argentine nationality. In order to become an Argentine citizen the defend-

Case No. 130 *Contd.* ant should have applied for Argentine nationality. No such application had ever been made. The defendant, through her marriage, had lost her German nationality without acquiring Argentine nationality, and had therefore become stateless.

(*b*) The Court could not accept the view that according to a general principle of law the wife shared the nationality of her husband. The principle that the family constituted a unit in regard to nationality laws was by no means common to all civilised peoples. The principle of the unity of the family from the point of view of nationality had lost ground and could no longer be regarded an an international principle.

[Report : *Danziger Juristische Monatsschrift*, vol. 12, p. 38.]

Loss of Nationality—Naturalisation—Conflict of Nationality.

See Case No. 98 (*Salem Case : United States and Egypt*, (3)).

Nationality—Renunciation of—Renunciation of Nationality Acquired by Option.

See Case No. 131 (*Option of Nationality* (*Austria*) *Case*).

VIII.—Double Nationality

Double Nationality—Principle of Effective Nationality.

See Case No. 98 (*Salem Case : United States and Egypt*, (3)).

IX.—Option

Case No. 131 **Option of Nationality—Nature of—Legal Effect of—Recognition by the Other State—Withdrawal of Option.**

Option of Nationality (Austria) Case.

Austria, Administrative Court. May 17, 1932.

The Facts.—Otto P. was born at Bautsch (Czechoslovakia), and was still resident there at the time of the present action. While in Vienna he gave notice in 1920 of his intention to exercise the right of opting for Austrian citizenship under Article 80 of the Treaty of St. Germain. The option was subsequently recognised as legally valid by an administrative decree. In 1927 the Federal Chancery certified that Otto P. had not acquired Austrian nationality under Article 80 of the Treaty of

St. Germain. Thereupon, by an order of the Federal Chancery under the Act concerning the allocation of homeless citizens, he was allocated to the parish of Liebenau.

Both Otto P. and the parish of Liebenau appealed to the Administrative Court against the order. They based their appeal on the contention that he was still a Czechoslovak citizen seeing that Czechoslovakia had not recognised the option, that the certificate given by the Federal Chancery stated expressly that he had not acquired Austrian nationality, and that he had made a declaration to the parish council of Bautsch to the effect that he desired to retain his Czechoslovak nationality.

Held: that the allocation was legal. The Convention of Brünn between Czechoslovakia and Austria provided expressly that the option under the Treaty of St. Germain was a "unilateral act of the person exercising the option, and as such created a right," and that "the certificate of this act has merely a declaratory effect." It was immaterial for the validity of the option proceedings whether or not the Czechoslovak Republic recognised them. A nationality acquired by way of option could not be given up by withdrawing the option, but only by way of proceedings instituted with a view to renouncing the nationality acquired as the result of it.

[Report: *Sammlung der Erkenntnisse des Verwaltungsgerichtshofes*, 1932 (Administrative Part), p. 322.]

Nationality—Acquisition and Loss of—Option—Germano-Polish Convention of August 30, 1924 (so-called Vienna Convention)—"Return to Territory"—Meaning of—Operation of Treaties—How Far Covering Acts Done Prior to the Treaty. **Case No. 132**

OPTION OF NATIONALITY (GERMANY) CASE.

Germany, Court of Appeal of Hamm. March 4, 1932.

THE FACTS.—The accused was born in 1892 at Posen, in the former Prussian Province of Posen. In 1912 he went to Essen (Germany) where he took up residence. During the War he was taken prisoner by the French army. In April 1920 he was sent back to Posen, which meanwhile had been ceded to Poland. In May 1920 he returned to the Ruhr district and established his residence at Düsseldorf. Subsequently he applied for a Polish passport, which was issued to him by the Polish Consulate at Essen. The Düsseldorf police then ordered him to pro-

Case No. 132 *Contd.*

duce his passport in order to prove his identity and his Polish nationality. He refused to comply with this order on the ground that he was a German subject, whereupon the police fined him for not obeying the order. He then applied to the Court for a judicial decision. The relevant treaty provisions are referred to below. The lower Court acquitted him. The Court of Appeal confirmed this decision, on grounds different from those of the Court below. It

Held: that the accused had lost his Polish nationality and retained only his German citizenship. Article 91 (4) of the Treaty of Versailles provided that "Poles who are German nationals . . . habitually resident in Germany"—a class of persons to which the accused belonged—should remain German citizens, but that they should have the right within two years to opt in favour of Polish nationality. This provision was qualified by Article 4 of the Treaty for the Protection of Minorities of June 28, 1919, between Poland and the Allied Powers. By the latter provision Poland recognised persons of German nationality, born on her territory of parents there domiciled, as Polish nationals *ipso facto* and without the requirement of any formality. It was not necessary for the persons in question to be domiciled there. They constituted a class of persons identical with the "Poles who are German nationals" of Article 91 (4) of the Treaty of Versailles; to this class was given the right to waive the Polish nationality thus acquired, within two years after the entry into force of the Treaty. As nationality questions became the subject of controversy between the two countries, a clarification of the position was brought about by Article 7 (1) of the German-Polish Convention concerning Questions of Option and Nationality, signed at Vienna on August 30, 1924, which expressly provided that German subjects who were born in districts subsequently ceded to Poland, of parents habitually residing there at the time of such birth, should acquire Polish nationality *ipso facto*. But Article 7 (3) laid down that the Polish nationality so acquired should be deemed to have been abandoned where a person had not returned to Poland by July 10, 1924, unless he should have claimed Polish nationality not later than February 28, 1925, before the Polish authorities referred to in Article 4 (2) of the Minorities Treaty, and should have proved that prior to July 10, 1924, he had applied in writing to a Polish authority for recognition of such nationality, and had received a refusal or a written answer equivalent to a refusal.

The effect of Article 7 (1) of the Vienna Convention was to

give the accused, as a Pole by birth, Polish, in addition to German, nationality. This Polish nationality he had renounced, if not expressly, at least by conduct, within the meaning of Article 7 (3). It was true that after the War, in April 1920, the accused was taken back to Poland by a French transport. However, even if he had consented to this, it could not be taken to imply a "return" as envisaged by Article 7 (3). "Not every coming back to Polish territory may be called a return under that provision. Considering what serious consequences, such as loss of nationality (for Art. 7 (4) provided for the divesting of German nationality in cases where Polish nationality was retained), are attached to a return, this condition may only be regarded as fulfilled if the person comes back with the intention of taking up residence in Polish territory." This was not the case with the accused. When he was brought back to Poland he remained there for only a very short period on a visit to his parents. He very soon returned to the Ruhr district, where he had worked and resided before the War.

Neither did the accused satisfy the conditions laid down in Article 7 (3) 1, by virtue of which a person might retain Polish nationality without returning to Poland, *i.e.*, by claiming it not later than February 28, 1925, before the authorities referred to in Article 4 (2) of the Minorities Treaty—"the competent Polish authorities in the country in which they are resident." His application for a Polish passport might be regarded as a "claim" within the meaning of this provision ; but this application had been made in 1923 (*i.e.*, before the Convention of Vienna).

"It follows from the wording of the provision that any claim to Polish nationality which shall result in loss of German nationality must have been made between the conclusion of the Vienna Convention and February 28, 1925. Earlier expressions of intention could not have produced that effect. This is clear if one bears in mind that the provisions speak only of "to claim" and not of "to claim or have claimed," and that the period during which such claims may be made is fixed by a period of time extending beyond the date of the coming into force of the Vienna Convention (January 31, 1925). This view also finds support in Article 7, paragraph 3 (2). There it is provided that the Polish Government shall communicate to the German Government the names of persons who, by exercising their right, shall have retained Polish nationality. It would be difficult to understand this provision if it related to former expressions of intention, for as no similar provision obtained

Case No. 132 *Contd.*

during the earlier period there would probably not exist any lists of such persons, and it would probably be impossible to determine who had expressed an intention amounting to a claim to retention of nationality. This construction is finally borne out by Article 7, paragraph 3 (1), proviso (*a*), whereby any person claiming to retain Polish nationality must further prove that he had taken steps, prior to July 10, 1924, with a view to having his Polish nationality recognised by a Polish authority. If a claim under paragraph 3 (1) was intended to cover also an earlier expression of intention, no meaning could be given to the requirement of further proof by proviso (*a*), inasmuch as both provisions would be in the same terms and would in certain circumstances be identical. Paragraph 3 (1) expressly lays down two conditions, *viz.* : first, the claiming of Polish nationality up to February 28, 1925, and secondly, proof of a similar act before July 10, 1924. It follows that the claiming of Polish nationality was regarded as something different from the action to be proved under proviso (*a*) and which had to take place prior to July 10, 1924."

[Report : *Juristische Wochenschrift*, 1932, p. 2305.]

NOTE.—This decision, which is apparently based on the interpretation of particular treaty provisions, has been reported in some detail as bearing on a typical case of nationality in connection with option.

On similar facts the Court of Appeal of Hamburg, on February 6, 1931 (*Juristische Wochenschrift*, 1931, p. 2873), made an order applying Article 17 of the Vienna Convention on grounds similar to those adopted by the lower Court in the above case. For an interpretation of Article 7, paragraph 3 (1), proviso (*a*), see also the decision of the Prussian Supreme Administrative Court of February 19, 1931 (*Entscheidungen des Preussischen Oberverwaltungsgerichts*, vol. 87, p. 262), where it was laid down that the words of that provision as well as its intention, as shown by its history, made it clear that two conditions were meant to be made for the acquisition of Polish nationality, namely, proof of unavailing steps taken before July 10, 1924, and a renewed claim before a Polish authority before February 28, 1925.

A case where Polish nationality was acquired by Poles by residence, under Article 91 (1) of the Treaty of Versailles in conjunction with Article 7 (1) of the Vienna Convention, was dealt with in the order of the Court of Appeal of Marienwerder of January 19, 1932 (*Juristische Wochenschrift*, 1932, p. 2347.).

Option—Acquisition and Loss of Nationality—Germano-Polish Treaty of August 30, 1924 (so-called Vienna Treaty)—"Return to Territory"—Meaning of—Operation of Treaties—How far Covering Acts Done Prior to the Treaty.

See Case No. 132 (*Option of Nationality* (*Germany*) *Case*).

X.—Statelessness

Statelessness—Legal Position of Stateless Persons—Poor Persons' Procedure—Privileged Treatment of Former Nationals. **Case No. 133**

POOR PERSONS' PROCEDURE CASE.

Germany, Court of Appeal of Düsseldorf. November 24, 1932.

THE FACTS.—By Article 114 of the German Code of Civil Procedure a poor party is entitled to the benefit of poor persons' procedure ; but where the poor party is a subject of a foreign State, reciprocity is required. The plaintiff was formerly a German subject. By marrying the defendant she lost her nationality and became stateless. She now petitioned for poor persons' procedure.

Held : that the petition must be granted. The general trend of judicial precedent had been to the effect that, owing to the terms of Article 114, stateless persons were disqualified from poor persons' procedure. They were placed in the same position as aliens generally, and they could not give any guarantee as to reciprocity. On the other hand, some courts did grant poor persons' procedure to stateless persons living in Germany. They held that the views concerning stateless persons had changed since the Peace Treaties and that, as it was impossible to expect reciprocity when a stateless person was concerned, Article 114 could not be applied in such cases.

It was now the opinion of the Court that the former view was the correct one. Generally speaking, stateless persons should not be granted poor persons' procedure. However, an exception was justified where a former German subject who by marriage had lost her nationality and had become stateless, sued for dissolution of that marriage before German courts. The Court laid down that under the German Nationality Act of July 22, 1913, a former German subject who had lost her nationality by marriage was in a more advantageous position than ordinary aliens. Section 10 of the Act provided that,

Case No. 133 *Contd.*

under certain conditions, a former German woman resident in Germany was entitled to be re-naturalised after divorce. It was probably not the intention of Article 114 (2) of the Code of Civil Procedure to exclude from the benefit of poor persons' procedure persons having an expectation of re-naturalisation.

[Report: *Rechtsprechung auf dem Gebiete des Internationalen Privatrechts*, 1933, No. 85.]

NOTE.—There is no uniformity in German judicial practice on this matter. See the previous decisions referred to in the note in *Annual Digest*, 1927-1928, Case No. 216. The following decisions are, in effect, in accordance with that reported above: Court of Appeal of Dresden, *Juristische Wochenschrift*, 1933, p. 1343; Court of Appeal of Stuttgart, *Rechtsprechung auf dem Gebiete des Internationalen Privatrechts*, 1931, No. 124; and Court of Appeal of Munich, *ibid.*, 1932, No. 125. See, on the other hand, Court of Appeal of Berlin, 13th Division, *Juristische Wochenschrift*, 1931, p. 1836. The Act for the Amendment of Civil Proceedings of October 27, 1933, closed the controversy. In future a stateless person is entitled to the benefits of poor persons' procedure under Article 114 (2) in cases where a German subject would have had a claim to it. Similarly, Article 110 of the Code of Civil Procedure provides in its new form that stateless persons, not resident in Germany, must, like subjects of a foreign State, give the defendant security for costs if he so desires. (Cp. to the same effect the decision, prior to the Act, of District Court No. 1 of Berlin of June 5, 1931: *Juristische Wochenschrift*, 1931, p. 2391.)

Statelessness—Deportation of Stateless Persons—Deportation to Last State of Domicile—Absence of Visa as a Ground for Deportation—Relevance of Consent of State to Receive the Person Deported.

See Case No. 152 (*Engel et Al.* v. *Zurbrick, District Director of Immigration*).

XI.—Nationality of Corporations

[See also Part XI, WAR AND NEUTRALITY : A. VI. *Enemy Character*.]

Corporations—Nationality of—The Test of Incorporation. **Case No. 134**

In re MADERA COMPANY (LIMITED).

Great Britain and Mexico : Claims Commission.

(Zimmerman, Stoker, Flores.)

May 13, 1931.

In this case the Commission, while admitting that there exists much controversy as regards the nationality of corporations, agreed with the view that a majority of States have in their legislation accepted as such the country of domicile.[1] The Commission accordingly adopted the same test, in conformity with its previous decisions.

[Report : *Decisions and Opinions of the Commissioners*, 1933, p. 67.]

NOTE.—See also *ibid.*, p. 118, the *Interoceanic Railway of Mexico* case, where the same principle was followed. The Commission pointed out that the Convention did not require that British companies should, in order to have standing before the Commission, show that British subjects have or have had an interest exceeding fifty per cent. of their total capital ; neither was it necessary, in case the company was British, that any allotment be produced.

Corporations — Nationality of — Jurisdiction of Arbitral Tribunals. **Case No. 135**

In re MEXICO PLANTAGEN G.m.b.h.

German-Mexican Claims Commission. January 25, 1930.

Decision No. 27.

THE FACTS.—This was a claim on behalf of a limited liability company established under the laws of Germany, with its head office in Hamburg and doing business in Mexico. The

[1] The ordinary rule is that the nationality of a company is determined by the law under which it is incorporated —(see the immediately following case),— and that law almost always requires that the company should maintain an office (in English law a registered office) in the country of incorporation. The registered office may be taken as the seat or domicile of the company, although sometimes the domicile is taken as the principal office, which may or may not be the same as the registered office.

Case No. 135 ***Contd.*** Mexican Agent contended that the Commission had jurisdiction only with regard to such German nationals as were physical persons; that the Company must be considered as Mexican because it did business in Mexico; and that it had no standing as a claimant because it failed to publish its balance sheet as required by Mexican law. The Claims Convention gave the Commission jurisdiction over claims for loss or damage suffered by "German societies, companies, associations or German juristic persons."

Held: (by Cruchaga, Presiding Commissioner, for the Commission): that the claim must be allowed. A company could have nationality, and its nationality was that of the State under whose laws it was established. Under Mexican law, failure to publish the balance sheet did not result in depriving a foreign company of juristic personality, but merely exposed it to liability to a penalty. The President said: "No plausible reason can be conceived for limiting nationality only to natural persons. A company is a person created by the law, owing its existence to a contract which, entered into in accordance with legal forms in effect in the State in which it is created, renders it capable of acquiring rights and assuming obligations like a natural person. Thus, just as a natural person is tied to the State by nationality acquired through birth or naturalisation, a tie from which rights and duties are derived, so a company is tied to the State in whose territory it is created and acquires rights and obligations."[1]

[Unreported.]

[1] The President discussed the merits of the various tests of nationality of corporations as follows:

"(*a*) A corporation has the nationality of its members. This is an unreasonable system because a corporation is a person distinct from its members, because the members of a corporation may have different nationalities, and because it is almost impossible to determine the nationality of the members of the innumerable corporations which have shares payable to bearer, etc.

(*b*) A corporation has the nationality of the place where it is created . . . This rule seems the most reasonable, since the laws imposed by that country must be observed in the creation of the corporation. If these laws are infringed, the corporation becomes a nullity; it has no personality, and consequently will have no nationality.

(*c*) A corporation has the nationality of the place of its domicile or *siège social*. This system does not seem acceptable because the principal seat of the business of a corporation may change frequently in accordance with the needs or convenience of the corporation, and because, not infrequently, the *siège social* is not the real centre of the business."

Corporations—Nationality of—Effect of Transfer of Territory. **Case No. 136**

ASSICURAZIONI GENERALI *v.* SELIM COTRAN.

British Empire, Judicial Committee of the Privy Council, on appeal from the Supreme Court of Palestine. November 27, 1931.

(Lords Blanesburgh, Darling, and Russell of Killowen.)

THE FACTS.—The Treaty of Lausanne, made between the Allied Powers, including Italy, and the Ottoman Empire, was signed on July 24, 1923, and became part of the municipal law of Palestine in 1924. The Treaty, as translated, contained certain provisions concerning "life assurance policies . . . entered into before October 29, 1924, between companies possessing at this date [actuellement] the nationality of an allied power and Turkish nationals." The question at issue was whether these provisions applied to a policy issued in 1909 to the respondent, a Turkish national, by the appellants, an insurance company whose principal place of business had at all material times been at Trieste. Trieste was Austrian territory in 1909, but in 1920 it became Italian territory under the Treaty of St. Germain. The Supreme Court of Appeal of Jerusalem decided that the expression "at this date" referred to the time when the insurance policy was effected, and that as the company had remained an Austrian company throughout the War, the provision in question had no application.

Held : that on the proper interpretation of the Treaty of Lausanne it applied to companies possessing the nationality of an Allied Power at the date of the signing of the Treaty, July 24, 1923. The material provision was that contained in the first sentence of paragraph 7 of the translation in which the words "at this date" represented the French word "actuellement" and referred to the date on which the Treaty was signed. At that date Trieste (where the head office and control of the insurance company were situate) had become Italian territory by virtue of the Treaty of St. Germain. Whatever the previous nationality of the company may have been, it therefore undoubtedly possessed Italian nationality at that date and was entitled to take advantage of the provisions of the Treaty of Lausanne.

[Report : *L.R.*, [1932] A.C. 268.]

Case No. 137 **Corporations—Nationality of—Suez Canal Corporation—Jurisdiction of Mixed Tribunals—Double Status of Company—Payment of Dividends.**

J. Shallam & Sons and Others *v.* Compagnie Universelle du Canal Maritime de Suez.

Egypt, Mixed Court of Appeal of Alexandria. June 18, 1931.

The Facts.—This was a rehearing of certain questions arising out of the proceedings in Case No. 94 above. The Court was asked to say by what standard the payment of dividends was to be measured—by the value of the franc in Egypt or in France.

Held: that, although the administrative headquarters of the Company were in Paris, its *siège social* was in Egypt. Accordingly, the Company had a double status, and was governed, in regard to its corporate activity, by the laws of Egypt, but, in regard to the relations of its members *inter se*, by the laws of France. The dividends must be paid in gold francs as stabilised by Egyptian law.

[Report: *Gazette des Tribunaux Mixtes d'Egypte*, XXIII (1932-1933), p. 304.]

Note.—It will be noted that the Suez Canal Company was incorporated under Egyptian law. Compare a decision of the Commercial Tribunal of Cairo of May 6, 1933: *ibid.*, p. 297, and several decisions in 1933 on the gold clause: *ibid.*, pp. 257-280.

C.—ALIENS

I.—Admission of Aliens

Case No. 138 **Aliens—Admission of—Right of Re-Admission of Alien into the United States after He Had Left the United States Temporarily.**

United States *ex rel.* Polymeris *et al.* *v.* Trudell, Immigration Inspector.

United States, Supreme Court. January 4, 1932.

(Hughes, C. J.; Holmes, Van Devanter, McReynolds, Brandeis, Sutherland, Butler, Stone, Roberts, JJ.)

The Facts.—Aspasia Polymeris and her daughter were Greek citizens who lawfully entered the United States in 1909 and lived for a number of years in New York City, which became and remained their domicile. In 1923, because of the illness of Aspasia's husband, they went back to Greece, with the intention, which they retained, of making only a temporary visit. The death of the husband prolonged their stay until 1924. They made several unsuccessful applications to the United States Consul General at Athens for documents which would permit their return to New York. In 1929 they obtained authority to cross Canada on a pretended trip from Greece to Japan, and, in 1930, presented themselves at St. Albans, Vermont, for admission to the United States. They were taken into custody by the immigration inspector, and sought release by *habeas corpus*, on the ground that they were entitled to enter the country. It was held that they "were properly excluded under §13 (*a*) of the Immigration Act of May 26, 1924, 43 Stat. 153, 161, since the Secretary of Labor did not admit them in his discretion, . . and [they] neither presented an unexpired valid immigration visa or an unexpired valid permit to re-enter in accordance with the regulations promulgated under §13 (*b*) of that Act." 49 F. (2d) 730. On *certiorari* to the United States Supreme Court,

Held: that the judgment must be affirmed. In delivering the Opinion of the Court, Mr. Justice Holmes said: "The relators have no right to enter the United States unless it has been given to them by the United States. The burden of proof is upon them to show that they have the right. Immigration Act of 1924, §23, 43 Stat. 165; Code, Title 8, §221. By §13 and the regulations under it, as remarked by the court below, a returning alien can not enter unless he has either an immigration visa or a return permit. The relators must show not only that they ought to be admitted but that the United States, by the only voice authorized to express its will, has said so. Obviously it has not done so."

[Report: 284 U.S. 279.]

Treatment of Aliens—Admission of Aliens—Visa—Agreement by Government with a Foreigner—Act of State. **Case No. 139**

FRISINA *v.* EGYPTIAN GOVERNMENT.

Egypt, Civil Tribunal of Alexandria. April 14, 1931.

THE FACTS.—The plaintiff claimed damages from the Egyptian Government and an order for the publication (at the expense of the Government) of the present judgment in three local papers chosen by the plaintiff. The claim was based on

Case No. 139 ***Contd.*** the fact that the inspector of police at Alexandria had (on the instructions of the Minister for the Interior) erased the visa on his passport and refused him permission to land. His passport had been visa-ed by the Egyptian representative at Buenos Aires. The Government pleaded the incompetence of the Tribunal on the ground that an act of State was involved ; and with regard to the merits, the Government claimed a right, in virtue of its "police powers," to refuse to admit undesirables on its territory, and, further, that visas given by Egyptian representatives abroad were given at the risk of the applicant.

Held : (1) that the plea to the jurisdiction must be rejected for, even admitting that an act of State was in question, there was also in question the violation of the vested right of a foreigner, which could not escape scrutiny by the Court.

(2) As to the merits, that the plea that visas were given at the applicant's risk must be rejected. The fact that the Egyptian Government had the right to prevent undesirables landing on its territory did not justify the violation of an agreement made with a private individual. The plaintiff's claim must succeed in so far as it related to these questions.

[Report: *Gazette des Tribunaux Mixtes d'Egypte,* XXII (1931-1932) p. 353.]

NOTE.—The Civil Tribunals are competent to consider administrative acts violating private rights guaranteed by "treaties, laws or agreements." It was so held on June 14, 1932, by the Civil Tribunal of Alexandria : *ibid.*, p. 350 ; and by the Civil Tribunal of Cairo, on June 8, 1931 : *ibid.*, p. 343.

It will be noted that the view of the Tribunal that a consular visa creates an agreement with the holder of the visa is not generally held.

Case No. 140 **Aliens—Admission of—Right of Aliens Formerly Resident to Re-Enter—The Law of Argentina.**

In re BERTONE.

Argentina, Federal Supreme Court. April 13, 1932.

THE FACTS.—This was a petition on behalf of an Italian whom the immigration officials refused to admit on the ground that medical officers held him incapable of working. Law 817 of 1876, which regulated immigration, excluded persons who were found physically unfit for work. Bertone claimed that he was not an immigrant within the meaning of that Law, since he had previously lived in Argentina for eight years. The

Federal District Judge refused the petition. The Cámara Federal affirmed that decision. On appeal to the Supreme Court,

Held : that the judgments of the Courts below be reversed. The evidence showed that Bertone was not an immigrant in the meaning of Article 12 of the Law of 1876.[1] He was not an alien who now came to Argentina for the first time in order to establish himself there. He sought to return to it after a period of absence and after having resided there for eight years "as a member of the social life of the nation, forming part of its working population." Bertone was still an inhabitant of Argentina, since he lived there with the intention of remaining, and enjoyed in that capacity all the rights which the Constitution gave to residents without distinction of nationality. These included expressly, as provided in Article 14 of the Fundamental Charter, the right "to enter, remain, sojourn, and depart from the country." Accordingly, his entry could not be prevented, since he had been a resident.

[Report : 164 *Fallos de la Corte Suprema*, 290.]

II.—Position of Aliens

i.—Subjection to Territorial Sovereignty of the Receiving State

Aliens—Duty of Foreigners to Appear as Witnesses—Foreigners Permanently Resident Abroad. **Case No. 141**

JURISDICTION (FOREIGN WITNESSES) CASE.

Germany, District Court of Göttingen. September 2, 1932.

THE FACTS.—While on a temporary visit to Germany the appellant, who was a French citizen and resident in Paris, was subpœnaed to attend a trial as a witness. He wrote to the local Court that it was doubtful whether he would be in Germany when the action was heard, but that in any case he would let the Court know a week before the trial whether he would be able to attend. Up to the day of the trial no notice was

[1] That Article provided as follows : "For the purposes of this law, there shall be deemed to be immigrants, any alien labourer, artisan, industrialist, farmer, or teacher, under seventy years of age, approved as to morality and conduct, who comes to the Republic to establish himself there, on steam or sailing vessels, paying second or third class passage or having his passage paid by the Nation, the Provinces, or the particular enterprises protecting immigration and colonisation."

Case No. 141 ***Contd.*** received by the Court, but on the day of the trial the Court received a letter from a company to the effect that the appellant, who was a director of the company, would not be present at the hearing. The local Court did not regard this letter as a sufficient excuse. It therefore imposed on the appellant a fine of 50 Reichsmark or two days' arrest, and ordered him to pay the costs occasioned by his non-attendance. He appealed.

Held: that the appeal must be dismissed. The Court said: "Section 380 of the Code of Civil Procedure empowers the Court to fine a witness who fails to appear after subpœna. It is beyond any doubt that it is not only German subjects who are obliged to attend German courts as witnesses, but that the same applies to foreigners staying in Germany. The duty to attend as a witness is not of the same nature as a duty imposed on a national as such, as, *e.g.*, the duty to serve in the armed forces or to attend trials as lay assessors. It is rather in the nature of a compulsion which the State exercises for the maintenance of law and order. Accordingly, that duty is owed by anybody who in fact, *i.e.*, physically, is subject to German jurisdiction, whether or not he be a German citizen. Likewise, it is immaterial whether the foreigner who has been subpœnaed as a witness resides in Germany or abroad. The only condition of a foreigner's duty to appear before a German court is that he should have been served with the subpœna on German territory.

"If the foreigner fails to attend without excuse he may be fined on whichever territory he may be staying at the time. The order is therefore valid even though the appellant was actually in Paris when it was made. It does not constitute any extension of German jurisdiction if a foreign witness is ordered to pay a fine although he has already left Germany. The order to pay a fine is merely connected with the subpœna. If the latter was admissible, *i.e.*, if it was served on him while he was in Germany, then the fine imposed on the witness on account of his unexcused non-attendance is only to be regarded as the consequence of an event which happened at a time when he was subject to German jurisdiction."

[Report: *Juristische Wochenschrift*, 1929, p. 3833.]

Aliens—Jurisdiction—Over Non-Resident Aliens with regard to Property within the Jurisdiction—Double Taxation.

See Case No. 65 (*Burnet, Commissioner of Internal Revenue* v. *Brooks et Al., Executors*).

ii.—Protection by the National State

Position of Aliens—Protection by the Home State—The Calvo Clause—Foreign Companies as Shareholders in National Company—How Far Affected by Calvo Clause—Losses Suffered by Aliens through Measures Affecting a National Corporation. **Case No. 142**

THE UNITED STATES OF AMERICA ON BEHALF OF INTERNATIONAL FISHERIES COMPANY

v.

THE UNITED MEXICAN STATES.

United States and Mexico : Special Claims Commission.

(Alfaro, MacGregor, Nielsen.)

July 1931.

THE FACTS.—This was a claim on behalf of the International Fisheries Company, a United States corporation, for damage alleged to have been suffered as the result of the cancellation by the Mexican Government of the concession of a Mexican company, "La Pescadora," in which the claimant Company possessed a considerable number of shares. The concession granted to "La Pescadora" contained the so-called Calvo Clause couched in wide terms and referring to the concessionary company or whosoever shall succeed to its rights.

Held (by the majority of the Commission, Nielsen, Commissioner, dissenting) : that the claim must be rejected.

(1) *The Calvo Clause.*—The Commission adhered fully to its decision in the *North American Dredging Company* case (*Annual Digest*, 1925-1926, Case No. 218) which the American Agent now questioned. The Commission pointed out that that decision had since been followed in a number of cases. Referring to the preparatory work of the Codification Conference of 1930 the Commission said : "There are other circumstances favorable to the contention that the Calvo Clause has already been accepted by the usage of nations." (At p. 209.)

(2) *Foreign Companies as Shareholders. How Far Affected by Calvo Clause.*—With regard to the contention of the United States that the American Company was merely the possessor of a certain number of shares in "La Pescadora" and that it could not, therefore, be said that it had relinquished the right to diplomatic intervention in matters relating to the concession,

Case No. 142 ***Contd.***

the Commission said that it was not "debatable that the holder of shares of stock therein is in the last analysis the beneficiary of a fixed part of the rights of the company, with the limitation that they cannot be exercised directly at any time except through the procedure and in the words established by the company's constitution and by-laws. This being the case it is clear that the stockholder not only *derives*, but directly has, (subject to the aforementioned limitation) all the rights accruing to him as a stockholder therein. By virtue thereof, it must be recognized that the International Fisheries Company, a stockholder of the Mexican fishing company which owned the contract-concession of March 10, 1909, had the same rights and obligations which are derived from the contract-concession granted to the "Pescadora" itself, with the limitation that the exercise thereof appertained to the appropriate company authorities." (At pp. 214, 215.)

(3) *Cancellation and Nullification of Concessions.*—The present case was not one of unilateral nullification of the concession without reasons; it concerned the exercise of the right of cancellation identical with that possessed by any party to a private contract in cases where the other party fails to comply with his obligations. Accordingly, the cancellation of a concession could not be regarded as being *prima facie* a violation of international law calculated to bring the case within the exception laid down in the *North American Dredging Company* case. The Commission said: "If every non-fulfillment of a contract on the part of a Government were to create at once the presumption of an arbitrary act, which should therefore be avoided, governments would be in a worse situation than that of any private person, a party to any contract. The latter could cease to fulfill his contractual obligations when he believed that his co-contractor had first violated the contract, in the expectation of being sued by him in the courts if he was not satisfied. In that case he assumes the role of defendant, which is the more advantageous position in a suit. But according to the contention of the American Agency, Mexico could not cancel the contract for non-fulfillment on the part of "La Pescadora, S.A.," without first having had recourse to the courts; which means that it would always have to continue fulfilling the contract and to assume the difficult role of plaintiff, never enjoying the advantage that a private person would have under the same circumstances. In the instant case the Government made use therefore of a right given to it by the contract, and so any question as to the grounds which the Government of Mexico had for

acting in that sense or as to the interpretation of the clause of the contract upon which it based its reason for acting in that manner, were the matters specially provided for by Article 32 of the contract-concession respecting which diplomatic agents could not intervene." (At pp. 219, 220.)

(4) *Losses Suffered by Aliens through Measures Affecting a National Corporation.*—The Convention of September 8, 1923, by which the Commission was set up, provided in Article 1 that among the claims upon which the Commission was to adjudicate were claims of "citizens of either country by reason of losses or damages suffered by any corporation, company, association or partnership in which such citizens have or have had a substantial and bona fide interest, provided an allotment to the claimant by the corporation, company, association or partnership of his proportion of the loss or damage suffered is presented by the claimant to the Commission hereinafter referred to. . . ." (At p. 221.) The Commission interpreted that Article as follows with regard to the case before it. "In a case of this nature it is not sufficient that the Company, a national of the respondent country, has suffered a loss of any kind, and that it has made to the claimant of another country a proportionate allotment thereof; that would not be a cause for international action. It is necessary that the loss which the national entity of the respondent country has suffered be of the kind which gives rise or ground to an international claim in the supposition that that entity were an alien and therefore had the right to make claim. States according to a thoroughly established rule of international law, are responsible only for those injuries which are inflicted through an act which violates some principle of international law." (At pp. 221, 222.) As the action of the Mexican Government with regard to "La Pescadora" would not, if that Company had been a foreign company, be contrary to international law, no claim on behalf of International Fisheries Company was admissible.

[Report: *Opinions of Commissioners*, October, 1930, to July, 1931, p. 207.]

Aliens—Protection by the Home State—Nature of the Legal Relation between the Home State and the National in Whose Favour Diplomatic Protection is Exercised—Discretion of the Political Department—Claim against the State on account of Inadequate Protection—Nature of the Claim against the Foreign State.

See Case No. 120 (*Gschwind* v. *Swiss Confederation*).

iii.—Treatment by and Responsibilities of the Receiving State

[See also Part V STATE RESPONSIBILITY.]

Case No. 143 **Aliens—Legal Position of—Free Access to Courts—Security for Costs—Treaties Providing for Equal Treatment—Interpretation by Reference to Other Treaties.**

SECURITY FOR COSTS (GERMANY) CASE.

Germany, Court of Appeal of Karlsruhe. January 14, 1931.

THE FACTS.—By Article 1 (5) of the Germano-Yugoslav Treaty of Commerce and Navigation the subjects of each of the contracting States were granted free access to the courts of the other State on an equal footing with nationals and with citizens of the most-favoured-nation. The appellant claimed that it followed from this provision that he could not be ordered to give security for costs under Article 110 of the Code of Civil Procedure.

Held: that the appeal must be dismissed. The Supreme Court had previously laid down (*Entscheidungen des Reichsgerichts*, vol. 104, p. 191) that the expression "free access to the courts" did not imply an exemption from giving security for costs. This followed, *inter alia*, from Conventions made by Germany with Austria and Poland respectively (*Reichsgesetzblatt*, 1924, II, pp. 55 and 91), in which aliens were granted free access to the courts and in which it was further provided that they shall be allowed to appear in such courts under the same conditions as the subjects of the country concerned. But these Conventions also provided expressly that aliens, when suing or intervening in an action in the courts, shall not be ordered to furnish security for costs. It followed that the parties to these Conventions were of opinion that "free access" to the courts did not, as such, comprise freedom from the obligation to give security. Rather did such freedom appear as a special privilege which must be expressly stipulated. The Convention in question had been concluded some years after those made with Austria and Poland. It contained no provision to that effect. This circumstance seemed to indicate conclusively that in this case Germany was not prepared to grant the aliens in question the additional privilege.

[Report: *Juristische Wochenschrift*, 1931, p. 751.]

Aliens—Treatment of—Actual Reciprocity in Treatment—Whether Conferring a Legal Right. **Case No. 144**

HEDDING *v.* STEISEL.

Belgium, Civil Tribunal of Brussels. January 3, 1931.

THE FACTS.—A British subject claimed the right of free legal assistance in Belgium, alleging that in certain cases British Courts had granted similar assistance to Belgian subjects.

Held: that the claim must be dismissed. "Under the terms of Article 4 of the Law of June 29, 1929, on legal aid, aliens can invoke it, in conformity with international treaties, in the Belgian Courts, when the subjects of the country to which they last belonged enjoy a treaty right in this respect. But there is no such treaty between Belgium and Great Britain . . . and the fact that in certain cases British Courts have allowed Belgian subjects the facility of free legal assistance is of little significance if the right has not been given legal form by a convention between the two countries."[1]

[Report: *Pasicrisie,* III (1931), p. 170.]

Aliens—Position of—Equality with Nationals—Constitutional Guarantees of—Attachment of Property—The Law of Cuba. **Case No. 145**

Ex parte LARREA Y FERNÁNDEZ.

Cuba, Supreme Court. June 30, 1932.

THE FACTS.—In this case the State had brought an action against several debtors, including the appellant, and had obtained a preliminary attachment against the appellant's property. The attachment was granted on the sole ground that he was an unnaturalised alien.[2] The appellant claimed that the relevant provision of the Law on Civil Procedure was

[1] Such a convention has now been concluded.

[2] Article 1398 of the Cuban Law on Civil Procedure provides: "For the issuance of a preliminary attachment it is necessary:

1. That with the request there is presented a document proving the existence of the debt.

2. That the debtor against whom it is sought comes within one of the following cases:

(2) That he be an alien not naturalised in Cuba.

(3) That, whether he be a Cuban or a naturalised alien, he has no known domicile, or real property, or agricultural, industrial or commercial establishment in the place where the demand for payment of the debt should be made in Court against him . . .

(4) When he has disappeared from his domicile . . ."

Case No. 145 *Contd.*

unconstitutional, being in violation of Article 10, Sect. 3, of the Constitution. That article provided as follows: "Aliens resident in the territory of the Republic shall be on a basis of equality with Cubans: . . . 3. As to the enjoyment of civil rights, on the conditions and with the limitations established by the Law on Alienage."

Held (by seven judges against four): that the relevant provision of the Law on Civil Procedure was unconstitutional. There was under that Law a decided inequality in the treatment of aliens as compared with that of citizens. The Court said: "That inequality of rights, explicable and perhaps necessary in the far off times when the Law on Civil Procedure was promulgated, when political relations and means of communication between peoples were very different from those at the present time, is contrary to Section 3 of Article 10 of the Constitution, which places Cubans and aliens residing in the territory of the Republic on a level of equality 'as to the enjoyment of civil rights, on the conditions and with the limitations established by the Law on Alienage'."

[Report: 4 *Revista Cubana de Derecho* (jurisprudencia civil), 681.]

Case No. 146

Aliens—Treatment of—Foreign Corporations—Recognition of Foreign Religious Societies.

GEWAKHOFF AND THE ORTHODOX SOCIETY OF PALESTINE *v.* CHLENOW AND THE RUSSIAN SOCIETY OF PALESTINE.

Italy, Court of Cassation. March 11, 1930.

THE FACTS.—In April 1922 Prince Nicholas Gewakhoff, as representative of the Orthodox Society of Palestine, founded in Russia in 1882, summoned before the court of Bari one Alexeeff and one Kamenski, demanding the delivery of property, real and personal, belonging to the Society, and an account of its management. In the proceedings which had been instituted Professor Chlenow intervened on behalf of the Russian Society of Palestine, and declared that the latter Society was a continuation of the old Orthodox Society and consequently the property in dispute belonged to it. The Court of Bari rejected this contention, pointing out that the new Russian Society had not obtained recognition in Italy. The Court of Appeal of Bari denied the necessity for such recognition on the part of Italy, and found in favour of Chlenow.

Held (by the Court of Cassation): that a foreign society

does not need to be recognised in Italy in order to acquire legal personality there, and that likewise changes in its constitution do not need to be recognised in Italy. "The Supreme Court is of the opinion that . . . a new recognition is not indispensable in connection with every modification that a foreign legal entity undergoes after admission to the exercise of civil rights in Italy, as long as its distinctive features are not destroyed or fundamentally altered. But it is also of the opinion that it is necessary to go further than this and to rule out the need for new recognition even when it is a case of radical changes, because, in Italy, foreign legal entities are admitted to the enjoyment of civil rights in virtue of Article 3 of the Civil Code. By the terms of this article a foreign religious society has legal existence in relation to our law when its State of origin has been recognised in Italy, even if the legal personality of the society had not received confirmation in Italy. . . . If foreign individuals, by reason solely of the fact that they exist in the sight of the law, are admitted to the enjoyment of civil rights, it is difficult to conceive why the same should not be the case with legal entities which have come into legal existence abroad. . . ." There was no ground for the fear that, by freeing foreign religious societies from the obligation to obtain confirmation, in Italy, of their legal status, the danger might arise of having to tolerate harmful activities of undesirable societies, since the State was protected against such danger, both by the possibility of adopting the police measures which the law applied to foreigners who neglect the duties of hospitality, and by the power given by statute to withdraw recognition of the juridical personality obtained abroad."

[Report: *Rivista italiana di diritto internazionale privato e processuale*, 1931, p. 191.]

Aliens—Legal Position of—Acquisition of German Real Property by Foreign Companies—Meaning of the Term "National." **Case No. 147**

FOREIGN COMPANIES (ACQUISITION OF PROPERTY) CASE.

Germany, Court of Appeal of Berlin. July 9, 1931.

THE FACTS.—The point in issue in the present case was whether an English company had to obtain the consent of the Prussian Cabinet, under Article 7 (2) of the Prussian Act to give effect to the German Civil Code, in order to acquire real property situate in Prussia, or whether that provision had been super-

Case No. 147 *Contd.* seded by Article 5 of the Anglo-German Treaty of Commerce and Navigation of December 2, 1924, which acquired statutory force. Article 5 conferred on subjects of the contracting parties full liberty to acquire real property in the territory of the other party provided that the subjects of another foreign State were entitled to do so.

Held: that the Treaty had not altered the provisions of the Act. Article 5 applied only to individuals. This followed from the expression "*Staatsangehöriger*" (national) in the German text. Under the Nationality Act of July 22, 1913, nationality applied only to individuals. As regards companies and corporations, the term "nationality" was used only in a figurative sense. Moreover, the German Foreign Office had certified that the expression "subjects or citizens" in the English text usually applied only to individuals. In addition, other provisions of the Convention which spoke of "the subjects of each of the Contracting Parties," showed that it was intended to apply the term only to individuals. Thus Article 2 read: "The subjects or citizens of the two Contracting Parties in the territory of the other shall enjoy, in respect of their *persons*, their property, rights and interests. . . ." Article 6 provided: "The subjects or citizens . . . shall be entitled to *enter and reside* in the territory of the other. . . ." Article 7 prescribed that "the subjects or citizens . . . in the territories of the other shall be exempted from all *compulsory military service* whatsoever." Article 28 dealt with the case "when a subject or citizen dies within the territories of the other . . . ." Finally, it was important to bear in mind, when construing this term, that Article 16 contained special provisions for limited companies and trading partnerships, and that in Article 16 (3) companies and subjects and citizens were mentioned simultaneously, thus implying that each expression had a different meaning.

[Report: *Juristische Wochenschrift*, 1932, p. 598.]

Case No. 148 **Aliens—Legal Position of—Applicability of Revenue Laws to Aliens—Equal Treatment of Aliens and Subjects ("Non-Discrimination Clause")—Aliens and Political Rights.**

ALIENS (NON-DISCRIMINATION CLAUSE) CASE.

Germany, Supreme Revenue Court. November 24, 1931.

THE FACTS.—Paragraph 4 (1), No. 1, of the Second Chapter of the President's Decree of July 26, 1930, provided for the payment of a so-called Citizen Tax by all persons over 20 years of age and resident within the parish or borough. Paragraph 6 of the Regulations made for the carrying out of that Decree exempted from the duty to pay the tax all persons who could claim exemption from personal taxes under general rules of international law or under special international conventions. The appellants, who were aliens, were assessed for citizen tax; the lower Court upheld the assessment. The appellants contended that, as aliens, they were exempt from the tax. They invoked Paragraph 4 (2), No. 1, according to which no person shall be assessed for citizen tax who at the material date is by law prevented from exercising his right to vote. They argued that, on a literal reading of the law, a German subject who, at the material date, had been arrested for taking part in an unlawful assembly or a riot, was exempt from the citizen tax, whereas an alien who was so arrested along with Germans could not claim that exemption inasmuch as he had no right to vote at all. This, they said, involved a breach of the generally accepted rule, which was also specially laid down in international conventions, that an alien should be in no worse a position than a German subject. It followed, therefore, they contended, that the Statute could not be read literally and that it was unlawful to assess an alien for the citizen tax.

Held (by the Supreme Revenue Court): that the appeal must be dismissed. In no event could an interpretation be adopted which would have the result of exempting aliens from the citizen tax. That would mean putting them in a position more favourable than that of German subjects. Such a conclusion could not possibly be drawn from the Statute.

The words "general rules of international law," as used in the Regulations, were primarily intended to cover the representatives of foreign Powers accredited to Germany and entitled to the privileges of exterritoriality. There certainly did not exist a generally accepted rule of international law exempting all aliens from the duty to pay personal taxes.

Neither did the provision for non-discrimination between aliens and Germans, as stipulated in numerous conventions (the so-called "non-discrimination clause"), allow an inference to the effect that aliens should not be obliged to pay the citizen tax. That clause was not intended to apply to political rights of the citizen, such as the right to vote, nor to matters arising therefrom. Nor was it possible to interpret the "non-discrimination clause" as exempting aliens from the citizen tax on the ground of their having no right to vote.

[Report: *Entscheidungen des Reichsfinanzhofs*, vol. 30, p. 1.]

Case No. 149 **Aliens—Legal Position of—Principle of Equal Treatment of Aliens and Subjects ("Non-Discrimination Clause")—Protection of Trade Names of French Subjects in Germany.**

SOCIÉTÉ À RESPONSABILITÉ LIMITÉE CHAUSSURES MANON v. B. & Co., G.m.b.H.

Germany, Supreme Court for Civil Matters. April 30, 1931.

THE FACTS.—Article 28 (1) of the Trade Agreement between France and the German Customs Union of August 2, 1862, provided that, in respect of the description and labelling of goods, the citizens of each contracting State shall enjoy the same protection as is enjoyed by the subjects of the other State. Since April 1914, the plaintiffs had carried on business in the shoe trade in Paris under the name of "Chaussures Manon." In March 1919, the word "Manon" was registered as a trade mark for the plaintiff company. Since 1925 the defendants had sold shoes in Germany under the description "Manon-Shoes." In June of that year they had the word "Manon" registered by the Patent Office as a trade mark. The plaintiffs alleged that their business had become known also outside France, and that the name "Manon" had acquired a secondary meaning as a trade name and was associated with their business throughout the world. They claimed, by virtue of Article 28 of the Agreement of 1862, that the name should be removed from the German Register at the Patent Office. They also demanded an injunction to restrain the defendants from using the word "Manon" in connection with their business.

Held: that the action must be dismissed. The plaintiffs could succeed only if they could prove that the defendants, by causing the registration at the Patent Office in 1925, infringed the plaintiffs' right to the trade name in Germany. To establish such an infringement the word "Manon" must have acquired a secondary sense in Germany at the time of the registration. This was not so in the present case. To adopt a different view "would infringe the principle of equal treatment of aliens and subjects inasmuch as it would amount in practice to giving an advantage to aliens at the expense of nationals."

It was not necessary for all the conditions entitling a foreign undertaking to claim the protection of its trade name in Germany to be present at the relevant date. The possibilities of a future expansion of the business must be taken into account. However, in such a case there must always be a high probability that such expansion will occur within a reasonable time.

[Report : *Entscheidungen des Reichsgerichts in Zivilsachen*, vol. 132, p. 374 ; *Z. für a. ö. R. und V.*, III (1932-1933), No. 1, Part 2, p. 149 ; *Juristische Wochenschrift*, 1932, p. 579.]

NOTE.—See also the comments by Mandelsloh in *Z. für a. ö. R. und V.*, *loc. cit.* ; and compare, to the same effect, the decision of the Supreme Court of May 12, 1931 : *Juristische Wochenschrift*, 1932, p. 595.

Aliens—Position of—As Compared with Nationals.

PERMANENT COURT OF INTERNATIONAL JUSTICE.

See the Advisory Opinion rendered by the Court on February 4, 1932,[1] in the case of the *Treatment of Polish Nationals and Other Persons of Polish Origin or Speech in the Danzig Territory* (*P.C.I.J.*, Series A/B, No. 44), for the statement that "the distinction between citizens and non-citizens obtains to a greater or less extent in almost all countries, and is the standard adopted in all the Minorities treaties ; it may not be entirely satisfactory from the point of view of a certain group or groups of foreigners, but it cannot be said to be unreasonable or unjust." (At p. 40.)

Aliens—Position of Aliens—Treatment by the Receiving State—Whether Entitled to Use their Own Language before Courts and Authorities on the Same Conditions as Members of a National Minority.

The view relied upon in the decision Váž. 9854 civ. (*Annual Digest*, 1929-1930, p. 295) and other previous decisions to the effect that aliens are not entitled to use their own language before the courts and administrative authorities on the same conditions as members of a national minority, was re-affirmed by the Czechoslovak Supreme Court of Justice in its decision of November 23, 1932, No. Rv. I 786/31 (Váž. 12.126 civ.).

Aliens—Position of—Right to Sue—Effect of Non-Recognition of Governments.

See Case No. 24 (*Russian Volunteer Fleet* v. *United States*).

Aliens—Treatment of—Diplomatic and Legislative Reciprocity.

See Case No. 204 (*Sanchez* v. *Consorts Gozland*).

[1] For the composition of the Court see p. 209.

Aliens—Position of—Foreign Corporations as Shareholders in National Company—Losses Suffered by Aliens through Measures Affecting a National Corporation.

See Case No. 142 (*United States of America on behalf of International Fisheries Company* v. *United Mexican States*).

Aliens—Treatment of—Arrest and Detention.

See Case No. 102 (*Chevreau Case,* (2)).

iv.—Plea of Non-Discrimination

[See also Part V, STATE RESPONSIBILITY.]

PERMANENT COURT OF INTERNATIONAL JUSTICE.

Aliens—Position of—Obligation of Non-Discrimination—Meaning of.

See the Advisory Opinion given by the Court on February 4, 1932,[1] in the case of the *Treatment of Polish Nationals and Other Persons of Polish Origin or Speech in the Danzig Territory* (*P.C.I.J.*, Series A/B, No. 44), where the Court said: "the prohibition against discrimination, in order to be effective, must ensure the absence of discrimination in fact as well as in law. A measure which in terms is of general application, but in fact is directed against Polish nationals and other persons of Polish origin or speech, constitutes a violation of the prohibition. A similar view has already been expressed by the Court in its Advisory Opinion No. 6 relating to German settlers in Poland. Whether a measure is or is not in fact directed against these persons is a question to be decided on the merits of each particular case. No hard and fast rule can be laid down." (At p. 28.)

Aliens—Treatment of—Responsibility for Loss to Aliens as the Result of Measures Adopted with regard to Nationals.

See Case No. 115 (*United States of America on behalf of Dickson Car Wheel Company* v. *United Mexican States*).

Aliens—Treatment of—Property Rights—Non-Discrimination.

See Case No. 33 (*Niederstrasser* v. *Polish State*).

[1] For the composition of the Court see p. 209.

v.—Respect for Property. Expropriation

[See also Part IV, JURISDICTION : I. *Territorial*.]

Aliens—Treatment of—Right to Compensation for War Damage Granted to Nationals—French Law of April 17, 1919—Registered Joint Stock Company Exclusively Composed of Aliens—Exclusion of Aliens from the Benefits of the Law. **Case No. 150**

In re MOREAUX.

France, Conseil d'Etat. February 12, 1932.

THE FACTS.—A joint stock company having its *siège social* in France but exclusively composed of aliens, claimed from the French Government, under the Law of April 17, 1919, on Reparation for War Damage, an indemnity for damage suffered in France during the War of 1914-1918.

Held: that the claim must be dismissed. Aliens were entitled to indemnification for war damage only under the conditions established by treaties.

[Report: *Sirey*, 1932, Part 3, p. 49, with a note by P. de F.R.]

NOTE.—The Law of April 17, 1919, on Reparation for War Damage confined the right to reparation to persons of French nationality, *i.e.*, individuals, private groups and public concerns (*patrimonies*) other than those belonging to the State. Aliens and naturalised French nationals enjoyed the right only under the conditions laid down in the treaties concluded with the States of which they were originally the subjects. Hitherto, treaties had been concluded with two States only, Great Britain (Anglo-French Agreement of August 2, 1929) and Belgium (Franco-Belgian Convention of November 7, 1929, on the indemnification of the civil victims of the War). Both these States were Allies. No treaties were concluded with neutral Powers. Serious difficulties arose between France and Switzerland in this connection, with which the Council of the League of Nations refused to deal in view of the prevailing doubt as to the law applicable to the question (Council, Sessions of September 25, 1934, January 17 and May 25, 1935). See *Le séquestre de la propriété privée en temps de guerre*, vol. II (Geneva, 1933); Friedmann in *R.I.* (Paris), 1935, pp. 90-103; Maupas in *Clunet*, 62 (1935), pp. 277-304, and *ibid.*, 63 (1936), pp. 560-570.

On the question as to whether companies possessing French nationality, but composed of aliens, can enjoy the benefit of the provisions of the Law of April 17, 1919, see the decision of the Conseil d'Etat of July 29, 1932, *In re Société Graf et Cie.*: *Sirey*, 1932, Part 3, p. 85.

Case No. 151 **Aliens—Treatment of—Property of—Currency Laws—How far Affecting Contracts with Aliens made prior to that Legislation—Statutes Inconsistent with Prior Treaties—Egypt and Turkey.**

DAMASCUS (MUNICIPALITY OF) *v.* LIQUIDATOR OF X. COMPANY.

Syria, Court of Cassation. December 30, 1931.

THE FACTS.—A company incorporated in Egypt was declared bankrupt by the Mixed Commercial Court of Alexandria in 1913. The Municipality of Damascus was at that time a debtor of the Company on account of work which had been carried out by it for the Municipality. The debt was incurred in Turkish pounds. The Egyptian Court appointed a Liquidator for the Levant, but he was prevented by the War from communicating with the Municipality and recovering the debt. After the ratification of the Treaty of Lausanne in 1924, the Municipality of Damascus claimed that it was entitled to pay the debt in the paper currency which had been introduced by an Ottoman law during the War. Article 84 of the Treaty of Lausanne provided that debts should be paid in the currency stipulated in the contract at the rate current in the country of origin. A decree of the High Commissioner of Syria, enacted after the coming into force of the Treaty, prescribed a rate of exchange in Syria for contracts made in Turkish pounds. The Municipality contended also that Egypt was in law a part of the Turkish State during the War, and that the Turkish Law concerning currency was binding upon Egypt.

Held : that the plea of the Municipality must be rejected. The debt was payable in the equivalent of the gold pounds in which it was incurred before the War. A law fixing legal tender does not affect contracts between a government and foreign subjects made before the enactment of the law. There was an international rule by which such a law only applied internally ; and foreign contracts remained subject to the terms of payment contained in them. Egypt could not be regarded as a part of Turkey in this connection. It had its own currency, and was in fact independent of Turkey, even before the War. The provisions of the Treaty of Lausanne did not mean that the debt incurred in Turkish gold pounds could be paid in Turkish paper pounds of the same amount, but that payment might be made in paper pounds at the rate of exchange for gold pounds. The decree of the High Commissioner concerning the rate of exchange for Turkish gold pounds had no bearing on the matter. The provision of the Treaty prevailed over any internal law passed subsequently to it, even if that legislation only modified indirectly the application of the Treaty.

[Report: *Gazette des Tribunaux Libano-Syriens* (1932), p. 47.]

Aliens — Property of — State Responsibility — Executive Action—Responsibility for Damage Done to the Property of Aliens in the Course of Suppression of Rebellion.

See Case No. 103 (*In re Heyn, Wislicenus and Schmidt*).

III.—Expulsion of Aliens

Aliens—Deportation of—Deportation of Stateless Persons—Deportation to Last State of Domicile—Absence of Visa as a Ground for Deportation—Relevance of Consent of State to Receive the Person Deported. **Case No. 152**

ENGEL *ET AL. v.* ZURBRICK, DISTRICT DIRECTOR OF IMMIGRATION.

United States, Circuit Court of Appeals, Sixth Circuit.

June 30, 1931.

(Denison, Hicks, Hickenlooper, Circuit Judges.)

THE FACTS.—This was a petition against deportation brought by three aliens, John Engel, his daughter and his stepson. Engel went from a place in Russia, which was now a part of Poland, to Canada, in 1909. In Canada he married in 1912 a widow of Russian nationality who had come there in 1911 with her son. A daughter was born in Montreal in 1914. After continuous residence in Canada, the family entered the United States in 1922 or 1923, without passports and without inspection. In June 1925, warrants of arrest were issued and the family was held for deportation. The sole charges against the father and children were that they entered without inspection and were likely to become public charges. In December 1925, warrants of deportation to Poland were issued. As to Engel and his wife, these warrants recited the additional ground for deportation that they had entered without properly visaed passports, as required by the Passport Law of 1918 (22 U.S.C.A. §§223-226) and the President's Proclamation

Case No. 152 ***Contd.***

(40 U.S. Stat. L. 1829). Deportation was delayed until August 1930, when the Polish Government consented to Engel's repatriation. Engel's wife had died in the meantime. Writs of *habeas corpus* were taken out and it was contended by the petitioners that the three year statute of limitations applicable to entry without inspection (8 U.S.C.A. §155) had expired. The writs were refused. On appeal,

Held : that the order must be reversed. Assuming the three year statute to be applicable, the petitioners did not have a fair trial upon this issue, and the deportation warrants must be annulled for this reason if no other. There was no evidence to support the findings that the petitioners were, at the time of entry, likely to become public charges. Furthermore, the deportation could not be justified merely because the petitioners, entering in 1922 or 1923, did not have visaed passports : *U.S.* v. *Smith*, 36 F. (2d) 503 ; 46 F. (2d) 229, 230.

The impropriety of deporting to Poland the daughter born in Canada was conceded. As regards the father and stepson, they had been domiciled in Canada for more than ten years. Without doubt Canada was, following *Gorcevich* v. *Zurbrick*, 48 F. (2d) 1054, the country "whence they came." If Canada had refused to receive them, they might have been sent to the country of their allegiance ; but since, on March 18, 1921, they were not residing in the Russian territory which later became a part of Poland, and since they did not file their option for Polish citizenship before September 24, 1924, they did not become Polish citizens and they had lost the right to acquire that status : Treaty of Riga, March 18, 1921, Art. 6. Poland could doubtless permit a later acquisition of citizenship, but the Court was not advised as to how it could compel them to accept Polish citizenship. In any event, the deportation authorities must show a clear justification for their action, and this they had not done.

Leaving aside the question of limitation, the warrants could be amended to direct deportation to Canada, as in the *Gorcevich* case, *supra*, but this was hardly the "ordinary case" there mentioned. The Court was inclined rather to follow the *Wenglinsky* case, 282 U.S. 798, and discharge absolutely. The order to deport to Poland was so obviously wrong, and the petitioners had been kept under restraint for so long, that the invalid warrant did not appeal strongly to the Court's discretionary aid. In such a matter it was not without importance that the petitioners were not of any excluded class but, on the contrary, except for want of passports, were entitled to enter.

The case was remanded with instructions to discharge the petitioners from custody.

[Report : 51 F. (2d) 632.]

Aliens—Deportation of—Unlawful Entry—Re-Entry from an American Ship Without Touching Foreign Soil—Whether Constituting a New Entry—Territorial Character of Ships. **Case No. 153**

UNITED STATES *ex rel.* STAPF *v.* CORSI, COMMISSIONER OF IMMIGRATION.

United States, Supreme Court. November 7, 1932.

(Hughes, C.J.; Van Devanter, McReynolds, Brandeis, Sutherland, Butler, Stone, Roberts, Cardozo, JJ.)

THE FACTS.—This was a petition against the deportation of an alien alleged to have remained in the United States in violation of the terms of §14 of the Immigration Act of 1924 (c. 190, 43 U.S. Stat. L. 153, 162). The petitioner, a German citizen, deserted his ship in 1923 in the port of New York and remained in the United States until 1929, when he made a trip to Germany as a member of the crew of a vessel of United States registry. It did not appear whether the petitioner went ashore in Germany. When the ship returned to the United States, the petitioner was discharged from it but was not examined by any immigration officer, nor did he possess an immigration visa or pay a head tax. In 1931 he was arrested and, after a hearing, was ordered to be deported. The District Court dismissed his petition and the Circuit Court of Appeals affirmed the decision : 54 F. (2d) 1086. On *certiorari* to the United States Supreme Court,

Held (*per* Roberts, J.) : that the judgment must be affirmed. The petitioner's entry in 1923 was irregular[1] and he was liable to deportation, but such action could only be taken within

[1] Section 32 of the Act of February 5, 1917, c. 29, 39 U.S. Stat. L. 874, 895, then in force, but since repealed by the Immigration Act of 1924, provided : "That no alien excluded from admission into the United States by any law . . . and employed on board any vessel arriving in the United States from any foreign port or place, shall be permitted to land in the United States, except temporarily for medical treatment, or pursuant to regulations prescribed by the Secretary of Labor providing for the ultimate removal or deportation of such alien from the United States . . ."

Case No. 153 *Contd.* three years of his entry.[1] The Immigration Act of 1924 did not alter the status of one who had unlawfully entered the country or remained after the passage of the Act of 1917,[2] but abolished the three year period of limitation only as to those entering after 1924: Section 14 of the Immigration Act of 1924, c. 190, 43 U.S. Stat. L. 153, 162 ; *Philippides* v. *Day*, 283 U.S. 48. The petitioner was entitled to invoke immunity under the Act of 1917, therefore, unless he had lost it by making the voyage to Germany in 1929.

The petitioner's arrival in the United States in 1929 was a new entry into the United States, although he was at the time a member of the crew of an American ship which had made a round trip voyage. He came from a place outside the United States, and from a foreign port or place, within the meaning of the immigration law: *United States ex rel. Claussen* v. *Day*, 279 U.S. 398. He was therefore subject to deportation under §14 of the Immigration Act of 1924.

It was urged that the statutes requiring the master of a ship, under penalties, to bring back to the United States a seaman who signs for a round trip voyage, made the petitioner's entry in 1929 lawful. That argument, in substance based upon the theory that an American vessel is American soil, was effectively answered, as regards the requirements of the Immigration Acts, in *United States ex rel. Claussen* v. *Day*, *supra*.

The petitioner did not in 1929 comply with the statutory provisions and regulations for temporary sojourn as an alien seaman. Even if the Court were to disregard his status as an alien seaman, the law required that he should have submitted himself to inspection, should have produced an immigration visa, and should have paid a head tax, if as an immigrant he desired to apply for citizenship (U.S.C., Tit. 8, §§132, 167 (*a*), 202, 203, 204, 205, 208). He did none of these things and therefore remained in the United States in violation of law.

[Report: 287 U.S. 129.][3]

[1] Section 34 of the Act of February 5, 1917, c. 29, 39 U.S. Stat. L. 874, 896 provided: "That any alien seaman who shall land in a port of the United States contrary to the provisions of this Act shall be deemed to be unlawfully in the United States, and shall, at any time within three years thereafter, upon the warrant of the Secretary of Labor, be taken into custody and brought before a board of special inquiry for examination as to his qualifications for admission to the United States, and if not admitted said alien seaman shall be deported. . . ."

[2] Section 20 (d) of the Immigration Act of 1924, c. 190, 43 U.S. Stat. L. 153, 165, provided: "Section 32 of the Immigration Act of 1917 is repealed, but shall remain in force as to . . . all seamen, arriving in the United States prior to the enactment of this Act."

[3] See also *George Washington Law Review*, vol. I, p. 113 ; *Illinois Law Review*, vol. 27, p. 822.

Aliens—Deportation of—Securing of Acquiescence of Country of Citizenship—International Comity. **Case No. 154**

Re JANOCZKA.

Canada, Manitoba Court of Appeal. August 4, 1932.

THE FACTS.—The plaintiff, a Polish subject, had been ordered to be deported in accordance with Sections 40 and 42 of the Canadian Immigration Act of 1927. His appeal against the order was dismissed. Subsection 2 of Section 19 of the Immigration Act provided as follows: "In case of the appeal being dismissed by the Minister, the appellant shall forthwith be deported." After the appeal had been dismissed, the authorities took up the matter with the Polish Consul in February 1931, with a view to obtaining a Polish passport for the petitioner. It was not until November 1931 that they received an intimation that the passport would be granted. Thereupon they took steps to apprehend the petitioner and to deport him. The present petition was based on the ground that the deportation order, not having been carried out "forthwith", was no longer valid.

Held : that the petition must be dismissed. There had been no undue delay in making the order for deportation. After referring to authorities on the matter of the right of the State to expel aliens,[1] the Court said (*per* Robson, J.A.) : "The right of expulsion of a foreign citizen whose presence is found to be objectionable does not seem to be conditional on the acquiescence of the country of the foreign citizenship but apparently international comity requires that communication take place. Such communication takes the form of passport application. At all events the practice to that effect does exist and must be recognized. I do not see how, in these circumstances, the Canadian officials can be held to be chargeable with unjustifiable delay if in order to carry out such an important matter of communication they spent considerable time in seeking and obtaining the passport."

[Report : [1933] 1 *D.L.R.*, p. 123.]

NOTE.—See also *Re Veregin*, decided by the Supreme Court of Nova Scotia on February 25, 1933 : [1933] 2 *D.L.R.* 362. The petitioner, an alien, had been sentenced to a term of imprisonment. After having served part of his sentence he received a royal pardon. He was then ordered to be deported by virtue of Section 43 (1) of

[1] In particular *Attorney-General for Canada* v. *Cain*, [1906] A.C. 542, at p. 546, and Hall, *International Law* (7th ed., 1917), pp. 223-224.

Case No. 154 *Contd.*

the Canadian Immigration Act authorising deportation of prisoners "after the sentence or term of imprisonment of such person has expired." The petitioner asked to be discharged from the imprisonment in which he was held with a view to deportation, claiming that in his case the sentence of imprisonment had not "expired." It was *held* (by Mellish, J.) that the petitioner was unlawfully detained for deportation and must be discharged. "Freedom from deportation is incident to pardon because deportation was incident to the imprisonment." The pardon could not be used for what would be in effect the acceleration of the prisoner's deportation.

Case No. 155

Aliens—Expulsion of—Subsequent to Cancellation of Naturalisation.

In re SÁNCHEZ.

Mexico, Supreme Court. November 17, 1932.

THE FACTS.—Sánchez was a naturalised Mexican who sought relief against expulsion from the country. The lower Court held that the power of expulsion was confined to aliens, and that, since Sánchez had been naturalised, he could not be deported. Subsequently, his certificate of naturalisation was revoked.[1] On appeal by the Government,

Held: that the judgment must be reversed, and expulsion allowed. The Court said: "During the course of the case there has arisen a reason which makes the relief improper, namely, extinction of the right which señor Sánchez believed was violated in his expulsion from the country. He has lost his status as a Mexican national as the result of the cancellation of his certificate of naturalisation, and the present case no longer involves a question of his guaranteed rights."[1]

[Report: 36 *Semanario Judicial* (5th ep.), 1740.]

Aliens—Deportation of.

See Case No. 102 (*Chevreau Case*).

[1] Compare the case of *Wong Yin*, decided on October 26, 1932 (36 *Semanario Judicial* (5th ep.), 1321) in which it was held that an alien who had received a certificate of naturalisation could not be expelled.

D.—EXTRADITION

I.—In General

Extradition—In General—Extradition in the Absence of a Treaty—Extradition of Fugitive Taking Refuge on a Warship of the Requested State in Waters under the Jurisdiction of the Requesting State. **Case No. 156**

In re VILCA.

Chile, Supreme Court. May 15, 1929.

THE FACTS.—This was a question of the extradition of one Vilca, a Chilean, on a charge of homicide in the Chilean port of Arica. He had taken refuge on a Peruvian naval transport stationed in the neighbourhood of Arica in connection with the attempted plebiscite in Tacna-Arica. There was no extradition treaty with Peru. A warrant of arrest had been issued, and the Court had to decide whether extradition of Vilca should be requested from Peru.

Held: that, although there was no extradition treaty, the request should be made. The accused was on a Peruvian warship which, under the rules of international law, enjoyed the privileges of extraterritoriality. The crime with which the accused was charged was "in the nature of a serious crime against humanity, which compromises good order and social tranquility. These are circumstances in which extradition of fugitives is proper, according to the rules of public international law, uniformly accepted by both States."

[Report: *Gaceta de los Tribunales*, 1929 (1st sem.), 327.]

NOTE.—See also the decision of the Supreme Court in *Silva's case*, decided on April 23, 1929: *Gaceta de los Tribunales*, 1929 (1st sem.), 319. In *Huerta's case*, decided on June 10, 1929, *ibid.*, 334, the Supreme Court decided to ask for extradition from Argentina for rape, since "it is a crime against public morality and family relations, which all peoples have an interest in not leaving unpunished."

Case No. 157

Extradition—Conditions of—Extradition in the Absence of a Treaty—Persons Convicted *in absentia* in Requesting State—Statute of Limitations.

In re LEPAGE.

Argentina, Federal Supreme Court. December 7, 1932.

THE FACTS.—France sought the extradition of a French national, one Lepage, who was charged with embezzlement committed in France in 1928. Lepage had been convicted of this crime, *in absentia*, by a French Court and sentenced on July 12, 1929, to one year's imprisonment. There was no extradition treaty between France and Argentina,[1] but the French Government produced the documents required, under the Argentine Code of Criminal Procedure, for extradition. Extradition was refused by the Federal District Judge on the ground that the period of limitation had run. This was affirmed by the Cámara Federal. On appeal to the Supreme Court,

Held: that the judgments of the lower Courts must be affirmed and extradition refused. The Court said: "As there is no extradition treaty with the French Republic, it is proper to apply to the present case the principles of reciprocity and of the uniform practice of nations.[2] . . . In dealing with an accused person convicted *in absentia* or by default, the effect of the judgment is that we must consider him, according to the principles of our legislation, merely as a person accused of a crime, with the case still open in the requesting country, since in ours the right of defence in Court is inviolable.[3] The crime with which Lepage is charged is of a 'correctional' nature, for which the period of limitation for prosecution expires in three years, according to Article 638 of the French Code of Criminal Procedure." Under the Argentine Code of Criminal Procedure extradition should not be granted if the

[1] On extradition in Latin-America without a treaty see Puente in *M.L.R.*, XXVIII (1930), p. 665.

[2] Article 646 of the Argentine Code of Criminal Procedure provided as follows: "Extradition of criminals, whether requested by the Republic or granted by it at the request of another State, shall only take place: (1) In the cases provided for by existing treaties; and (2) In the absence of treaties, in the cases in which extradition is proper according to the principle of reciprocity or the uniform practice of States."

[3] Argentine Constitution, Article 18.

period for prosecution has expired under the law of the requesting State (Article 655, No. 5).[1]

[Report : 167 *Fallos de la Corte Suprema*, 50.]

II.—Extradition of Nationals

Extradition—Nature of—Extradition and Re-Extradition—Re-Extradition of a State's Own Subjects—German Law. **Case No. 158**

In re UTSCHIG.

Germany, Supreme Court for Criminal Matters.

October 12, 1931.

THE FACTS.—Czechoslovakia was seeking the extradition of one Utschig, who was serving a term of eight years' imprisonment with hard labour in a German prison. Proceedings for murder were pending against him and another accused before a Czechoslovak District Court. In order to confront Utschig with the other accused, the District Court requested that he should "temporarily be put at this Court's disposal." The Supreme Court had in the first instance to decide the question whether such request was to be regarded as a request for extradition or for provisional extradition. Paragraph 4 (1) of the German Extradition Act provided that extradition shall be lawful only where reciprocity is guaranteed. Accordingly, a German court must examine in each case whether in the reverse case the municipal law of the other State would allow extradition. For this reason the Supreme Court had to answer the further question : If Germany were to request the provisional extradition of a German subject then serving a term of imprisonment in Czechoslovakia, would Article 112 (3) of the Constitution prevent the German Government from binding themselves, in respect of Czechoslovakia, to re-extradite such person ? Article 112 (3) of the Constitution provided that no German subject shall be extradited to a foreign government in

[1] A similar result was reached in *Re La Rocca*, decided on April 29, 1932 : 164 *Fallos de la Corte Suprema*, 330. Here Italy asked for the extradition, under treaty, of a man convicted *in absentia* and sentenced to a term of imprisonment. The crime was committed in July 1921, and conviction took place in September 1925. Under Argentine law, the period of limitation was ten years or less, and this time had elapsed since the commission of the crime. The proceedings *in absentia* against the accused did not affect the period. *In re Montauto*, decided on August 26, 1932 (166 *ibid.* 23), is to the same effect, again under the Treaty with Italy.

Case No. 158 Contd.

order that criminal proceedings may be taken against him or a sentence executed.

Held : that extradition must be granted.

(1) *As to the first question.*—The Czechoslovak request must be regarded as a request for extradition. The term "extradition" was not defined anywhere in the German Extradition Act. Paragraph 1 of that Act provided that extradition shall only be granted for the purpose of criminal proceedings and punishment. Considering the construction placed on the term "criminal proceedings" by the German Law on Criminal Procedure, any delivery must be regarded as "extradition" in the meaning of the German Extradition Act, whereby a person subject to German jurisdiction is handed over to the government of a foreign State in order either that proceedings instituted abroad against the accused in consequence of a criminal charge may be continued, or to enable the execution of a penalty imposed by reason of his having committed a criminal offence. Extradition for the purpose of confronting a person as *accused* fell within the terms of the definition. That construction was not ruled out by Paragraph 41 (3), No. 4, which authorised, under the heading of "other legal assistance," as opposed to extradition, the delivery of a person in order to confront him as a *witness*.

(2) *As to the second question.*—Re-extradition of a German subject after a previous extradition by a foreign State did not come within the term "extradition" in the meaning of Article 112. In consequence the German Government would not be prevented by the Constitution from guaranteeing re-extradition in case such request should be made.

The Supreme Court pointed out that extradition was not an abstract notion of international law which could be regarded apart from its motives. Not every delivery as such of a person to a foreign Government constituted an extradition. Only such deliveries constituted extradition as were made to enable criminal proceedings to be taken against the accused in the foreign country. The prohibition contained in Article 112 was directed only against cases of that nature. The Court said : "This object does not exist in the case of re-extradition after a provisional extradition. Of course, re-extradition also assists criminal proceedings against the accused in a foreign State, or the execution of a sentence which he has been serving there. However, the assistance thus rendered to *foreign* justice is not the purpose of the extradition in this case. Rather is it a necessary and inescapable result which must be accepted in the interest of justice *at home*. The promise of re-extradition after a provisional extradition—and consequently the re-extradition itself—has to be made for the purpose of proceedings pending in this country."

The idea underlying the prohibition to extradite one's own subjects was that, by extraditing such persons, the State would commit a breach of its obligations towards them. But this was not so in cases of re-extradition after a provisional extradition. For when the provisional extradition took place the citizen was already subject to foreign jurisdiction.

[Report: *Entscheidungen des Reichsgerichts in Strafsachen*, vol. 65, p. 374; *Juristische Wochenschrift*, 1932, p. 2341.]

Extradition—Extradition of Nationals—Carrying out of Foreign Sentence in Lieu of Extradition. **Case No. 159**

In re ALDANA.

Guatemala, Supreme Court. July 9, 1932.

THE FACTS.—Aldana, a Guatemalan national, had been tried by a Honduran Court for negligent homicide, and sentenced to a term of imprisonment. He escaped to Guatemala. Honduras thereupon requested his extradition. This was refused on the ground that he was a Guatemalan national.[1] Upon submission to the Supreme Court,

Held: that he must serve, in the Central Prison of Guatemala, the sentence passed on him by the Honduran Court. "The provisions of the Penal Code of Guatemala are applicable to Guatemalans who have committed abroad any extraditable crime, provided that there has been a request to that effect by the government of the country in which the crime was committed (Penal Code, Article 6, No. 5). For this purpose, the law provides that when a Guatemalan has been sentenced by a foreign Court and has not undergone his punishment, the case may be re-opened. However, the present case comes under the exception established by Article 8, No. 3, of the Penal Code, seeing that Honduran law imposes a milder punishment for the crime of negligent homicide. . . . It is accordingly proper to apply the foreign law, without re-opening the proceedings (Penal Code, Article cited, and Article 7, No. 2)."

[Report: 28 *Gaceta de los Tribunales*, 586.]

[1] Article 9 of the Guatemalan Penal Code provided as follows: "The extradition of a Guatemalan citizen shall not be granted to a foreign government."

III.—Conditions of Extradition. Extraditable Crimes

No. 160 **Extradition—Conditions of—Principle of Double Criminality—Evidence of Crime and Principle of Double Criminality—Interpretation of Treaties—Liberal Interpretation—Negotiations Preceding the Treaty—Practical Construction by Governmental Department.**

LAUBENHEIMER *ET AL. v.* FACTOR.

United States, Circuit Court of Appeals, Seventh Circuit; Supreme Court. October 15, 1932; *December* 4, 1933.

(Alschuler, Evans, Sparks, Circuit Judges; Hughes, C.J.; Van Devanter, McReynolds, Brandeis, Sutherland, Butler, Stone, Roberts, Cardozo, JJ.)

THE FACTS.—This was a petition against extradition to Great Britain, where the petitioner was charged with the crime of receiving money knowing it to have been fraudulently obtained. The treaty provisions involved were Article 10 of the Webster-Ashburton Treaty of 1842 (8 U.S. Stat. L. 576) and Article 1 of the Blaine-Pauncefote Treaty of 1889 (26 U.S. Stat. L. 1508). Article 10 of the Webster-Ashburton Treaty, after specifying by name seven crimes for which extradition might be granted, proceeded: "Provided that this shall only be done upon such evidence of criminality as, according to the laws of the place where the fugitive or person so charged shall be found, would justify his apprehension and commitment for trial, if the crime or offence had there been committed." Article 1 of the Blaine-Pauncefote Treaty of 1889 added ten further classifications of crimes which would subject the offender to extradition. Classification 3, which embodied the crime here charged, was as follows: "Embezzlement; larceny; receiving any money, valuable security, or other property, knowing the same to have been embezzled, stolen or fraudulently obtained." Classification 4 ran as follows: "Fraud by bailee, banker, agent, factor, trustee, or director or member or officer of any company, made criminal by the laws of both countries." Classification 10 was as follows: "Crimes and offences against the laws of both countries for the suppression of slavery and slave-trading." Article 1 also provided: "Extradition is also to take place for participation in any of the crimes mentioned in this Convention or in the aforesaid Tenth Article, provided such participation be punishable by the laws of both countries." None of the classifications of Article 1 of the Treaty of 1889, except the three quoted above, made any reference to the "laws of both countries." It was maintained on behalf of the British Government that since only classifications 4 and 10 of the ten numbered classifications stipulated that the offences therein named be made criminal "by the laws of both countries," it followed that there was no such requirement as to the other classifications, and that in this case it was sufficient that the acts charged were made criminal by the laws of England. In line with this contention, it was further contended that the above-quoted provision of Article 10 of the Treaty of 1842 had application, not to the crime itself as an offence under the laws of both countries, but only to the evidence of criminality required for apprehension and commitment of the alleged criminal. It was also contended that the acts charged were criminal under the laws of Illinois, where Factor was apprehended. The District Court discharged the petitioner.

Held (by the Circuit Court of Appeals[1]) : that the order of the District Court should be reversed. The acts charged must be a crime under the laws of both countries : *Collins* v. *Loisel*, 259 U.S. 309 ; *Kelly* v. *Griffin*, 241 U.S. 6 ; *Wright* v. *Henkel*, 190 U.S. 40. It was not sufficient that the acts charged were criminal under the laws of the United States (18 U.S.C. §467). They must be criminal under the laws of the State of the United States in which the offender was found : *Pettit* v. *Walshe*, 194 U.S. 205. Although no statute of Illinois expressly made criminal the acts charged, it was found by the United States Supreme Court in *Kelly* v. *Griffin*, 241 U.S. 6, that receiving money knowing it to have been fraudulently obtained was a crime under the laws of Illinois and the federal courts were bound by that decision.

[Report : 61 F. (2d) 626.]

Held (by the United States Supreme Court[2]) : that the judgment of the Circuit Court of Appeals should be affirmed. It was urged by the petitioner that it was a general principle of international law that an offence for which extradition could be granted must be a crime both in the demanding country and in the place where the fugitive was found and that the applicable treaty provisions, interpreted in the light of that principle, excluded any right of either country to demand the extradition

[1] *Per* Alschuler, J., Evans, J., dissenting.

[2] *Per* Stone, J., Butler, J., dissenting.

Case No. 160 *Contd.*

of a fugitive unless the offence with which he was charged was a crime in the particular place of asylum. See *Wright* v. *Henkel*, 190 U.S. 40, 61. But the principles of international law recognised no legal right to extradition apart from treaty. See *United States* v. *Rauscher*, 119 U.S. 407, 411, 412; *Holmes* v. *Jennison*, 14 Pet. 540, 569, 582; *United States* v. *Davis*, 2 Sumner 482. To determine the nature and extent of the right, the Court must look to the treaty which created it.

The crime charged in this case was specified in the supplemental Convention of 1889. That Convention recited that it was desired by the high contracting parties that the provisions of Article 10 of the earlier Treaty should be made applicable to an added schedule of crimes specified in ten numbered classes of offences and one un-numbered class. In the case of certain offences, namely, those enumerated in the classes numbered 4 and 10 and in the un-numbered class, Article 10 applied only if they were, in the former case, "made criminal," and, in the latter, "punishable," by the laws of both countries. No such limitation was expressed with respect to the crimes enumerated in the other eight classes, one of which, the third, included the crime with which the petitioner was charged. It was thus clear that it was not intended that the offences in the other eight classes must be made criminal by the laws of both countries. It was sufficient that they be made criminal by the laws of the demanding country. The provision of Article 10 of the Webster-Ashburton Treaty concerning evidence of criminality sufficient to justify apprehension and commitment related only to procedure.

"In ascertaining the meaning of a treaty we may look beyond its written words to the negotiations and diplomatic correspondence of the contracting parties relating to the subject matter, and to their own practical construction of it. *Nielsen* v. *Johnson*, 279 U.S. 47, 52; *In re Ross, supra*, 467; *United States* v. *Texas*, 162 U.S. 1, 23; *Kinkead* v. *United States*, 150 U.S. 483, 486; *Terrace* v. *Thompson*, 263 U.S. 197, 223. And in resolving doubts the construction of a treaty by the political department of the government, while not conclusive upon courts called upon to construe it, is nevertheless of weight. *Nielsen* v. *Johnson, supra*, 52; *Charlton* v. *Kelly*, 229 U.S. 447, 468." However, an exhaustive search by counsel through available diplomatic records and correspondence, disclosed nothing in the diplomatic history of the treaties in question which would support a different conclusion. It was not without significance that the suggested construction would limit the reciprocal action of the Treaty. Under that construction the right to extradition from the United States would vary with the State or territory where the fugitive was found, although extradition could be had from Great Britain with respect to all the offences named in the Treaty. Treaties should be liberally construed to secure equality and reciprocity between the parties. If a treaty fairly admitted of two constructions, one restricting the rights which could be claimed under it, and the other enlarging them, the more liberal construction was to be preferred: *Jordan* v. *Tashiro*, 278 U.S. 123, 127; *Geofroy* v. *Riggs*, 133 U.S. 258, 271; *In re Ross*, 140 U.S. 453, 475; *Tucker* v. *Alexandroff*, 183 U.S. 424, 437; *Asakura* v. *Seattle*, 265 U.S. 332. It was unnecessary to determine whether or not the Dawes-Simon Treaty of 1932 was yet in force, since the crime charged was an extraditable offence also under the Treaty, which by its terms included offences committed before its effective date: 47 U.S. Stat. at L. 2125.

[Report: 290 U.S. 276; *A.J.*, XXVIII (1934), p. 149.][1]

Extradition—Conditions of—Principle of Double Criminality—Sufficiency of Evidence—Extradition Treaty between the United States and Italy. **Case No. 161**

UNITED STATES *ex rel.* DI STEFANO *v.* MOORE.

United States, District Court, E.D. New York. June 6, 1930. (Campbell, District Judge).

THE FACTS.—This was a petition to secure the discharge of the petitioner from custody upon a warrant for his extradition to Italy. The crime charged was an attempt to commit murder by firing a gun at one Guiseppe Sutera. An attempt to commit murder was among the offences included in the Extradition Treaty with Italy. Section 2 of the Penal Law of the State of New York Consolidated Laws, c. 40, provided that an act done with intent to commit a crime and tending but failing to effect its commission is an attempt to commit that crime. Section 240 provided that a person who, with intent to kill a human being, assaults another with a loaded firearm, is guilty of assault in the first degree. The petitioner contended that the only offence with which he could be charged under the laws of the State of New York was that of assault in the first degree and that, since assault in the first degree was not enumerated in the Treaty, he could not be extradited.

[1] See Hudson in *A.J.*, XXVIII (1934), p. 274; *Columbia Law Review*, 34 (1934), p. 177; *H.L.R.*, 46 (1933), p. 859; *M.L.R.*, 32 (1934), p. 417.

Case No. 161 Contd.

Held: that the petition should be dismissed and the petitioner remanded to the custody of the United States Marshal. Section 2 of the New York Penal Law was broad enough to include an attempt to commit murder: *People* v. *Pisano*, 142 App. Div. 524. On the evidence offered there was present every element necessary to sustain the charge of an attempt to commit murder in the first degree, as defined by the laws of the State of New York. Even if the evidence received would be insufficient to support a charge of attempt to commit murder under the laws of New York, the act charged was an attempt to take the life of a human being; and that was a crime both in Italy and in New York, whether it be called assault in the first degree, or, as defined in the Treaty, attempted murder. Therefore the offence was extraditable. As the Court said in *Collins* v. *Loisel*, 259 U.S. 309: "The law does not require that the name by which the crime is described in the two countries shall be the same; nor that the scope of the liability shall be coextensive, or, in other respects, the same in the two countries. It is enough if the particular act charged is criminal in both jurisdictions."

[Report: 46 F. (2d) 308.]

Case No. 162

Extradition—Conditions of—Commission of Crime within the Territory of the Requesting State as Condition of Extradition.

KOSSEKECHATKO AND OTHERS *v.* ATTORNEY-GENERAL FOR TRINIDAD.

British Empire, Judicial Committee of the Privy Council. October 22, 1931.

(Viscount Dunedin, Lords Blanesburgh, Atkin, Russell of Killowen, and Macmillan.)

THE FACTS.—The appellants were members of a party of nine men who had landed in a small boat on the island of Trinidad on August 7, 1930. They had come, they said, from the French penal settlement at Cayenne, French Guiana. They were subsequently arrested and detained in custody under a local ordinance, and proceedings were commenced by the Governor of French Guiana for their surrender under the Extradition Acts, 1870 and 1873, and the Extradition Treaty with France of 1878. Article 1 of the Treaty read as follows: "The High Contracting Parties engage to deliver up to each other those persons who are being proceeded against or who have been convicted of a crime committed in the territory of the one Party, and who shall be found within the territory of the other

Party, under the circumstances and conditions stated in the present treaty."

In the course of the proceedings evidence was produced that the appellants had been convicted in France of various crimes, but no direct evidence was given that those crimes had been committed in French territory.

Held: that extradition could not be granted and that the appellants must be released. In addition to certain irregularities in procedure, the Treaty applied only "to crimes committed within the territory of the Power which is seeking extradition." "In their Lordships' opinion no one of the appellants was liable to be extradited under the treaty, unless the crime of which he was convicted was, in fact, committed within the territory of the French Republic." This had not been proved. It might have been unnecessary to do so "if it could have been shown that under French law no conviction in France of any of the appellants would have been possible unless the crime of which he had been convicted had, in fact, been committed in French territory." On the evidence before the Court, however, it was quite clear that in the case of each appellant conviction in France did not necessarily involve that the crime of which he had been convicted had been committed in the territory of the French Republic.

[Report: *L.R.* [1932] A.C. 78.]

NOTE.—A "fugitive criminal" who may be surrendered under the Extradition Act, 1870, is defined (Sect. 26) as "any person accused or convicted of an extradition crime committed within the *jurisdiction* of any foreign state . . ." Is the phrase "committed within the *jurisdiction*" appreciably wider than "committed in the *territory*"? The former is the phrase to be found in recent British extradition treaties. The case digested is of little assistance on this point. In the first place the Court seems to have ignored the discrepancy between the wording of the Extradition Act and the wording of the Treaty, and in any case (though again the Court omitted to stress this point) by Sects. 2 and 5 of the Act itself the application of the Act to any particular State is modified and limited by the terms of the Treaty which brings it into operation. The decision is therefore only authoritative as an interpretation of a particular treaty, and not as an interpretation of the phrase used in the Extradition Act and in recent treaties.

Case No. 163 **Extradition—Conditions of—Principle of Double Criminality—Distinction between Substantive and Adjective Law.**

In re SCHWARZ.

Germany, Supreme Court for Criminal Matters. April 27, 1931.

THE FACTS.—The Austrian Legation in Berlin requested the extradition of the accused, who was charged with a criminal offence punishable in both Germany and Austria. The accused had been acquitted of the offence in question many years before, but new facts and new evidence of his guilt had emerged, which justified a re-trial under the Austrian, but not under the German, law of criminal procedure.

Held : that the extradition could be granted in spite of the fact that German law did not allow a re-trial. The Court considered the wording of Section 4 (2) of the German Extradition Act, which prohibited [*sic*] the extradition of a person who could not be indicted under German law. It pointed out that extradition was essentially a procedural matter, although "the requested State must not grant a request for extradition, where the facts of the case do not furnish adequate grounds for an indictment, in other words, where under the prevailing law no 'right of punishment' arises on the part of the requested State." Under Section 4 (2) of the German Extradition Act, however, only such grounds may be taken into consideration as a bar to extradition which affect the existence of the right of punishment, that is to say, substantive law. Provisions of adjective law which prevented an indictment from being brought—as, for instance, under German law, a mental disease of the wrongdoer developing after he has committed the offence, or, here, the rules as to re-trial—were immaterial to the issue of extradition. The German judge who, under the Extradition Act, was called upon to examine the case which had given rise to the request for extradition, must do so from the point of view of German law, but he must limit the scope of his inquiry to the province of substantive law.

[Report : *Entscheidungen des Reichsgerichts in Strafsachen*, vol. 65, p. 269.]

Extradition—Conditions of—Admissibility of Examination of Legality of Extradition Granted by a Foreign State. **Case No. 164**

In re BECKER AND HAUSCHKE.

Germany, Supreme Court for Criminal Matters. July 11, 1932.

THE FACTS.—At the request of the German Government, the accused had been extradited by Austria on the charge of manslaughter. They were then convicted by the lower Court for that crime. They now appealed against the conviction on the ground that the extradition was illegal inasmuch as the crime in question was political. On appeal,

Held: that the appeal must be dismissed. The trial judge rightly declined to examine the question whether the crime was to be regarded as a political one under Austrian law. Previous decisions of the Supreme Court had established that a judge is not allowed to examine the question whether the extradition was justified by substantive law (*Entscheidungen des Reichsgerichts in Strafsachen*, vol. 60, pp. 202, 205). The appellants were wrong in contending that a more exact and more detailed exposition of the facts ought to have been submitted to the foreign Government, so as to enable the latter to decide whether or not the crime in question was to be regarded as political. It was for the foreign Government to decide whether the warrants of arrest were sufficient. It was not for German Courts to go behind the decision of the foreign Government and to examine whether the latter ought to have refused the extradition on the ground that the request did not reveal sufficient cause (*Entscheidungen des Reichsgerichts in Strafsachen*, vol 65, p. 111).

[Report: *Entscheidungen des Reichsgerichts in Strafsachen*, vol. 66, p. 346; *Juristische Wochenschrift*, 1933, p. 983.]

NOTE.—See also *In re Mück*, decided by the Court of Appeal of Karlsruhe on January 9, 1931: *Juristische Wochenschrift*, 1931, p. 2878.

Extradition—Conditions of—Conviction for an Offence Other than that for which Extradition is Granted. **Case No. 165**

EXTRADITION (FRAUD AND FORGERY) CASE.

Germany, Supreme Court for Criminal Matters. March 15, 1932.

THE FACTS.—The accused was extradited from France for fraud. The Court of Appeal convicted him of fraud and forgery. The accused appealed.

Case No. 165 *Contd.*

Held : that the appeal must be dismissed. It had been laid down in decisions of the Supreme Court that there was no objection to an extradited accused being convicted under a provision of a criminal statute other than that mentioned in the request for extradition and the extradition warrant, unless in a given case the words of the warrant or of the extradition treaty in question circumscribed the right to effect such changes (*Entscheidungen des Reichsgerichts in Strafsachen*, vol. 64, pp. 183, 189, and the decisions there quoted).

The Court agreed that, although no express provision to that effect existed in any of the extradition treaties, an extradited person could be punished for an offence other than that for which he had been extradited only if such other offence was included in the list of offences which had been made extraditable by the extradition treaty in question. That condition was fulfilled in the present case.[1]

[Report : *Entscheidungen des Reichsgerichts in Strafsachen*, vol. 66, p. 172 ; *Juristische Wochenschrift*, 1932, p. 2344.]

Case No. 166

Extradition—Conditions of—Statutes of Limitation.

In re ADDIS.

Belgium, Court of Appeal of Brussels. December 19, 1931.

THE FACTS.—Addis, an Italian subject by birth, fled to Belgium on being sentenced by Italian Courts, after protracted proceedings, to two years' imprisonment with hard labour. The Italian Government demanded his extradition by the Belgian Government. It was admitted that at the time of the judgment the action was barred by a Belgian statute of limitations. The Court of Appeal of Brussels was asked to give an opinion on the request for extradition.

Held : that the request should not be granted. "It is a principle of law common to all civilised nations that in questions of extradition the Government of the State to which the application is made, is not called upon to co-operate within its territory . . . with the applicant Government when such co-operation is requested in connection with an act which, if committed within the territory of the former State, could not

[1] See also, to the same effect, the decision of the Supreme Court for Criminal Matters in *Entscheidungen des Reichsgerichts in Strafsachen*, vol. 65, pp. 106, 111. This case goes a step further than the one reported above, in that it establishes, as an additional condition of conviction, the requirement that the offence, in the altered form in which it is proved at the trial, must satisfy the conditions which the *foreign law* lays down as an element of the offence.

give rise to a prosecution (even if this should be due merely to the operation of prescription). As Article 7 of the two Belgian Laws on Extradition provides, extradition cannot take place if, since the alleged commission of the act, the prosecution or sentence has become barred under Belgian law by a Belgian statute of limitations."

[Report: *Pasicrisie*, II (1932), p. 71.]

Extradition—Conditions of—Extradition of Nationals—Nationality at the Time of the Request for Extradition as Distinguished from Nationality at the Time of the Commission of the Offence or of the Conviction. **Case No. 167**

In re DEL PORTO.

Switzerland, Federal Court. March 6, 1931.

THE FACTS.—This was a request for the extradition of a person who had lost her Swiss nationality after the commission of the offence in respect of which extradition was sought. Article 5 (1) of the Swiss-Italian Extradition Treaty read as follows: "In no case and for no reason whatsoever shall the two contracting parties be bound to extradite one of their own subjects." Article 2 of the Swiss Law of January 22, 1892, concerning extradition, provided as follows: "The extradition of a Swiss citizen shall not be consented to."

Held: that extradition must be granted. It followed clearly from the words of the Treaty that, as regards the nationality of the person to be extradited, the material moment was that of the extradition proceedings. As in this case the accused alleged that she had lost her Swiss nationality already before the present proceedings, it could not be said that, by handing her over, Switzerland "extradites a national." Neither did the terms of the Law of 1892 leave any doubt that the material time for possessing Swiss nationality as a bar to extradition was that of the extradition proceedings. The delivering up of a former subject, that is to say, of a person who was a Swiss subject when the crime was committed or when he was convicted but who later lost Swiss nationality, could not be called the extradition of a Swiss citizen.

After having observed that the prohibition to extradite the State's own nationals was a maxim of Continental public law and unknown to Anglo-American law, the Court pointed out that the question whether that principle applied also to persons who had acquired the nationality of the State of refuge after the

Case No. 167 *Contd.* offence for which extradition was requested, was very controversial in legal literature,[1] but that that question was clearly answered in the Italo-Swiss Treaty and the Extradition Law. Both recognised that the material criterion was nationality at the time of the extradition proceedings, and that the newly created subject could not be extradited (except where he acquired the new nationality by fraud, *e.g.* by way of a fictitious marriage). However, the Court observed that no writer held the opinion that in the reverse case, *i.e.* when an ex-subject was concerned, such person could object to extradition by invoking his former nationality.[2] This was also the interpretation usually placed on paragraph 9 of the German Criminal Code (see also Article 112 (3) of the German Constitution), which provided that "no German shall be extradited to a foreign government for the purpose of his prosecution or punishment." (Cf. Hegler, *Prinzipien des internationalen Strafrechts*, p. 159.)

Opinions differed as to the reason why the extradition of nationals should be prohibited. The rule was largely due to the special ties which bind the subject to the State, and to his unconditional right to remain in his own country. Neither of these reasons obtained with regard to a person who had lost his nationality.

[Report: *Entscheidungen des Schweizerischen Bundesgerichts*, 57 (I), p. 12.]

Case No. 168 **Extradition—Conditions of—Grant of Extradition—Whether to be Interpreted by the Law of the Extraditing State—*Locus delicti commissi* under French Law with regard to Offences Committed at a Distance—Fraud—The General Rule of International Criminal Law in the Matter.**

In re MEHLING.

Switzerland, Upper Court of the Canton of Zürich. March 8, 1932.
Court of Cassation of the Canton of Zürich. June 7, 1932.

THE FACTS.—This was a prosecution for fraud. The false representations constituting the fraud were made partly in Zürich (Switzerland) and partly in Graz (Austria). Some of the payments made by the defrauded persons were effected in cash

[1] The Court referred here to Lammasch, *Auslieferungspflicht und Asylrecht*, (1887), pp. 376 *et seq.*; Wettstein, *Die Staatsangehörigkeit im schweizerischen Auslieferungsrecht* (1905), pp. 41 *et seq.*

[2] The Court referred here to Lammasch, *op. cit.*, p. 403; v. Martitz, *Rechtshilfe in Strafsachen*, vol. I (1888), p. 302; Wettstein, *op. cit.*, p. 42; Lanza, *Estradizione*, No. 143; Kohler, *Internationales Strafrecht* (1917), p. 171.

at Graz ; others were effected by transfer from Zürich to Graz. While residing in France the accused was extradited by the French Government to the Zürich authorities on account of "*escroqueries commises à Zürich.*" The accused now contended that the Zürich Courts had no jurisdiction in respect of the false representations made in Graz.

Held (by the Zürich Court of Cassation, in conformity with the decision of the Court below) : that Swiss Courts could not prosecute the accused for false representations made abroad. The decisive question was on what grounds France had granted the extradition of the accused to the Zürich judiciary and what meaning French law attributed to the expression "*escroqueries commises à Zürich.*" The meaning of that expression must be determined according to French law and not according to the law of the country to which the criminal was extradited. However, owing to the fact that French statutes did not refer specially to this point, it could not be definitely stated what view French law took as to the *locus delicti commissi* in regard to a fraud committed at a distance. The Court referred here to Roux, *Cours de Droit pénal et de Procédure pénale* (1920), p. 513, and Kitzinger, *Vergleichende Darstellung des deutschen und ausländischen Strafrechts*, General Part, I, pp. 154 *et seq.* "On the other hand, writers on international criminal law have often put forward the so-called act or deed theory, according to which in international matters the decisive criterion should be the place where the wrongdoer [was when he] committed the offence as opposed to the place where the effect had occurred. See Meili, *Lehrbuch des internationalen Strafrechts*, pp. 118, 229 *et seq.* ; *Entscheidungen des Bundesgerichts*, 43 (I), pp. 75 *et seq.* [where the Court refused to follow the effect theory "*notamment en matière internationale*"] ; Hafter, *Lehrbuch des schweizerischen Strafrechts*, General Part, p. 79, n. 2. It is accordingly possible to speak of a widely recognised rule of international law in these matters, a rule which has also a place in the law of extradition. In these circumstances the view taken by the Court below, according to which the expression "*escroqueries commises à Zürich*" used in the French extradition warrant meant that the accused must have made the false representations in Zürich, is in conformity with substantive law."

[Report : *Blätter für Zürcherische Rechtsprechung*, vol. 32, No. 54 ; *Schweizerische Juristenzeitung* (*Revue suisse de Jurisprudence*), vol. 29, p. 83].

NOTE.—See the note in *B.Y.*, IX. (1928), pp. 131-134.

Case No. 169 **Extradition—Conditions of—Prosecution for Crimes Other than those for which Extradition has been Requested.**

In re REINER.

Hungary, Supreme Court. No. B.I. 1246. 1930.

THE FACTS.—The Royal District Court of Veszprém (Hungary) issued a warrant against the accused on a charge of embezzlement. The accused then fled to Antwerp (Belgium). The Hungarian Minister of Justice asked for his extradition, and he was arrested in Belgium. In the meantime the criminal proceedings against the accused were extended to cover fraudulent bankruptcy. Before the amended request reached the Belgian authorities the accused was surrendered to Hungary. The High Court of Veszprém sentenced the accused to eight months' imprisonment for embezzlement and fraudulent bankruptcy. He appealed on the ground that extradition was granted by the Belgian authorities only on account of embezzlement.

Held: that the judgment could not stand. The Court said: "In our Extradition Treaty with Belgium fraudulent bankruptcy is not enumerated under extraditable crimes. It seems clear therefore that the accused cannot be sentenced for such a crime in Hungary unless, after the conclusion of the criminal proceedings instituted as a consequence of extradition or after he has served a term of imprisonment, he has had a month during which to leave the country, or unless he has voluntarily returned thereto. No importance can be attached to the fact that the Court subsequently asked for extradition also on account of fraudulent bankruptcy since, on the basis of the information received from the Hungarian Minister of Justice, the Belgian Government granted extradition only on account of embezzlement. Accordingly, criminal proceedings for other crimes should not have been commenced against the accused, even if fraudulent bankruptcy had been included in the Extradition Treaty."

[Report: *Magyar Törvénykezés*, vol. V, p. 71.]

Case No. 170 **Extradition—Conditions of—Extraditable Offences—Proof of Offence—Principle of Double Criminality—Crimes Committed in the Territory of a Third State.**

In re HUGO.

Venezuela, Court of Federal Affairs and of Cassation.

April 4, 1932.

THE FACTS.—Colombia requested the extradition of one Hugo, a German, for the crime of "abuse of trust," under an

Extradition Treaty usually referred to as the Acuerdo del Congreso Boliviano.[1] Hugo objected that the Colombian Government had failed to present such proof of the crime as would justify detention for trial if the crime had been committed in Venezuela ;[2] that the crime with which he was charged was not punishable under Venezuelan law ; and that the crime, if any, had been committed in Germany rather than in Colombia. The report is not clear on the matter, but it appears that although the alleged crime was committed in Germany, some of the persons defrauded were Colombian nationals or residents.

Held : that extradition should be granted. The Court said : "It is not necessary, as claimed, under Article 8 of the Agreement on Extradition, that the request for extradition of a fugitive who has been proceeded against, should be accompanied by originals or certified copies of the statements or other proofs on the basis of which the warrant of arrest was made out ; for, as clearly appears from a reading of the aforesaid text,[2] all that is required is an exact designation of the crime."

Although in Venezuela there was no crime exactly corresponding to that for which extradition was requested (Colombian Penal Code, Article 844), the Venezuelan Penal Code, Article 468, referring to "unlawful appropriation," covered the same ground as the offence here charged. Although the accused was a German and the crime was in part committed in Germany,[3] enough of the crime took place in Colombia to allow extradition.

[Report : *Memoria*, 1933, p. 152.]

[1] An extradition treaty between Bolivia, Colombia, Ecuador, Peru, and Venezuela, signed at Caracas, July 18, 1911. The Spanish text is printed in Venezuela, Ministerio de Relaciones Exteriores, *Tratados Públicos y Acuerdos Internationales de Venezuela*, II, 435 ; the English translation in *A.J.*, XXIX, Supp. (1935), p. 282.

[2] Article 1 of that Treaty provides : ". . . For extradition to take place, it is necessary that the proofs of the crime be such that the laws of the place where the fugitive or condemned man is located would justify his detention or delivery to justice, if the commission, attempt at, or frustration of the crime or misdemeanor had taken place there."

Article 8 provides : "The request for extradition shall be accompanied by the sentence of conviction, if the fugitive has been tried and sentenced ; or by the order for detention issued by the proper court, with the exact designation of the offence or crime which motivated the order, and of the date of its commission, as well as by the statements or other proofs by virtue of which the order for detention was issued, in case the fugitive has only been indicted."

[3] Article 3 of the Treaty provides : "When the crime or misdemeanor which motivates the extradition has been committed or attempted or frustrated, outside of the requesting State, the request shall be considered only when the laws of the requested State authorise the trial of such crimes when committed outside its jurisdiction."

Case No. 171 **Extradition—Conditions of—Place where Crime Committed —Acts in Requested State in Complicity with Crime in Requesting State.**

In re RODRIGHIERO.

Brazil, Federal Supreme Court. May 2, 1930.

THE FACTS.—This was a request by Italy for extradition from Brazil. The accused was charged with complicity in a fraudulent bankruptcy in Pisa. He objected to extradition on the ground, *inter alia,* that the acts with which he was charged had been committed in Brazil, although they might have been done in connection with the bankruptcy in Pisa.

Held[1]: that extradition must be refused. "If the person requested committed illegal acts as an agent of the firm Dante Angeli & Co., of São Paulo [Brazil], it is in the Courts of that city that such acts ought to be considered and punished. . . . Acts committed in Brazil ought to be punished by Brazilian authorities; it makes no difference that the effects of those crimes have repercussions in another country."[2]

[Report: 101 *Revista de Direito,* 381.]

[1] Four Judges dissenting, on the grounds that sufficient evidence of the crime was presented, and that "the warrant of arrest sent by the Judge of Pisa . . . declared that Rodrighiero was accused of *complicity in the crime of fraudulent bankruptcy of the firm Dante Angeli & Co. of Lucca.* Though resident in Brazil, he committed acts violating Italian penal laws, *acts which were to produce their injurious effects there, harming the property interests of creditors domiciled in Italy.* The judicial authorities of the Kingdom [of Italy] do not lack competence to try or judge him, without prejudice to the possibility of his trial in Brazil with respect to the branch of the firm established in São Paulo."

[2] In the Case of *Alvares Pereira,* decided on August 1-15, 1932, 16 *Revista de Jurisprudencia Brasileira,* 167, it was decided that *habeas corpus* could still be brought against extradition, despite decrees of the Provisional Government in 1930 which limited *habeas corpus* to trials of common crimes. But the Court, although it granted *habeas corpus* because the request for extradition was supported by insufficient documents, allowed a second request for extradition, and approved surrender to Portugal. The provisions of Article 11 of the Brazilian Extradition Law (Law 2416, of 1911) did not prohibit a second arrest, except where the accused had been surrendered to the requesting State and then not removed by it within 20 days. To the same effect see *In re Friesman,* decided on October 19, 1931, 105 *Revista de Direito,* 114. But in the Case of *Nogueira,* decided on May 9, 1930, 99 *ibid.* 334, the surrender of the accused had been requested by Portugal in 1924, and his extradition refused; a second request in 1925 was granted, but the Portuguese Embassy failed to remove him within 20 days after he was turned over to the Portuguese authorities. Therefore another arrest for this same offence, and another attempt at extradition, was held improper. The provisions of Article 11 of Law 2416 seemed clear: "Extradition having been granted, if within 20 days from the date of the communication stating that the accused is at the disposal of the requesting State, the respective diplomatic agent of the latter has not sent him to the

Extradition—Conditions of—Copies of Laws of the Requesting State—Statute of Limitations—The Principle *non bis in idem*. **Case No. 172**

In re TOMASELLI.

Argentina, Federal Supreme Court. October 17, 1932.

THE FACTS.—In this case Italy sought the extradition, under treaty, of one Tomaselli for the crimes of robbery and participation in murder. The request was not accompanied by a copy of the relevant Italian statute of limitations. Tomaselli contended that he had previously been tried in Italy for this murder, and acquitted. The Federal Court of Bahía Blanca held that extradition should not be granted, since the Treaty with Italy required that the request be accompanied by a copy of the legal provisions applicable to the crime.[1] The Cámara Federal reversed this decision, holding that the period of prescription had not run under Argentine law, and that the Treaty did not specifically require the requesting State to send a copy of the legal provisions bearing on prescription.[2] It also held that the defence of *res judicata* had not been proved, seeing that the identity of the former case with that for which Tomaselli's extradition was now sought had not been shown.

Held: that the decision of the Cámara Federal must be affirmed. (*a*) The period of limitation had not run under Argentine law, and the accused had failed to prove that it had run under Italian law.

(*b*) As to the prior acquittal, the Court said: "The defence of *res judicata* . . . is out of place before the Courts of the requested State, since its consideration belongs to the territorial

requesting State, he shall be set at liberty and shall not again be seized for the same reasons for which his extradition was requested."

In the case of *Marius* decided on May 16, 1930, 99 *Revista de Direito*, 334, extradition was granted to France, for violation of laws and of the International Convention of Paris of May 4, 1910, prohibiting the "white slave" traffic. In the cases of *Rodriguez* (June 21, 1930), 99 *ibid.* 346, and *De la Plata* (June 27, 1930), 100 *ibid.* 87, extradition was refused because the requests contained insufficient information about the crime with which the accused were charged and the legislation of the requesting State applicable to it.

[1] Article 12 of the Extradition Treaty of 1886 between Argentina and Italy (*Tratados de la Republica Argentina* (1901), vol. I, p. 295; Italian text in Martens, *N.R.G.*, 2nd ser., XXVIII, p. 3; English translation, *ibid.*, XXXIII, p. 47), provided: "The demand for extradition shall be . . . accompanied by the following documents: . . . 3. Copy of the legal dispositions applicable to the fact charged, according to the legislation of the requesting State."

[2] Citing *In re Kwintkieviecz*: *Annual Digest*, 1929-1930, Case No. 182; *In re Naceradsky and Hitschamann* and *In re Degloria*, *ibid.*, n. 3.

Case No. 172 *Contd.* judge of the case in the appropriate proceedings. Extradition does not constitute a true criminal trial, but merely a proceeding calculated to establish the defendant's identity and to ensure the carrying out of the respective treaties or laws in force."[1]

[Report: 166 *Fallos*, 173.]

NOTE.—In *Re Nervi*, decided on May 18, 1932 (164 *Fallos*, 429), the Supreme Court approved the surrender to Italy of the accused, who had served his prison sentence in Argentina. For an earlier action in this case see 157 *Fallos*, 116; *Annual Digest*, 1929-1930, Case No. 183. In *Re Mazzeo*, decided on July 18, 1932 (165 *Fallos*, 227), extradition was granted to Italy, although no copy of the Italian law as to limitations accompanied the request. In *Re Lestruzzi*, decided on February 20, 1931 (160 *ibid.*, 67), extradition was granted to Italy although the request was not accompanied by a copy of the applicable Italian penal law, seeing that the Italian Commercial Code made it clear that the acts alleged amounted to fraudulent bankruptcy. In the case of *Ranulfo and Juan Vicente Benitez*, decided on March 4, 1932 (164 *ibid.*, 42), extradition was granted to Paraguay in respect of homicide. However, since the death penalty for homicide was imposed by the law of Paraguay but not by that of Argentina, extradition was granted subject to the undertaking that the death penalty would not be inflicted on the persons extradited. (On this practice see Reeves in *A.J.*, XVIII (1924), p. 298; Puente in *M.L.R.*, XXVIII (1930), p. 665.)

Extradition—Conditions of—Extradition of Nationals—Extradition and Re-Extradition.

See Case No. 158 (*In re Utschig*).

Extradition—Acts Done Outside the Jurisdiction but Producing Effects Within It.

See Case No. 66 (*Ex parte Hammond*).

Extradition—Conditions of—Identity of Request for Extradition and Prosecution—The Designation of the Offence and the Facts which Constitute It.

See Case No. 177 (*The King* v. *Corrigan*).

[1] The Court referred here to a passage from its decision in *Re Foglia*, quoted in *Annual Digest*, 1929-1930, p. 288, n. 1.

IV.—Procedure of Extradition

Extradition—Procedure—Amount of Necessary Evidence—Hearsay. **Case No. 173**

UNITED STATES *ex rel.* KLEIN *v.* MULLIGAN.

United States, Circuit Court of Appeals, Second Circuit. June 25, 1931.

(Manton, Swan, Chase, Circuit Judges.)

THE FACTS.—This was a petition before a United States District Court against the extradition of Arthur J. Klein, a British subject, sought as a fugitive from justice. An information, supported by depositions charging the defendant with the receipt of money "knowing the same to have been obtained under circumstances which amount to a misdemeanor, to wit, conspiracy to defraud, in each case contrary to section 33 (1) of the Larceny Act, 1916," had been lodged against Klein in London. Klein was arrested upon complaint of the British Consul-General at New York. At the hearing before a United States Commissioner, copies of the British documents, duly authenticated, were received in evidence. Klein offered no evidence and was committed to the custody of the Marshal to await the receipt of an extradition warrant from the Secretary of State. The Treaty of 1842 (8 U.S. Stat. L. 572, 576), as amended in 1889 (26 U.S. Stat. L. 1508, 1509), provided that the crime of "receiving any money, . . . knowing the same to have been embezzled, stolen or fraudulently obtained" is an extraditable offence. Article 10 of that Treaty also provided that extradition may be granted only "upon such evidence of criminality as, according to the laws of the place where the fugitive or person so charged shall be found, would justify his apprehension and commitment for trial, if the crime or offense had there been committed." The acts with which Klein was charged would have been criminal under the laws of the State of New York had the offence been committed there. (Consol. Laws N. Y. c. 40, §1308.) Klein contended that there was insufficient evidence to warrant a finding of reasonable ground to believe him guilty of the crime charged. The District Judge dismissed writs of *habeas corpus* and *certiorari* after a hearing. On appeal,

Held (*per* Swan, J.) : that the order appealed from must be affirmed. The commitment for extradition was proper, provided

Case No. 173 Contd.

that there was evidence to warrant a finding of reasonable ground to believe the accused guilty. It was clear that competent evidence to establish reasonable ground was not necessarily evidence sufficient to convict, nor only such as could pass technical rules governing the admissibility of evidence in criminal trials: *Glucksman* v. *Henkel*, 221 U.S. 508, 512; *Collins* v. *Loisel*, 259 U.S. 309, 312; *Fernandez* v. *Phillips* 268 U.S. 311, 312.

Klein contended that there was a failure of proof that the money he was accused of receiving was obtained fraudulently, since the only evidence thereof was hearsay. This contention was unfounded. By virtue of the Act of August 3, 1882 (18 U.S.C.A. §655), the depositions taken in England and properly authenticated were competent evidence. Indeed, the objection urged was not to their reception in evidence, but to the sufficiency of what they contained. The hearsay character of a statement was, of course, a factor to be considered in determining the weight to be accorded to it. It was not a decisive objection.

After reviewing the evidence, the Court concluded that it was sufficient to warrant a finding of reasonable ground to believe that the money was obtained fraudulently and that Klein had knowledge of the fraud.

[Report: 50 F. (2d) 687.]

Case No. 174 **Extradition — Procedure — Nature of — Evidence by the Accused.**

EXTRADITION OF MERTZ.

United States, District Court, S.D. Texas, Galveston Division.

August 8, 1931.

(Kennerley, District Judge).

THE FACTS.—This was an extradition proceeding brought against Mertz, a United States narcotics officer, who was charged in the Dominion of Canada with the crime of murder. At the hearing Mertz objected that certain depositions lodged by the Canadian Government, tending to show that the alleged offence was committed in Canada, were inadmissible since they were taken without cross-examination by Mertz. The Canadian Government objected that the testimony of Mertz and that of other witnesses offered by him, tending to show that the alleged offence was committed in the United States and that the shooting was accidental, was not admissible.

Held: that the defendant must be discharged. The depositions complied fully with Section 655, title 18, U.S.C.A., and were admissible: *Bingham* v. *Bradley*, 241 U.S. 511; *Rice* v. *Ames*, 180 U.S. 371. The testimony of Mertz and that of other witnesses offered by him was also admissible. A proceeding of this character was not a trial by which the prisoner was convicted or acquitted; it partook of the character of a preliminary examination before an examining or committing magistrate to determine whether or not the accused shall be held for trial. The issue was whether a *prima facie* case of guilt was presented; and although generally the defendant's witnesses were not heard, a distinction could be made between evidence presented to contradict that of the prosecution and the testimony of witnesses present at the time the offence was said to have been committed and offered to explain what was said by the witnesses for the prosecution. See *United States* v. *White*, Fed. Cas. No. 16,685; *Benson* v. *McMahon*, 127 U.S. 457; *Charlton* v. *Kelly*, 229 U.S. 456. Here the evidence of Mertz and Vaccaro, who were present at the time the offence was said to have been committed, was admissible to explain the statements of the witnesses for the Canadian Government. Commenting unfavourably upon the credibility of the witnesses for the Canadian Government, the Court concluded that the offence, if committed, was committed in the United States, that the shot was fired accidentally, and that Mertz was not extraditable.

[Report: 52 F. (2d) 241.]

Extradition—Procedure—Remand in Prison Pending Examination. **Case No. 175**

UNITED STATES *ex rel.* MCNAMARA *v.* HENKEL.

United States, District Court, S.D. New York. January 26, 1912.[1]

(Hough, District Judge.)

THE FACTS.—This was a *habeas corpus* proceeding. The petitioner was held pending examination for extradition to Great Britain, and asked for bail.

Held: that the writ should be discharged and the petitioner remanded. It was within the spirit of all extradition treaties concluded by the United States to arrest and hold for a reasonable time, pending examination, a person accused of having

[1] This case, although decided in 1912, was reported in the period covered by the present issue of the *Digest*. Possibly it is reported because of its relevancy to *In re Klein*, decided on November 24, 1930 and reported in 46 F. (2d) 85.

Case No. 175 *Contd.* committed a crime abroad. This could be done on telegraphic request, provided that the request was made by such person or persons that officials in the United States representing both the contracting parties were justified in believing the statements made in the telegram: *Yordi* v. *Nolte*, 215 U.S. 227. As for admitting the prisoner to bail, the Court undoubtedly had that power. It was inadvisable, however, to admit to bail prior to the date of a reasonably early examination. If, when the examination day arrived, the complainant was not ready to proceed after having had a reasonable opportunity to communicate with the region from whence the request for extradition emanated, it would then be time enough to ask for bail.

[Report: 46 F. (2d) 84.]

NOTE.—See also, to the same effect, *In re Klein*, decided by the United States District Court, S.D. New York, on November 24, 1930, where the Court pointed out that the prisoner was not entitled to bail as of right: *Wright* v. *Henkel*, 190 U.S. 40. The power to grant bail, the Court said, must be exercised sparingly and only when the justification was plain: *In re Mitchell*, 171 Fed. 289; *U.S. ex rel. McNamara* v. *Henkel*, 46 F. (2d) 84. Otherwise, the Courts might frustrate the efforts of the Executive branch of the Government to fulfil treaty obligations. [Report: 46 F. (2d) 85.]

Case No. 176

Extradition—Procedure of—Proof of Criminality.

In re TRINIDAD.

Mexico, Supreme Court. September 19, 1932.

THE FACTS.—The United States asked for extradition, under treaty,[1] of the accused, a citizen of the United States, for the crime of counterfeiting American money. The request was accompanied by detailed sworn statements of an American Secret Service agent and other witnesses. The accused objected to extradition on the ground that the evidence of criminality was not such as would justify commitment for trial if the offence had been committed in Mexico; such evidence was required under the treaty.[2]

Held: that extradition might properly be granted. The evidence adduced was sufficient. The indictment was supported

[1] Treaty of February 22, 1899: *Tratados y Convenciones Vigentes*, 1931, I, 177; Malloy, *Treaties, Conventions, &c. of the United States*, vol. I (1910), p. 1184.

[2] Article 3 of the Treaty provided: "Extradition shall not take place in any of the following cases: 1. When the evidence of criminality presented by the requesting party would not justify, according to the laws of the place where the fugitive or person so charged shall be found, his or her apprehension and commitment for trial, if the crime or offence had been there committed."

by the statement of three witnesses, whose testimony was apparently worthy of belief, and by authenticated copies of the document [the counterfeit note] in question. That evidence showed, *prima facie*, that the accused was guilty. Under the Treaty[2] it was not necessary, in order to grant extradition, to prove "the existence of the crime." What was necessary was to satisfy the requirements for the issuance of a warrant of arrest.[1]

[Report: 36 *Semanario Judicial* (5th ep.), 357.]

Extradition—Procedure of—Surrender as distinguished from Voluntary Return—Interpretation of British-French Extradition Treaty of 1876—Identity of Request for Extradition and Prosecution—The Designation of the Offence and the Facts which Constitute it. **Case No. 177**

THE KING *v.* CORRIGAN.

England, Court of Criminal Appeal. November 6, 1930.

(Swift, Acton and Talbot, JJ.)

THE FACTS.—In October 1929, and again in November, warrants were issued in London for the arrest of the defendant on three separate charges of obtaining money by false pretences. The defendant was then in France, and requests were made by the Government of the United Kingdom to the French Government for his extradition under the Extradition Treaty of August 14, 1876. The defendant was arrested in Paris on November 13, 1929, and brought before a French Court on two occasions, when the charges upon which his extradition was required were made known to him. The defendant expressed his willingness to be returned to England to be tried upon all three charges, was brought from Paris in custody to Boulogne, handed over to the English police on the boat and brought to England. The French Government informed the British Embassy in Paris that he had been shown the three charges against him, and had consented to be sent back "without the fulfilment or accomplishment of the formalities of extradition."

On his arrival in England the defendant was committed for trial at the Central Criminal Court on the three charges of false pretences, but when the case was tried he was charged, in respect of each of the three offences, under a further indictment for fraudulent conversion. This further indictment charged him with a different and more serious offence, but one based upon

[1] On this question of the extent of proof necessary see *Michigan Law Review*, 31 (1933), p. 544; *Cornell Law Quarterly*, XVIII (1932), p. 608.

Case No. 177 *Contd.*

the same set of facts as the earlier charges. The defendant was convicted upon two of the charges of fraudulent conversion, and appealed against his conviction on the ground, *inter alia*, that the Central Criminal Court had no jurisdiction to try him on the indictment for "fraudulent conversion." The defendant submitted that Section 19 of the Extradition Act of 1870 only provided that, where a person had been surrendered under an extradition treaty, he "shall not, until he has been restored or had an opportunity of returning to [the] foreign state, be triable or tried for any offence committed prior to the surrender . . . other than such of the said crimes as may be proved by the facts on which the surrender is grounded." Nevertheless the Act only became applicable to France by reason of an Order in Council made under Sections 2 and 5 of the Act, and power was given under those sections to restrict by Order in Council the application of the Act and to render its application subject to such "conditions, exceptions and qualifications as may be deemed expedient." The Order in Council dated May 1878, which applied the Act to France, recited the provisions of the Treaty of 1876 with France, and accordingly rendered the application of the Act subject to the conditions or qualifications of Article 4 of the Treaty, which provided that "a person surrendered shall not be tried for any crime or offence committed in the other country before the extradition, other than the crime for which his surrender has been granted." The defendant contended that he had been extradited from France under the Treaty of 1876 on charges of obtaining money by false pretences, and therefore could not be tried on charges of the different crime of fraudulent conversion.

On behalf of the Crown it was contended: (1) that the defendant had not been surrendered or extradited in that he consented to be returned to England, and by his waiver relieved the French Court of the necessity of making any order for his surrender under the Treaty. If he had been surrendered under French law, a formal order from the President of the Republic would have been necessary. Since there was no surrender, neither Section 19 of the Act nor Article 4 of the Treaty applied to the case;

(2) That, even if it was a surrender, Article 4 of the Treaty had, and was intended to have, the same meaning as Section 19 of the Act. The Article referred, by the words "crime or offence," not to the manner in which the charge was formulated in accordance with the law of one or other country, but to the

substance of the allegations—the state of facts on which the extradition was granted.

Held (*per* Swift, J.): (1) that Corrigan had not been extradited under the Treaty, and that therefore neither Article 4 of the Treaty nor Section 19 of the Act applied to the case;

(2) that Article 4 of the Treaty did not have the effect of limiting the power given by Section 19 of the Act to try a surrendered person upon any charge based on the facts contained in the depositions and information on which his surrender had been obtained.[1]

[Report: *L.R.* [1931] 1 K.B. 527 (C.C.A.).]

Extradition—Procedure of—Time for Removal by Requesting State—Treaties—Enforcement of—How Far Abrogated by Subsequent Inconsistent Statutes.

See Case No. 5 (*In re Brooks*).

Extradition—Procedure of—Evidence of Crime.

See Case No. 170 (*In re Hugo*).

V.—Political Criminals

Extradition—Political Offences—Admissibility of Examination of Legality of Extradition Granted by a Foreign State.

See Case No. 164 (*In re Becker and Hauschke*).

[1] The learned judge said: "With regard to the misdirection, it is pointed out that in a particular passage the learned Commissioner in telling the jury what amounted to fraudulent conversion, did not actually use the word 'fraud.' I agree that in the particular passage to which our attention was called he did not use the word 'fraud' or 'fraudulent,' but he put before the jury a state of facts which, if they were true, could compel ordinary reasonable people to but one conclusion, and that was that what had been done had been done fraudulently. If the matter stood there, I should have hesitated a long time before I thought that in that there was any misdirection, but it does not stop there, for within a few sentences later the learned Commissioner goes on to point out to the jury that before they can convict the prisoner they must be satisfied that what he did was in truth done fraudulently."

E.—MINORITIES (PROTECTION OF MINORITIES)

I.—Minorities Treaties and their Interpretation

Case No. 178

Minorities—Obligation of Non-Discrimination—Meaning of—Polish Minorities Treaty of June 28, 1919.

PERMANENT COURT OF INTERNATIONAL JUSTICE.

See the Advisory Opinion rendered by the Court on February 4, 1932,[1] in the case of the *Treatment of Polish Nationals and Other Persons of Polish Origin or Speech in the Danzig Territory* (*P.C.I.J.*, Series A/B, No. 44), for a re-affirmation of the view that the expression "all inhabitants" used in that Article (2)[2] refers also to minorities consisting of non-citizens of the State. "This interpretation is in conformity with the practice of the Council and with the Court's Advisory Opinion No. 7 on the question concerning the acquisition of Polish nationality. The members of minorities who are not citizens of the State enjoy protection—guaranteed by the League of Nations—of life and liberty and the free exercise of their religion, while minorities in the narrow sense, that is, minorities the members of which are citizens of the State, enjoy—under the same guarantee—amongst other rights, equality of rights in civil and political matters, and in matters relating to primary instruction." (At p. 39.)

Minorities—Regional Protection of—Geneva Convention of May 15, 1922—Articles 69 and Others—Minority Schools —Language Declarations.

ACCESS TO GERMAN MINORITY SCHOOLS IN UPPER SILESIA.

Advisory Opinion of May 15, 1931.[3]

This Opinion (*P.C.I.J.*, Series A/B, No. 40) does not seem to raise general questions either of international law or of protection of minorities, and it has therefore not been considered necessary to report it in this volume.

[1] For the composition of the Court see p. 209.

[2] That Article provides, *inter alia*, as follows : " Poland undertakes to assure full and complete protection of life and liberty to all inhabitants of Poland without distinction of birth, nationality, language, race or religion."

[3] The Court was composed as follows : Adatci (President) ; Guerrero (Vice-President) ; Kellogg, Baron Rolin-Jaequemyns, Count Rostworowski, Fromageot, Altamira, Anzilotti, Sir Cecil Hurst, Schücking, Negulesco, van Eysinga (Judges).

V.—Treatment of Minorities Apart from Treaty

Minorities—Aliens not Protected by Minorities Treaties—Whether Entitled to Use their Own Language before Courts and Authorities on the Same Conditions as Members of a National Minority—Aliens in Czechoslovakia.

See p. 283.

Minorities—Miscellaneous—Territorial Autonomy—Memel Territory—Question of Division of Sovereignty.

See Case No. 7 (*Interpretation of the Statute of the Memel Territory*).

PART VII

DIPLOMATIC AND CONSULAR INTERCOURSE AND PRIVILEGES

A.—PERMANENT DIPLOMATIC ENVOYS

III.—Privileges and Immunities of—

i.—Diplomatic Envoys and Their Staff

Diplomatic Immunities—Combination of Diplomatic and Consular Functions—Limits of Extraterritoriality—Voluntary Submission to Jurisdiction—Whether Involving Submission to Execution. **Case No. 179**

AFGHAN MINISTER (CONSULAR ACTIVITIES) CASE.

Germany, Court of Appeal of Berlin. October 13, 1932.

THE FACTS.—The Afghan Minister in Berlin had brought two actions against the appellant. Both actions, which arose out of the Minister's consular activities, were dismissed with costs. An order was made fixing the amount of costs, and the appellant thereupon applied for a compulsory mortgage to be registered on the Minister's property in Germany. The District Court refused the application. On appeal,

Held : that the appeal must be dismissed. The Court said : "Section 18 (1) of the Judicature Act provides that the jurisdiction of German Courts does not extend to the heads of embassies and legations accredited to Germany. This provision reproduces a principle generally recognised by international law. Such a principle must, as is now expressly laid down in Article 4 of the Constitution, be applied by German Courts even if not expressed in a municipal statute. The principle means that the head of the embassy or legation, as the case may be, shall be extraterritorial in the receiving State, *i.e.* that he shall be exempt from that State's jurisdiction. . . . (See *Entscheidungen des Reichsgerichts in Zivilsachen*, vol. 111, p. 150.) This applies to criminal and civil jurisdiction, to the trial itself, and to the execution of judgments. Where the head of a foreign mission is so exempt he enjoys the immunity absolutely and to its full extent. His personality under international law cannot be split up so that he may be treated as extraterritorial in his capacity as diplomatic representative, but not generally as a private

Case No. 179 *Contd.*

person. For this reason it is immaterial that the Afghan Minister had sued the appellant not in his capacity as Minister but in his capacity as Consul. For if the head of a foreign mission is exempt from the jurisdiction of the receiving State in his capacity as a private individual, this is certainly so if he acts in his official capacity as Consul. It follows that Section 21 of the Judicature Act, by virtue of which consuls are subject to the jurisdiction of German Courts, is not applicable to the facts of this case. That provision concerns only persons who are nothing else but consuls, and not diplomatic members of foreign missions simultaneously exercising consular functions. Consuls are at times entrusted with the entire (including the diplomatic) representation of their State (so-called chargés d'affaires); they have then diplomatic status, and therefore enjoy the protection of extraterritoriality. Equally, in the converse case, the minister does not lose his extraterritorial privilege when acting as consul. Section 18 of the Judicature Act exempts persons enjoying extraterritoriality from the internal jurisdiction also with regard to the execution of judgments. For this reason any act of execution against a person possessing the privileges of extraterritoriality is prohibited. In this class of acts must be reckoned the registration of a compulsory mortgage."

[Report: *Rechtsprechung auf dem Gebiete des Internationalen Privatrechts*, 1933, No. 97.]

NOTE.—The Court pointed out, *obiter*, that the immunity of an extraterritorial person from the jurisdiction of the receiving State was without effect in an action *in rem* concerning real property owned by such person and situate in the territory of the receiving State. It was true that extraterritoriality ceased in cases in which the diplomatic envoy voluntarily submitted to the jurisdiction of the receiving State, and that the bringing of an action could be regarded as such voluntary submission. However, the unanimous opinion at least of German case law and of German writers went to show that the submission to internal judgments did not imply a submission to execution, inasmuch as the proceedings leading up to the judgment were distinct from and independent of the proceedings leading up to its execution.

Diplomatic Immunities—Criminal Jurisdiction after Termination of Mission in respect of an Act Committed during the Mission. **Case No. 180**

In re GARCÍA Y GARCÍA.

Guatemala, Supreme Court. June 25, 1932.

THE FACTS.—This was a prosecution for an attempt to defraud the customs. García had imported from Spain dutiable merchandise which was introduced into Guatemala as sent to the Minister of Salvador, Florentin Souza. García, when tried, claimed that the merchandise was imported for Souza, but had remained in his name since Souza wanted to see it before paying for it ; and that, as the parties could not agree on the terms, he retained the merchandise and paid a thousand dollars to Souza. García claimed that Souza had promised to arrange with the Government about the duty. Souza, who appeared as a witness, said that he thought García would pay the duty, and that he had originally sought the exemption because he thought that the packages were some which he had ordered for himself. Souza was now no longer Minister.

The Court of first instance found García guilty. On appeal, the Court of Appeals reversed the decision and held him not guilty. On appeal to the Supreme Court,

Held : that the judgment of the Court of Appeals be reversed, the sentence of the Court of first instance carried out against García, and Souza placed on trial for his part in the offence. The Supreme Court was satisfied that both García and Souza knew of and participated in the attempt to defraud the customs.

[Report : 28 *Gaceta de los Tribunales,* 577.]

Diplomatic Immunities—In General—Absence of Express Provisions of Municipal Law—The Law of Chile. **Case No. 181**

In re CHAYET.

Chile, Supreme Court. October 6, 1932.

THE FACTS.—The facts are stated in the report only very summarily, but it appears that a trial Court ordered the appellant, the French Commercial Attaché in Chile, to give up to its new owner certain property which he had rented. He invoked his diplomatic immunity.

Held : that the appeal must be granted. The appellant's "inviolability protects not only his person but his house and the

Case No. 181 ***Contd.***

movable property for his personal use or necessary for the performance of his duties."

The Court said: "The immunities from jurisdiction are founded upon the reciprocal interests of States, which demand that their diplomatic representatives be in a position to carry out with the fullest liberty the missions entrusted to them. . . . The inviolability of diplomatic agents, which is the direct and necessary consequence of the rights of external sovereignty and of mutual respect of the States which they represent, shields these agents from any proceeding, whether against their persons or against the things necessary for the performance of their mission or destined for their personal use, such as residence, furniture, papers, and personal effects."

Although there was no express Chilean legislation granting immunity from civil jurisdiction, such immunity must be recognised as imposed by international law. Rules of international law, "co-existent with those of internal law, are applicable in the sphere of relations governed by it, whatever may be the form of the constitution, unless in the written legislation of a State there exist provisions which expressly exclude some of these rules." Chilean legislation clearly did not exclude the operation of the rules of international law concerning diplomatic immunity. (The Court observed that, in any case, diplomatic immunity could not be renounced by the agent without authorisation of his Government, and that such authorisation could not be presumed except when the agent himself brought the action.)

[Report: 30 *Revista de Derecho, Jurisprudencia y Ciencias Sociales*, 70.]

Diplomatic Immunities—In General—Acts of a Public Law and Private Law Character.

See Case No. 187 (*Consular Premises (Greece) Case*).

iv.—The Official Residence of a Diplomatic Envoy

Diplomatic Immunity—Immunity from Taxation—Taxation of Immovable Property Subsequent to Cessation of Diplomatic Mission—Property Purchased for Private Purposes. **Case No. 182**

In re KHAN.

Austria, Administrative Court. December 10, 1932.

THE FACTS.—In 1922 Nirza Mustapha Khan, the then Persian Minister in Austria, acquired a house in Austria. He ceased to be Minister in 1926. The house was sold after his death in 1930. The difference between the price paid for the house in 1922 and that received for it in 1930 was taken by the tax authorities as the basis for the assessment of the Lower Austria Increased Value Tax, and levied on the estate. The heirs appealed on the ground that the house in question was protected from taxation by reason of diplomatic privilege.

Held : that the appeal must be dismissed. According to a statement of the Department for Foreign Affairs of the Federal Chancery, the former Minister, by reason of international comity (*sic*), enjoyed the privileges of extraterritoriality until the end of 1926. After that date he had to be regarded as a private individual. Accordingly, the exemption provided for by the Lower Austria Increased Value Tax Act in case of extraterritoriality did not apply. This was particularly so seeing that the house had not been purchased for the purposes of the legation.

[Report : *Sammlung der Erkenntnisse des Verwaltungsgerichtshofes*, 1932, *Finanzrechtlicher Teil*, p. 509.]

IV.—Termination of Appointment of Diplomatic Envoy

Diplomatic Relations — Suspension of — Influence on Operation of Treaties.

See Case No. 17 (*N. and M. Shipoff* v. *Elte*), and Case No. 16 (*Lowinsky* v. *Receiver in Bankruptcy of the Egyptische-Türksche Handwerksigarettenfabriek "Jaka", Ltd.*).

B.—SPECIAL ENVOYS: DELEGATES AT INTERNATIONAL CONFERENCES: TRADE DELEGATIONS

Case No. 183 **Consuls—Immunities of—Action against a Consul concerning the Lease of Consular Premises—Competence of French Courts.**

FAUCOMPRÉ v. POLISH CONSUL-GENERAL.

France, Civil Tribunal of Lille. May 7, 1932.

THE FACTS.—An action was brought before the "*Président des référés*"[1] against the Polish Consul-General, in his capacity as representative of the Polish Government, with regard to the lease of the consular premises. The Consul invoked jurisdictional immunity.

Held: that the French courts had no jurisdiction. "A foreign State is in general immune from the jurisdiction of another State." The *Président des référés* had no competence to hear the action brought against the Consul. "The inclusion in the lease of a clause providing for submission to the jurisdiction of the place of domicile is without effect in view of Article 4 of the Franco-Polish Consular Convention of December 30, 1925, which provides that the courts will refrain from jurisdiction when an agent invokes diplomatic [*sic*] immunity."

[Report: *Le Nord judiciaire*, 1932, p. 99; *Recueil des Sommaires*, 1933, No. 160; *R.G.*, 42 (1935), p. 223.]

NOTE.—This decision conforms with other French decisions on the subject. Before 1840 the French Courts refused to grant immunity from jurisdiction to consular agents, but from 1840 onwards this attitude has been reversed (see the decisions mentioned in Challine, *Le droit international public dans la jurisprudence française de 1789 à 1848* (1934), pp. 208-222). Contemporary jurisprudence has confirmed this change: see the decision of the Conseil d'Etat of March 22, 1929, in *Ministre des Finances* v. *Héritiers X* (*Annual Digest*, 1929-1930, Case No. 213); and the decision of the Civil Tribunal of the Seine of October 30, 1929 (*Dalloz hebdomadaire*, 1930, p. 15). It will be noted that the immunity granted to consuls applies only to their official activities, as distinguished from purely personal acts.

[1] This is a summary jurisdiction concerned mainly with decreeing conservatory measures.

Trade Delegations—Immunities of—Commercial Representation of the Union of Soviet Socialist Republics in Norway. **Case No. 184**

KOPYTOFF *v.* THE COMMERCIAL REPRESENTATION OF THE U.S.S.R.

Norway, Court of Oslo. November 7, 1932.

THE FACTS.—On January 15, 1926, the head of the Commercial Representation of the Union of Soviet Socialist Republics engaged the plaintiff, who was a citizen of the U.S.S.R., as a member of the Commercial Representation in Oslo. On April 1, after his engagement had been terminated, the plaintiff brought an action against the Representation claiming the balance of his salary and compensation with regard to the salary which he had received but had been forced to place in Russian State loans.

The Commercial Representation of the U.S.S.R. pleaded to the jurisdiction of Norwegian Courts. It relied on the Treaty between Norway and the U.S.S.R. of December 15, 1925, Article 4 (3) of which ran as follows:

> "In accordance with paragraphs 1 and 2, the Commercial Representation shall be under the direction of a person (the Commercial Representative) attached to the Soviet Legation at Oslo. The offices of the Commercial Representation shall enjoy extraterritoriality whether they are situated in the same building as the Legation or elsewhere."

Held: that the Court had no jurisdiction. [Unreported.]

Trade Delegations—Jurisdiction—Legal Position of the Commercial Representation of the U.S.S.R. in Berlin—Submission to German Jurisdiction—Trade Agreement of October 12, 1925.

Article 9 (2) of the Trade Agreement of October 12, 1925, between Germany and Russia provided that the acts of the Commercial Representation in Germany must be governed by German law. Article 5 of the Trade Agreement provided that the premises occupied by the Commercial Representation for the purposes of its business, shall be extraterritorial.

In its judgment of April 9, 1931 (*Rechtsprechung auf dem Gebiete des Internationalen Privatrechts*, 1931, No. 22), the German District Court of Berlin *held* that the effect of these provisions was that, while the premises of the Commercial

Representation must be deemed extraterritorial and therefore Russian soil, German law must be applied to the acts done on those premises and having legal effect in Germany ; and that the latter provision was adopted for the protection of German undertakings and citizens and to avoid the contingency of contracts entered into with the Commercial Representation being invalid or not subject to German jurisdiction by reason of their having been actually made on extraterritorial, *i.e.*, on Russian, territory.

See also the decision of the German Supreme Labour Court of December 21, 1932 (*Entscheidungen des Reichsarbeitsgerichts*, vol. 12, p. 184).

Case No. 185 **Trade Delegations—Immunities of—Russian Commercial Representation in Greece.**

Russian Commercial Representation (Greece) Case.

Greece, Council of State. 1932.

The Facts.—This was an appeal by the Commercial Representation of the U.S.S.R. against certain assessments by the Greek tax authorities. Article 7 of the Treaty of Commerce and Navigation of June 11, 1929, between Greece and the U.S.S.R., provided for diplomatic immunities for the head of the Commercial Representation, and for the extraterritoriality of its premises. The same article laid down that commercial transactions of the Representation shall be subject to Greek legislation and jurisdiction, but that the property of the Representation shall not be subject to seizure as a preliminary measure of security.

Held : that these provisions did not have the effect of granting to the Commercial Representation immunity in fiscal matters.

[Report : *Thémis,* vol. 44, p. 198.]

Note.—See to the same effect the decision of the Court of Athens of 1935 : *Thémis*, vol. 46, p. 692, and *Clunet*, 63 (1936), p. 46. It appears that not only the Commercial Representation but also the U.S.S.R. as such, does not enjoy jurisdictional immunities in Greece in matters other than acts of a public character. See the decision of the Court of Athens, 1928, No. 1681, and 1920, No. 672 : *Thémis*, vol. 40, pp. 486 and 842.

Trade Delegations—U.S.S.R.—Commercial Representations Abroad—Whether Distinguishable from the U.S.S.R.

See Case No. 28 (*Société Despa et Fils* v. *U.S.S.R.*).

Trade Delegations—Status of—Right to Sue.

See Case No. 26 (*Cibrario* v. *Russian Trade Delegation in Italy and the National City Bank of New York*).

Trade Delegations—Status of—Russian Trade Delegation in Italy.

See Case No. 86 (*Slomnitzky* v. *Trade Delegation of the U.S.S.R. in Italy*).

D.—CONSULS

II.—Position and Functions of Consuls

Consuls—Functions of—Right to Represent Parties without Special Power of Attorney.

See on this question the decision of the Supreme Court of Lithuania of September 28, 1932 (unreported), where it was held that, having regard to the existing Treaty with Soviet Russia, the Russian consul was entitled, without a special power of attorney, to apply to the courts with a view to protecting the interests of Russian subjects in an inheritance action.

Consuls—Functions of—With regard to Subjects Abroad—How Far Dependent upon Express Treaty Provisions.

See Case No. 92 (*Blackmer* v. *United States*).

Consuls—Consular Certificates—Proof of Nationality.

See Case No. 123 (*Boubez* v. *Dame Edra Sabbagh Bey*).

Consuls—State Responsibility—Responsibility for Act of Consul Acting on Behalf of a Foreign Consul.

See Case No. 102 (*Chevreau Case*).

III.—Privileges and Immunities of Consuls

Case No. 186 **Consuls—Immunity of—Acts Done on Behalf of the State—Acts of a Public Character—Immunity from Italian Jurisdiction.**

MAZZUCCHI *v.* AMERICAN CONSULATE.

Italy, Court of Appeal of Naples. April 7, 1931.

THE FACTS.—Mazzucchi, who had been employed at the American Consulate at Naples, was dismissed in August 1930. The nature of his duties is stated below. On October 30 he brought an action before the Court of Naples asking for compensation for wrongful dismissal. The Court dismissed the action on account of lack of jurisdiction. On appeal,

Held: that the Court had no jurisdiction. "Consuls do not possess the true and proper quality of representing the State in its international political relations; neither are they diplomatic agents. Nevertheless, in fulfilling their mission and in exercising the powers belonging to them they must be considered as official agents of the governments by whom they are appointed. It follows that, if consuls enter into relations with private persons in order to carry out duties which appertain to the political activity of the State which they represent, no action in respect of such relations can be brought before the Courts since a foreign State cannot, in the exercise of its political functions, be subjected to the jurisdiction of another State without suffering a denial of its sovereignty. If, on the other hand, consuls engage in private activities, then they assume the character of foreign private persons and as such are admitted to the enjoyment of the civil rights which the law confers upon citizens. In such a case consuls are subject to the jurisdiction of the Italian Courts.

"In the dispute in question the plaintiff maintains that this Court can hear his claim having regard to the fact that the modest duties entrusted to him were not of a consular character. In fact he asserts that he had first the task of disinfecting emigrants, and then that of stamping the papers issued by the American Consul so as to make it possible to ascertain, at the moment of embarkation, that the emigrants had been medically examined by the sanitary officer of the Consulate. He does not appreciate that, although his duties were simple, they were nevertheless still relative to a service of a political nature which the American State carries on in Italian territory by means of its consuls.

"In order to be able to declare whether Mazzucchi should have a right to compensation, the Labour Court would have to ascertain, as a preliminary step, whether the cause of the dismissal was just. It would have to submit to examination the motives which led the Consul to dismiss a person employed in a service of a political nature. It would have to give judgment on a step taken by the Consul with regard to the execution of a duty which has its origin in the sovereignty of a foreign State. Such examination and judgment lie outside the jurisdiction of the Italian Courts."

[Report : *Monitore dei tribunali*, 1931, p. 621.]

Consular Archives—Immunity of.

The Swiss Federal Political Department was asked by a judge of a Court of the Canton of Berne whether it was permissible to attach a bond deposited with a foreign consulate. The Political Department, in a letter dated January 30, 1930, gave the following ruling :

In principle consuls are subject to the jurisdiction of the receiving State except with regard to acts done in the exercise of their official duties and within the sphere of their authority. A seizure or attachment of property in the possession of a consul is permissible as in the case of any other third party, unless the property in question is held by the consul in the exercise of his internationally recognised official capacity or unless the consulate as such is the debtor.

This distinction may entail certain difficulties. If, as may be assumed, the bond is in the office of the consulate, the attachment cannot be effected under the provisions of Articles 91-109 of the Federal Execution and Bankruptcy Act. The consular archives enjoy immunity not only under general rules of international law, but also under positive provisions of particular conventions to which Switzerland is a party. For this reason representatives of the authorities of the receiving State are not allowed access to the consular archives without the consent of the principal officer in charge. Accordingly, a writ of execution against a consulate can never be issued in the usual form ; in practice it will be couched in the form of a simple notice of the writ of attachment, thus being in substance a request for judicial assistance.

[Report : *Verwaltungsentscheide der Bundesbehörden*, VI (1932), No. 5.]

Case No. 187 **Consular Immunities—Distinction Between Acts of a Private Law and Public Law Nature—Renting of Consular Premises—Whether Covered by Jurisdictional Immunity.**

CONSULAR PREMISES (GREECE) CASE.

Greece, Court of Athens. 1931.

THE FACTS.—This was a case of distress levied for rent of the premises occupied by the British Consul-General in Athens. The Consul appealed on the ground of immunity from jurisdiction.

Held (by a majority) : that the distress was invalid. Although a foreign State did not enjoy jurisdictional immunities with regard to acts of a private law nature, such as contracts of sale, relations of landlord and tenant, lending of money, etc., the renting of premises for the purposes of consular service was an act of a public character having reference to the exercise of sovereign rights of the foreign State. Such acts were covered by the privilege of immunity from jurisdiction.

The Court also pointed out : (*a*) that diplomatic representatives, including consuls performing diplomatic functions, enjoyed immunity with regard to all acts whatsoever, including acts in the field of private law. This was so in order to safeguard the inviolability of diplomatic envoys and the unhampered exercise of their duties ; (*b*) that it was not necessary to go into the question whether execution was admissible with regard to such acts of foreign States as were of a private law nature seeing that "one must assume that a foreign State will voluntarily submit to execution."

[Report : *Thémis*, vol. 42, p. 833.]

Consular Privileges and Immunities—Combination of Diplomatic and Consular Functions.

See Case No. 179 (*Afghan Minister* (*Consular Activities*) *Case*).

PART VIII

TREATIES

I.—Conception and Function of Treaties

Treaties — Functions of — As Evidence of Undisputed Sovereignty.

See Case No. 49 (*Legal Status of Eastern Greenland*).

II.—Forms of International Agreements and Methods by Which They Are Concluded

Treaties—Forms of—Resolutions of the Council of the League as International Engagements.

See Case No. 215 (*Railway Traffic between Lithuania and Poland*).

Treaties—*Pactum de contrahendo*—Obligation to Negotiate —How Far Implying the Duty to Conclude an Agreement.

See Case No. 215 (*Railway Traffic between Lithuania and Poland*).

Treaties—Form of—Oral Declarations in the Course of Judicial Proceedings—Binding Force of—Absence of Ratification.

See Case No. 202 (*Case of the Free Zones of Upper Savoy and the District of Gex,* (7)).

Treaties—Conclusion of—Parties to Treaties—Undertakings Given by Minister for Foreign Affairs—Binding Force of.

See Case No. 49 (*Legal Status of Eastern Greenland*).

IV.—Conditions of Validity of Treaties. Registration of Treaties

Treaties—Validity of—Essential Error—Withdrawal of Consent to Arbitrate.

See Case No. 218 (*Italian State Railways* v. *Polish State Railways*).

V.—Parties to Treaties. Right to Conclude Treaties. Composite and Dependent States and Territories

Treaties — Operation of — British Dominions — Treaty-Making Power—Canada—Power to Implement Treaties in Matters Not Expressly Reserved to the Federation.

See Case No. 19 (*In re the Regulation and Control of Aeronautics in Canada ; In re the Regulation and Control of Radio Communication in Canada*).

VI.—Constitutional Limitations

Treaties — Constitutional Limitations — Procedure by Boundary Commission Instead of Cession.

See Case No. 55 (*San Lorenzo Title & Improvement Co.* v. *City Mortgage Co. ; The Same* v. *Clardy et Al. ; The Same* v. *Caples et Al.*).

Treaties—Conclusion of—Constitutional Limitations—United States of America.

See Case No. 114 (*Santovincenzo* v. *Egan*, Note).

VIII.—Ratification of Treaties. Entry into Force

Case No. 188 **Treaties—Operation and Enforcement of—Authorisation to Ratify Distinguished from Publication of the Treaty.**

LISZKOWICZ *v.* POLISH STATE RAILWAYS.

Poland, Supreme Court, Third Division (*Court* 1).

October 22, 1931.

THE FACTS.— Article 275 of the Peace Treaty of St. Germain provided as follows :

"... the Austrian Government undertakes ... to hand over to any Power to which territory of the former Austro-Hungarian Monarchy is transferred ... such portion of the reserves ... as is attributable to the carrying on of Social or State Insurance in such territory.

"The Powers to which these funds are handed over must apply them to the performance of the obligations arising from such insurances.

"The conditions of the delivery will be determined by special conventions to be concluded between the Austrian Government and the Governments concerned."

A convention bearing on this matter was subsequently concluded between Poland and Austria, but before it had been ratified the plaintiff brought the present action claiming to be entitled to an annuity under the Austrian insurance scheme established for the benefit of former Austrian railway employees. After the action had been dismissed by the Court of first instance a Law was published in the Polish *Journal of Laws* authorising the President to ratify the Convention. The Court of Appeal dismissed the plaintiff's appeal. On his appeal to the Supreme Court,

Held: that the appeal must be dismissed. The Court said: "Like every statute, the Convention will be binding after its publication by the Polish Government in the *Journal of Laws*. This has so far not taken place, although the statute authorising the ratification has been published . . . since the decision of the lower Court in the present case was given. . . . Thus there is no legal and no treaty basis" for the appellant's claim.

[Report: *Zb.O.S.N.*, III (i) (1931), Part 2, p. 89.]

Treaties—Effect of—Actions Instituted Prior to the Conclusion of the Treaty—Unratified Treaty. **Case No. 189**

HASSAN CHALABY BADR AND OTHERS *v.* ABDEL RAHMAN MOUSSA AND OTHERS.

Egypt, Mixed Court of Appeal of Alexandria. December 17, 1931.

THE FACTS.—This was an appeal from a judgment of the Mixed Civil Tribunal of Alexandria, based on a plea to the jurisdiction of that Tribunal, in an action to which Egyptians and Persians were parties. The appellants relied on a Treaty of November 28, 1928, which provided by Article 5 that Egyptians and Persians in each other's territory were placed respectively under the territorial jurisdiction. The Treaty provided that it should come into force on the exchange of ratifications. The present proceedings began on November 14, 1928, and ratifications were not exchanged until January 30, 1929.

Held: that the appeal must be dismissed. The proceedings

Case No. 189 Contd.

were started "not merely before the ratification of the Treaty invoked, but even before its existence."

[Report: *Clunet*, 59 (1932), p. 502; *Gazette des Tribunaux Mixtes d'Egypte*, XXIV (1933-1934), p. 91.]

Treaties—Ratification—Treaties Passed by Parliament but not Ratified.

See Case No. 196 (*German-Polish Revaluation Convention Case*).

Ratification—Absence of—Oral Declarations in the Course of Judicial Proceedings—Binding Force.

See Case No. 202 (*Case of the Free Zones of Upper Savoy and the District of Gex*, (7)).

IX.—Operation and Enforcement of Treaties. Necessity of Municipal Legislation

[See also Part I, INTERNATIONAL LAW IN GENERAL: V. *Relation to Municipal Law*; and Part VI, THE INDIVIDUAL IN INTERNATIONAL LAW: A. *In General*.]

Case No. 190

Treaties—Operation of—Retroactive Effect of—Treaties Terminating the Jurisdiction of Arbitral Tribunals—Effect on Pending Actions.

X. *v.* GERMANY.

Germano-Roumanian Mixed Arbitral Tribunal. January 4, 1932.

THE FACTS.—Article 305 of the Treaty of Versailles provided for the jurisdiction of Mixed Arbitral Tribunals with regard to such decisions of municipal courts of the contracting parties as were alleged to be contrary to certain provisions of the Treaty. In 1928 Roumania and Germany concluded an Agreement, Article 4 of which read as follows: "Le Gouvernement allemand de même que le Gouvernement Royal roumain renoncent *l'un contre l'autre* à toutes actions devant le Tribunal arbitral mixte germano-roumain ou devant l'Arbitre constitué en vertu du paragraphe 4 de l'Annexe à la Section IV de la Partie X du Traité de Versailles."[1]

[1] Translation: The German Government and the Royal Roumanian Government mutually renounce all actions before the Germano-Roumanian Mixed Arbitral Tribunal or before the arbitrator appointed in virtue of paragraph 4 of the Annex to Section IV of Part X of the Treaty of Versailles: *L.N.T.S.*, 91 (1929), p. 101.

In the present case, in which the proceedings before the Mixed Arbitral Tribunal began before the conclusion of the Agreement of 1928, the defendant pleaded that, in view of the Agreement, the Tribunal had no jurisdiction.

Held : that the Tribunal had jurisdiction. "According to its clear wording, this article [Article 4 of the Agreement of 1928] concerns claims of State against State and does not exclude the right of a German national to sue the Roumanian State, nor the right of a Roumanian national to sue the German Reich. If that wording were to have the wider sense attributed to it by the plaintiff Company, then it should contain a reservation as regards the numerous suits brought by Roumanian citizens against the German State before the Mixed Arbitral Tribunal or before the Single Arbitrator and which have not been decided up till now."

[Report : *Zeitschrift für Ostrecht,* VI (1932), p. 834.]

Treaties—Effect in Municipal Law—Interpretation of Orders in Council putting Treaty into Effect—Reference to Treaty itself—Subsequent Treaties with Third Parties Irrelevant and *res inter alios acta*—Strict Interpretation in Favour of Party Obliged. **Case No. 191**

WHITTALL *v.* THE ADMINISTRATOR OF GERMAN PROPERTY.

England, High Court of Justice. November 11, 1932.

THE FACTS.—The plaintiffs were British subjects with claims against the Turkish Government in respect of (*a*) the requisitioning of their property in Turkish territory before the date of the coming into force of the Treaty of Versailles (January 10, 1920), (*b*) the destruction of such property during the Graeco-Turkish hostilities after 1920. Under Article 58 of the Treaty of Lausanne of 1923 His Majesty's Government had renounced as against Turkey all pecuniary claims for loss and damage suffered by British subjects in Turkey between August 1, 1914, and the coming into force of the Treaty of Lausanne in 1923. The plaintiffs had received certain payments, in respect of their claims, from the International Commission appointed under the Paris Convention of 1919 and from the Sumner Commission set up by the Treasury of the United Kingdom, but, in respect of the balance of their claims, they now sought a declaration that they were entitled to the benefit of the charge created by Article 1, paragraph 16 (b), of the Treaty of Peace Order in Council on the proceeds of the liquidation of the property of German nationals

Case No. 191 *Contd.*

in British territory under Article 297 (b) of the Treaty of Versailles. Article 1, paragraph 16 (b), of the Treaty of Peace Order in Council, substantially reproducing paragraph 4 of the Annex to Article 297 of the Treaty of Versailles, charged these proceeds "Secondly with payment of the amounts due in respect of claims by British nationals . . . with regard to their property, rights and interests in the territories of Austria, Hungary, Bulgaria and Turkey, in so far as these claims are not otherwise satisfied."

Held (by Maugham, J.): As to (*a*): In respect of damage suffered before January 10, 1920, the plaintiffs were entitled to the benefit of the charge. They were not restricted to claims ascertained and determined as the result of the procedure provided for this purpose under the Peace Treaties with Austria, Hungary, Bulgaria and Turkey respectively, since these arrangements were, as regards Germany, *res inter alios acta*, and could not have been contemplated at the time of the Treaty of Versailles. The charge was in substance a guarantee by Germany, which could not be deemed to be dependent on subsequent arrangements between the creditor and the principal debtor. [The renunciation of British claims in the Treaty of Lausanne seems to have been regarded as another such "subsequent arrangement."] But the guarantor would be entitled to argue that it must be a condition of his liability that the amounts claimed under the guarantee were truly owed by the principal debtor, so that the claims must be limited to those which could be proved to be valid under Turkish municipal law at the date of the coming into force of the Treaty of Versailles.

As to (*b*), the plaintiffs were not entitled to the benefit of the charge in respect of damage suffered after 1920. The words "amounts due" in the Annex to Article 297 meant "amounts due at the date of the coming into force of the Treaty of Versailles."

[Report: *B.Y.*, 15 (1934), p. 180.]

Case No. 192

Treaties—Execution of—Treaties Providing for Future Detailed Regulation of their Subject-Matter—Legal Position in the Absence of Such Detailed Regulation.

Ex parte DOVE.

United States, District Court, D. Minnesota. August 14, 1925. (Cant, District Judge).

THE FACTS.—This was a petition to secure the discharge of the petitioner, who was arrested for fishing on that part of Rainy Lake which lies within the State of Minnesota, in violation of the law of that State. The petitioner contended that, by reason of treaty relations between the United States and Great Britain, the State law was invalid. The Treaty of July 1, 1908, between the United States and Great Britain, relating to fisheries in the waters contiguous to the United States and Canada, provided for the appointment of an International Fisheries Commission which was to prepare a system of detailed regulations for the preservation of the food fishes in the waters in question. These regulations were to be enforced by legislative and executive action ; and the regulations were to go into effect when a concurrent proclamation should be made by the proper executive officers of the respective Governments. No regulations were ever agreed upon by the Commission or proclaimed by the respective Governments.

Held : that the petition must be dismissed. The petitioner was subject to the State laws. This was a matter concerning which the State could act until such time as the federal authorities should act in reference thereto by legislation or treaty. Until the regulations and restrictions contemplated by the Treaty had been agreed upon and proclaimed, the Treaty was of no effect in displacing or superseding the authority of the State.

[Report : 49 F. (2d) 816.]

Treaties — Application of — Whether Self-Executing — Application in Municipal Law of International Labour Conventions—Geneva Convention of June 5, 1925, on Equality of Treatment for National and Foreign Workers as Regards Workmen's Compensation for Accidents—Reciprocity—Whether Dependent on the Conclusion of Special Agreements. **Case No. 193**

VEUVE ATLIMAS BEN MOHAMED *v.* SANCHIS ET CIE. LA ZURICH.

France, Civil Tribunal of Oran. November 5, 1932.

THE FACTS.—Article 1 of the International Convention of Geneva of June 5, 1925, provided as follows :

"Every member of the International Labour Organisation which ratifies this Convention undertakes to grant to the nationals of any other member which shall have ratified the Convention who suffer personal injury as a result of industrial accidents happening on its territory, or to their dependents, the same treatment in respect of workmen's compensation as

Case No. 193 *Contd.*

it grants to its own nationals. This equality of treatment shall be guaranteed to foreign workers and their dependents without any condition as to residence."

Atlimas ben Mohamed, a Moroccan workman from the Spanish Protected Zone, died in France as the result of an accident occurring in the course of his work. Thereupon his widow, who did not reside in France, claimed the benefit of the French Law of April 9, 1898, on workmen's compensation for accidents. Both States had ratified the Convention of June 5, 1925 (France by a Law of March 30, 1928) and their ratifications had been registered with the Secretariat of the League of Nations on August 4, 1928 (for France) and February 22, 1929 (for Spain).

Held: that the claim must be rejected. Ratification of the Convention of Geneva of June 5, 1925, by Spain and France was not sufficient, without a special treaty of reciprocity between the two countries, to alter the French Law of April 9, 1898. To enable the widow and children (not residing in French territory) of a Moroccan workman from the Spanish Protected Zone, who died in France as the result of an accident occurring in the course of his work, to benefit by the provisions of the said Law, a special arrangement between Spain and France was necessary.

[Report: *Sirey*, 1933, Part 2, p. 91.]

NOTE.—See, for a discussion of the whole question, the article of Professor Niboyet in *Revue générale des assurances terrestres*, 1933, Nos. 4-5, and the notes by Professor Ch. Rousseau in *R.G.*, 42 (1935), pp. 208-210, and *ibid.*, 43 (1936), pp. 491-492.

The terms of Article 1 of the Convention of June 5, 1925, would seem to rule out any possibility of a dispute arising as to the binding character of the text. A difference of opinion, however, arose, soon after ratification, between French Courts as to the interpretation to be given to the Article. The decisions of certain appeal courts adopted the "principle of assimilation" (*i.e.*, of equality of treatment of French and Moroccan workers) pure and simple (Court of Appeal of Riom, December 24, 1930, *Puig* v. *Vve. Sales-Quérol: Sirey*, 1931, Part 2, p. 54, and *Revue générale des assurances terrestres*, 1931, pp. 418 *et seq.*, with a note by Professor Rouast); other courts, on the other hand, gave judgments similar to that rendered by the Tribunal of Oran, which concluded that in the Convention of 1925 the grant of reciprocity was subject to the conclusion of special agreements, and that reciprocity did not exist in their absence (see the decisions mentioned by Professor Raynaud in *Clunet*, 58 (1931), pp. 329 *et seq.*). The controversy has now been settled in favour of the doctrine of automatic reciprocity, since a decision of the Court of Cassation given in *Castanié* v. *Veuve Hurtato* (*Sirey*, 1935, Part 1, p. 1, with a note by Professor Niboyet).

Treaties—Execution of—Cases in which the Performance of the Treaty by the Other Party is Doubtful—The Function of Courts as Distinguished from that of the Political Departments. **Case No. 194**

DEUTSCHE FEUERVERSICHERUNGS A.G. *v.* LUCAS AND OTHERS.

Switzerland, Federal Court. November 25, 1932.

THE FACTS.—The President of the District Court in the Canton of Baselland (Switzerland) ordered the Deutsche Feuerversicherungs A.G. of Berlin, plaintiffs in an action tried by that Court, to give security for costs. The plaintiffs appealed against this order to the Federal Court. They contended that the security was ordered in contravention of Article 17 of the Hague Convention concerning Civil Procedure of July 17, 1905/April 27, 1909. That Article prohibited "security or a deposit for costs, whatever it might be termed, to be ordered from subjects of contracting States who appear as plaintiffs or third persons . . . by reason of their being aliens or having no domicile or residence in the country." The security had been required on account of the general economic and legal position in Germany which made it uncertain whether German debtors would in the future be able to make any payments at all. The Cantonal Court referred in its order to the increasing restrictions on payments from Germany under the German foreign exchange laws.

Held: that the order must be reversed and the plaintiffs exempted from the obligation to give security. The plaintiffs were subject to the restrictions made by the law of the German Reich in regard to payments between Germany and foreign countries. They were subject to these restrictions because they were registered in Germany, a fact which in view of Article 17 of the Convention should not have been considered as a ground for ordering the deposit of security for costs. The Court also pointed out that the lower Court had not enquired whether and to what extent those restrictions would affect the plaintiffs' ability to pay.

"The restriction of payments from Germany, effected by the foreign exchange administration, might perhaps induce the political federal authorities (*i.e.*, the Federal Assembly or the Federal Council) to take appropriate retaliatory measures or, in certain circumstances, to terminate a convention which by

Case No. 194 *Contd.*

reason of a permanent or temporary change of conditions can no longer be sustained. However, as long as this has not been done, the judicial authorities are bound to observe the law as laid down by international conventions and are not entitled to depart from it. (*Entscheidungen des Schweizerischen Bundesgerichts*, 49 (I), pp. 194 *et seq.*)."

[Report: *Entscheidungen des Schweizerischen Bundesgerichts*, 58 (I), p. 307.]

NOTE.—See also *In re Lepeschkin*: *Annual Digest*, 1923-1924, Case No. 189.

Case No. 195

Treaties—Enforcement of—Agencies of Interpretation—Competence of Courts to Enquire into Political Questions Arising out of Conventions—Swiss Courts—Protectorates.

SARASIN AND PICTET *v.* FOURNIER.

Switzerland, Federal Court. May 13, 1932.

THE FACTS.—The question at issue was whether or not the Convention of 1869 between Switzerland and France concerning the execution of judgments in civil cases was applicable to the dispute over the estate of a Swiss subject who had died in Morocco. The appellants contested the applicability of the Convention on the ground that Morocco was not a colony (and therefore part of France), but a protectorate. They contended that Morocco, which had by special treaties with Switzerland adhered to a number of international conventions, had never, properly speaking, adhered to the Franco-Swiss Convention of 1869.

Held: that the Convention was applicable. The application of the Convention would in any case follow from Article 3 of the Reciprocal Declaration of June 11, 1914, by virtue of which Switzerland and France agreed "to extend to the French zone of the Sherifian Empire" all treaties and conventions of any kind in force between Switzerland and France. "It follows from the Federal Resolution of April 15, 1921, by which the Federal Chambers ratified that arrangement, that the Federal Court is not entitled to investigate whether the nature of the relations flowing from the protectorate confers upon France authority to act in the name of the Sherifian Empire. As far as concerns the relations between Switzerland and France, the arrangement has acquired the force of law, and binds the Swiss judge."

[Report: *Entscheidungen des Schweizerischen Bundesgerichts*, 58 (I), p. 104.]

NOTE.—See also *In re Lepeschkin*: *Annual Digest*, 1923-1924, Case No. 189.

Treaties—Operation of—Treaties Passed by Parliament and Published, but not Ratified—International Law and Domestic Law—Nature of Ratification—International Application of Conventions. **Case No. 196**

GERMAN-POLISH REVALUATION CONVENTION CASE.

Germany, Supreme Court for Civil Matters. February 9, 1931.

THE FACTS.—Since 1903 the plaintiffs had been mortgagees of property situate in Upper Silesia. The defendants had bound themselves by a written promise to guarantee the mortgagor's debt and interest service. In May 1923 the owners of the land and debtors of the original loan repaid the loan in devalued money. In the present action the plaintiffs claimed interest calculated on the revalued debts. They contended, *inter alia*, that the German-Polish Revaluation Convention of July 17, 1929, was applicable to the case in dispute. At the time of the action the Convention had received the consent of the German Parliament and had been promulgated in the official *Gazette*. However, no exchange of ratifications had yet taken place.

Held (on final appeal): that the action must be dismissed. The Polish-German Revaluation Convention was not in force. The fact that the Convention had been ratified by the consent of Parliament and published in the *Gazette* was irrelevant. The reason for legislating with regard to a convention prior to the exchange of ratification declarations between Germany and a foreign State was to obviate uncertainty after the ratification. Such uncertainty might arise from Article 45 (3) of the Constitution, which entitled Parliament to declare its consent to international conventions. Apart from the legal situation under German constitutional law and under international law (*Entscheidungen des Reichsgerichts in Zivilsachen*, vol. 111, p. 42), Article 3 of the Introductory Provisions and Article 76 of the Convention provided expressly that the Convention shall not come into force until after one month shall have elapsed from the date of the exchange of ratifications. This exchange of ratifications had not yet taken place, and the Convention was therefore not applicable to the present dispute. It was immaterial that the Government had already made preparations for the carrying out of the Convention in case it should be ratified.

[Report: *Juristische Wochenschrift*, 1932, p. 582; *Zeitschrift für ausländisches öffentliches Recht und Völkerrecht*, vol. 3, No. 1, Part 2, p. 147.]

See also the note by Mandelsloh, *ibid.*, p. 147.

Case No. 197 **Treaties—Operation and Enforcement of—Necessity of Promulgation—Promulgation of Cessation of Operation of Treaties—Retroactive Effect—Polish Law.**

FEDEROWICZ AND ANOTHER *v.* MINISTRY OF FINANCE.

Poland, Supreme Administrative Court. May 15, 1931.

THE FACTS.—A Polish Law (in the form of a Presidential decree) of 1927 concerning the publication of the *Journal of Laws* provided that there must be published in that Journal, *inter alia*, international agreements as well as governmental proclamations concerning the fulfilment of the conditions on which depended the binding force of the several international agreements. The decree also provided that acts which require publication in the *Journal of Laws* shall be deemed duly published as from the day on which was published that issue of the *Journal of Laws* in which they are included.

A Polish-Greek Trade Convention, concluded and published in the *Journal of Laws* in 1925, provided that it could be denounced by either High Contracting Party at any time, on three months' notice. The Greek Government having denounced the Convention on May 31, 1928, it ceased to be binding on September 1, 1928. However, the declaration of the Polish Government to that effect, dated June 6, 1929, was not published in the *Journal of Laws* until June 17, 1929.

The plaintiffs imported from Greece certain quantities of wine on which, in December 1928, January 1929 and March 1929, they were charged customs duties according to the Trade Convention of 1925. In April 1929 they were summoned to pay additional amounts in view of the fact that the Trade Convention had expired and that consequently the reduced scale of customs duties provided for by the Convention was no longer applicable. An appeal to the Ministry of Finance was dismissed. On further appeal to the Supreme Administrative Court,

Held : that the appeal must succeed. The Court said : "The express legal provisions quoted above make it clear that where the binding force of . . . a convention depends on suspensive or dissolvent conditions, the coming into existence of the facts on which depends either the continuation or the cessation of the binding force of the international convention must be proclaimed by an act which takes the form of a declaration by the Government. None of the legal provisions mentioned above authorise the Government to make *ex post facto* declarations notifying the public that an international convention has begun or has ceased to be binding so as to impose on private parties retroactive obligations resulting from the fact that the convention has begun or has ceased to be in force. Hence such a promulgation, which is an indispensable condition for the establishment of the binding force of the convention, has effect only as from the moment when public notice was given in the Government declaration, that is, from the day of the publication of that issue of the *Journal of Laws* in which the declaration in question was printed. While this literal interpretation favours the contention of the plaintiffs, . . . a logical interpretation confirms that contention even more strongly. For the plaintiffs may, of course, have had no information concerning the exchange of diplomatic notes between the Polish and Greek Governments to the effect that the time limit of three months provided for in Article 11 of the Convention in question was to expire on August 31, 1928, especially since even the Polish customs authorities themselves applied at the end of March 1929, *i.e.*, seven months after the Trade Convention had expired, the customs tariffs based on that Convention."

[Report : *Zb.W.N.T.A.*, IX (1931), No. 461 S, p. 148.]

Treaties—Operation of—Relation to Municipal Law—Indirect Repeal of Municipal Law by Subsequent Treaty. **Case No. 198**

RENNERT *v.* MINISTRY OF THE INTERIOR.

Poland, Supreme Administrative Court. September 23, 1931.

THE FACTS.—The plaintiff claimed to be a Polish citizen by virtue of a Polish Law on Citizenship of January 20, 1920. The administrative authorities contended that by virtue of the Peace Treaty of Riga of March 18, 1921, published in the Polish *Journal of Laws* on June 18, 1921, the plaintiff was a citizen of Russia or the Ukraine, having lost his Polish citizenship as from April 30, 1921 (the date of the exchange of ratifications of the Treaty). The plaintiff maintained that the Law of 1920 provided that a Polish citizen who was liable to active military service could not acquire the citizenship of a foreign country without the consent of the Polish Minister for Military Affairs, that he was liable to active military service, and that he had not obtained the required consent.

Held : that the provision in question of the Law of 1920 "has, so far as acquisition of Russian or Ukrainian citizenship by virtue of the Treaty of Riga is concerned, been indirectly repealed by that Treaty, which is a later law."

[Report : *Zb.W.N.T.A.*, IX (1931), No. 427 A, p. 270.]

Case No. 198 Contd.

NOTE.—The same rule was applied in *Widrewicz* v. *Governor of Warsaw*, decided by the Supreme Administrative Court on October 23, 1931: *Zb.W.N.T.A.*, IX (1931), No. 447 A, p. 326.

Case No. 199

Operation of Treaties—Treaty of Paris of April 24, 1926, concerning Motor-Car Traffic—Necessity of Municipal Legislation—Relation of Treaty to Municipal Law—Whether Directly Applicable by Courts.

PUBLIC PROSECUTOR *v.* J.V.

Holland, Cantonal Court of Amsterdam. August 11, 1932.

THE FACTS.—The accused was prosecuted, *inter alia*, for having driven a motor-car which was not fitted with two independent brakes, contrary to the then obtaining Article 14 of the Dutch Motor-Cars and Cycles Regulations of 1927, but without infringing the relevant Article 3 (1) (b) of the Treaty of Paris of April 24, 1926, concerning Motor-Car Traffic, assented to by a Dutch Act of Parliament of July 21, 1928 (*Staatsblad* No. 291).

Held: that the accused was guilty. As laid down in the decision of the Supreme Court of May 25, 1906,[1] the Treaty of

[1] Since the decision of the Supreme Court of May 25, 1906 (*Weekblad van het Recht* No. 8383), it has been definitely established by Dutch Courts that an international treaty, regularly ratified by the Crown according to the Dutch Constitution and duly promulgated, needs no further transformation into municipal legislation in order to become binding upon the Courts and the subjects of the Netherlands. The decision of 1906 had a bearing on the original Hague Convention on Civil Procedure of November 14, 1896, approved by an Act of Parliament of December 31, 1897 (*Staatsblad* No. 275), and harmonised fully with the view of the Dutch Government, which had repeatedly taken up the same attitude in previous parliamentary debates and otherwise. The decision of the Supreme Court was based mainly on the consideration that, according to the Constitution of the Netherlands, the Crown, apart from its power to issue Orders in Council (*algemeene maatregelen van bestuur*) on the advice of the State Council, has a twofold legislative authority over the subject: (1) to participate in the legislative process; (2) to conclude treaties with other States. This governmental and judicial thesis, according to which a treaty is immediately binding upon the Courts and the subject without the necessity of any further transformation into municipal law, has given rise to much discussion on constitutional doctrine, but has never been superseded either by judicial or by governmental practice. In 1937 the question was discussed by the Netherlands Lawyers Association. See on this matter Levy, *Wet of tractaat?* (1880); Van Eysinga, *Proeve eener inleiding tot het Nederlandsch tractatenrecht* (1906), pp. 125 *et seq.*; De Marez Oyens, *Het normatieve karakter van internationale tractaten* (1907); De Savornin Lohman, *Onze Constitutie* (2nd ed., 1907), pp. 106 *et seq.*; editorial in *Weekblad van het Recht*, No. 8487; and, in more recent years, Kosters in *Bulletin de l'Institut Intermédiaire International*, IX (1923), pp. 1 *et seq.*; François, *Handboek van het Volkenrecht*, I (1931), pp. 333 *et seq.*; and the two reports of 1937, by Professors Telders and Verzijl, in *Handelingen der Nederlandsche Juristen-Vereeniging*, 1937, vol. I, Part I, debates in vol. II.

Paris of 1926, assented to by an Act of the Dutch Parliament, supplemented the Dutch Motor-Cars and Cycles Act without any further municipal legislation being necessary. As a special and, at the same time, posterior law, it derogated from the Act.[1] However, no evidence had been adduced showing the applicability of that international treaty to the case under consideration. No element of the case whatsoever (*e.g.*, nationality of the accused, origin of the car, etc.) pointed to the relevancy of the Treaty of Paris to this breach of Dutch regulations by a Dutch subject in Holland.[2]

[Report: *Weekblad van het Recht*, No. 12607.]

NOTE.—This in itself insignificant criminal case has been reported here on account of the general principle involved.

[1] This was a case of the application of the principle *lex posterior derogat legi priori* to the question of the relation between a previous law and a conflicting subsequent treaty. The reverse case, namely, the question whether in a Dutch Court a previous treaty must yield to a subsequent conflicting law, has not so far come before the Supreme Court. A definite ruling on the matter has been avoided by the finding that there was no inconsistency between statute and treaty. In particular, the Act of Mannheim of October 17, 1868, concerning Navigation on the Rhine, has on occasions engaged the attention of the Dutch Courts in this connection. Thus, in 1915, incompatibility was alleged, before the Supreme Court, between certain provisions of the Dutch Ships Act of 1909 and the Convention. The Cantonal Judge, like the District Court of Rotterdam, had admitted the inconsistency of the legal provisions in question with the Act of Mannheim and therefore considered them as not binding upon the Court, on the ground that "in case of conflict between a municipal law and a treaty, the latter ranks above the former and the law must be left without application, even where a Dutch subject is involved." The Supreme Court, however, by its judgment of February 8, 1915 (*Weekblad van het Recht*, No. 9792; *Nederlandsche Jurisprudentie*, 1915, p. 655), denied the alleged incompatibility and made an express reservation with regard to the main thesis of the lower Courts, which it was unnecessary to examine in the case under consideration.

Another case of the same kind presented itself in 1934 in connection with a new Dutch law of May 8, 1933, purporting to effect a fair distribution of freight-traffic on the Dutch inland waterways. In this case also, which will be digested in due course, the question of principle was not decided by the Supreme Court (*Weekblad van het Recht*, No. 12849).

[2] The case digested raises the question: should an international convention, in case of doubt, be interpreted as tending to govern cases in which no international element whatsoever is involved? Contrary to the opinion of the Cantonal Judge with regard to the Paris Convention of 1926 in the case cited above, the Supreme Court held, in a case decided in 1934 and cited above in n. 1, that the principle of freedom of navigation sanctioned by the Act of Mannheim was applicable even to purely Dutch navigation in Holland. The Supreme Court had already in 1919 interpreted in the same sense the scope of Article 33 of the Netherlands-Prussian Boundary Treaty of Aachen of June 26, 1816: judgment of March 3, 1919 (*Weekblad van het Recht*, No. 10402). In that case the Supreme Court acquitted a Dutch subject of the charge of infringement of a Dutch emergency law of August 3, 1914 (*Staatsblad* No. 344), prohibiting the exportation of certain specified goods, on the ground that the accused was entitled by treaty to export to Germany crops grown on the

Case No. 200 **Treaties—Operation of—Municipal Statutes Inconsistent with Treaties.**

THURN UND TAXIS *v.* YUGOSLAV STATE.

Yugoslavia, State Council (Supreme Administrative Court).

May 20, 1932.

THE FACTS.—Prince Albert Maria Lameral von Thurn und Taxis was the proprietor of large estates situated in the territory of the former Austro-Hungarian Empire and now part of the Kingdom of Yugoslavia. Under the Law of June 19, 1931, concerning the liquidation of the agrarian reform, the Yugoslav Ministry of Agriculture made an order on February 19, 1932, expropriating part of the Thurn und Taxis estates. This order was subsequently confirmed by the legislative authorities and was thus invested with the character of a special law. Thereupon Prince von Thurn und Taxis lodged a complaint with the State Council, requesting that the expropriation order be reversed. He contended, *inter alia*, that the confiscation of the property of a German national was contrary to the provisions of the Treaty of Versailles and the Hague Convention of January 20, 1930, *i.e.*, international treaties which upon ratification had become at the same time the recognised law of Yugoslavia. The plaintiff contended that the legislative and administrative powers of Yugoslavia had been limited by the Treaty of Versailles, and that in ratifying the Treaty she had renounced of her own will a portion of the liberty which she would otherwise have enjoyed in this respect.

Held : that the appeal must be dismissed. The State Council "cannot enter into an examination of the question whether the laws concerned are or are not in contradiction with the existing international engagements [of Yugoslavia]. These

Dutch parts of his estates, which lay partly in Germany and partly in Holland. That treaty provision (the text of which is printed in the Dutch *Staatsblad* of 1850, No. 10) was considered as operating to the benefit not only of German nationals in Holland and of Dutch subjects in Germany, but also of Dutch subjects *vis-à-vis* their own Government. The same principle would have exonerated another Dutch subject who in the same year had grown beets on the Dutch part of estates which extended also into Belgium—contrary to another Dutch emergency law prohibiting the growing of certain crops—if the Supreme Court had held beet growing to be covered by a corresponding provision (Article XX of the Austro-Russian Treaty of Vienna of May 3, 1815 : de Martens, *N.R.*, II, pp. 225 *et seq.*), incorporated in Article 37 of the Netherlands-Belgian Boundary Treaty of August 8, 1843 (*Staatsblad* of 1844, No. 12) : judgment of May 12, 1919 (*Weekblad van het Recht*, No. 10420).

Cf. also concerning this general question *Annual Digest*, 1919-1922, Case No. 233 ; *ibid.*, 1927-1928, Case No. 280.

engagements are open to such examination only in so far as they are proclaimed to be the law of the country, and, in a case of a conflict of laws, the later and special law derogates from the earlier and general law. In the present case the administrative decision in question became law at a later date than the special law said to be applicable to the case at issue."

[Unreported.]

Treaties — Operation of — Abrogation of Inconsistent Statutes—Jurisdiction of Municipal Courts with regard to Seizures Effected in Violation of Treaties.

See Case No. 1 (*The Mazel Tov*).

Treaties—Operation of—Applicability of Treaties Prior to Incorporation into Municipal Law—Retroactive Effect of Municipal Legislation—Brussels Convention on Salvage of December 23, 1910.

See Case No. 3 (*Olivo* v. *Mordini, Giovanni and Others*).

Treaties—Effect of—Treaty between Cuba and the United States concerning the Limits of Territorial Waters—Whether Binding upon Cuba in relation to Other States.

See Case No. 62 (*The Hallmoor*).

Treaties—Operation of—Non-Recognition—Suspension of Diplomatic Relations.

See Case No. 17 (*N. and M. Shipoff* v. *Elte*), and Case No. 16 (*Lowinsky* v. *Receiver in Bankruptcy of the Egyptische-Türksche Handwerksigarettenfabriek "Jaka," Ltd.*).

Treaties—Operation of—How far Covering Acts Done Prior to the Treaty.

See Case No. 132 (*Option of Nationality (Germany) Case*).

Treaties—Operation of—Reference to Domestic Law for the Purpose of Interpretation.

See Case No. 210 (*Swiss-German Mortgage Agreement Case*).

Treaties—Operation of—Municipal Laws Inconsistent with Treaty Obligations.

See Case No. 4 (*Société Régie* v. *Greek Government*).

Treaties—Operation of—How far Conferring Rights upon Individuals—Governments as Trustees of Individuals.

See Case No. 119 (*Administrator of German Property* v. *Knoop*, (2)).

Treaties—Operation of—Whether Conferring Rights Directly upon the Individual.

See Case No. 118 (*Civilian War Claimants Association Ltd.* v. *The King*).

Treaties—Operation of—Necessity of Municipal Legislation.

See Case No. 119 (*Administrator of German Property* v. *Knoop*, (1)).

Treaties — Operation of — Non-Discrimination against Aliens.

See Case No. 2 (*Re Arrow River & Tributaries Slide & Boom Co. Ltd.*, Note).

Treaties—Operation of—Public Debt—Treaty Obligation in Respect of—How Far Executory without Further Municipal Regulation.

See Case No. 32 (*Kaiser-Ferdinand North Railway Case*).

Treaties—Effect of—Recognition of the Treaty of Versailles by Austria.

See Case No. 15 (*Ettinger* v. *Ministry of the Interior*).

Treaties—Operation of—Restrictive Interpretation of Treaty Provisions of an Exceptional Nature.

See Case No. 205 (*The Kronprins Gustaf Adolf ; The Pacific. United States and Sweden*).

Treaties—Effect of—Indirect Recognition of Sovereignty.

See Case No. 49 (*Legal Status of Eastern Greenland*).

Treaties—Operation of—Relevance of Date of Signature for the Operation of Treaty Provisions.

See Case No. 136 (*Assicurazioni Generali* v. *Selim Cotran*).

X.—Effect of Treaties on Third Parties

Treaties—Effect on Third Parties—Effect on Russia of the Minorities Treaty of 1919—Nationality—Acquisition and Loss of—Effect as against Third States—Interpretation of Treaties—Filling of Gaps by Construction—Russo-Polish Peace Treaty of March 15, 1921. **Case No. 201**

MINORITIES TREATY (RUSSIAN SUBJECTS) CASE.

Germany, District Court of Torgau. January 8, 1931.

THE FACTS.—The defendant, a male, was born in 1869 at Lódź, then part of Russian Congress Poland. In 1915 he emigrated to Germany and there married in 1918 the plaintiff, a Prussian subject. After the War he did not opt either for Poland or for Russia. The spouses now brought an action against one another for divorce. The husband produced a Polish passport. He invoked the Minorities Treaty of 1919 and contended that he possessed Polish nationality since the coming into existence of the Polish State. The relevant Treaty provisions are stated below.

Held : that the defendant was a Russian subject. He was originally a Russian subject by birth : when he was born, Lódź, his birth-place, belonged to Czarist Russia. Thus when he came to Germany he was a Russian. He never acquired German nationality. His position was in no way affected by the events after the War or by the international conventions concluded in connection therewith. It was true that the so-called Treaty concerning the Protection of Minorities made between the Allied Powers and Poland on June 28, 1919, provided in Article 4 that all persons of German, Austrian, Hungarian or Russian nationality who were born in Poland of parents habitually resident there, should *ipso facto* acquire Polish nationality even if, at the date of the coming into force of that Treaty, such persons were not habitually resident in Poland. However, that Convention had no legal effect as against Russia. If it were otherwise, these Russian subjects would have lost their nationality. Had this effect been desired, it would at least have been necessary for Russia to declare her renunciation of them by becoming a party to the Treaty. But Russia was not a party to the Treaty ; in consequence she could not be bound by it. Moreover, the Treaty could not be regarded as the decisive legal basis for the regulation of the problem of nationality. Its intention was to secure generally an adequate treatment of minorities.

Case No. 201 *Contd.*

The law applicable to these nationality questions was to be gathered from Article VI of the Russo-Polish Peace Treaty of March 15, 1921 (the Treaty of Riga). There it was provided, quite independently of the Minorities Treaty, that all persons over eighteen years of age who shall be resident in former Russian, now Polish, territory at the date of the ratification of the said Treaty, shall acquire Polish nationality unless they exercise an option for Russia. Conversely, all persons resident in territory, adjacent to Poland, which belonged and still belongs to Russia shall retain their Russian nationality, unless they exercise an option for Poland. The same Article VI provided that provisions with regard to option are applicable also to persons who were resident neither in Russia nor in Poland. When the Treaty of Riga was ratified, the defendant was no longer in Łódź (that is to say, in Polish territory), but in Germany. He had therefore not acquired Polish nationality under Article VI. As he had not opted for Poland, no change of nationality ever occurred. It could not be assumed that persons like the defendant must have exercised an option in favour of Russia if they wished to retain Russian nationality. If that had been necessary, failure to exercise the option would have rendered them stateless. The obvious gap in the provisions of the Treaty must be filled by construction, and it must be held that the nationality of the persons in question did not change where no option had been exercised. Accordingly, the defendant was still a Russian subject.

[Report : *Rechtsprechung auf dem Gebiete des Internationalen Privatrechts*, 1931, No. 82.]

NOTE.—See to the same effect the decision of the Court of Appeal of Berlin of March 21, 1932 : *ibid.*, 1932, No. 82.

Treaties—Effect on Third States—Effect of the Treaty of St. Germain on Holland.

See Case No. 18 (*Billig v. Handelsvennootschap onder de Firma S. Einhorn's Söhne*).

Treaties—Effect on Third Parties—Treaties in Favour of Third Parties—Treaties of 1815 and 1816 Creating the Free Zones of Gex and Geneva.

See Case No. 202 (*Case of the Free Zones of Upper Savoy and the District of Gex*, (3)).

Treaties—Effect on Third Parties—Treaties Imposing Burdens on Third Parties—Treaties of 1815 and 1816 Creating the Free Zones of Gex and Geneva—Effect of Article 435 of the Treaty of Versailles.

See Case No. 202 (*Case of the Free Zones of Upper Savoy and the District of Gex*, (2)).

Treaties—Effect on Third Parties—Berlin Act of 1885.

See Case No. 50 (*Clipperton Island Award*).

Treaties—Effect of—Subsequent Treaties with Third Parties.

See Case No. 191 (*Whittall* v. *The Administrator of German Property*).

XI.—Termination of Treaties

i.—By Operation of Law

Treaties — Termination of — Obsolescence of — State Succession—Conduct as Showing Intention to Terminate.

See Case No. 38 (*Flensburger Dampfercompagnie* v. *United States*).

(*d*) THE *CLAUSULA REBUS SIC STANTIBUS*. RECONSIDERATION OF TREATIES UNDER ARTICLE 19 OF THE COVENANT

Case No. 202

PERMANENT COURT OF INTERNATIONAL JUSTICE.

Abrogation of Treaties as the Result of Changes in Circumstances—Interpretation by Reference to the Context—Two Paragraphs of One Article—Treaties Imposing Burdens upon Third States—Treaties in Favour of Third Parties—Partial Impossibility of Execution of Treaties—Clauses of the Arbitration Agreement—Impossibility of Applying One of the Clauses—Whether Invalidating the Whole Agreement—Re-Adaptation of Treaties to New Conditions—Opinion, as Distinguished from Judgment, of the Permanent Court of International Justice—Oral Declarations in the Course of Judicial Proceedings—Binding Force—Execution of the Judgment.

CASE OF THE FREE ZONES OF UPPER SAVOY AND THE DISTRICT OF GEX.

Judgment of June 7, 1932.[1]

THE FACTS.—See *Annual Digest*, 1929-1930, Cases Nos. 276 and 277. The other facts are more conveniently stated in the *Held*, below.

Held (Altamira, Hurst, Yovanovitch, Negulesco, Judges, and Dreyfus, Judge *ad hoc*, dissenting): (1) *Interpretation by Reference to the Context. Two Paragraphs of One Article.*—In holding that paragraph 2 of Article 435 of the Treaty of Versailles, with its Annexes, had not abrogated the régime of free zones as between Switzerland and France, the Court attached decisive importance to the fact that, while both

[1]The Court was composed as follows: Anzilotti (President); Loder, Altamira, Oda, Huber, Sir Cecil Hurst, Kellogg, Yovanovitch, Beichmann, Negulesco (Judges); Dreyfus (Judge *ad hoc*).

paragraphs invoked the change in conditions as a reason for abrogating the existing arrangements, the first paragraph of that Article, relating to the neutralized zone of Savoy, provided in express terms for the abrogation of the latter, whereas no such abrogation was stipulated in the second paragraph. The Court said: "It must not be overlooked that Article 435, both by reason of its position in the Treaty of Versailles and of its origin, forms a complete whole: it would therefore be impossible to interpret the second paragraph without regard to the first paragraph. But, in the first paragraph, the High Contracting Parties, after noting that the provisions of these 'treaties, conventions, declarations and other supplementary acts concerning the neutralized zone of Savoy . . . are no longer consistent with present conditions,' go on to declare that 'for this reason' they 'take note of the agreement reached between the French Government and the Swiss Government for the abrogation of the stipulations relating to this zone,' and add that these provisions 'are and remain abrogated.' It follows that the expression 'no longer consistent with present conditions,' when used in the first paragraph of the Article, constitutes the ground on which the High Contracting Parties acquiesce in an agreement already concluded between France and Switzerland for the abolition of the neutral zone. When used in the second paragraph, these same words 'are no longer consistent with present conditions' constitute the ground on which the High Contracting Parties declare that they acquiesce in a future agreement between France and Switzerland. Hence, no matter what its significance might be in other contexts, it is scarcely possible to regard the expression 'are no longer consistent with present conditions' as *ipso facto* involving in the second paragraph of the Article the abolition of the free zones, since in the first paragraph its meaning is not such as automatically to involve the abolition of the neutralized zone." (At pp. 140, 141.) In the view of the Court the provision of that Article that the existing régime of the free zones was no longer in accordance with present conditions and that France and Switzerland were to settle between themselves the status of the zones was tantamount "to a declaration of disinterestedness in regard to their status on the part of the High Contracting Parties other than France." (At p. 140.)

(2) *Treaties Imposing Burdens upon Third States.*—"Even supposing that the words [of Article 435 of the Treaty of Versailles] 'it is for France and Switzerland to come to an agreement together with a view to settling between themselves

Case No. 202 *Contd.*

the status of these territories under such conditions as shall be considered suitable by both countries' were interpreted as a mandate involving an obligation for France and Switzerland to proceed to abrogate provisions acknowledged to be no longer consistent with present conditions—rather than as an authorization resulting from the disinterested attitude assumed by the Powers which had signed the old treaties—this mandate would not be enforceable as against Switzerland, which has not accepted it."[1] (At p. 143.)

(3) *Treaties in Favour of Third Parties.*—For reasons stated in *Annual Digest*, 1929-1930, Case No. 277, *Held* (*d*), the Court re-affirmed the view that the creation of the Gex Zone formed part of a territorial settlement in favour of Switzerland, made as a result of an agreement between that country and the Powers, including France, which agreement conferred on the stipulations in question the character of a contract to which Switzerland was a party. This being so, the Court did not consider it necessary to examine the legal nature of the Gex Zone from the point of view of whether it constituted a stipulation in favour of a third Party. The Court then added: "But were the matter also to be envisaged from this aspect, the following observations should be made: It cannot be lightly presumed that stipulations favourable to a third State have been adopted with the object of creating an actual right in its favour. There is however nothing to prevent the will of sovereign States from having this object and this effect. The question of the existence of a right acquired under an instrument drawn between other States is therefore one to be decided in each particular case: it must be ascertained whether the States which have stipulated in favour of a third State meant to create for that State an actual right which the latter has accepted as such." (At pp. 147, 148.)

(4) *Abrogation of Treaties as the Result of Changes in Circumstances.*—It was contended by France that, with regard to all the zones, there had taken place, since their establishment, a change in circumstances which justified the Court in holding that

[1] See, however, the following passage in the Dissenting Opinion of Judges Hurst and Altamira: "We wish to make every reservation in regard to a theory seeking to lay down, as a principle, that rights accorded to third Parties by international conventions, to which the favoured State is not a Party, cannot be amended or abolished, even by the States which accorded them, without the consent of the third State; such a theory would be fraught with so great peril for the future of conventions of this kind now in force, that it would be most dangerous to rely on it in support of any conclusion whatever." (At p. 185.) It will be noted that, in the opinion of the Court, Switzerland was in effect a party to the instruments in question (see *Annual Digest*, 1929-1930, Case No. 277).

the treaties had lapsed. In particular it was contended by France that in 1815 the Canton of Geneva was to all intents and purposes an area of free trade, that the withdrawal at that time of the French and Sardinian customs line made Geneva and the zones an economic unit, but that the institution of the Swiss Federal Customs in 1849 destroyed this economic unit. The Court held that the French argument failed on the ground that France had not proved that the zones were actually set up, having regard to the circumstances which ceased to exist in 1849. The Court said : "To establish this position it is necessary, first of all, to prove that it was in consideration of the absence of customs duties at Geneva that the Powers decided, in 1815, in favour of the creation of the zones. There is nothing in the text of the treaties to support this, and the only occasion on which the Swiss representative at the Allied gatherings in 1815 is shown to have relied on the absence of customs at Geneva was when he endeavoured to secure the withdrawal of the French customs along the whole frontier from Basle to Geneva—an effort in which he was not successful. . . . Nor can the Court assume that what the Powers had in view in 1815 was a condition of things under which modest customs duties might be imposed, but not substantial duties, with the result that a serious increase would justify a claim that the relevant stipulations had lapsed. The resulting situation would have been much too precarious to constitute the basis of a part of the European settlement after the Napoleonic wars." (At pp. 156, 157.) The Court also pointed out that although there had doubtless been other changes, for instance, in connection with the requirements of the food supply of Geneva, with the development of communications and with technical progress, these changes had no bearing on the whole body of circumstances which the Parties to the Treaties of 1815 had in mind at the time when the free zones were created. These circumstances were essentially governed by the geographical configuration of the Canton of Geneva and of the surrounding region. These had not changed.[1]

(5) *Treaties. Partial Impossibility of Execution of Treaties. Clauses of Arbitration Agreement. Impossibility of Applying One of the Clauses. Whether Invalidating the Whole Agreement.*—

[1] In view of this finding the Court did not consider it necessary to examine "any of the questions of principle which arise in connection with the theory of the lapse of treaties by reason of change of circumstances, such as the extent to which the theory can be regarded as constituting a rule of international law, the occasions on which and the method by which effect can be given to the theory if recognized, and the question whether it would apply to treaties establishing rights such as that which Switzerland derived from the treaties of 1815 and 1816." (At p. 158.)

Case No. 202 ***Contd.*** Article 2 of the Special Agreement provided that after pronouncing its decision on the question whether the stipulations as to the free zones had been abrogated by the Treaty of Versailles, the Court was to settle all the questions involved in the execution of that paragraph. Switzerland, but not France, declared that she would be willing to accept in advance the measures indicated by the Court with regard to certain aspects of the future régime. The Court held in a previous Order (see *Annual Digest,* 1929-1930, Case No. 276), now affirmed (at p. 161), that it could not give judgment in pursuance of that paragraph inasmuch as it would be incompatible with the Statute and its position as a court of justice to give a judgment which would be dependent for its validity on the subsequent approval of the Parties. France contended that as the Court found itself unable to carry out the whole mission entrusted to it by the Special Agreement, it should declare itself incompetent as to the whole dispute ; that for the Court to limit its judgment to one part of the mission entrusted to it would be to run counter to the will of the Parties ; and that as one Party was particularly interested in judgment being given with regard to paragraph 1 and the other in judgment being given with regard to paragraph 2, to give judgment with regard to paragraph 1 only would amount to destroying the balance between two Parties and would therefore be unjust.

Held : that the French contention must be rejected. "It is the Special Agreement which represents, so far as the Court is concerned, the joint will of the Parties. If the obstacle to fulfilling part of the mission which the Parties intended to submit to the Court results from the terms of the Special Agreement itself, it results directly from the will of the Parties and, therefore, cannot destroy the basis of the Court's jurisdiction for the reason that it was counter to the will of the Parties.

"As regards the second argument, it must not be forgotten that one of the Governments concerned has agreed in advance to whatever measures of permeability the Court might impose as to goods passing through the customs barriers. For the Government which finds itself unable for constitutional reasons to make a similar declaration to claim that the Court should, because of the consequences which the Court is bound to attribute to this provision in the Special Agreement, declare itself incompetent as to the whole dispute, would not be just to the other Government." (At pp. 163, 164.)

(6) *Treaties. Re-Adaptation to New Conditions. Opinion, as Distinguished from Judgment, of the Permanent Court of Inter-*

national Justice.—After having rejected the French contention that Article 435 of the Treaty of Versailles had abrogated the régime of the zones as not being in accordance with present conditions and that the instrument which created the free zones had lapsed as the result of "change in conditions," the Court stated : "The Court does not hesitate to express its opinion that if, by the maintenance in force of the old treaties, Switzerland obtains the economic advantages derived from the free zones, she ought in return to grant compensatory economic advantages to the people of the zones." (At p. 169.) (In the course of the proceedings the Swiss Government had in fact declared that it was prepared to agree to the establishment of a more stable and more liberal régime for the admission of zone produce into Switzerland).

(7) *Treaties. Form of. Oral Declarations in the Course of Judicial Proceedings. Binding Force of. Absence of Ratification.*—In the course of the oral argument before the Court the Swiss Agent declared on behalf of his Government that should the zones be maintained Switzerland would, if so desired by France, be prepared to agree that, in the absence of agreement between the Parties, the terms of the exchange of goods between the zones and Switzerland should be settled by a binding decision of experts which would not, so far as Switzerland was concerned, require ratification. The French Agent did not make a similar offer. He considered the Swiss offer to be unacceptable and expressed doubts as to the binding character, from the point of view of Swiss constitutional law, of the Swiss declaration. *Held* : that "having regard to the circumstances in which this declaration was made, the Court must . . . regard it as binding on Switzerland." (At p. 170.)

(8) *Execution of the Judgment.*—After having held in its final judgment "that the French Government must withdraw its customs line in accordance with the provisions of the said treaties and instruments ; and that this régime must continue in force so long as it has not been modified by agreement between the Parties" (at p. 172), the Court considered it appropriate that a reasonable period should be accorded to the French Government in which to comply with the terms of that judgment. It fixed January 1, 1934, as the date by which the French Government must withdraw the customs line so as to re-establish the free zones in accordance with the stipulations of the Treaties of 1815 and 1816.

[Report : *P.C.I.J.*, Series A/B, No. 46.]

NOTE.—I. See also entries on p. 430 on the Reconstitution of the

Case No. 202 Contd. Court (Article 25 of the Statute) and p. 431 on the Contents of the Judgments of the Court in relation to alternative submissions put forward by the Parties.

II. And see *Annual Digest*, 1929-1930, Case No. 6, on the Question of Restrictive Interpretation of Treaties (subject to the exception of abuse of rights) and *ibid.*, Case No. 276, on the Competence of the Court to Give Judgments Dependent for their Validity on the Approval of the Parties.

Treaties—Re-Adaptation to New Conditions—Opinion, as Distinguished from Judgment, of the Permanent Court of International Justice.

See Case No. 202 (*Case of the Free Zones of Upper Savoy and the District of Gex*, (6)).

Treaties—Partial Impossibility of Execution—Clauses of Arbitration Agreement—Impossibility of Applying One of the Clauses—Whether Invalidating the Whole Arbitration Agreement.

See Case No. 202 (*Case of the Free Zones of Upper Savoy and the District of Gex*, (5)).

Treaties—Termination of—*Clausula rebus sic stantibus*—Changed Conditions.

For an example of a refusal of a municipal court to take into account a vital change in conditions with regard to a State guarantee of a loan see Case No. 31 (*Sch.* v. *Germany*).

ii.—By Act of Party.

(*c*) Unilateral Denunciation. Result of Non-Performance by the Other Party

Treaties—Termination of—Changed Conditions—Non-Performance by the Other Party—How Far to be Considered by Municipal Courts.

See Case No. 120 (*Gschwind* v. *Swiss Government*).

iii.—Effect of Termination.

Treaties—Termination of—Effect of Treaties after Termination—Jurisdiction over Foreigners in Egypt—Customs Statute—Lapse of Commercial Conventions—Recognition of Customs Statute by Foreign Powers. **Case No. 203**

GRUNBERG *v.* ADMINISTRATION DE DOUANES EGYPTIENNES.
SIGNORINI AND OTHERS *v.* THE SAME.

Egypt, Commercial Tribunal of Alexandria.

February 9, 1931; *April* 25, 1932.

THE FACTS.—In the first case, a Roumanian subject, in the second, an Italian, disputed the power of the Egyptian Customs Commission to inflict certain fines. The Commission relied on the Customs Statute, but it was contended that the Statute was ineffective against foreigners because commercial treaties of foreign Powers recognising it were no longer in force.

Held: that the convictions must be upheld. "The Powers concerned and the Egyptian Government appear to have recognised for nearly half a century that the Customs Law had an independent character which enabled it to survive these commercial conventions."

[Report: *Gazette des Tribunaux Mixtes d'Egypte*, XXII (1931-1932), p. 344.]

NOTE.—The Tribunal pointed out that in any event the Powers had made independent protocols of adhesion to the Statute.

XII.—Interpretation of Treaties

i.—Agencies of Interpretation. Construction in Accordance with the Intention of the Parties.

Treaties—Agencies of Interpretation—Authority Competent to Interpret Treaties in connection with Actions concerning Private Rights—Distinction between Actions Involving the Public Interest and Actions Involving Private Rights—Franco-Spanish Convention of January 7, 1862—Diplomatic and Legislative Reciprocity—French Law of June 30, 1926, on Commercial Property. **Case No. 204**

SANCHEZ *v.* CONSORTS GOZLAND.

France, Court of Cassation, Civil Chamber. December 22, 1931.

THE FACTS.—The case before the Court raised the question of the right of aliens to invoke the Law of June 30, 1926,

Case No. 204 ***Contd.***

commonly called the Law on Commercial Property, which regulated the relations between tenant and landlord with regard to the renewal of leases for premises used for commercial or industrial purposes. Article 19 of the Law, as amended by the Law of April 22, 1927, provided that the Law itself could not be invoked, with certain exceptions, by persons of foreign nationality engaged in commercial or industrial enterprises and being nationals of States which had not enacted similar legislation in their territories for the protection of the commercial property of French nationals. In the present case, Sanchez, a tenant of Spanish nationality, invoked the Franco-Spanish Convention of January 7, 1862, arguing that it provided for reciprocity and thereby enabled him under the Law of 1926 to claim that his landlord should renew his lease for commercial premises.

Held: that the petition should be dismissed. The plaintiff could not invoke the Law of June 30, 1926, in his favour and claim the renewal of his lease. The terms of Article 19 clearly expressed the intention, which was repeatedly mentioned in the course of the parliamentary discussion of the Bill, to create a new civil right for French citizens alone, which right could not be invoked by the nationals even of a country with which France had concluded a treaty of establishment, unless the general condition set forth in Article 11 of the *Code Civil* was fulfilled, *viz.*, that a similar right existed for French citizens in that country. The Franco-Spanish Convention of January 7, 1862, implied, not that the nationals of each contracting Party should enjoy all the rights enjoyed by nationals, but only that their recognised rights, derived from international law alone, should be exercised by Spaniards in France under the same conditions as by Frenchmen in Spain. The Court was competent to interpret that Convention. "In litigation concerning private civil rights the ordinary courts are competent to determine the meaning and scope of treaties." Legislation similar to the French Law of June 30, 1926, did not exist in Spain.

[Report: *Sirey*, 1932, Part 1, p. 257, with a note by Niboyet.]

NOTE.—See the conclusions of Matter, Procurator-General, on the case, and the note of Professor Niboyet on the decision, both in the same *Recueil Sirey*. For an analysis of the decisions of French courts on the interpretation of treaties see Chailley, *La nature juridique des traités internationaux* (1932), pp. 266-277; Bioux, *La position de la jurisprudence française vis-à-vis des traités internationaux* (1933); Mestre, "Les traités et le droit interne," in *Hague Recueil*, vol. 38 (1931) (iv), pp. 290-302. As a rule French courts distinguish between actions (or clauses) involving private rights and actions (or clauses) involving the public interest. The courts are competent to interpret treaties in connection with the former type of action only. The distinction appears for the first time in the judgment in *Séguin* v. *Héritiers du duc Guillaume Looz*, given on December 11, 1816, by the Court of Cassation; it is clearly expressed in the decision in *Napier and Others* v. *Duc de Richmond*, given on June 24, 1839, by the Court of Cassation: *Sirey*, 1839, Part 1, p. 577. (On the origins of this rule see Challine. *Le droit international public dans la jurisprudence française de* 1789 *à* 1848 (1934), pp. 71-79.) For recent instances see Court of Cassation, Civil Chamber, decision of June 2, 1923, *Concession française de Shanghaï* v. *Compagnie française de tramways et d'éclairage électrique de Shanghaï* (*Annual Digest*, 1923-1924, Case No. 190); Court of Cassation, Criminal Chamber, March 22 and August 9, 1923, *In re Thyssen and Others, In re Krupp and Others* (*ibid.*, Case No. 191); the decisions mentioned in *Annual Digest*, 1929-1930, Note to Case No. 233; Court of Cassation, *Chambre des requêtes*, February 8, 1932, *Lebas and Others* v. *Verdet and Others* (*Dalloz hebdomadaire*, 1932, p. 146): "the ordinary courts are necessarily competent to decide the meaning and scope of a treaty of establishment in actions involving private civil rights." Professor Mestre (*loc. cit.*, pp. 293-295) and Professor Niboyet (note mentioned above) have expressed views critical of the attitude adopted in this matter by French courts.

See also *Huber* v. *Maître Bollack ès-qualités*, decided by the Court of Cassation, Civil Chamber, on December 29, 1932. This case concerned the sequestration by the French Government, after the World War, of the property of German subjects in Alsace-Lorraine. Article 1 (3) of the Convention of Baden-Baden of November 15, 1919, provided that, subject to the payment of a covering indemnity of 25 million francs by Germany, the household effects, "*i.e.*, the furniture, household utensils, family jewellery, etc.," should be excepted from this measure. The Court of Cassation was asked to define the term "family jewellery." It *held* that it was competent to give the interpretation requested by the plaintiff. The term "family jewellery" was held to include ornamental objects treasured, as a result of their origins and family history, with a respect and affection which is quite apart from their intrinsic value. This does not apply to jewellery belonging to a commercial concern or bought for purely speculative purposes." [Report: *Sirey*, 1933, Part 1, p. 91.]

Treaties—Interpretation of—Agencies of—Interpretation of Treaties Concluded Between Third States.

See Case No. 47 (*Van Blarkom C.S.* v. *Ordo Fratrum Minorum Sancti Francisci Capucinorum*).

Treaties—Interpretation—Agencies of—Competence of Courts to Enquire into Political Questions Arising out of Conventions—Swiss Courts—Protectorates.

See Case No. 195 (*Sarasin and Pictet* v. *Fournier*).

ii.—Restrictive Interpretation.

(*a*) Restrictions of Sovereignty

Case No. 205 **Interpretation of Treaties—Treaties and Limitations of Sovereignty—The Preamble—Meaning of "Embargo"—Contemporaneous Interpretation—Use of Dictionaries—Reference to Other Treaties—Bilingual Treaties—Limits of the Duty of Non-Interference with Ships and with the Freedom of Commercial Transactions—Restrictive Interpretation of Treaty Provisions of an Exceptional Nature—Necessity of an Actual Decision as a Basis for a Claim for Compensation—Insufficiency of Oral Ruling—Conditions of a Valid Renunciation of Rights—The Law Applicable—Treaties as Exclusive Sources of Arbitral Decision.**

The Kronprins Gustaf Adolf ; The Pacific.

(*United States and Sweden*).

July 18, 1932.

(Borel, Arbitrator).

The Facts.—Article 7 of the Treaty of 1783 between Sweden and the United States provided as follows:

"All and every the subjects & inhabitants of the Kingdom of Sweden, as well as those of the United States, shall be permitted to navigate with their vessels in all safety and freedom and without any regard to those to whom the merchandizes and cargoes may belong, from any port whatever. And the subjects and inhabitants of the two States shall likewise be permitted to sail and trade with their vessels and, with the same liberty and safety, to frequent the places, ports and havens of Powers enemies to both or either of the contracting parties, without being in any wise molested or troubled, and to carry on a commerce not only directly from the ports of an enemy to a neutral port, but even from one port of an Enemy to another port of an Enemy, whether it be under the jurisdiction of the same or of different Princes. . . ."

Article 5 of that Treaty stipulated that, once on board, goods the export of which is forbidden can no longer be stopped and that no embargo can be laid on the ships on account of such goods.

The Treaty was renewed in 1827, and the second paragraph of the relevant Article 17 ran as follows:

> "Merchants, masters and owners of ships, seamen, people of all sorts, ships and vessels, and in general all merchandises and effects of one of the allies or their subjects, shall not be subject to any embargo nor detained in any of the countries, territories, islands, cities, towns, ports, rivers, or domains whatever, of the other ally, on account of any military expedition or any public or private purpose whatever, by seizure, by force, or by any such manner; much less shall it be lawful for the subjects of one of the parties to seize or take anything by force from the subjects of the other party, without the consent of the owner."

One part of the Preamble to the Treaty of 1783 ran as follows:

> "Desiring to establish, in a stable and permanent manner, the rules which ought to be observed relative to the correspondence and commerce which they have judged necessary to establish between their respective countries and subjects, they have thought that they could not better accomplish that end than by taking for a basis of their arrangements the mutual interest and advantage of both nations, thereby avoiding all those burthensome preferences which are usually sources of debate, embarrassment and discontent, and by leaving each party at liberty to make, respecting navigation and commerce, those interior regulations which shall be most convenient to itself."

Sweden invoked these provisions as a ground for her claim for compensation on account of the detention by the United States in June and July 1917, respectively, of the Swedish ships the *Kronprins Gustaf Adolf* and the *Pacific*, belonging to the Johnson Line, and their cargoes in American ports. These ships were prevented from departing from American ports without export licences for the bunker oil carried on board these ships on their arrival in the United States, such licences to be granted on conditions set forth in regulations issued by the United States governing the export of certain commodities in war time.

By a Special Agreement signed on December 17, 1930, the two Governments, in pursuance of the Hague Convention of 1907 for the Pacific Settlement of International Disputes, submitted to arbitration the question of the responsibility of the

Case No. 205 ***Contd.***

United States under the above-mentioned Treaties and of eventual compensation.

It is convenient to state the other relevant facts in the part of the digest which follows below.

Held: that the detention of the ships in question by the United States was not in contravention of the Treaties of 1783 and 1827.

(1) *The Law Applicable. Treaties as the Exclusive Sources of Arbitral Decision.*—It was contended by the United States that, in view of the wording of the Arbitration Agreement, the function of the Arbitrator was confined to the examination of the compatibility of the action of the United States with the Treaties in question and that he was not therefore expected to base his decision on principles of international law as such. The Arbitrator dealt with that contention as follows: "However just in itself, this observation must not be allowed to lead to a misapprehension. The decision to be given is undoubtedly to be governed by the treaties, and the Arbitrator is not asked to look for other rules in the field of international law. On the other hand, it is clear that the treaties themselves are part of the international law as accepted by both contracting powers and it may be safely assumed that, when the said treaties were concluded, both parties considered them as being agreed upon as special provisions to be enforced between them in what may be called the atmosphere and spirit of international law as recognized by both of them. Particularly, it may also be assumed that it was not the intention of the parties to adopt provisions which would give their respective nationals rights inferior to those which they already possessed by virtue of rules of international law recognized as binding by both states." (At pp. 839, 840.)

(2) *Interpretation of Treaties. Treaties and Limitations of Sovereignty. The Preamble.*—The Arbitrator could not wholly accept the contention of the United States, based on the Preamble as quoted above, that the chief object of the Treaty was to maintain and safeguard the sovereignty of each contracting party. "This certainly goes too far, for, if such had been the aim contemplated by the parties, no treaty was needed in order to reach it. In the opinion of the arbitrator the parties wanted to lay down principles which in their mutual interest were to be accepted as henceforth governing their mutual relations, but that their respective liberty remained entirely reserved whenever and as far as it could be reconciled with what was clearly and unambiguously stated in the treaty."

(At p. 847.) The Arbitrator considered it unnecessary to examine whether the Treaties of 1783 and 1827 imposed undue limitations on the two parties. He said: "Their very existence is a manifestation of the sovereign will of the Powers which had deemed it convenient to stipulate the said provisions and to accept them as governing their mutual relations. That these provisions, produced by the sovereign will, cannot be considered as incompatible therewith is moreover shown by the fact that, according to the terms of the treaty, each of the contracting parties remained at liberty to recede from it, if and when it deemed it convenient to do so, a right of which the United States of America has made use, as aforementioned. On the other hand it must be observed that, considering the natural state of liberty and independence which is inherent in sovereign states, they are not to be presumed to have abandoned any part thereof, the consequence being that the high contracting parties to a treaty are to be considered as bound only within the limits of what can be clearly and unequivocally found in the provisions agreed to and that those provisions, in case of doubt, are to be interpreted in favor of the natural liberty and independence of the party concerned." (At p. 846.)

(3) *The Meaning of 'Embargo.' Contemporaneous Interpretation. Use of Dictionaries.*—The Arbitrator could not accept the contention of the United States that, although the Treaty of 1827 prohibited in comprehensive terms both embargo and detention, it actually aimed at prohibiting only requisition by right of angary and that such prohibition of requisition was intended to cover only persons, ships or goods mentioned in the relevant Article. In particular the Arbitrator could not accept the contention that the reference in the Treaty to 'detention' and 'embargo' was intended by the makers of the Treaty to show clearly the meaning of the word 'embargo' which during the eighteenth century had often been used as meaning requisition. The Arbitrator said: "It is true that in several works which appeared on international law during the 18th century and even later the meaning of the word 'embargo' was extended as far as to include a requisition, implying the use of what is seized by the state proceeding to requisition, but there can be no doubt that at the time of the treaty the proper meaning of the word 'embargo' was common enough to lead to the conclusion that the framers of the treaty used it in its ordinary and proper sense." (At p. 849.) The Arbitrator then referred to Law Dictionaries published in 1792, 1816 and 1848 as

Case No. 205 *Contd.*

showing that 'embargo' was used in the sense of detention generally in peace time and war. He also referred to United States Statutes passed in 1794 and 1807 as showing the wider meaning of the term 'embargo' as applying to the detention of ships, crews, persons or goods.

(4) *Reference to Other Treaties.*—"There can be no doubt but that the framers of the treaty contemplated here two different measures, both of which they wanted to prohibit and this is confirmed by a similar provision in numerous other treaties, prior, contemporaneous with and posterior to the Treaty of 1783.

"Article XVI of the treaty between the United States and Prussia (1785), (Miller: *Treaties and other international acts of the United States of America*, Vol. II, Washington, 1931, p. 173), provides that 'the subjects or citizens, etc., shall not be liable to any embargo or detention.' The same words appear in Article VII of the treaty between the United States and Spain (1795) (Miller *eodem*, page 323).

"The use of the two words shows that the framers of the treaty meant to exclude both the embargo as such and any other detention of the kind contemplated by the terms used in Article 17." (At p. 851.)

(5) *Bilingual Treaties.*—The Arbitrator could not accept the contention of the United States that the French text militated in support of the view that the detention contemplated by the Treaty meant detention for public or private 'use,' *i.e.*, a requisition. That contention was based on the fact that while the English text used the phrase "on account of any military expedition or any public or private *purpose* whatever," the French text read "pour quelque expédition militaire, *usage* public ou particulier de qui que ce soit." It was true that the original of the Treaty of 1783 was in French. But the evidence showed that it was understood and ratified by the United States as it stood in the English text. It must therefore be assumed that the word 'purpose' was not due to inadvertence. Also it was not without importance that in other treaties concluded at that time by the United States the word 'purpose' was used in this connection.

(6) *The Limits of the Duty of Non-Interference with Ships and with the Freedom of Commercial Transactions.*—The following part of the award, although referring to the interpretation of particular treaty provisions, seems of sufficient general importance to warrant quotation in full. "Article 17 contemplates and prohibits the embargo or detention of ships, together with

what they have on board, but it does not impose on one of the signatories the obligation of enabling the ships of the other to sail. . . . Nor does Article 17 affect the liberty of either signatory to make, respecting navigation and commerce, such regulations which it may deem fit. In this respect the preamble of the Treaty of 1783, though formally no longer in force as such, remains effective; and Article 1 of the Treaty of 1827, which guarantees to the nationals of one signatory the most complete security and protection in their mercantile transactions, subjects them to the obligation of submitting to the laws and ordinances of the other signatory. A similar provision is to be found in Article 11 of the same Treaty.

"It follows therefrom that the prohibition to export goods issued by one of the signatories is not contrary to Article 12, even if it actually has the effect of preventing the departure of ships of the other signatory, because such ships cannot navigate without some of the said goods. For the same reasons Article 17 cannot be relied upon against the regulations which subjected to a license the exportation from the territory of the United States of the commodities enumerated in the proclamations." (At pp. 879, 880.)

(7) *Restrictive Interpretation of Treaty Provisions of an Exceptional Nature.*—The Arbitrator could not accept the Swedish interpretation of Article 5 (see above, *Facts*) to the effect that goods once loaded were freed from the regulations requiring an export licence. "The general rule that limitations imposed by a treaty on the natural liberty of a state are to be strictly interpreted applies with special emphasis to provisions of so exceptional a nature as those of Separate Article 5." (At p. 882.) Accordingly, that Article did not allow any inference beyond its strict terms. An inference within its terms was that a licence for the goods in question ought to have been granted, when properly applied for, for its refusal would amount to stopping the goods and detaining the vessel. But that Article did not mean that no application for a licence was necessary.

(8) *The Necessity of an Actual Decision as a Basis for a Claim for Compensation. Insufficiency of Oral Ruling.*—The Arbitrator could not accept the contention of Sweden that the required application was not made for the reason that it appeared to the owners as useless in view of certain declarations made by the authorities and in view of the relevant war regulations as interpreted by the owners of the ships in question. "A claim for damages asserted by a government on behalf of a national

Case No. 205 *Contd.*

cannot rest on mere declarations of intentions or of policy on the part of the authorities. The proper foundation for such a claim is an act, a decision taken with regard to such national and of a nature incompatible with his treaty rights.

"In the present case, the claim is based on the alleged detention of the *Kronprins Gustaf Adolf* and the *Pacific*. Detention means that departure was not permitted. According to then existing United States statutes, an application for clearance was to be addressed to the Collector of Customs of the port. The anticipation of a refusal, however justified, cannot be accepted as relieving one from the obligation of making the application. On the contrary, the application is the proper way to call forth the decision of the official concerned and, in case of refusal, to give the proper foundation for a claim." (At pp. 886, 887.) A claim based on alleged detention must be based on an actual decision concerning the very ship in question and resulting in its detention. Neither was it sufficient to invoke, as Sweden did, an oral ruling or intimation of the competent official. "This would mean that an oral intimation by an official as to how he will act in a case has the effect of dispensing with the procedure validly prescribed and the making of applications properly required by regulations in force. Such a rule, which could not but be of a general character, would lead to consequences which immediately show that it cannot be adopted and unreservedly applied. The communications relied upon by the Swedish Government as to the policy and the intentions of a board may properly call for a protest and entirely justify a note. . . . But they cannot do away with the procedure prescribed by the regulations in force. The belief that an application will meet with a refusal cannot be considered as a just and sufficient reason for not making that application according to the regulations, . . . However natural such a belief may have been in the light of the above-mentioned circumstances, it cannot amount to positive evidence as to what the War Trade Board would have decided ultimately, especially if the application had, as might have been desirable and helpful, called attention to Separate Article 5 of the Treaty of 1783. Should an application, properly made pursuant to the regulations in force, have met with a refusal, or the issuance of a license been based on unacceptable conditions, then the Johnson Line, and, on its behalf, the Swedish Government, would have had a case against the United States, on the strength of the above-named Separate Article 5. Failing an application, it is impossible for the Arbitrator to base his decision on the fact that there were reasons to believe that an application, which was not made, would have been denied." (At pp. 889, 890.)

(9) *Conditions of a Valid Renunciation of Rights.*—The Arbitrator rejected the contention of the United States that the conclusion of a *modus vivendi* on January 29, 1918, between Sweden and the Allied and Associated Powers amounted to a renunciation of any claims on account of the detention of the ships in question. The object of that Agreement, which consisted of a number of separate points, was to provide Sweden with commodities which she needed badly at that time in consideration of facilities granted by the Swedish Government for the use of Swedish ships by the Allied and Associated Powers. It could not be admitted that the Agreement amounted to a waiver of claims arising out of events prior to that date. "A renunciation to a right or a claim is not to be presumed. It must be shown by conclusive evidence, which in this case does not exist." (At p. 896.)

[Report: *A.J.*, XXVI (1932), p. 834.]

Interpretation—Restrictive Interpretation—Limits of.

See Case No. 205 (*The Kronprins Gustaf Adolf; The Pacific. United States and Sweden*).

Treaties—Restrictive Interpretation—Arbitration Agreements.

See Case No. 211 (*Greece* v. *Bulgaria: Article* 181 *of the Treaty of Neuilly, Preliminary Question,* (4)).

Treaties—Restrictive Interpretation.

See Case No. 208 (*Access to, or Anchorage in, the Port of Danzig, of Polish War Vessels*).

Treaties—Interpretation of—Various Rules of—Strict Interpretation in Favour of Party Obliged.

See Case No. 191 (*Whittall* v. *The Administrator of German Property*).

Treaties—Interpretation of—Rules of—Restrictive Interpreation of Treaties Limiting Sovereign Rights.

See Case No. 64 (*Polish Officials in Danzig Case*).

Treaties—Interpretation of—Restrictive Interpretation of Arbitration Agreements.

See Case No. 202 (*Case of the Free Zones of Upper Savoy and the District of Gex*).

Treaties—Construction of—Restrictive Interpretation—International River Commissions—The Rhine Navigation Convention.

See Case No. 56 (*Rhine Navigation Commission Case*).

(*b*) INTERPRETATION AGAINST THE PARTY RESPONSIBLE FOR THE DRAFTING

Case No. 206 **Treaties—Interpretation of—Intention of the Parties—Interpretation *contra proferentem*.**

SCH. *v*. GERMANY.

Germany, Supreme Court for Civil Matters. April 14, 1932.

THE FACTS.—See Case No. 31.

Held: that Article 257 (1) of the Treaty of Versailles, which provided, with regard to the former German colonies, that neither those territories nor the Powers on whom a mandate over them was conferred, should be liable for any part of the interest service on or redemption of loans taken by Germany and the Federal States, did not affect the liability of the colonies for the loans contracted by them with the guarantee of Germany. The colonies continued to be liable as principal debtors. It did not matter that the Allied Powers believed that Germany was exclusively or principally liable for the repayment of the colonial loans, and that no liability attached to the colonies themselves. "This Division of the Supreme Court has laid down before (decision of February 27, 1930, IV 910/28) that in construing the Treaty of Versailles it is necessary to enquire what purpose both parties had in mind when incorporating a given provision. What is relevant is only the objective meaning of the provision. In case of ambiguity the provision must be construed *contra proferentem*. Article 257 was not drafted by Germany. In view of the doubts existing as to the proper meaning of that article, it cannot be admitted that it had the result of freeing the colonies from their liabilities arising from the loans of 1908, 1909 and 1913."

[Report: *Entscheidungen des Reichsgerichts in Zivilsachen*, vol. 137, p. 1.]

iii.—Bilingual Treaties.

Treaties—Bilingual—Interpretation of—Interpretation of a Decision of the Council of the League, given in French, under Article 312 of the Treaty of Versailles—Reference Back to National Law. **Case No. 207**

GRAF H. VON D. AND OTHERS *v.* LANDESVERSICHERUNGSANSTALT SCHLESIEN.

Germany, Supreme Court for Civil Matters. February 2, 1931.

THE FACTS.—The plaintiffs, the Provincial Insurance Institution of Silesia, were mortgagees of property belonging to the defendants and situate in Polish Upper Silesia. In 1922 and 1923 the defendants repaid the loan, which had been secured by the mortgage, in devalued currency. The plaintiffs sued for revaluation of the amount. They contended that neither Article 312 of the Treaty of Versailles nor Article 2 of the decision of the Council of the League of Nations of December 9, 1924, constituted a bar to the action. By Article 312 Germany bound herself to make over to any State to which German European territories were ceded, a proportionate part of reserves, accumulated by public or publicly supervised corporations, for social and State insurances in those territories. The Article laid down that, should the interested Governments be unable to agree on the conditions of such assignment, the League Council should decide the matter by arbitration, and that the decision of the Council should be final and "have immediate effect." Subsequently, Poland and Germany being unable to agree, the Council of the League gave a decision on December 9, 1924. Article 2 of the decision laid down that the ownership in all movable things held by insurance corporations in Polish Upper Silesia should be transferred to Poland. The plaintiffs contended that those words did not cover their mortgage on the defendants' property.

Held (by the Supreme Court) : that the decision of the Court of Appeal allowing the plaintiffs' action must be affirmed. The Court said that the decision in the present dispute turned on the construction of Article 2 of the decision of the League Council. According to the German translation, as published in the *Gazette*, there was no difficulty in holding that Article 2 did not apply to the plaintiffs' claim. For in modern German legal terminology "movable things" (*bewegliche Sachen*) referred only to corporeal things and not to debts. Even the authoritative French version

Case No. 207 ***Contd.***

"*tous biens meubles*" did not comprise rights or claims. It was true that in the French Civil Code "*biens meubles*" was also intended to apply to property which was deemed to be movable in virtue of statutory provisions. However, neither the fact that the League Council's decision was drawn up in French, nor the fact of its having been made in France, proved conclusively that terms of private law used in the decision must be understood in the meaning attributed to them by French private law. "It must depend on the circumstances of each case how terms of private law employed in declarations of the League of Nations should be interpreted. . . . In the present case the question presents no difficulties. The Council of the League of Nations decided that 'property should be transferred to Poland with respect to social insurance.' This transfer became necessary in consequence of the partition of Upper Silesia. However, at the date of the decision German private law still prevailed on both sides of the new frontier. This being so, the Council of the League must be taken to have adapted to German law the description of objects to be transferred to Poland as a means of carrying on social insurance. Thus it is assumed that the expression '*biens meubles*' signified what the German Civil Code meant by movable things, *i.e.*, corporeal things of a movable nature." Accordingly, a mortgage on land was not covered by the term '*biens meubles*.'

The Court also pointed out that it followed from Articles 297 and 298 of the Treaty of Versailles, on Article 312 of which the decision of December 9, 1924, was based, that "*biens*" did not in any event comprise rights ("*droits*"), as in the heading to those Articles as well as in their context the words "*biens*" and "*droits*" were used together.

[Report: *Entscheidungen des Reichsgerichts in Zivilsachen*, vol. 131, p. 250.]

Bilingual Treaties—Original French Text—English Text before Ratifying Authorities.

See Case No. 205 (*The Kronprins Gustaf Adolf; The Pacific. United States and Sweden*).

iv.—Consideration of Preparatory Work.

Treaties—Interpretation of—Historical Antecedents of the Treaty—Intention of the Authors of the Treaty Unexpressed in its Provisions—Special Rights and Privileges in Foreign Territory—Necessity of Clear Provisions to that Effect—Article 104 of the Treaty of Versailles—Poland and Danzig.

Case No. 208

PERMANENT COURT OF INTERNATIONAL JUSTICE.

ACCESS TO, OR ANCHORAGE IN, THE PORT OF DANZIG, OF POLISH WAR VESSELS.

Advisory Opinion of December 11, 1931.[1]

THE FACTS.—On September 19, 1931, the Council of the League of Nations adopted a Resolution requesting the Court to give an Advisory Opinion on the following question :

"Do the Treaty of Peace of Versailles, Part III, Section XI, the Danzig-Polish Treaty concluded at Paris on November 9th, 1920, and the relevant decisions of the Council of the League of Nations and of the High Commissioner, confer upon Poland rights or attributions as regards the access to, or anchorage in, the port and waterways of Danzig of Polish war vessels ? If so, what are these rights or attributions ?"

Section XI of Part III of the Treaty of Versailles provided for the cession by Germany of the territory now constituting the Free City of Danzig to the Allied and Associated Powers, who undertook to establish that territory as the Free City of Danzig. Article 104 (2) of the Treaty provided that Poland and Danzig shall negotiate a treaty with the purpose of "ensuring to Poland without any restriction the free use and service of all waterways, docks, basins, wharves and other works within the territory of the Free City necessary for Polish imports and exports." In support of the view that she had a right to access and anchorage for war vessels in the port of Danzig, Poland invoked, *inter alia*, the provisions of that Article and, in particular, the principles underlying the establishment of the Free City and the promise made to Poland of a free and secure access to the sea.

Held : that the natural interpretation of the terms of Article 102 (2) was that Poland was to enjoy the unfettered use of the port and its equipment for commercial purposes only.

[1] The Court was composed as follows : Adatci (President) ; Guerrero (Vice-President) ; Baron Rolin-Jaequemyns, Count Rostworowski, Fromageot, Altamira, Anzilotti, Urrutia, Sir Cecil Hurst, Schücking, Negulesco, van Eysinga, Wang (Judges) ; Bruns (Judge *ad hoc*).

Case No. 208 *Contd.*

"The promise to Poland at the time of the peace settlement after the war of 1914-1918 of a free and secure access to the sea is a matter of history of which the Court is prepared to take notice, but no materials and no reasons have been submitted to it for assuming that the contents of Section XI of Part III of the Treaty of Versailles, as carried into effect by the Convention concluded in pursuance of Article 104 of that Treaty, do not constitute a complete fulfilment of the promise. The Court is not prepared to adopt the view that the text of the Treaty of Versailles can be enlarged by reading into it stipulations which are said to result from the proclaimed intentions of the authors of the Treaty, but for which no provision is made in the text itself." (At p. 144.) The Court said: "The fact that Poland claims special rights and privileges for her war vessels in the port of Danzig, renders it necessary to find some juridical basis for the claim. The port of Danzig is not Polish territory, and therefore the rights claimed by Poland would be exercised in derogation of the rights of the Free City. Such rights must therefore be established on a clear basis." (At p. 142.)

[Report: *P.C.I.J*, Series A/B, No. 43.]

PERMANENT COURT OF INTERNATIONAL JUSTICE.

Treaties—Interpretation of—Preparatory Work.

See the Advisory Opinion rendered by the Court on February 4, 1932,[1] in the case of the *Treatment of Polish Nationals and Other Persons of Polish Origin or Speech in the Danzig Territory* (*P.C.I.J.*, Series A/B, No. 44) for the statement that the text of the Treaty before the Court "not being absolutely clear, it may be useful, in order to ascertain its precise meaning, to recall here somewhat in detail the various drafts which existed prior to the adoption of the text now in force." (At p. 33.) A substantial portion of the Opinion was devoted to an examination of the various drafts and other preparatory work leading to the adoption of Article 33 of the Convention of Paris between Poland and Danzig (see Case No. 104). But see *ibid.*, p. 48 for the Dissenting Opinion on this matter. And see *ibid.*, p. 40, for the statement that "the duty of the Court is to interpret the text as it stands, taking into consideration all the materials at the Court's disposal."

PERMANENT COURT OF INTERNATIONAL JUSTICE.

Treaties—Interpretation of—Preparatory Work.

See the Judgment concerning the *Interpretation of the Statute of the Memel Territory*, given by the Permanent Court of Inter-

[1] For the composition of the Court see p. 209.

national Justice on June 24, 1932[1] (*P.C.I.J.*, Series A/B, No. 47), where the Court pointed out that, "as it has constantly held, the preparatory work cannot be adduced to interpret a text which is, in itself, sufficiently clear." However, the Court examined in detail the preparatory work leading to the adoption of the disputed Article 17 of the Memel Convention as showing that its history "provides no material which conflicts with the interpretation of the terms of the Article standing by themselves."

Treaties—Interpretation of—Preparatory Work—Article 10 of the Brussels Convention of September 1910 concerning Collisions between Vessels. **Case No. 209**

BRUSSELS CONVENTION CASE.

Germany, Court of Appeal of Hamburg. June 29, 1932.

THE FACTS.—A ship owned by a German shipping company collided in German waters with another vessel; several ships were to blame, among them that belonging to the defendants. The Court below held that, in view of the wording of Article 10[2] of the Brussels Convention, all the defendants were jointly and severally liable. The defendants contended that, according to the intention of the parties to the Convention, which was not expressed in the Convention as adopted but which was referred to during the negotiations preceding it, they were only liable severally.

Held: that the appeal must be dismissed. The Court said: "The defendants argue that international conventions, as opposed to statutes, should not be construed by merely looking at the words of the convention, but by taking into account the intention of the contracting parties, even if that intention cannot be gathered from the actual words. This proposition is open to doubt as a general principle of international or municipal law of contract. In any event, it is obviously wrong in a case

[1] The Court was composed as follows: Guerrero (Vice-President, acting as President); Kellogg, Baron Rolin-Jaequemyns, Count Rostworowski, Fromageot, de Bustamante, Altamira, Anzilotti, Urrutia, Adatci, Sir Cecil Hurst, Schücking, Negulesco, van Eysinga, Wang (Judges); Römer'is (Judge *ad hoc*).

[2] That Article provided as follows: "Without prejudice to any Conventions which may hereafter be made, the provisions of this Convention do not affect in any way the law in force in each country with regard to the limitation of shipowners' liability, nor do they affect the legal obligations arising from contracts of carriage or from any other contracts."

Case No. 209 *Contd.*

like the present one. What happened was this: after negotiations extending over many years, an international convention acquired the form of a statute. It had to be ratified subsequently by numerous States which had contributed in an unequal degree to the actual drafting. It remains uncertain which declarations of whose representatives shall obtain for which States; this is all the more so as the systems of law of the States in question may approach the problems involved from different angles. The defendants rely on Oppenheim, *International Law*, Vol. I, p. 702 [who refers to] '. . . intentions of all the parties as *unanimously* declared . . .', and on Calvo, *Droit des Nations*, Section 652 [who refers to negotiations] '. . . which immediately preceded the signature of the agreement . . .'; but it is difficult to apply these quotations to the present case. . . . The defendants quote declarations made by certain delegates at the Conference; but those declarations appear to refer exclusively to Franco-Belgian law. . . . Moreover, the declarations referred to were made only by some members of the Conference, and they were made in 1905, that is to say, not 'immediately' before the conclusion of the Convention. Neither were the said declarations expressly or generally adopted in the course of the subsequent negotiations in 1909/1910."

[Report: *Rechtsprechung auf dem Gebiete des Internationalen Privatrechts*, 1932, No. 61.]

Case No. 210

Interpretation of Treaties—Preparatory Work—Reference to Domestic Law—Interpretation of Statutes by Reference to Underlying International Conventions.

SWISS-GERMAN MORTGAGE AGREEMENT CASE.

Germany, Supreme Court for Civil Matters. February 4, 1931.

THE FACTS.—Article 1 of the Swiss-German Gold Mortgage Agreement of December 6, 1920, laid down that all debts secured by mortgages and created prior to July 31, 1914, shall be regarded as gold mortgages, provided that a gold clause is added to the covenant to repay so as to protect the foreign creditor against a devaluation of the Mark. Under German law the debt is created when the money has actually been paid to the borrower, whereas Swiss law causes it to arise as soon as the loan agreement is made. The plaintiffs sued for a declaration that the Treaty applied to their mortgage on the defendants' property, because under Swiss law the debts had been created prior to July 31, 1914.

The Court of Appeal dismissed the action, holding that the Treaty dealt with mortgages on German property; that it thus formed part of the German law of mortgages; and that it followed that German law applied.

Held (by the Supreme Court): that the case must be sent back to the Court of Appeal for a re-hearing.

In order to construe international agreements the intention common to the contracting States was of primary importance. That intention must be gathered from the Treaty as a whole, from the object it had in view, and from its history. "The German judge must first exhaust all sources which might inform him about the intention of the parties. Only if these sources are of no avail is he permitted to take into consideration German rules of conflict of laws, and to apply German law on that basis." The Court of Appeal had not reviewed the history of the Treaty when trying to find out the intention of the contracting States.

The Supreme Court, on the other hand, agreed with the view of the Court of Appeal that special statutes, like the Treaty under consideration, which was made for the benefit of individual sets of creditors, were not capable of a wide construction which would result in detriment to debtors. If the contracting States when using the word "created" had in fact intended this term to be understood in the Swiss meaning as referring to the making of the loan agreement, it would have been easy to express such intention by simpler and clearer words.

[Report: *Juristische Wochenschrift*, 1932, p. 243.]

NOTE.—See also the decision of the Supreme Court printed in *Entscheidungen des Reichsgerichts in Strafsachen*, vol. 66, p. 165, concerning the construction of the term "place of business" in Articles 17 and 24 of the German-Polish Convention of December 30, 1924, concerning Facilities in respect of Traffic in Frontier Districts. The Court said there: "Though the Frontier Convention is an international enactment, it has been adopted by the German legislature. The German draftsman used the term in connection with exemption from customs duty without giving any special explanation. In doing so he must be taken to have employed it in the same meaning which this term has acquired in modern German statutes regulating related subjects, particularly statutes dealing with revenue laws."

Treaties—Interpretation of—Preparatory Work—Historical Circumstances.

See Case No. 211 (*Greece* v. *Bulgaria: Article* 181 *of the Treaty of Neuilly, Preliminary Question,* (1) and (2)).

Treaties—Preparatory Work—Sixth Hague Convention of 1907.

See Case No. 228 (*The Tibor*).

Treaties—Preparatory Work—Staff Regulations of the League of Nations.

See Case No. 216 (*Lhoest, Souc, Gordon and Grote* v. *Secretariat of the League of Nations*).

Treaties—Interpretation of—Preparatory Work—Historical Circumstances.

See Case No. 1 (*The Mazel Tov*).

Treaties—Preparatory Work—Note of the Allied and Associated Powers to Germany of June 16, 1919.

See Case No. 31 (*Sch.* v. *Germany*).

Treaties—Preparatory Work—As Element of Interpretation.

See Case No. 55 (*San Lorenzo Title & Improvement Co.* v. *City Mortgage Co.; The Same* v. *Clardy et Al.; The Same* v. *Caples et Al.*).

Treaties—Interpretation of—Preparatory Work—Practical Construction of Treaties by Governmental Departments.

See Case No. 160 (*Laubenheimer et Al.* v. *Factor*).

Treaties—Interpretation of—Preparatory Work—Part XIII of the Treaty of Versailles—Convention of 1919 concerning Employment of Women during the Night.

See Case No. 217 (*Interpretation of the Convention of* 1919 *concerning Employment of Women during the Night,* (2)).

Treaties—Interpretation of—By Reference to Circumstances Obtaining at the Time of the Conclusion of the Treaty—Effect of Changes since the Conclusion of the Convention.

See Case No. 217 (*Interpretation of the Convention of* 1919 *concerning Employment of Women during the Night*).

Preparatory Work—Consideration of—Successive Drafts of Treaties.

See Case No. 49 (*Legal Status of Eastern Greenland*).

Treaties—Interpretation of—Preparatory Work.

See Case No. 98 (*Salem Case : United States and Egypt*, (1)).

Treaties—Interpretation of—Miscellaneous—Interpretation of Treaties by Reference to Circumstances at the Time of the Conclusion of the Treaty.

See Case No. 81 (*The May* v. *The King*).

v.—Various Other Rules of Interpretation.

Treaties—Interpretation—Rules of—Presumption against Redundancy—Preparatory Work—Historical Circumstances —Interpretation of Arbitration Clauses. **Case No. 211**

GREECE *v.* BULGARIA.

(Article 181 of the Treaty of Neuilly. Preliminary Question.)

Undén, Arbitrator.

November 4, 1931.

THE FACTS.—In the Treaty of London of May 17, 1913, Turkey ceded most of her possessions in Europe to Bulgaria, Greece, Serbia and Montenegro. In the Treaty of Bucharest of August 10, 1913, these States divided among themselves the territory in question. Separate treaties were also concluded between Turkey and Bulgaria, Greece, and Serbia. These were the Treaties of Constantinople, Athens and Stamboul, respectively.

Article 181 of the Treaty of Neuilly of 1919 provided as follows :

"Transfers of territory made in execution of the present treaty shall not prejudice the private rights referred to in the Treaties of Constantinople, 1913, of Athens, 1913, and of Stamboul, 1914.

"All transfers of territory made by or to Bulgaria in execution of the present treaty shall, equally and on the same conditions, ensure respect for these private rights.

Case No. 211 Contd.

"In case of disagreement as to the application of this article, the difference shall be submitted to an arbitrator appointed by the Council of the League of Nations."

Articles 10 and 11 of the Treaty of Constantinople between Bulgaria and the Turkish Empire provided as follows:

Article 10.

"Rights acquired previous to the annexation of the territories, as well as judicial documents and official titles emanating from the competent Ottoman authorities, shall be respected and held inviolable until there is legal proof to the contrary."

Article 11.

"The right of holding landed property in the ceded territories by virtue of the Ottoman law on urban and rural properties shall be recognized without any restriction.

"The proprietors of real or personal property in the said territories shall continue to enjoy their property rights, even if they fix their personal residence temporarily or permanently outside of Bulgaria. They shall be able to lease their property or administer it through third parties."

Similar clauses were inserted in Articles 5 and 6 of the Treaties of Athens and Stamboul.

The subject of the present dispute was certain forests situated near Dospat-Dag in Central Rhodopia, a district ceded by Turkey to Bulgaria in 1913. Between 1908 and 1911, the Dospat-Dag Company acquired from the Turkish Government the right to exploit the forests in question. The Bulgarian Government refused to recognise the rights of the Company. In 1926 it granted to an international group the right of exploitation. The persons owning the Dospat-Dag Company became Greek subjects after the World War.

In the present case the Arbitrator was called upon to decide whether the resulting dispute between Bulgaria and Greece constituted a disagreement with regard to the application of Article 181 of the Treaty of Neuilly although the private rights alleged to have been infringed were connected with territories which had not been ceded by the Treaty of Neuilly.

Held: that Article 181 was applicable with regard to the territory where the disputed forests were located.

(1) *Interpretation of Treaties. Presumption against Redundancy.*—The Arbitrator arrived at this conclusion after having examined the various interpretations submitted by both

parties and after having found that "the difficulties raised by the thesis of the Greek Government are less serious than those which would result from the adoption of the thesis of the Bulgarian Government." (At p. 772.) The principal consideration which seems to have weighed with the Arbitrator was the presumption against redundancy. He said: "If [as contended by Bulgaria] Article 181 actually had for its purpose the protection of private rights acquired in those territories only which had been transferred in execution of the Treaty of Neuilly, the first paragraph of that article, taken in connection with the second paragraph, would be quite useless and redundant, as the Greek Government has pointed out. . . . If we accept the first argument of the Bulgarian Government—that is, the interpretation according to which the provisions of Article 181 would apply only to the protection of rights arising in the regions ceded by the Treaty of Neuilly—it must still be explained why the first paragraph mentions the Treaties of Athens of 1913 and of Stamboul of 1914. According to the information furnished by the parties during the oral arguments, none of the territories acquired by Serbia and Greece under these two treaties were transferred under the Treaty of Neuilly. It would have been, therefore, entirely superfluous and illogical to stipulate in the Treaty of Neuilly that the transfers of territory made in conformity with that treaty should not affect the private rights contemplated in the Treaties of Athens and Stamboul." (At pp. 771, 772.)

(2) *Preparatory Work.*—The Arbitrator requested the Secretariat of the League of Nations to communicate with the French Minister for Foreign Affairs, with whom the archives of the Peace Conference had been deposited, to find out whether there existed any preparatory documents concerning Article 181 of the Treaty likely to throw light on the question before the Arbitrator. In the answer of the French Foreign Minister it was stated that "there was no discussion of the Supreme Council on this article, nor any observation of the Bulgarians as to the insertion of this provision in the conditions of peace, the draft of the conditions being on this point identical with the text of the treaty." Accordingly, the Arbitrator formally declared the negative result of the enquiry.

(3) *Historical Circumstances.*—The Arbitrator found a corroboration of his interpretation of Article 181 in the fact that after the Balkan War there was set up in accordance with the Treaty of London an international commission to settle the various financial questions arising out of the territorial changes

Case No. 211 Contd.

effected by the Treaty and that there was an intention to establish an international arbitral machinery for the settling of the conflicts arising under this head. "This work not having been accomplished, it does not seem improbable that the authors of Article 181 of the Treaty of Neuilly—in the first place the Great Powers—may have wished to take up again the idea of arbitral settlement of claims relative to private rights acquired in all the territories ceded by Turkey in 1913 and 1914." (At pp. 772, 773.)

(4) *Interpretation of Arbitration Clauses.*—It was contended by Bulgaria that in case of doubt as to the meaning of an arbitral clause the Arbitrator ought to assume that he had no jurisdiction seeing that there was a general rule that, in the absence of a formal agreement to that effect, States were not obliged to have recourse to arbitration. *Held:* that the suggested principle of interpretation of arbitration clauses could not be accepted. "Such a clause should be interpreted in the same way as other contractual stipulations. If analysis of the text and examination of its purpose show that the reasons in favor of the competence of the Arbitrator are more plausible than those which can be shown to the contrary, the former must be adopted." (At p. 773.)

[Report: *A.J.*, XXVIII (1934), p. 760.]

NOTE.—See also *ibid.*, p. 765, for the statement that "the Treaty of Neuilly expressly sanctions a general principle of common international law, that concerning respect for private rights in annexed territory, regularly acquired under the former government," and again p. 771 for a reference to "the well-known principle of respect for acquired rights in ceded territory, that is, the novation by the annexing state of an obligation incumbent upon the ceding state."

Case No. 212

Treaties—Interpretation of—Various Rules of—Liberal and Narrow Interpretations—Restrictive Interpretation—Treaties and Subsequent Statutes.

CLARK *v.* PIGEON RIVER IMPROVEMENT SLIDE & BOOM CO.

United States, Circuit Court of Appeals, Eighth Circuit.

August 27, 1931.

(Kenyon, Booth, Circuit Judges; Dewey, District Judge.)

THE FACTS.—This was an action for an injunction brought by the plaintiff, a Canadian citizen, against the defendant, a Minnesota corporation. The plaintiff claimed the right to the free and unobstructed use of the Pigeon River, which is an international boundary line between Minnesota and the Province of Ontario, for the purpose of driving logs. The defendant claimed the right under Minnesota statutes to obstruct the river with a boom and to collect tolls upon logs driven down the river. The plaintiff relied on the Webster-Ashburton Treaty between the United States and Canada, ratified on August 22, 1842 (8 U.S. Stat. L. 572), which established the international boundary line between the United States and Canada. The Treaty provided "That all the water communications and all the usual portages along the line from Lake Superior to the Lake of the Woods, and also Grand Portage, from the shore of Lake Superior to the Pigeon river, as now actually used, shall be free and open to the use of the citizens and subjects of both countries." The trial Court dismissed the complaint. On appeal,

Held: that the judgment must be reversed. The respondent contended that the words of the article, "as now actually used," limited water communications and the usual portages to such traffic as they were used for at that time, *i.e.*, as a fur-trader's route, and had no reference to the floating of logs. As a matter of grammatical construction, an argument might have been made that the term "as now actually used" applied to all the water connections and early portages, and not merely to Grand Portage, but it appeared from the record that Grand Portage alone of all the portages was not "along the line." It was thought, therefore, that the term "as now actually used" referred only to Grand Portage. Any other construction would give the Treaty a narrow and apparently distorted construction. Treaties are to be fairly and liberally construed to carry out the intentions of the parties thereto at the time the Treaty was concluded. Since the treaty-making power was superior to the legislative power of the States (U.S. Constitution, Article 6), there was no necessity, in construing treaties, to avoid possible conflict with State legislation. The Treaty prevailed over inconsistent State legislation.

[Report: 52 F. (2d) 550.]

NOTE.—In 1934 the Supreme Court of the United States had occasion to interpret the same provision of the Arbitration Treaty in the case *Pigeon River Improvement Slide and Boom Co.* v. *Charles W. Cox, Ltd.* (291 U.S. 138). See Hunter Miller in *A.J.*, XXIX (1935), pp. 118-123.

Case No. 213

Treaties—Interpretation of—Authentic Interpretation—How Far Binding upon Courts—Bilateral Interpretation of the Franco-Swiss Treaty of February 23, 1882, by an Exchange of Notes between the French Minister for Foreign Affairs and the Swiss Minister at Paris.

HUCKENDUBLER *v.* HOEFFLEUR.

France, Commission Supérieure de Cassation (*Rent Cases*).

December 22, 1932.

THE FACTS.—Difficulties arose concerning the application to aliens of the new French legislation on Rent (Article 4 of the Law of February 1, 1926, as amended by the Law of June 29, 1929), in particular with regard to the question as to how far alien tenants could take advantage of the provisions for prolongation of the lease. After diplomatic protests had been made against various judgments, the French Minister for Foreign Affairs exchanged Notes with the British Government (May 21 and 25, 1929) and the Swiss Government (July 11 and 26, 1929) in which the treaties concluded with these States in 1882 were interpreted in the sense that the High Contracting Parties declared that their purpose was to secure for their subjects or nationals the advantages of rent-legislation. The Courts were notified of this interpretation by a ministerial circular dated July 22, 1929, inserted in the *Journal Officiel* of August 13, 1929 (and slightly amended in another letter of April 29, 1930), and agreed to conform to it in their decisions. The circular stated that "the Minister is competent to intervene and decide diplomatic disputes" and added that "when he declares officially in the name of the Government the meaning to be attached to a clause, his interpretation becomes part of the treaty and is binding upon the ordinary and the administrative courts." The Courts—in this case the Commission Supérieure de Cassation—were therefore called upon to decide the value to be attached to this declaration of interpretation, particularly in the relations between France and Switzerland.

Held: that the interpretation was binding on the Courts. "The States which sign a diplomatic convention are competent to decide its meaning and scope." The Exchange of Notes between France and Switzerland of July 11-26, 1929, was in this respect "a contractual interpretation. . . . This bilateral interpretation, irrespective of its form, is part of the convention itself and should be observed and applied as though it expressed officially the common intention of the governments concerned."

[Report: *Dalloz hebdomadaire*, 1933, p. 39.]

NOTE.—On the question of the value to be given by municipal courts to governmental interpretations see Chailley, *La nature juridique des traités internationaux* (1933), p. 268; Mestre in *Hague Recueil*, vol. 38 (1931) (iv), pp. 295-299. On the special problem of the application to aliens of the French legislation on Rent see Judenstein-Le Bonheur, *La législation française des loyers et les étrangers* (1931); and Pigasse in *Recueil de l'Académie de législation de Toulouse*, 1931, pp. 9-27. French Courts have shown two tendencies in connection with the issue decided in this case (see Ch. Rousseau in *R.G.*, 41 (1934), pp. 78-79): the first, exhibited especially by the lower Courts (Court of Appeal of Paris, January 18, 1930: *Gazette du Palais*, 1930, Part 1, p. 275, with the conclusions of Lagarde, Avocat Général; Tribunal civil des Basses-Pyrénées, February 1, 1930: *Dalloz hebdomadaire*, 1930, p. 238; Tribunal civil of the Seine, February 18, 1930, *Leroy* v. *Rockwell*, *ibid.*, p. 221), has been to refuse to regard a ministerial interpretation as binding. However, the majority of decisions seem to favour the opposite view (see Court of Appeal of Paris, November 21, 1929: *Sirey*, 1930, Part 2, p. 161, with a note by Audinet). The Commission Supérieure de Cassation has always taken this view, and before the present case had given similar judgments: January 2, 1930, *Burnup* v. *Dolphens*: *Dalloz hebdomadaire*, 1930, p. 70; January 8, 1931, *Lepeut* v. *Toussaint*; July 2, 1931, *Rockwell* v. *Leroy*: *Sirey*, 1932, Part 2, p. 161; March 26, 1931, *Conner* v. *Thouret*: *Dalloz hebdomadaire*, 1931, p. 319.

Treaties — Interpretation — *Expressio unius est exclusio alterius*—Geneva Convention of May 15, 1922.

See Case No. 33 (*Niederstrasser* v. *Polish State*).

Treaties—Interpretation—Requirement of Effectiveness.

See Case No. 7 (*Interpretation of the Statute of the Memel Territory* (2)).

Treaties — Interpretation — *Expressio unius est exclusio alterius*.

See Case No. 215 (*Railway Traffic between Lithuania and Poland*).

Treaties—Interpretation—By Reference to Context—Two Paragraphs of One Article.

See Case No. 202 (*Case of the Free Zones of Upper Savoy and the District of Gex*, (1)).

Treaties—Interpretation of—Various Rules of Interpretation—Liberal Construction—"Ordinary Meaning" of Words.

See Case No. 114 (*Santovincenzo* v. *Egan*).

Treaties—Interpretation of—By Reference to Conduct of State Authorities.

See Case No. 38 (*Flensburger Dampfercompagnie* v. *United States*).

Treaties—Interpretation of—Leaning to Construction which Makes Treaty Legal rather than Illegal—Constitutional Limitations.

See Case No. 55 (*San Lorenzo Title & Improvement Co.* v. *City Mortgage Co.; The Same* v. *Clardy et Al.; The Same* v. *Caples et Al.*).

Treaties—Interpretation of—Various Rules of—Liberal Interpretation—Extradition Treaties.

See Case No. 160 (*Laubenheimer et Al.* v. *Factor*).

vi.—Miscellaneous.

PERMANENT COURT OF INTERNATIONAL JUSTICE.

Treaties—Interpretation—Preamble—Authority of.

For frequent references to the Preamble in interpreting Part XIII of the Treaty of Versailles see the Advisory Opinion of the Court of November 15, 1932,[1] on the *Interpretation of the Convention of* 1919 *concerning Employment of Women during the Night*: *P.C.I.J.*, Series A/B, No. 50, pp. 373-375.

Treaties—Interpretation of—Treaties Providing for Equal Treatment of Aliens—Interpretation by Reference to Other Treaties.

See Case No. 143 (*Security for Costs* (*Germany*) *Case*).

Treaties—Interpretation—Customary International Law as an Element of.

See Case No. 205 (*The Kronprins Gustaf Adolf; The Pacific. United States and Sweden*).

[1] For the composition of the Court see p. 410.

Treaties—Interpretation—Geographical Terms—Technical Meaning of—Burden of Proof.

See Case No. 49 (*Legal Status of Eastern Greenland*).

Treaties—Interpretation—Miscellaneous—Interpretation of Treaties Enacted as Municipal Statutes.

See Case No. 7 (*Interpretation of the Statute of the Memel Territory*, (2)).

Treaties—Interpretation of—Equivalence of Consideration as an Element of Interpretation—Rules of Interpretation—Rejection of Presumption of Redundancy.

See Case No. 8 (*Customs Régime between Germany and Austria*).

Treaties — Interpretation — Miscellaneous — Errors in Wording.

See Case No. 102 (*Chevreau Case*).

Treaties—Interpretation of—Miscellaneous—Filling of Gaps by Construction.

See Case No. 201 (*Minorities Treaty (Russian Subjects) Case*).

Treaties—Interpretation of—Miscellaneous—Meaning of the Expression "Free and Open."

See Case No. 2 (*Re Arrow River & Tributaries Slide & Boom Co. Ltd.*).

Treaties — Interpretation of — Miscellaneous — English Doctrine of Equity of Redemption.

See Case No. 119 (*Administrator of German Property* v. *Knoop*, (3)).

XIII.—Special Kinds of Treaties

i.—Commercial Treaties. Most-Favoured-Nation Clause.

Case No. 114 **Treaties—Most-Favoured-Nation Clause—Interpretation of —Rules of Interpretation—Liberal Construction.**

SANTOVINCENZO *v.* EGAN.

United States, Supreme Court. November 23, 1931.

(Hughes, C. J.; Holmes, Van Devanter, McReynolds, Brandeis, Sutherland, Butler, Stone, Roberts, JJ.).

THE FACTS.—This was a proceeding in the Surrogate's Court of the State of New York to administer the estate of a deceased Italian subject who had been domiciled in New York and who died intestate. No heirs or next of kin were discovered. The Consul-General of Italy claimed to be entitled to receive the net assets of the estate for distribution to the Kingdom of Italy. The claim was based upon the Consular Convention of 1878 between the United States and Italy which provided that consular officials of the two nations shall enjoy in both countries all the rights, prerogatives, immunities and privileges which are or may hereafter be granted to officers of the same grade, of the most favoured nation (20 U.S. Stat. L. 725, 732). The Italian Consul-General, pursuant to this agreement, sought the application of Article VI of the Treaty of 1856 between the United States and Persia, which provided: "In case of a citizen or subject of either of the contracting parties dying within the territories of the other, his effects shall be delivered up integrally to the family or partners in business of the deceased; and in case he has no relatives or partners, his effects in either country shall be delivered up to the consul or agent of the nation of which the deceased was a subject or citizen, so that he may dispose of them in accordance with the laws of his country." (11 U.S. Stat. L. 709, 710.) This Treaty was terminated on May 10, 1928.

The Surrogate's Court decreed, pursuant to c. 230 of the Laws of New York of 1898, that the balance of the estate after payment of debts and the sums allowed as commissions and expenses of administration be paid into the Treasury of New York City for the use and benefit of the unknown kin of the decedent. Ultimately the amount would go to the Treasury of the State of New York: *In re Comincio's Estate,* 135 Misc. Rep. 733;

affirmed, 229 App. Div. 862. On appeal to the United States Supreme Court,

Held (*per* Hughes, C. J.): that the decree must be reversed. The provision of Article VI of the Treaty with Persia did not contain the qualifying words "conformably with the laws of the country" (where the death occurred) as in the case of the Treaty between the United States and the Argentine Confederation of 1853 (Art. IX, 10 U.S. Stat. L. 1001, 1009: *Rocca* v. *Thompson*, 223 U.S. 317, 326, 330); or the phrase "so far as the laws of each country will permit," as in the Consular Convention between the United States and Sweden of 1910 (Art. XIV, 37 U.S. Stat. L. 1479, 1487, 1488: *Rocca* v. *Thompson, supra*; *Matter of D'Adamo*, 212 N. Y. 214, 222, 223). The requirement that the property be delivered to the consul of the nation of which the deceased was a subject must therefore be complied with unless a different rule was to apply simply because the decedent was domiciled in the United States. No distinction between residence and domicile was suggested by the language of Article VI of the Treaty with Persia, nor by other articles of the same Treaty, which used the words "citizens" or "subjects" without qualification. "It is not necessary to invoke the familiar rule with respect to the liberal construction of treaties[1] as the instant case merely calls for a reading of the provision as to 'citizens' and 'subjects' according to its terms. There is no applicable principle which permits us to narrow them. As treaties are contracts between independent nations, their words are to be taken in their ordinary meaning 'as understood in the public law of nations.' *Geofroy* v. *Riggs*, 133 U.S. 258, 271." The purpose of the Treaty afforded no reason to differentiate between residence and domicile. Its objective as a commercial treaty was to promote intercourse, which was facilitated by residence. The rights and privileges granted to the citizens or subjects of one party who were permitted under the Treaty to reside in the territory of the other party were not expressly made to depend upon the acquisition of a domicile, and there was no reason to infer such a qualification.

[Report: 284 U.S. 30; *A.J.*, XXVI (1932), p. 395.][2]

NOTE.—It appears that the appellants questioned the power of the Government of the United States to conclude with Persia or

[1] *Hauenstein* v. *Lynham*, 100 U.S. 483, 487; *Geofroy* v. *Riggs*, 133 U.S. 258, 271; *Tucker* v. *Alexandroff*, 183 U.S. 424, 437; *Asakura* v. *Seattle*, 265 U.S. 332, 342; *Jordan* v. *Tashiro*, 278 U.S. 123, 127; *Nielsen* v. *Johnson*, 279 U.S. 47, 52.

[2] See also *Columbia Law Review*, 32 (1932), p. 381.

Case No. 214 *Contd.* Italy treaties on subjects regulated in a different manner by State legislation. The Court said: "The treaty-making power is broad enough to cover all subjects that properly pertain to our foreign relations, and agreement with respect to the rights and privileges of citizens of the United States in foreign countries, and of the nationals of such countries within the United States, and the disposition of the property of aliens dying within the territory of the respective parties, is within the scope of that power, and any conflicting law of the State must yield. *Hauenstein* v. *Lynham*, 100 U.S. 483, 489; *Geofroy* v. *Riggs*, *supra*, at p. 266; *Missouri* v. *Holland*, 252 U.S. 416, 434; *Sullivan* v. *Kidd*, 254 U.S. 433, 440; *Asakura* v. *Seattle*, 265 U.S. 332, 343; *Todok* v. *Union State Bank*, 281 U.S. 449, 453."

XIV.—Miscellaneous

Treaties — Miscellaneous — "Unilateral" or "Unequal" Treaties—Compensation for Breach of.

See Case No. 98 (*Salem Case: United States and Egypt*).

Treaties—Miscellaneous—Undertakings Given in the Course of Negotiations.

See Case No. 49 (*Legal Status of Eastern Greenland*).

Treaties—Miscellaneous—Renunciation.

See Case No. 49 (*Legal Status of Eastern Greenland*).

PART IX

INTERNATIONAL ORGANISATION AND ADMINISTRATION

A.—LEAGUE OF NATIONS

III.—The Council

Council of the League of Nations—Resolutions of—Binding Force of.

See Case No. 215 (*Railway Traffic between Lithuania and Poland*).

IV.—Interpretation of the Covenant of the League

Covenant of the League of Nations—Interpretation of—Article 23(e)—Freedom of Communications—Binding Force of Resolutions of the Council—*Pactum de contrahendo*—*Expressio unius est exclusio alterius*—Reprisals—Necessity of a Breach of an International Obligation. **Case No. 215**

PERMANENT COURT OF INTER-NATIONAL JUSTICE.

RAILWAY TRAFFIC BETWEEN LITHUANIA AND POLAND.

Advisory Opinion of October 15, 1931.[1]

THE FACTS.—On January 24, 1931, the Council of the League of Nations adopted a Resolution requesting the Permanent Court of International Justice to give an Advisory Opinion on the following question :

> "Do the international engagements in force oblige Lithuania in the present circumstances, and if so in what manner, to take the necessary measures to open for traffic or for certain categories of traffic the Landwarów-Kaisiadorys railway sector ?"

The sector in question, which lay in Lithuanian territory, formed part of the railway between Vilna (the sovereignty over which was exercised by Poland but claimed by Lithuania), and Libau, a commercial port of Latvia. It had not been in use since the War. As a result of the controversy with Poland con-

[1] The Court was composed as follows : Adatci (President) ; Baron Rolin-Jaequemyns, Count Rostworowski, Fromageot, de Bustamante, Altamira, Anzilotti, Urrutia, Sir Cecil Hurst, Schücking, Negulesco, Wang (Judges) ; Stašinskas (Judge *ad hoc*).

Case No. 215 *Contd.*

cerning the sovereignty over Vilna, Lithuania did not maintain diplomatic relations with Poland and refused to maintain any direct transport or other communications with Poland.

The international obligations referred to in the request of the Council and relied upon by Poland were as follows:

(*a*) The Resolution of the Council of December 10, 1927, which recommended the two Governments "to enter into direct negotiations as soon as possible in order to establish such relations between the two neighbouring States as will ensure 'the good understanding between nations upon which peace depends' ";

(*b*) Article 23 (*e*) of the Covenant, which provides as follows: "Subject to and in accordance with the provisions of international conventions existing or hereafter to be agreed upon, the Members of the League . . . (*e*) will make provision to secure and maintain freedom of communications and of transit and equitable treatment for the commerce of all Members of the League. . . .";

(*c*) The Memel Convention of May 8, 1924, of which Article 3 of Annex III provides as follows: "The Lithuanian Government shall ensure the freedom of transit by sea, by water or *by rail,* of traffic coming from or destined for the Memel territory or in transit through the said territory, and shall conform in this respect with the rules laid down by the Statute and Convention on the Freedom of Transit adopted by the Barcelona Conference. . . ."

The Statute of Barcelona laid down in Article 2 that the contracting Parties "shall facilitate free transit, by rail or waterway, on routes *in use convenient for international transit.*"

In Article 3 of that Annex the Lithuanian Government agreed "to permit and to grant all facilities for the traffic *on the river* to or from or in the port of Memel, and not to apply, in respect of such traffic, on the ground of the present political relations between Lithuania and Poland, the stipulations of Articles 7 and 8 of the Barcelona Statute on the Freedom of Transit and Article 13 of the Barcelona Recommendations relative to Ports placed under an International Régime." Article 7 of the Barcelona Statute permitted measures of suspension of traffic on account of national safety and vital interests.

Held (unanimously): that the international engagements in force did not oblige Lithuania in the present circumstances to take the necessary steps to open for traffic or for certain categories of traffic the Landwarów-Kaisiadorys railway sector." (At p. 122.)

(1) *The Binding Force of Resolutions of the Council. Pactum de contrahendo.*—(i) As the representatives of Lithuania and Poland participated in the adoption of the Resolution of the Council of December 10, 1927, the two Governments were bound by their acceptance of the Council's Resolution, which constituted an engagement between them.

(ii) The Court could not accept the contention of Poland that the obligation to negotiate as laid down in the Resolution constituted an engagement to come to an agreement. "The Court is indeed justified in considering that the engagement incumbent on the two Governments in conformity with the Council's Resolution is not only to enter into negotiations, but also to pursue them as far as possible, with a view to concluding agreements. . . . But an obligation to negotiate does not imply an obligation to reach an agreement, nor in particular does it imply that Lithuania, by undertaking to negotiate, has assumed an engagement, and is in consequence obliged to conclude the administrative and technical agreements indispensable for the re-establishment of traffic on the Landwarów-Kaisiadorys railway sector." (At p. 116.)

(2) *Article* 23 (*e*) *of the Covenant.*—That Article did not imply any specific obligation for these States to open any particular lines of communication. "Specific obligations can therefore only arise, as this text clearly states, from 'international conventions existing or hereafter to be agreed upon,' for instance from 'general conventions to which other Powers may accede at a later date,' as is stated in the Preamble to the Barcelona Convention on freedom of transit. If this interpretation is correct, it is impossible to deduce from the general rule contained in Article 23 (*e*) of the Covenant an obligation for Lithuania to open the Landwarów-Kaisiadorys railway sector for international traffic, or for part of such traffic; such obligation could only result from a special agreement." (At p. 119.)

(3) *The Memel Convention. Expressio unius est exclusio alterius. Exception of National Safety and Vital Interests.*—The Memel Convention did not apply on the ground that the sector in question was not *in use* at the time of the conclusion of the Convention. It was inadmissible to say that the railway as a whole was in use, although one of its sectors was not.

The fact that Article 3 of Annex III expressly referred to rivers meant that it did not apply to railways. Having regard

Case No. 215 *Contd.*

to the existing political relations between Lithuania and Poland, the former "would be entitled to invoke Article 7, as a ground for refusing to open this sector for traffic or for certain categories of traffic, in case of an emergency affecting *her safety* or *vital interests*." (At p. 122.)

(4) *Reprisals.*—In view of the decision of the Court that there had been no breach of an international obligation on the part of Lithuania, it was unnecessary to consider the contention of Lithuania justifying her action on the ground of pacific reprisals against Poland. That question could only arise if it were shown that the international engagements in force obliged Lithuania to open this sector for traffic.

[Report: *P.C.I.J.*, Series A/B, No. 42.]

League of Nations—Covenant—Article 10 of the Covenant.

See Case No. 8 (*Customs Régime between Germany and Austria*).

V.—The Secretariat of the League

Case No. 216

League of Nations—Secretariat—Conditions of Service of Members of the Secretariat—League of Nations Administrative Tribunal—Law Applied by—*Travaux préparatoires*.

LHOEST *v.* SECRETARIAT OF THE LEAGUE OF NATIONS.

SOUC *v.* THE SAME.

GORDON *v.* THE SAME.

GROTE *v.* THE SAME.

League of Nations Administrative Tribunal. January 13, 1932.

(Judgments Nos. 5-8).

(Devèze, Montagna and Froelich, Judges.)

THE FACTS.—As from January 1, 1931, the Staff Regulations of the Secretariat of the League of Nations were modified and new contracts were offered to certain officials. In the case of certain grades of staff a distinction was drawn between locally recruited and internationally recruited officials, and expatriation was one of the factors taken into account when fixing the conditions of service of internationally recruited officials. The 1931 Staff Regulations, for the first time, established detailed statutory criteria for distinguishing between locally and internationally recruited officials, and the complainants in these cases (who had accepted as locally recruited officials new contracts which had been offered to them by the Secretary-General but had reserved their rights under the Staff Regulations), claimed that, on the basis of the criteria in the new Staff Regulations, they were entitled, when offered new contracts, to be offered contracts as internationally recruited officials. The main qualification prescribed by the 1931 Staff Regulations for appointment as internationally recruited officials was that the candidates should not have been resident for five years prior to appointment in French-speaking Switzerland or in French territory within fifteen kilometres of Geneva. The complainants in these cases had been resident in Geneva for more than five years at the time when the 1931 contracts were concluded, but claimed that the material date for determining whether they were entitled to be regarded as internationally recruited was the date of their first engagement and not the date of the conclusion of their new contracts in 1931.

Held : that the complaints must be dismissed. The relations between the League of Nations and its officials were in principle governed by the Staff Regulations in force at the time when the official had been engaged and, in so far as the Staff Regulations did not regulate any matter or left a question to be settled by agreement between the parties, by the special agreements entered into between the League and each official. If, during the currency of an engagement, new Staff Regulations came into force, it was for the new Regulations, subject to the application of general legal principles, to determine whether, and if so subject to what conditions and restrictions, current contracts should be affected by the new provisions. The Secretary-General was not required by the new Staff Regulations to offer new contracts to existing staff, but, if he chose to do so, he could only do so subject to the terms of the new Staff Regulations.

[Unreported.]

NOTE.—I. The Tribunal observed that the Secretariat was not entitled to invoke the fact that no provision had been made in the Budget to meet certain expenses, as an argument against the complainants, since the existence of obligations incumbent upon public administrations was not conditional upon the existence of budgetary provision to meet those obligations.

The fact that an official, when accepting one contract, had reserved any rights which he might have under the Staff Regulations to be offered a different contract did not deprive his acceptance of its definitive character or destroy the consensus *ad idem* required

Case No. 216 *Contd.*

for the creation of the contract. Although considerations of equity appeared to support the contention of the complainants that the material time for determining whether an official was internationally or locally recruited should be the time of his first engagement, the Tribunal was required to decide cases according to law and could not uphold a contention which could not be supported either by the terms of the Staff Regulations or by general legal principles. As the new Staff Regulations applied to the case not because they were of retroactive operation but because a new contract had been concluded, it necessarily followed that the date of the new contract was the date upon which the official must have fulfilled the conditions laid down by the new Staff Regulations for classification in the international category.

II. With regard to the interpretation of the new Staff Regulations of 1931, the Tribunal remarked that, according to generally recognised principles of law, the *travaux préparatoires* of a law were not an authentic interpretation of it. They served to indicate its general objects and even to clarify the meaning of an ambiguous provision, but, where the text of the law was clear, the preparatory work could not be invoked in support of an interpretation inconsistent with the text.

III. The Tribunal pointed out that it was unnecessary to consider the complainants' contention that, in view of the extraterritorial status of League officials, the physical presence of officials at Geneva did not make them resident in Geneva for the purpose of determining whether, when entering into a new contract, they were eligible to be recruited as international or only as local officials. Only officials of the first category[1] had extraterritorial status, and the complainants did not belong to that category.

IV. In this connection it is convenient to summarise in some detail the Opinion, dated October 8, 1932, of the Committee of Jurists appointed by the Chairman of the First Committee of the Thirteenth Ordinary Session of the Assembly of the League of Nations to report upon the power of the Assembly to reduce the salaries of officials of the Secretariat of the League of Nations, the International Labour Office and the Registry of the Permanent Court of International Justice. The Committee was composed as follows: Andersen, Basdevant, Huber, Sir William Malkin, and Pedroso.

1. League officials "form part of an international public service" and "the legal relationship which exists between them and the Secretariat, the International Labour Office or the Registry, as the case may be, is not a legal relationship of private law within the meaning of the civil law of any country."

2. The legal position of the officials of each organisation is governed by the Staff Regulations of the organisation which in

[1] For an explanation of the categories into which the staff of the League are divided see *Annual Digest*, 1929-1930, p. 315.

each case provide that an official entering the service receives a letter of appointment and replies by a letter of acceptance. The letter of appointment refers to the Staff Regulations and specifies, *inter alia*, the salary which the official will receive. It follows that, although the League could have chosen a different system under which the official by voluntarily entering its service thereby brought himself under conditions of service which were laid down by regulation and were subsequently capable of being altered by authority of the League, it has preferred a different system which makes the official's right to his salary rest upon a contract. This view that the nature of the relationship is contractual is confirmed by various provisions of the regulations.

3. Under "the general principles of law which are recognised by the Members of the League of Nations" both parties to a contract are bound thereby and one party cannot alter the contract without the consent of the other party. "The result, therefore, of the relevant provisions and of general legal principles is that . . . the official possesses a right of a contractual character, no interference with which is possible without his consent."

4. The same view is confirmed by the decisions of the Administrative Tribunal of the League which has stated that while the administration is "entirely free to make in regard to its staff any rules that it considers desirable," this power is "subject to its not infringing the acquired rights of any member of the staff," and that while it is for new Regulations substituted during the course of officials' periods of service for the Regulations previously in force to determine whether, under what conditions, and within what limitations, contracts in force will be affected by the new provisions, this is so "subject always to application of the general principles of law." Such general principles obviously include respect for rights acquired by contract.

5. The question as to whether the Assembly has any right to derogate from the contractual rights of officials in the exercise of its budgetary authority "does not arise in the same manner as it arises for a Parliament which besides its budgetary authority has power to legislate—that is to say, to make rules of law which can override other rules of law." The Assembly finds itself in the presence of contracts which fix the salaries of the officials and create rights to such salaries. These contracts are made in consequence of an appointment approved or made by the authority competent to make such appointments under the constituent instruments of the three organisations. There can be no presumption that one organ of an association has the power to nullify the decision of another organ. The obligation which flows from the official's contract is an obligation resting upon the League and all the organs of the League are therefore bound to conform to it. Accordingly, in providing for expenditure the Assembly is bound to take as a basis the contractual rights of officials.

Case No. 216 *Contd.*

[Report: League of Nations, *Official Journal*, Special Supplement No. 107, Records of the Thirteenth Ordinary Session of the Assembly, Minutes of the Fourth Committee. Geneva 1932, pp. 206-208.]

In view of the above report, which was unanimous, the Assembly refrained from taking any action with a view to reducing the salaries of officials. Since 1931 it has been customary to include in new letters of appointment a provision that "the terms of this contract are subject to such modifications, if any, as may result from the decisions of the Assembly."

B.—INTERNATIONAL LABOUR ORGANISATION

Case No. 217

PERMANENT COURT OF INTERNATIONAL JUSTICE

International Labour Organisation—Scope of—Whether Restricted to Manual Labour—Convention of 1919 concerning Employment of Women during the Night—Interpretation of Treaties—Preparatory Work—Interpretation by Reference to Circumstances Obtaining at the Time of the Conclusion of the Treaty—Effect of Changes since the Conclusion of the Convention.

INTERPRETATION OF THE CONVENTION OF 1919 CONCERNING EMPLOYMENT OF WOMEN DURING THE NIGHT.

Advisory Opinion of November 15, 1932.[1]

THE FACTS.—Article 3 of the Convention of 1919 concerning employment of women during the night provides as follows:

> "Women without distinction of age shall not be employed during the night in any public or private industrial undertaking, or in any branch thereof, other than an undertaking in which only members of the same family are employed."

On May 9, 1932, the Council of the League of Nations adopted a Resolution requesting the Court to give an Advisory Opinion on the following question:

> "Does the Convention concerning employment of women during the night, adopted in 1919 by the International Labour Conference, apply, in the industrial undertakings covered by the said Convention, to women who hold positions of supervision or management and are not ordinarily engaged in manual work?"

Held (Baron Rolin-Jaequemyns, Count Rostworowski, Fromageot, Anzilotti and Schücking, Judges, dissenting):

[1] The Court was composed as follows: Adatci (President); Guerrero (Vice-President); Baron Rolin-Jaequemyns, Count Rostworowski, Fromageot, Anzilotti, Urrutia, Sir Cecil Hurst, Schücking, Negulesco, van Eysinga (Judges).

that the Convention "applies, in the industrial undertakings covered by the said Convention, to women who hold positions of supervision or management and are not ordinarily engaged in manual work." (At p. 382.)

(1) *Scope of the Activity of the International Labour Organisation. Whether Applying to Manual Workers Only.*—"The Court has considered whether it could be maintained that, in view of the fact that the improvement of the lot of the manual worker was the aim of Part XIII, a provision in a Labour convention couched in general terms must be assumed to be intended to apply only to manual workers unless the opposite intention is made manifest by the terms of the Convention. This would be tantamount to saying that, as no such contrary intention is shown to exist in the case of this Convention, Article 3 must be regarded as applying only to manual workers.

"The Court holds that it would not be sound to argue thus.

"It is certainly true that the amelioration of the lot of the manual worker was the main preoccupation of the authors of Part XIII of the Treaty of Versailles of 1919; but the Court is not disposed to regard the sphere of activity of the International Labour Organization as circumscribed so closely, in respect of the persons with which it was to concern itself, as to raise any presumption that a Labour convention must be interpreted as being restricted in its operation to manual workers, unless a contrary intention appears." (At p. 374.)

"To justify the adoption of a rule for the interpretation of Labour conventions to the effect that words describing general categories of human beings such as 'persons' or 'women' must *prima facie* be regarded as referring only to manual workers, it would be necessary to show that it was only with manual workers that the Labour Organization was intended to concern itself." (At p. 375.)

The Court referred to its previous Advisory Opinions (Nos. 2, 3 and 13) concerning the competence of the Organisation, and stated that "an examination of the Opinions referred to above is sufficient to show that the limits of the sphere of the Labour Organization are not fixed with precision or rigidity in Part XIII, and a study of the text of Part XIII provides ample material for arriving at the same conclusion." The words used in the Preamble and in the operative articles of Part XIII were not words confined to manual workers. "The words used are '*travailleurs*,' 'workers,' 'workpeople,' '*travailleurs salariés*,' 'wage-earners,' words which do not exclude employed persons doing non-manual work, as perhaps might have been held to be

Case No. 217 *Contd.*

the case if the words used had been '*ouvrier*' or 'labourer.' "

(2) *Interpretation of Treaties. Preparatory Work.*—With regard to the contention that the preparatory work of the Conference showed its essential uniformity with the Berne Convention of 1906 on the prohibition of night work for women employed in industry, which was in terms limited to manual workers,[1] the Court examined in detail the preparatory work of the Convention and reached the following conclusion. "The impression derived from a study of the preparatory work is that, though at first the intention was that the Conference should not deviate from the stipulations of the Berne Convention, this intention had receded into the background by the time that the Draft Convention was adopted on November 28th, 1919. The uniformity of the terms of this Draft Convention with those of the other draft conventions which were being adopted, and which had their origin in the programme set forth in Part XIII of the Versailles Treaty, had become the important element. The preparatory work thus confirms the conclusion reached on a study of the text of the Convention that there is no good reason for interpreting Article 3 otherwise than in accordance with the natural meaning of the words." (At p. 380.)

With regard to recourse to preparatory work in general the Court said: "In doing so, [*i.e.*, in examining in the present case the preparatory work of the Conference] the Court does not intend to derogate in any way from the rule which it has laid down on previous occasions that there is no occasion to have regard to preparatory work if the text of a convention is sufficiently clear in itself." (At p. 378.)[2]

[1] This was the sole reason for the dissent of the five judges referred to above, at p. 410.

[2] See on this the following passage in the Dissenting Opinion of Judge Anzilotti: "If Article 3, according to the natural meaning of its terms, were really perfectly clear, it would be hardly admissible to endeavour to find an interpretation other than that which flows from the natural meaning of its terms. But I do not see how it is possible to say that an article of a convention is clear until the subject and aim of the convention have been ascertained, for the article only assumes its true import in this convention and in relation thereto. Only when it is known what the Contracting Parties intended to do and the aim they had in view is it possible to say either that the natural meaning of terms used in a particular article corresponds with the real intention of the Parties, or that the natural meaning of the terms used falls short of or goes further than such intention. In the first alternative it may rightly be said that the text is clear and that it is impossible, on the pretext of interpretation, to endow it with an import other than that which is consistent with the natural meaning of the words. In the other alternative, since the words have no value save as an expression of the intention of the Parties, it will be found either that the words have been used in a wider sense than normally attaches to them (broad interpretation) or that they have been used in a narrower sense than normally attaches to them (narrow interpretation)." (At p. 383.)

(3) *Interpretation of Treaties by Reference to Circumstances Obtaining at the Time of the Conclusion of the Treaty. Effect of Changes since the Conclusion of the Convention.*—With regard to the contention that in interpreting the Convention account must be taken of the fact that at the time of its conclusion in 1919 very few women held positions of supervision or management in industrial undertakings and that the application of the Convention to women thus engaged had not been considered, the Court said: "Even if this were so, however, it does not by itself afford sufficient reason for ignoring the terms of the Convention. The mere fact that, at the time when the Convention on Night Work of Women was concluded, certain facts or situations, which the terms of the Convention in their ordinary meaning are wide enough to cover, were not thought of, does not justify interpreting those of its provisions which are general in scope otherwise than in accordance with their terms." (At p. 377.)

[Report: *P.C.I.J.*, Series A/B, No. 50.]

C.—OTHER ORGANS OF INTERNATIONAL ADMINISTRATION

[See also Part II, B. *Territories under Joint or International Government*; and Part III, B. *Functions and Competence of International Commissions on International Rivers.*]

International Unions—Telegraphic Convention of 1875—Interpretation of Article 3 of the Convention—Immunity of Private Companies Acting Under Sovereign Authorisation. **Case No. 217a**

See *Elias and Abdou Noujaim* v. *Eastern Telegraph Co.*, decided by the Egyptian Summary Tribunal of Port Said on December 19, 1931, and December 31, 1932, in which it was held that Article 3 of the International Telegraph Convention of St. Petersburg of 1875, in which the contracting States declared that they would not accept any responsibility in respect of the international telegraphic service, must be interpreted so as to cover not merely cases of accident or *force majeure*, but also, in certain cases, of human negligence. It was held that the protection given by the Article extended not only to States themselves, but also to private companies, such as the defendant company, who must be deemed to benefit by it in virtue of being allowed to carry on the telegraphic service in Egypt on the same conditions as the Egyptian Government.

Case No. 217a *Contd.*

[Report: *Gazette des Tribunaux Mixtes d'Egypte,* XXIV (1933-1934), p. 35.]

Compare the judgment of the Summary Tribunal of Alexandria of June 12, 1933: *ibid.*, p. 34.

International Administration—Sanitary Council in Egypt.

For a case bearing on the Sanitary Council without, however, raising any question of general international law, see *Ayoub* v. *Conseil Sanitaire, Maritime et Quarantenaire d'Egypte,* decided by the Egyptian Mixed Court of Appeal of Alexandria on April 8, 1931: *Gazette des Tribunaux Mixtes d'Egypte,* XXI (1930-1931), p. 407.

PART X

DISPUTES

A.—ARBITRATION

I.—In General

ii.—The Law Applied by Arbitral Tribunals. Arbitration and Judicial Settlement.

Arbitration—The Law Applied by Tribunals—Relative Authority of Treaties and of Customary International Law.

See Case No. 205 (*The Kronprins Gustaf Adolf; The Pacific. United States and Sweden*).

International Arbitration—Law Applicable—Law Applicable by Domestic Tribunal Set Up to Decide on a Controversy of an International Character—The Court of Claims of the United States.

See Case No. 229 (*Royal Holland Lloyd* v. *United States*, (*a*)).

Arbitration—Law Applicable—Administrative Tribunal of the League of Nations.

See Case No. 216 (*Lhoest, Souc, Gordon and Grote* v. *Secretariat of the League of Nations*).

iii.—The Arbitration Treaty. Appointment and Withdrawal of Arbitrators.

Arbitration—*Compromis*—Withdrawal of Consent to Arbitrate on the Ground of Essential Error—Central Office for International Transport as Arbitrator under the Berne Convention—Competence to Pass on the Scope and Validity of the Special Agreement. **Case No. 218**

ITALIAN STATE RAILWAYS *v.* POLISH STATE RAILWAYS.

Central Office for International Transport. January 21, 1931.

THE FACTS.—On July 18, 1914, one Bozzi, an Italian national resident in Milan, sent a wagon-load of silk waste as ordinary freight to Warsaw. The wagon crossed the Austro-Russian

Case No. 218 *Contd.*

frontier on July 29, 1914. Apparently it reached Warsaw, but beyond Warsaw it could not be traced. The Italian Railways paid to Bozzi 230.000 lire damages. Under Article 47 of the International Convention on Transport of Goods by Railway of October 14, 1890,[1] they claimed reimbursement of this sum from the Russian State, the Polish Railways, the Czechoslovak Railways, and the Austrian Railways. All these refused to accept responsibility. The Polish refusal was based on the provisions of the Treaty of Riga between Poland and Russia of March 18, 1921,[2] by virtue of which Poland was expressly released from liability for the obligations of the Russian Empire. On June 9, 1929, the Italian State Railways informed the Central Office for International Transport by Rail at Berne that they wished to resort to arbitration by that Office between them and the Polish State Railways, as provided for in Article 57 of the Convention of 1890. The Italian Railways produced letters from the Polish State Railways in which they declared that they did not object to the dispute being referred to the Central Office.

On June 28, 1929, the Central Office requested the Polish State Railways to confirm their willingness to submit to the arbitral procedure provided for in the Convention. Thereupon the Polish State Railways declared that they "submitted the case to arbitration by the Central Office under Article 57 (1) of the International Convention."[3]

The Arbitral Tribunal was then constituted[4]; the documents submitted by Italy were sent to the Polish State Railways on December 21, 1929; and a time limit was fixed for the Polish answer. In that answer the Polish State Railways withdrew their consent to submit the dispute to arbitration. They pointed

[1] The old Berne Convention.

[2] *L.N.T.S.*, vol. 6 (1921), p. 123:

Article 4: "Poland shall not, in view of the fact that a part of the territories of the Polish Republic formerly belonged to the Russian Empire, be held to have incurred any debt or obligation towards Russia, except as provided in the present Treaty. . . ."

Article 19: "Russia and the Ukraine hereby discharge Poland from all responsibility in respect of debts and obligations of whatever nature incurred by the former Russian Empire. . . ."

[3] Article 57 (1) provided as follows: "In order to facilitate and ensure the carrying out of the present Convention, a Central Office for International Transport by Rail shall be established and shall have the following duties:

". . . (*c*) To give awards at the request of the parties concerned regarding any disputes which may arise between railway administrations."

[4] The Tribunal was composed as follows: President: Lohner, Director of the Central Office; *Juge arbitre*: Meckenstock, Judge at Neufchâtel, Switzerland; *Juge suppléant*: Merz, Councillor of State, Head of the Judicial Department of the Canton of Berne.

out that the Central Office could not adjudicate on a dispute which had arisen prior to the adhesion of the Polish State to the International Convention. The Italian State Railways replied, in substance, that Poland having adhered to the Convention by Article 366 of the Treaty of Versailles, and an arbitration agreement having in fact been concluded under that Convention, Poland could not validly withdraw her consent. The Polish State Railways maintained their new position on the ground that it was only after December 23, 1929, that the true facts had become known to the Ministry of Communications. When the latter, it was said, had at first declared its willingness to submit the case to arbitration, it was on the assumption that one of the private railway companies whose lines, bought up by the Government, were now part of the Polish State Railways, had taken part in the disputed transport. It appeared now that carriage had been effected by the Warsaw-Vienna railway which, at the time, was owned by the Russian Empire.

Held: that the Arbitral Tribunal was not competent to decide on the binding character of the special agreement, and that the proceedings must be suspended. The arbitral jurisdiction under Article 57 of the Convention was not compulsory. It was based on a request by both parties. If this common request was not forthcoming, or if it subsequently became void, the Court which would normally be competent under Article 53 [1] of the Convention, had jurisdiction. As regards the legal effect of the revocation of its consent by the Polish State Railways, the principle was that arbitral tribunals are not empowered to decide on the obligatory force and scope of the special agreement, these questions falling within the jurisdiction of the Court which would normally be competent. This was a rule which was generally recognised and approved by the teachings of the leading authorities in the matter of procedure. It had been applied more than once by the Swiss Federal Court. [2] "It follows that, also in the present case, the Arbitral Tribunal is

[1] "All actions on the right of recourse are exclusively justiciable by a judge of the district within which the railway against which proceedings are taken has its chief office."

[2] The Office referred here to judgments reproduced in the official publication of the Judgments of the Swiss Federal Court, vol. 41 (I), p. 276, and vol. 41 (II), pp. 308-309; and to the following writers: Kohler, "Über prozessrechtliche Verträge und Kreationen," in *Beiträge zur Erläuterung des Deutschen Rechts* (1887), p. 510; Garsonnet et César, *Traité de procédure*, 3rd ed., vol. VIII, pp. 558-559; Rivier, *Droit des gens*, vol. II, p. 174; Leuch, *Zivilprozessordnung des Kantons Bern*, Note 1 to Article 385.

Case No. 218 Contd. not empowered to decide on the admissibility of the unilateral revocation of the consent previously given."

[Report : *Bulletin des transports internationaux par chemins de fer*, 1931, p. 49.]

NOTE.—It is a generally recognised rule of international arbitral law that an arbitral tribunal is competent to interpret the scope of the special agreement and to decide whether it has jurisdiction under it. The present case, which, strictly speaking, is neither a case of international arbitration proper nor of a clear special agreement, is concerned with the validity of the original submission to arbitration challenged on the ground of alleged essential error. It will be noted that the Central Office for International Transport refused to decide the question of the validity of the original submission to arbitration for the reason, apparently, that there existed another Court normally competent in these matters.

Arbitration Agreement—Interpretation—Partial Impossibility of Execution—Impossibility of Applying One of the Clauses—Whether Invalidating the Whole Arbitration Agreement.

See Case No. 202 (*Case of the Free Zones of Upper Savoy and the District of Gex*, (5)).

Arbitration Agreement—Error in Wording—Interpretation.

See Case No. 102 (*Chevreau Case*).

Arbitration—Arbitration Agreement—Interpretation of—Restrictive Interpretation.

See Case No. 211 (*Greece* v. *Bulgaria : Article* 181 *of the Treaty of Neuilly, Preliminary Question*, (4)).

II.—Procedure

i.—Procedure before the Tribunal (Oral and Written Arguments).

Case No. 219 **Arbitration—Procedure—Amendment of Claim—Change in the Nationality of the Claim Resulting from the Amendment.**

In re LAUE Y CIA., IN LIQUIDATION.

German-Mexican Claims Commission. February 12, 1930.

Decision No. 35.

THE FACTS.—This was a claim concerning damage suffered by a company, the members of which were German nationals.

The German Agent filed the claim in the name of the company. The Mexican Agent interposed the objection that the company was Mexican and that the Commission had no jurisdiction. The German Agent thereupon moved to amend the pleadings by substituting the names of the members, since the Claims Convention conferred jurisdiction on the Commission in respect of claims of companies in which German nationals had an interest in excess of 50 per cent. of the capital. The Mexican Agent objected to the motion on the ground that such an amendment was inadmissible because the nationality of the claimant was being changed.

Held (by Cruchaga, Presiding Commissioner, for the Commission): that the motion must be granted. The Commission had full liberty to decide on the allowance of amendments, and although this motion involved a change in the nationality of the claimant, the substance of the claim remained the same.

[Unreported.]

Arbitration—Procedure—Re-Hearing.

See the Decision on a Petition for Re-hearing given on March 30, 1931, by the United States-German Mixed Claims Commission in *Lehigh Valley R. R. Co. and Others* v. *Germany*, where the Commission stated that although its rules, in conformity with the practice of international commissions, made no provision for a re-hearing after a final decree had been entered, it had nevertheless considered carefully a petition for re-hearing submitted by the American Agent but not accompanied by fresh evidence. The Commission found no reason to depart from its former finding: *A.J.*, XXVII (1933), p. 339.

ii.—Competence. Competence to Determine Jurisdiction

Arbitration—Jurisdiction—Jurisdiction of Mixed Commissions—How Far Affected by Concurrent Jurisdiction of National Commission to which Claimant had Submitted his Claim. **Case No. 220**

In re Roy.

British-Mexican Claims Commission.

(Zimmerman, Stoker, Flores.)

April 24, 1931.

The Facts.—The claimant in the present case, before submitting to the Mixed Commission his claim in respect of property

Case No. 220 *Contd.*

taken away by some Mexican revolutionary forces, had filed a claim before the National Claims Commission set up by the Mexican Government. An award by that Commission had been given in his favour and partly paid by the Mexican Government. Before the Mixed Commission the Mexican Government contended that the Commission had no jurisdiction seeing that the present claim was in part one for the execution of a judgment and as such outside the terms of the Convention; that as to the other part it was *res judicata*; and, finally, that the claim having been merged in the award of the National Claims Commission, it could only be made the subject of direct negotiations between the two Governments.

Held: that the Commission had jurisdiction. The National Commission was created and rendered judgments before the Claims Convention was concluded. If the intention of the contracting parties had been that the work of the National Commission was in any way to interfere with the jurisdiction of the International Tribunal which they were about to create, they would have expressed their intention in the Convention. This was not done. On the contrary, it was agreed in Article 6 that no claim should be set aside or rejected on the ground that all legal remedies had not been exhausted prior to the presentation of the claim. The National Commission was an institution set up to examine and decide all claims for compensation for revolutionary losses and damage, whether suffered by Mexican citizens or by aliens. The various Claims Conventions were concluded because the foreign Governments desired that a means of redress of an impartial and neutral character be open to their subjects.

The Convention gave to British subjects a right which they did not possess under the Decree which created the National Commission. They received a new right in so far as the payment of compensation was no longer an act dependent on the discretion of one Government or on that of the authorities of one State. It was converted into an international liability, *i.e.*, a liability of one State towards another State.

The view taken by the Mexican Government would mean that those British subjects who—at a time when no other court existed—had resorted to the National Commission, had *ipso facto* and beforehand waived rights which the Convention subsequently concluded granted to other British nationals. In view of this the Commission could not attach importance to the fact that the claimant agreed to the award given before the Claims Convention was concluded, *i.e.*, at a time when he could seek no other means of redress than the National Commission. Moreover, as the total amount of the award had not been paid, the Commission would, by declaring themselves incompetent, place the claimant as regards the unpaid balance in a weaker position than that in which he would have found himself had he not sued before the National Commission.

In taking the view that the jurisdiction of the National Commission would have no effect on the jurisdiction of the Mixed Commission, the latter realised that the judgments of the former might have considerable weight for the decisions of the latter, merely because the examination of claims by the National Commission took place at a time less remote from the occurrence underlying the claim.

[Report: *Decisions and Opinions of the Commissioners*, 1933, p. 39.]

Arbitration — Jurisdiction — Extension of Jurisdiction subsequently to Arbitration Agreement.

See p. 425 (*Lehigh Valley R. R. Co. and Others* v. *Germany*).

Arbitral Tribunals—Jurisdiction—Right to Decree *restitutio in integrum*.

See Case No. 33 (*Niederstrasser* v. *Polish State*).

III.—Rules of Evidence. Burden of Proof

[As to Consideration ot Preparatory Work in the Interpretation of Treaties see Part VIII, TREATIES: XII. *Interpretation of Treaties*.]

Evidence—Technical Rules of Evidence—International and Municipal Tribunals. **Case No. 221**

In re ODELL.

British-Mexican Claims Commission.

(Zimmerman, Stoker, Flores.)

May 13, 1931.

THE FACTS.—This was a claim for damages brought by the claimant, a locomotive engineer, on account of injuries said to have been sustained as the result of the derailment of a train which he was compelled by some revolutionaries to drive. The Commission found that there was no evidence at all on such

Case No. 221 *Contd.* questions as whether the claimant conducted a military train; that he was induced against his will to drive it; and that the switch had been secretly tampered with by some other revolutionaries. In view of this the Commission

Held: that the claim must be rejected. The Commission said: "If an international tribunal were to accept all these allegations without evidence, it would expose itself to the not unjustifiable criticism of placing jurisdiction as between nations below the level prevailing in all civilized states for jurisdiction as between citizens. The Commission fully realize, as they have already expressed in their decision No. 2 (Cameron) No. 3, that in international jurisdiction technical rules of evidence may be less restricted and less formal than in lawsuits before a domestic tribunal. That in the admission of evidence greater liberality can obtain, has been shown by the Commission on several occasions, but in the present claim there is no question of the admission or the value of evidence: there is an absence of evidence and the greatest liberality cannot overcome this defect.

"The Commission also realize that the weighing of outside evidence, if any such be produced, may be influenced by the degree to which it was possible to produce proof of a better quality. In cases where it is obvious that everything has been done to collect stronger evidence and where all efforts to do so have failed, a court can be more easily satisfied than in cases where no such endeavour seems to have been made. This consideration has guided and will guide the Commission in other cases, for instance, as regards the fixing of the amount of the award. But in the claim now before them the Commission cannot believe that it would have been impracticable to produce at least some corroboration of the statements of the claimant." (At p. 63.)

[Report: *Decisions and Opinions of the Commissioners*, 1933, p. 61.]

Case No. 221a **Evidence—Certificate of a Notary Public—Evidential Value of—Compared with Consular Certificate.**

See *In re Carmichael*, decided by the British-Mexican Claims Commission (Zimmerman, Stoker, Flores), on April 29, 1931, in which the Commission pointed out that they could not attach to the certificate of a notary public the same value in matters of nationality as to a consular certificate. The Commission referred to the *Lynch case* which it decided some time before (*Annual Digest*, 1929-1930, Case No. 134, (*b*)) and said: "None of the guarantees which are offered by a consular certificate and which induced the Commission to accept it as *prima facie* evidence are presented by the document on which the British Agent relied. A notary public, although a public servant, cannot be considered as an agent working under the permanent control of, nor as being in continuous touch with, the Government. The keeping of a register of British subjects does not form part of his official duties. Neither does his normal professional work, nor his previous training therefor, include frequent contact with questions of nationality. His function gravitates in civil law, not in public or international law. To his declarations in matters of citizenship no preponderating value can be attached." (At pp. 47, 48.)

[Report: *Decisions and Opinions of the Commissioners*, 1933, p. 45.]

NOTE.—See also the *Bowerman and Burberry's Limited case, ibid.*, p. 17.

Arbitration—Evidence—Newly-Discovered Evidence—Re-Hearing.

For an example of a petition for re-hearing, on the ground of newly-discovered evidence, and of the dismissal of the petition on the ground that if the new evidence had been submitted at the time of the original decision it would not have substantially modified it, see the Decision of Roberts, J., Umpire in the United States-German Mixed Claims Commission, of December 3, 1932. The decision is exclusively concerned with an examination of the evidence submitted to the Commission, and does not call for a detailed digest.

[Report: *A.J.*, XXVII (1933), p. 345.]

Arbitration—Evidence—Subpœnas—United States Act of Congress of July 3, 1930—Extension of Jurisdiction of Commission by Statute Passed Subsequently to its Creation. **Case No. 221b**

In a petition for re-hearing submitted by the American Agent before the United States-German Mixed Claims Commission in the case *Lehigh Valley R. R. Co. and Others* v. *Germany* (see above, p. 421), the American Agent requested that subpœnas be issued by the Commission for the purpose of taking oral evidence in conformity with the Act of Congress approved on July 3, 1930, and having general application to international commissions. The Commission

Held: that the request must be rejected. The Agreement establishing the Commission did not authorise it to issue

Case No. 221b *Contd.* subpœnas for witnesses or to administer oaths. The jurisdiction conferred upon the Commission could not be extended by a later statute of the United States.

[Report: *A.J.*, XXVII (1933), p. 339.]

Arbitration—Evidence—Admissibility of Sworn Affidavits.

See Case No. 98 (*Salem Case: United States and Egypt*).

Evidence—Burden of Proof—Submission by Special Agreement.

See Case No. 426 (*Chevreau Case*).

Arbitration—Evidence—Burden of Proof—Evidence of Negative Facts—Failure to Prosecute.

See Case No. 101 (*In re Gill*).

Evidence—Treaties—Evidence of Undisputed Sovereignty.

See Case No. 49 (*Legal Status of Eastern Greenland*).

Evidence—Burden of Proof—Interpretation of Technical Terms.

See Case No. 49 (*Legal Status of Eastern Greenland*).

IV.—Admission of Liability. Waiver. Estoppel

Admissions—Treaties Containing Reservations as to Disputed Rights.

See Case No. 49 (*Legal Status of Eastern Greenland*).

Evidence—Admissions—In the Course of Diplomatic Negotiations.

See Case No. 49 (*Legal Status of Eastern Greenland*).

Estoppel—Undertaking by Foreign Minister in the Course of Negotiations—Undertaking Given as Consideration for Concession Made by the Other Party.

See Case No. 49 (*Legal Status of Eastern Greenland*).

Estoppel—Indirect Recognition of Sovereignty in Treaties.

See Case No. 49 (*Legal Status of Eastern Greenland*).

V.—The Award

Arbitration—Award—Participation of the Umpire in the Deliberations of the National Commissioners.

In a petition for re-hearing submitted by the American Agent in the case *Lehigh Valley R. R. Co. and Others* v. *Germany* (see above, p. 421), one of the grounds of the petition was that the Umpire had participated in the deliberations of the national Commissioners and in the opinion of the Commission. In its decision the Commission pointed out that this had been the usual practice of the Commission since its foundation in 1922, and that in any case the practice was not of "doubtful validity": Decision of March 30, 1931 (*A.J.*, XXVII (1933), p. 339).

B.—PERMANENT COURT OF INTERNATIONAL JUSTICE

I.—Organisation of the Court

Case No. 222

PERMANENT COURT OF INTERNATIONAL JUSTICE.

Permanent Court of International Justice—Statute of—National Judges—Parties Having the Same Interest—Article 31 of the Statute and Article 71, Paragraph 2, of the Rules of the Court.

CUSTOMS RÉGIME BETWEEN GERMANY AND AUSTRIA.

(Protocol of March 19, 1931.)

Order of July 20, 1931.[1]

THE FACTS.—See Case No. 8.

Article 31 of the Statute of the Court provided as follows:

"Judges of the nationality of each contesting party shall retain their right to sit in the case before the Court.

"If the Court includes upon the Bench a judge of the nationality of one of the parties only, the other party may select from among the deputy-judges a judge of its nationality, if there be one. If there should not be one, the party may choose a judge, preferably from among those persons who

[1] The Court was composed as follows: Adatci (President); Guerrero (Vice-President); Kellogg, Baron Rolin-Jaequemyns, Count Rostworowski, Fromageot, de Bustamante, Altamira, Anzilotti, Urrutia, Sir Cecil Hurst, Schücking, Negulesco, van Eysinga, Wang (Judges).

Case No. 222 *Contd.*

have been nominated as candidates as provided in Articles 4 and 5.

. . . .

"Should there be several parties in the same interest, they shall, for the purpose of the preceding provisions, be reckoned as one party only. Any doubt upon this point is settled by the decision of the Court. . . ."

Article 71, paragraph 2, of the Rules of the Court provided that in the hearing of requests for Advisory Opinions relating to an existing dispute between two or more States or Members of the League of Nations, Article 31 of the Statute shall apply.

The Austrian and Czechoslovak Governments informed the Court that should the Court decide that the above Articles were applicable to the dispute they would appoint judges *ad hoc*.

Held : that there was no ground for the appointment of judges *ad hoc*. "All governments which, in the proceedings before the Court, come to the same conclusion, must be held to be in the same interest for the purposes of the present case." (At p. 89.) The arguments advanced by the German and Austrian Governments lead to the same conclusion, whereas the arguments advanced by the French, Italian and Czechoslovakian Governments lead to the opposite conclusion. These two groups of Governments had, respectively, the same interest in the meaning of Article 31. The Court as composed included judges of German, French and Italian nationality.

[Report : *P.C.I.J.*, Series A/B, No. 41, Annex 1.]

III.—Contentious Jurisdiction

ii.—Procedure.

Case No. 223

Permanent Court of International Justice—Statute—Article 41—Interim Measures of Protection.

PERMANENT COURT OF INTERNATIONAL JUSTICE.

LEGAL STATUS OF THE SOUTH-EASTERN TERRITORY OF GREENLAND.

Order of August 3, 1932.[1]

THE FACTS.—On July 18, 1932, the Norwegian Government instituted proceedings against the Danish Government with

[1] The Court was composed as follows : Adatci (President) ; Guerrero (Vice-President) ; Baron Rolin-Jaequemyns, Count Rostworowski, Fromageot, de Bustamante, Altamira, Anzilotti, Urrutia, Sir Cecil Hurst, Schücking, Negulesco, van Eysinga, Wang (Judges) ; Vogt and Zahle (Judges *ad hoc*).

regard to the territory of South-Eastern Greenland and asked the Court to order interim measures of protection in accordance with Article 41 of the Statute. It based its application, *inter alia*, on statements which appeared in certain organs of the Danish Press and which caused the Norwegian Government to fear "that the Danish Government may proceed to acts of violence against Norwegian nationals . . . residing and exercising their calling in the territory." (At p. 278.) In the ensuing proceedings the Danish Government denied that it had any such intention and disclaimed responsibility for statements in the Press.

Held: that the Norwegian application for the indication of provisional measures must be dismissed, but that the Court reserved the right to consider later on whether circumstances had arisen justifying the indication of provisional measures. The Court stated that according to Article 41 it was entitled to indicate provisional measures both at the request of the parties (or of one of them) and *proprio motu*. With regard to the Norwegian application, the Court pointed out that it was "not based on the plea that the action which the Norwegian Government asks the Court to prevent would prejudice some recognized or alleged Norwegian right;" that "the incidents which the Norwegian Government aims at preventing cannot in any event, or to any degree, affect the existence or value of the sovereign rights claimed by Norway over the territory in question, were these rights to be duly recognized by the Court in its future judgment on the merits of the dispute;" and that "accordingly, so far as concerns the Norwegian request for the indication of interim measures of protection, no Norwegian rights, the protection of which might require the indication of such measures, are in issue." (At p. 285.)

The Court, having regard to the statements made before it by the two Governments, expressed the view that there was no occasion to fear that the incidents contemplated in the Norwegian request would actually occur; that these "declarations, taken together, are indicative of the existence in responsible circles in both countries of a state of mind and of intentions which are eminently reassuring;" and that "these intentions having been officially proclaimed before the Court, the latter must not and cannot presume that the two Governments concerned might act otherwise than in conformity with the intentions thus expressed." (At pp. 286, 287.)

Finally, the Court pointed out that, pending its decision on the merits of the dispute, "no act on the part of the said Govern-

Case No. 223 *Contd.*

ments in the territory in question can have any effect whatever as regards the legal situation which the Court is called upon to define" and that "accordingly, the Parties can have no interest in causing acts to be performed likely to give rise to incidents." (At p. 287.)

[Report: *P.C.I.J.*, Series A/B, No. 48, p. 277.]

Case No. 224

Permanent Court of International Justice—Procedure—Joinder of Actions.

PERMANENT COURT OF INTERNATIONAL JUSTICE.

LEGAL STATUS OF THE SOUTH-EASTERN TERRITORY OF GREENLAND.

Order of August 2, 1932.[1]

THE FACTS.—On July 18, 1932, the Norwegian Government, relying on the Optional Clause of Article 36 of the Statute of the Court, instituted proceedings, together with a request for interim measures of protection, against the Danish Government with regard to the legal status of certain parts of South-Eastern Greenland. On July 25, 1932, the Danish Government, equally relying on the Optional Clause, instituted proceedings against the Norwegian Government with regard to the same territory.

Held: that as "the situation with which the Court has to deal closely approximates, so far as concerns the procedure, to that which would arise if a special agreement had been submitted to it by the two Governments, parties to the dispute, indicating the subject of the dispute and the differing claims of the Parties . . . the two applications should be joined and the two applicant Governments held to be simultaneously in the position of Applicant and Respondent." (At p. 270.)

[Report: *P.C.I.J.*, Series A/B, No. 48, p. 268.]

PERMANENT COURT OF INTERNATIONAL JUSTICE.

Permanent Court of International Justice—Procedure—Article 25 of the Statute—Reconstitution of the Court.

For an instance of a reconstitution of the Court in accordance with Article 25 of the Statute and a waiver on the part of the Governments concerned of the demand that the whole case be argued, see the Judgment of June 7, 1932,[2] in the *Case of the Free Zones of Upper Savoy and the District of Gex*: *P.C.I.J.*, Series A/B, No. 46, p. 107.

[1] The Court was composed as follows: Adatci (President); Guerrero (Vice-President); Baron Rolin-Jaequemyns, Count Rostworowski, Fromageot, de Bustamante, Altamira, Anzilotti, Urrutia, Sir Cecil Hurst, Schücking, Negulesco, van Eysinga, Wang (Judges); Vogt and Zahle (Judges *ad hoc*).

[2] For the composition of the Court see p. 362.

Permanent Court of International Justice—Procedure—Contentious Jurisdiction—Form of Applications Instituting Proceedings before the Court.

See Case No. 7 (*Interpretation of the Statute of the Memel Territory*, (4)).

iv.—Judgment.

Permanent Court of International Justice—Judgments—Contents of—In Relation to Alternative Submissions Put Forward by the Parties—Interpretation of Arbitration Agreement. **Case No. 224a**

PERMANENT COURT OF INTER-NATIONAL JUSTICE.

See *Annual Digest*, 1929-1930, Case No. 277, The Facts and *Held* (*b*), and Judgment of June 7, 1932,[1] in the *Case of the Free Zones of Upper Savoy and the District of Gex* (*P.C.I.J.*, Series A/B, No. 46, p. 138), where the Court said: "From a general point of view, it cannot lightly be admitted that the Court, whose function it is to declare the law, can be called upon to choose between two or more constructions determined beforehand by the Parties, none of which may correspond to the opinion at which it may arrive. Unless otherwise expressly provided, it must be presumed that the Court enjoys the freedom which normally appertains to it, and that it is able, if such is its opinion, not only to accept one or other of the two propositions, but also to reject them both." (At p. 138.) The Court did not dispute the rule invoked by France that "every Special Agreement, like every clause conferring jurisdiction upon the Court, must be interpreted strictly," but pointed out that "that rule could not be applied in such a way as to give the Special Agreement, under the guise of strict interpretation, a construction according to which it would not only fail entirely to enunciate the question really in dispute, but would, by its very terms, have prejudged the answer to that question." (At pp. 138, 139.)

Permanent Court of International Justice—Judgment—Execution of.

See Case No. 202 (*Case of the Free Zones of Upper Savoy and the District of Gex*, (8)).

[1] For the composition of the Court see p. 362.

IV.—The Advisory Opinion

i.—Competence.

Case No. 225

PERMANENT COURT OF INTERNATIONAL JUSTICE.

Permanent Court of International Justice—Advisory Opinions—Request by Parties as Distinguished from Request by the Council.

INTERPRETATION OF THE GRECO-BULGARIAN AGREEMENT OF DECEMBER 9, 1927.

(*Caphandaris-Molloff Agreement.*)

Advisory Opinion of March 8, 1932.[1]

THE FACTS.—On September 19, 1931, the Council of the League of Nations adopted a Resolution requesting the Court to give an Advisory Opinion on the following questions :

"In the case at issue, is there a dispute between Greece and Bulgaria within the meaning of Article 8 of the Caphandaris-Molloff Agreement concluded at Geneva on December 9th, 1927 ?

"If so, what is the nature of the pecuniary obligations arising out of this Agreement ?"

For reasons which do not appear to have raised issues of a general character and which are therefore not reported in this volume, the Court answered the first question in the negative. In the course of the oral arguments before the Court, the Agents and Counsel of each of the Governments concerned declared that they wished the Court to give an Advisory Opinion on the second question regardless of the Court's answer to the first question.

Held : that the Court could not give an Advisory Opinion on the second question. "By the terms of Article 14 of the Covenant, the right to submit a question to the advisory jurisdiction of the Court is given only to the Assembly and to the Council of the League. The Court is therefore bound by the terms of the questions as formulated in this case by the Council. The second question is so worded as to be put to the Court conditionally upon an affirmative answer being given to the first question. To ignore this condition at the request of the Parties would be

[1] The Court was composed as follows : Adatci (President) ; Guerrero (Vice-President) ; Baron Rolin-Jaequemyns, Count Rostworowski, Fromageot, Altamira, Anzilotti, Urrutia, Sir Cecil Hurst, Schücking, van Eysinga, Wang (Judges) ; Caloyanni and Papazoff (Judges *ad hoc*).

in effect to allow the two interested Governments to submit a question for the advisory opinion of the Court." (At p. 87.)
[Report: *P.C.I.J.*, Series A/B, No. 45.]

C.—CONCILIATION

III.—Negotiation

Negotiations — Relevance of — Interpretation of Terms Used in the Course of.

See Case No. 49 (*Legal Status of Eastern Greenland*).

D.—UNILATERAL MEANS OF REDRESS SHORT OF WAR

I.—Retorsion

Disputes — Retorsion — Currency Regulations — Roumania and Czechoslovakia.

See Case No. 37 (*Rieber* v. *Kutzer et Cie. of Teschen* (*Czechoslovakia*)).

II.—Reprisals

Reprisals—Conditions of—Necessity for Breach of International Obligations.

See Case No. 215 (*Railway Traffic between Lithuania and Poland*).

PART XI

WAR AND NEUTRALITY

A.—WAR IN GENERAL

V.—Effects of Outbreak of War

iv.—On Enemy Subjects with regard to

(*a*) THEIR PERSONAL STATUS IN THE TERRITORY OF THE BELLIGERENT. *PERSONA STANDI IN JUDICIO*

War—Effects of—Enemy Aliens—Right to Sue—Operation of Statutes of Limitation—Termination of War—War Between the United States and Austria—Termination by Joint Resolution of Congress. **Case No. 226**

INDUSTRIAL COMMISSION OF OHIO *v.* ROTAR.

United States, Supreme Court of Ohio. November 18, 1931.

(Marshall, C.J.; Jones, Matthias, Day, Allen, Kinkade, Robinson, Stephenson, JJ.).

THE FACTS.—The plaintiff was the widow of a workman who was killed in 1919, in the course of his employment, in the United States, which at that date was at war with Austria-Hungary. At all material times the plaintiff herself resided at Straza, in the district of Banat, which was a district of Hungary up to the time of the dissolution of the Austro-Hungarian Monarchy. As a result of the Peace Treaty of Trianon, Banat became part of Yugoslavia. Under the Workmen's Compensation statute a two-year period of limitation was provided for claims (Ohio Gen. Code, Sections 1465-72a). The plaintiff's action was filed more than two years after the death of her husband, but within two years after the Joint Resolution of Congress of July 2, 1921 (42 U.S. Stat. at L., 105), terminating the war with Austria. The Industrial Commission dismissed the plaintiff's claim.

On appeal to the Court of Common Pleas, a verdict was entered for the defendant on the ground that the claim had been filed more than two years after the death of the decedent by a citizen of a country which had not been at war with the United States, namely, Yugoslavia.

Case No. 226 ***Contd.***

On appeal to the Court of Appeals this decision was reversed, and on further appeal,

Held (*per* Allen, J.): that the judgment of the Court of Appeals should be affirmed.

(1) The district in which the plaintiff resided remained a part of Hungary until after the termination of the World War. The plaintiff therefore remained a citizen of Austria-Hungary until the end of the War. It is a universally accepted rule, irrespective of statute, that when a state of war exists an alien enemy cannot prosecute a claim in the courts of a country at war with his own: *Hanger* v. *Abbott*, 73 U.S. 532; *Colorado Fuel & Iron Co.* v. *Industrial Commission*, 73 Colo. 579. But his right of action is merely suspended until the close of the war, at which time it revives and can be asserted (Ann. Cas., 1917 C, 213).

(2) There was, however, some confusion in the decisions as to when the war actually ended. It was held in *First National Bank of Pittsburgh* v. *Anglo-Oesterreichische Bank* (C.C.A.) 37 F. (2d) 564, that, as regards the statute of limitations, the Joint Resolution of Congress of July 2, 1921, did not terminate the war with Austria, seeing that the Resolution was not legally binding on Austria and that the restoration of peace could be accomplished only by a bilateral treaty. On the other hand, the fact that the war with Austria-Hungary was in fact ended by the Joint Resolution was recognised by the Supreme Court of the United States and by other federal courts in such cases as *Swiss National Insurance Co.* v. *Miller*, 267 U.S. 42; *Miller* v. *Camp* (D.C.) 280 Fed. 520; *In re Miller* (C.C.A.) 281 Fed. 764; *Zimmerman* v. *Hicks* (C.C.A.) 7 F. (2d) 443. The Court followed these decisions. The plaintiff had made her application within two years from the date of the Joint Resolution and her claim was therefore not barred under the statute.

[Report: 124 Ohio St. 418.]

v.—On Enemy Merchant Ships in Port

Case No. 227 **War at Sea—Hague Convention No. VI—Sinking of Enemy Vessel Provided with Safe-Conduct.**

The Bathori.

England, Prize Court. October 20, 1932.

The Facts.—The *Bathori* was a steamer owned by a Hungarian company and sailing under an Allied safe-conduct. In September 1914 she was captured and sunk (after removal of the crew) by a British cruiser, the captain of the cruiser having formed the erroneous opinion that she had violated her safe-conduct. At the trial it was not disputed that the sinking was unlawful, and the only question was whether the owners were entitled to compensation.

At the date of the Treaty of Trianon (June 4, 1920) Fiume was under the control of Gabriele d'Annunzio. From 1921 to 1924 it became a "free state," but in 1924 it was annexed to Italy by the Treaty of Rapallo, and by the terms of the Treaty the claimant Company acquired Italian nationality. The Company had been domiciled in Fiume since April 1920.

Held (by Lord Merrivale): that compensation was not payable. The case was governed by Article 53 of the Treaty of Trianon, whereby Hungary ceded all her rights over Fiume and agreed to accept any decision which the Allies might make as to its status. By Article 232 of the same Treaty Hungary renounced all claims which might be made by Hungarian subjects arising out of injuries done to them by the Allies. The learned Judge found that, apart from these articles, the claimants would have been entitled to compensation on the following grounds: (*a*) *Violation of safe-conduct*. The owner was entitled to have it respected for the time being. The right to compensation and restitution on account of violation of safe-conduct was clearly established (the judgments of Sir William Scott in *The Acteon*, 2 Dods. 48, 51, and of Dr. Lushington in *The Troija*, (1854) 1 Spink, 342, and *The Phoenix*, (1854) 1 Spink, 306, were cited). (*b*) *Article* 1 *of Hague Convention No. VI*, which provided that, when a merchant ship belonging to one of the belligerent Powers is at the commencement of hostilities in an enemy port, it is desirable that she should be allowed to depart freely, either immediately, or after a reasonable number of days of grace,and to proceed, after being furnished with a pass, direct to her port of destination or any other port indicated to her. The Court said: "As to the act of war which sank the *Bathori*, it may have been an 'independent act' of a naval officer acting within his commission, but in my judgment it was an act of war, not of piracy, and not of mere civil strife, and as an act of war committed by one of the commissioned officers of the State it was a breach of the obligation accepted by the State. . . . Whether the 'safe-conduct' or 'pass' under which the *Bathori* sailed be regarded as an act of a sovereign State independently of the Convention, or as an act of the State on the footing of the convention, the result practically seems to me to be that the *Bathori*, having been granted immunity, was sunk contrary

Case No. 227 *Contd.*

to the terms of the grant of safe-conduct, and that therefore a claim resulted to the owners to recover her value as soon as their disability to sue by reason of the state of war had been removed." (At pp. 32, 33.)

[Report: *L.R.* [1933], P. 22.]

NOTE.—The case was finally decided by the Judicial Committee of the Privy Council on other grounds (see Case No. 51).

Case No. 228

Sea Warfare—Hague Convention No. VI—Retention and Use of Enemy Merchant Vessels—Whether Amounting to Requisition.

THE TIBOR.

(*Navigazione Adria* v. *Minister of Marine*).

France, Civil Tribunal of the Seine. March 4, 1932.

THE FACTS.—The SS. *Tibor*, owned by the then Hungarian Company Adria, was seized by the French naval authorities on August 1, 1914, on her arrival at the port of Bordeaux. She was used for purposes of national defence until January 1918, when she was destroyed by fire off Port Said. The owners now sued for compensation in accordance with Hague Convention No. VI. A preliminary question of competence was raised, the question being whether the Courts were competent, to the exclusion of the administrative authorities, to deal with the claim for damages for use and loss of the vessel. The answer to this question depended on the further question whether the ship had or had not been requisitioned by the French State. According to French law requisitions fell within the competence of the judicial authorities.

Held: that the Court was competent, the *Tibor* having been requisitioned by the French State. "It was not the seizure of the vessel, an act of the sovereign power (*acte de gouvernement*) and therefore outside the jurisdiction of judicial tribunals, which caused her loss, but an act of management (*acte de gestion*), *viz.*, the subsequent use made of the vessel by the naval authorities in carrying out the public service of national defence. This act of management, which brought about the total and final extinction of private ownership, exhibits in effect the characteristics of requisition and, as such, comes within the jurisdiction of the judicial tribunals."

An examination of the Sixth Hague Convention of October 18, 1907, by which France was bound, led to the same conclusion.

In accordance with that Convention France could either seize the *Tibor* and return her, without indemnity, after the War, or make use of her, subject to indemnity. The latter course was adopted. There was a difference between confiscation, which was prohibited by the Convention, and the right to make use of the seized vessel on condition of indemnifying the owner. The latter constituted a requisition ; it was also what the parties to the Convention had in mind. When Article 2 came under discussion at the Hague Conference, one of the French representatives said : "A belligerent Power may wish to use these [seized] vessels, which may be of a kind suitable for purposes of warfare ; in the view of the French Delegation it is permissible in such a case for this Power to requisition the vessels provided that an indemnity is paid for them." It was considered preferable not to add a reference to national law concerning the exercise of the right of requisition and the obligation to pay an indemnity. This was not on account of any difference of opinion on a principle which had been unanimously agreed upon, but merely on account of the diversity and insufficiency or total absence of legislation on requisition in some countries. When putting Article 2, which was adopted by nine votes to two, to the vote of the Conference, the Chairman expressly pointed out that the draft implied the application of national law. No argument could be derived from the fact that no procedure of requisition was provided for by the Sixth Convention. The rule there adopted was one of principle and not of procedure. It was left to each Contracting Party to ascertain and settle damages. The omission by the French naval authorities of the formalities prescribed by national law in case of requisition, did not affect the situation.

[Report : *Le Droit maritime français*, vol. 10, p. 162.]

vi.—On Neutral Persons and Property. Embargo. The Right of Angary.

Case No. 229

Neutral Property—Detention of—Detention and Requisition of Neutral Ships—Duty of Compensation—Requisition of Dutch Ships in the United States—State Responsibility—Acts of Officials—Errors of Judgment—National Emergency and Duty of Compensation—Municipal Legislation and International Law—Measure of Damages—Award and Rate of Interest—Law Applicable by Domestic Tribunal set up to Determine a Claim of an International Character.

ROYAL HOLLAND LLOYD *v.* THE UNITED STATES.

United States, Court of Claims. December 7, 1931.

(Booth, C. J.; Green, Littleton, Williams, Whaley, JJ.).

THE FACTS.—This was an action against the United States for the wrongful detention of a vessel, the *Zeelandia*, belonging to the plaintiff, a Dutch corporation. The vessel was detained in 1917. In 1918, at which time the United States was at war with Germany and Austria, she was formally seized, requisitioned and placed in the active service of the United States. In March 1918 the United States entered into a bare-boat charter with the plaintiff, but refused to pay compensation for the detention and use of the vessel from October 1917 to March 1918. Following upon diplomatic correspondence with Holland in 1925, jurisdiction to entertain the action was granted to the Court of Claims by a special Act of Congress, which provided that the Court should have jurisdiction "to hear and determine such suit to judgment." Under municipal law the United States is not liable for the tortious or unauthorized acts of its officers.

Held: for the plaintiff,

(*a*) *The Law Applicable.*—In view of the fact that the plaintiff had no remedy against the Government of the United States according to the law of the United States, and in view of the circumstances which caused Congress to confer upon the Court of Claims jurisdiction to decide on the claim, the Court was bound to decide the issue as an international question in accordance with international law. "Indeed, since the primary ground of the alleged liability of the United States grows out of what are claimed to be the illegal and unauthorized acts of its officers, it is difficult to conceive of any theory upon which the Netherlands would have consented to a trial in this court, if the well-settled rule of law, consistently enforced in this court, that the United States is not liable for the tortious or unauthorized acts of its officers, was to be invoked as a bar to the plaintiff's claims. From the language of the jurisdictional act itself, as well as from the circumstances under which it was passed, and upon the plainest principles of justice and equity, we hold that the plaintiff is entitled to assert, and to have considered in its favor, to their fullest extent, such, if any, principles of the law of nations as may be applicable to the facts in the case."

(*b*) *Responsibility of the United States under International Law. Error of Judgment and State Liability.*—"In its relations with foreign nations, the United States bears what has been described as a 'wide, unlimited, unrestricted and vicarious responsibility' for the acts of its administrative officials and its military and naval forces. Oppenheim, International Law (second ed.) Vol. 1, sec. 163. Governments are responsible, in their international intercourse, for the acts of their authorized agents, and if such acts were mistaken, or wrongful, liability arises against the Government itself for the consequences of the error or wrong. Moses case (3 Moore, 3127); Deschamps & Renault's *Recueil* (1901), 706; the Labaun, 4 Moore, 3791; in the *Coquitlam* (15 Am. Jour. of Int. Law, 301); *Straughan* v. *United States*, 1 C. Cls. 324.

"Nor is it necessary, in order to sustain the liability of the United States, to show that the officers of the Government acted in bad faith, or with improper motives. While the bona fide nature of their conduct may be invoked by the officers in an explanation of their conduct to their own Government, its effect is merely to show that their conduct constituted an error in judgment. And any Government is responsible to other nations for error in judgment of its officials purporting to act within the scope of their duties. Schooner *Jessie* (XVI Am. Jour. Int. Law 115)."

(*c*) *Construction of Municipal Legislation in accordance with Treaties and International Law.*—The Court was unable to accept the contention of the United States that the detention of the vessel was justified under the relevant statutes of the United States, containing a prohibition to "export from" or "take out" from the United States certain categories of property. The vessel merely intended to "take out" such goods as she already had on board when she entered the United States. "The words 'carry out,' 'export from,' or 'take out of' must be held to apply only to an exportation or 'taking out' of goods which were a part of the general mass of goods belonging to the United States and to the loading of bunker coals and provisions, which, while not technically 'exports,' nevertheless came out of the general

Case No. 229 *Contd.*

mass of goods belonging to the United States. Whenever possible legislation should be so construed as not to violate or contravene treaty or international rights. Chew Heong *v.* United States, 112 U.S. 536; Johnson *v.* Browne, 205 U.S. 309. To hold that the espionage act applied to a situation, such as was the situation in regard to the *Zeelandia,* in which a vessel of a neutral, friendly power was about to depart from a port of the United States, having on board only cargo and stores loaded outside the United States and only temporarily within its confines, such cargo being consigned to ports outside of the United States, the vessel having neither cargo nor stores loaded within the United States nor out of the general mass of goods of the United States would, in our opinion, not only unduly extend the language of the act but would raise grave questions as to whether or not the act was in conflict with the rights of the neutral vessel under international law. We hold that such was not the intent of the Congress, and that no provision of the espionage act applied to the *Zeelandia* or justified the detention of the vessel. . . . By holding, and the language of the acts in question requires us to hold, that the Congress of the United States did not intend to go further than this we avoid any conflict, real or apparent, with the rules of international law. Such construction, under the authorities, is to be sought whenever possible and in this case is in harmony with the language and purposes of the acts in question. Chew Heong *v.* United States, *supra.*"

(*d*) *National Emergency and the Duty of Compensation.*—"However far the detention of the *Zeelandia* may have been justified, from the standpoint of the United States, by the existing emergency and the urgent need for additional ships for use by the United States; however beneficial to the United States and its associated governments in the conduct of the war may have been the acts of the officers of the port, it is clear that the rights of the plaintiff were disregarded and its property detained, to its damage, by the acts of the United States. Neither the need of the United States for additional shipping nor the good faith of its officers can be pleaded in defense of the claim of the plaintiff that it be made whole for the damage thereby sustained by it. Granting that the emergency did exist, and granting that the acts of the officers of the United States, whether done in an excess of zeal for the welfare of this country or in ignorance of the clear rights of the *Zeelandia* to be allowed clearance, were beneficial to the United States, the duty yet rests upon that Government to make restitution for the loss occasioned to the plaintiff by the acts in question."

(*e*) *Measure of Damages. Remoteness of Damage.*—While awarding damages for such items as loss of profits, wages to the crew, repairs, insurance, etc., the Court refused to award damages on account of the overhead expenses of the Company or advertising expenses. The Court said : "The overhead expense of the company was not increased or affected in any way by the detention of the vessel, and we regard this element of the plaintiff's claim as too remote to be chargeable to the United States. For similar reasons the general charge of an arbitrary portion of the advertising expense of the plaintiff to the *Zeelandia* does not constitute proof that the amount so charged was in fact lost to the plaintiff by any act of the United States. No part of the overhead expense of the company, or of its advertising expense, can be said to represent cash, or out-of-pocket, loss to the plaintiff. These expenses can not be said to have been directly and proximately attributable to the acts of the United States or to the enforced idleness of the *Zeelandia*. The burden of proof upon the question of the amount of damages, as well as upon all other questions in the case, is upon the plaintiff."

(*f*) *Award of Interest.*—In view of the international character of the issue before it and its duty to apply rules of international law to the determination of the case, the Court could not regard as decisive the contention that, according to the law of the United States, the latter is not liable to pay interest on claims in the absence of express statutory authority. "In the absence of a treaty between the United States and the Netherlands covering the point, we must have resort to the decisions of other tribunals to which have been submitted like controversies, for a determination of the rights of the plaintiff in this regard. The general rule appears to be that interest is allowable in all cases where the loss is either liquidated, or is capable of ascertainment by computation merely. Claims for 'property losses,' being claims for property taken, damaged, or destroyed, belong to this class. Claims for losses based on personal injuries, death, maltreatment to prisoners of war, or acts injurious to health, capacity to work, or honor, are of a class where the loss is neither liquidated nor can the amount thereof be determined by any method of computation. The claim of the plaintiff, being ascertainable by computation, is of the former class, and interest is properly allowable thereon. This holding is in accordance with the rules adopted by the Mixed Claims Commission, United States and Germany, one of the most recent

Case No. 229 *Contd.*

commissions of this character to function, and one to which were referred a large number of important controversies. See Administrative Decision III, United States and Germany Mixed Claims Commission."

(*g*) *The Rate of Interest. The dies a quo and dies ad quem.*—There was in this matter no rule of general application, and the Court deemed it proper to follow the rule adopted by the United States-Germany Mixed Claims Commission and to grant interest at 5 per cent per annum, interest to run from the date of the injury to the date of the judgment.

[Report: 73 Ct. Cl. 722; *A.J.*, XXVI (1932), p. 399.]

Case No. 230

Warfare at Sea—Requisitioning of a Neutral Ship by the French State—How Far Constituting an "Act of State"—Irregular Requisition—Competence of the French Courts.

In re CHAN PEK CHUN.

France, Conseil d'Etat. December 18, 1931.

THE FACTS.—Between February 8, 1917, and July 25, 1919, the French State detained and used, without requisitioning in the regular form, the neutral ship *Haïlan*, which lay in the port of Tourane in Indo-China. By a decision of the Minister of the Navy dated October 22, 1925, M. Chan Pek Chun, the owner of the ship, was granted an indemnity of 50,000 frs. for loss of use. The date taken as the basis for the calculation of the indemnity was fixed by this decision as September 10, 1924, while, according to the plaintiff, the date should have been October 27, 1919, when he applied to the Conseil du Contentieux administratif of Indo-China for reparation. The plaintiff, dissatisfied with the amount of the indemnity, applied to the Conseil d'Etat for a larger sum.

Held: that the Conseil d'Etat was competent and that the decision of the Minister of the Navy, dated October 22, 1925, which had granted inadequate compensation for "a requisition which had been irregularly effected," must be quashed.

[Report: *Sirey*, 1932, Part 3, p. 102.]

NOTE.—The French decisions on the requisitioning of neutral shipping in time of war are analysed by Bosc in *Revue du droit public*, 1926, especially pp. 224-226. The present decision marks some slight advance on previous decisions on the subject. Hitherto the Conseil d'Etat had invoked the theory of "acts of government" to dismiss claims brought by the owners of requisitioned neutral ships (see decision of May 6, 1921, *In re Pithis and Dallas, Recueil des arrêts du Conseil d'Etat*, 1921, p. 540; and decision of November 3, 1922, *In re Lichiardopoulos, ibid.*, 1922, p. 793).

XI.—Termination of War

War—Termination of—War between the United States and Austria—Termination by Joint Resolution of Congress.

See Case No. 226 (*Industrial Commission of Ohio* v. *Rotar*).

B.—WARFARE ON LAND

III.—Occupation of Enemy Territory

ii.—Legislative, Judicial and Administrative Functions of the Occupant.

Occupation in Time of War—Occupation of Alsace-Lorraine by the French Army between November 11, 1918, and January 10, 1920—Right to Annul German Legislation. **Case No. 231**

In re Ziwi.

France, Conseil d'Etat. November 4, 1932.

The Facts.—Article 32 of the German Law of June 21, 1916, authorised the inhabitants of Alsace-Lorraine to free themselves from liability for war-tax by means of payments in German War Loan Bonds. A Decree of the Commissioner-General of the French Republic in Alsace-Lorraine, dated June 18, 1919, annulled this provision. The plaintiff, in spite of this Decree, claimed that he was still entitled to take advantage of the offer provided in Article 32 of the Law of 1916 on the ground that the occupying French authority was not competent to annul local German law during the period intervening between the conclusion of the Armistice and the entry into force of the Peace Treaty.

Held : that the claim must be dismissed, and the Decree of June 18, 1919, upheld. By annulling Article 32 of the local Law of June 21, 1926, the Decree "had only stated the incompatibility of the said Article 32 with the position in fact and in law created by the Armistice Convention of November 11, 1918, and the reunion of the territories of Alsace and Lorraine with France."

[Report : *Dalloz*, 1933, Part 3, p. 4, with a note signed C.V.]

Note.—The formula used in the judgment is open to question inasmuch as it fails to recognise that an occupation in itself does

Case No. 231 *Contd.*

not bring about a transference of sovereignty. (See the more accurate view of the Hungarian-Yugoslav Mixed Arbitral Tribunal, of September 13, 1928, in *Kemeny* v. *Yugoslav State*, *Annual Digest*, 1927-1928, Case No. 374.) French legislation regarding Alsace-Lorraine equally upheld the doctrine of an immediate transfer of sovereignty (see Article 1 of the Decree of November 26, 1918, and Article 1 of the Law of October 17, 1919, on the temporary régime). In international law the territories of Alsace-Lorraine returned to French sovereignty in virtue of Article 51 of the Treaty of Versailles, and not of the Armistice Convention, Article 2 of which merely provided for the immediate evacuation of the territories. On the other hand, in the present case, the principle that the occupying authority can alter the law in force in the occupied country when circumstances require it (Article 43 of the Hague Regulations of October 18, 1907, on the Laws and Customs of War on Land) would be sufficient to ensure the legal validity of the decrees of the Commissioner-General between November 11, 1918, and January 10, 1920.

Case No. 232

Occupation of Enemy Territory—Judicial Functions of the Occupant—Sentences by Courts Set Up by the Occupant—How Far Constituting *res judicata*.

In re ANDRÁS.

Hungary, Supreme Court. September 14, 1932.

THE FACTS.—The accused was indicted for murder alleged to have been committed near the village of Nagyösz (Hungary) on February 27, 1920, at a time when the village was occupied by Roumanian troops. The accused was taken before a Roumanian Court set up by the Roumanian authorities in Temesvár (also occupied territory), where he was sentenced. Later he was released and settled down in territory which remained Hungarian. There he was again indicted and sentenced. He appealed on the ground that the matter was *res judicata*.

Held: that the appeal must be dismissed. "Both the place where the crime was committed and the city of Temesvár where the sentence was rendered belonged to Hungary until the coming into force of the Peace Treaty of Trianon. Up to the coming into force of this Treaty Hungarian Courts had exclusive jurisdiction to deal with ordinary crimes. . . . The Court of Temesvár which gave the sentence in this case received its commission not from the Hungarian but from the Roumanian State. It had no jurisdiction either by virtue of Hungarian law or according to the provisions of the Hague Convention.[1]

[1] Apparently Hague Convention of 1907 (No. IV).

Accordingly, a judgment given by such a Court does not possess the characteristics of a real *res judicata.*"

[Report : *Büntetöjogi Döntvénytár*, XXV, Case No 154.]

Occupation of Foreign Territory—Judgments of Courts.

See the *Occupation of Užice Case*, decided by the Yugoslav Court of Appeal on February 11, 1931. This case does not require a separate digest seeing that it was decided by reference to the Yugoslav Decree concerning the liquidation of the conditions created as a result of the World War, which gave a list of judgments and decisions of the occupant which were to be considered as having no legal force. The disputed judgments did not appear in the list and were therefore held valid.

[Report (incomplete) : Ivanović, *Sudska praksa u* 1931 *godini, sa Zbirkom načelnih odluka i mišljenja Opšte sednice Kasacionog suda od* 1931-1933 *godine* (*Jurisprudence of Yugoslav Courts in* 1931, *with Collection of the Doctrinal Decisions and Opinions of the General Division of the Court of Cassation,* 1931-1933), No. 208, pp. 257-259.]

iii.—Respect of Private Property. The Public Property of the Enemy State. Requisitions and Contributions

Warfare on Land—Occupation of Enemy Territory—Respect for Private Property—Article 56 of Hague Convention No. IV—Property of Municipalities. **Case No. 233**

WŁODZIMIERZ (CITY OF) *v.* POLISH TREASURY.

Poland, Supreme Court, First Division. July 1, 1931.

THE FACTS.—The City of Włodzimierz (in the part of Poland which was formerly under Russian rule) claimed the return of certain real property which it had possessed until 1915, at which date it was taken over by the military authorities of the army of occupation of the Central Powers. The Polish State authorities had subsequently taken over the property, and the Treasury now claimed to have acquired ownership by lapse of time. It was therefore material to determine whether the Treasury could claim possession leading to ownership as from 1915 or as from 1921 when it took over the property as its own.

Held : that time should run from the latter date. "The authorities of the army of occupation were only using the property in question and did not possess it as owners. Under Article 56 of the Rules annexed to the Hague Convention of

Case No. 233 *Contd.*

October 18, 1907, concerning the Laws and Customs of War on Land, to which Poland has acceded, . . . the property of a municipality is equivalent to private property."

[Report : *Zb.O.S.N.*, I (1931), Part 2, No. 146, p. 9.]

NOTE.—It was contended for the defendant Treasury that the property had become vested in the Treasury through lapse of time, counting the time of possession of the defendant as from 1915. The Court rejected that submission. It held that the Russian Treasury could not, since 1915, be deemed to have been in possession since the Russian authorities had withdrawn from the territory. Accordingly, the Polish Treasury could not calculate from that date its possession as successor to the rights of the Russian Treasury, and therefore it could only have become the possessor of the property as from 1921. Article XII of the Polish-Russian Peace Treaty of Riga (which vested in the Polish Government property of the Russian Government) could not apply in this case since it did not relate to property of private persons or of organs of self-government. Since the Russian Treasury had had no right in the property in question, there was no right which could pass to the Polish Treasury.

iv.—Inhabitants. Services. Deportations. Hostages

Occupation of Foreign Territory—Right to Take Measures for the Protection of Troops.

See Case No. 102 (*Chevreau Case*, (1)).

INDEX

D

U